Aproximación a la traducción de referentes culturales en el ámbito audiovisual y literario /

Approach to the translation of cultural references in the audiovisual and literary fields

IVITRA Research in Linguistics and Literature
Studies, Editions and Translations
ISSN 2211-5412

This series aims to publish materials from the IVITRA Research Project. IVITRA carries out research on literary, linguistical and historical-cultural studies, and on history of literature and translation, specially those related to the Crown of Aragon in the Middle Ages and the Renaissance. The materials in the series will consist of research monographs and collections, text editions and translations, within these thematic frames: Romance Philology; Catalan Philology; Translation and Translatology; Crown of Aragon Classics Translated; Diachronic Linguistics; Corpus Linguistics; Pragmatics & Sociolinguistics; Literary and historical-cultural studies; and E-Learning and IST applications.

A complete list of titles in this series can be found on *benjamins.com/catalog/ivitra*

Editor
Vicent Martines Peres
Universitat d'Alacant / IEC / RABLB / IULMA / IIFV

International Scientific Committee

Ignacio Aguaded	Juan Francisco Mesa
Carlos Alvar	Joan Miralles
Robert Archer	Josep Maria Nadal
Concepción Company Company	Veronica Orazi
Adelaida Cortijo	Maria Àngels Fuster Ortuño
Antonio Cortijo	Akio Ozaki
Ricardo Silveira Da Costa	José Antonio Pascual
Ramon Ruiz Guardiola	Hans-Ingo Radatz
Antoni Ferrando	Rosabel Roig-Vila
Sara Poot Herrera	Vicent Salvador †
Dominic Keown	Francisco Franco Sánchez
Coman Lupu	Ko Tazawa †
Enric Mallorquí-Ruscalleda	Joan Veny
Isidor Marí	Curt Wittlin †
Giuseppe Mazzocchi †	

Volume 45

Aproximación a la traducción de referentes culturales en el ámbito audiovisual y literario / Approach to the translation of cultural references in the audiovisual and literary fields
Editado por Pedro Mogorrón Huerta, Lucía Navarro-Brotons y Iván Martínez-Blasco

Aproximación a la traducción
de referentes culturales
en el ámbito audiovisual y literario /
Approach to the translation
of cultural references
in the audiovisual and literary fields

Edited by

Pedro Mogorrón Huerta
Lucía Navarro-Brotons
Iván Martínez-Blasco
University of Alicante

John Benjamins Publishing Company
Amsterdam / Philadelphia

The paper used in this publication meets the minimum requirements of the American National Standard for Information Sciences – Permanence of Paper for Printed Library Materials, ANSI Z39.48-1984.

DOI 10.1075/ivitra.45

Cataloging-in-Publication Data available from Library of Congress:

LCCN 2024060564 (PRINT) / 2024060565 (E-BOOK)

ISBN 978 90 272 1970 1 (HB)
ISBN 978 90 272 4494 9 (E-BOOK)

© 2025 – John Benjamins B.V.
No part of this book may be reproduced in any form, by print, photoprint, microfilm, or any other means, without written permission from the publisher.

John Benjamins Publishing Company · https://benjamins.com

Table of contents

Foreword	VII
Introducción	XI
Audiovisual translation & cultural references: May success lie at the roots? *Verónica Arnáiz-Uzquiza & Paula Igareda*	1
Culture-bound references in the Lithuanian-dubbed "Coco" *Jurgita Astrauskienė & Danguolė Satkauskaitė*	19
"La receta del pistou": Referencias culturales francesas en la TAV *Enora Lessinger*	42
Los antropónimos en la película cubana *Los dioses rotos*: Su traducción al inglés en la subtitulación *Geisy Labrada Hernández*	60
Kulturbezüge in der voice-over Übersetzung von multilingualen Filmen: Grenzen und Möglichkeiten der Übertragung *Eglė Alosevičienė*	72
Transposition of a distorted universe: Cultural elements in *The night is short, walk on girl* by Morimi Tomihiko and its English translation *Hiroko Inose*	90
Translating sociolinguistic traces of urban youth culture in contemporary fiction *Tiffane Levick*	109
Cultural awareness across time: A diachronic study of the use of cultural references in a corpus of translated novels *Virginia Mattioli*	123
Explotación didáctica del cómic en la formación de traductores: Adquisición de las subcompetencias lingüística, extralingüística, de transferencia y estratégica a partir de las viñetas de *Le Chat* *Tanagua Barceló*	142

El taller de traducción teatral del C.R.E.C. o una experiencia de traducción colectiva de un sainete español   164
Hélène Frison & Marie Salgues

Propuesta de traducción de «Un couteau dans la poche»   178
Esmeralda Vicente Castañares

"La Loba" irrumpe: La presentación del personaje en algunas traducciones al español y al catalán del relato de Giovanni Verga. Reflexiones y una nueva propuesta   198
Helena Aguilà Ruzola

Reigen y la traducción de los referentes culturales en teatro   211
Elena Serrano Bertos

El trasvase de los referentes culturales y la fraseología en las versiones españolas de "I Viceré"   230
Maria Carreras i Goicoechea

La metamorfosis del «lirio» (y del «lilio»): De flor a símbolo   253
Monica Savoca

L'intercompréhension en contexte universitaire: Traduction du *Petit Chaperon Rouge* de Charles Perrault dans différentes langues romanes   275
Alexandra Marti

La traducción al castellano de los culturemas de *Le pays des autres*   290
María del Mar Jiménez-Cervantes Arnao

Index   309

Foreword

The present volume titled *Aproximación a la traducción de referentes culturales en el ámbito audiovisual y literario* is made up by seventeen articles written by experts in the translation of cultural references in the audiovisual and literary fields. The audiovisual translation section starts with **Verónica Arnáiz-Uzquiza** and **Paula Igareda**'s contribution, titled "Audiovisual translation & cultural references: May success lie at the roots?" The authors present the findings of a study focused on the translation of the sitcom *The Big Bang Theory* (Lorre & Prady, 2007–2008). The study conducts a comparative analysis of the translation strategies employed in the French, German, and Spanish dubbing, and subtitling versions, with a particular emphasis on preserving the most representative aspects of the original version. For the authors the quality of their translations becomes crucial for their global expansion, making it a subject worthy of scholarly investigation. **Jurgita Astrauskienė** and **Danguolė Satkauskaitė**'s contribution titled "A translator's journey to the Land of the Dead and back: Rendition of culture-bound references in the Lithuanian-dubbed film 'Coco' (2017)" aims to investigate the translation of culture-bound references (CBRs) in the Lithuanian-dubbed version of the animated film *Coco* (2017). The significance and innovation of this work lie in its CBRs translation analysis model, which incorporates multiple procedures. **Enora Lessinger**'s article titled "La receta del pistou: Referencias culturales francesas en la TAV" explores the translation of cultural references in audiovisual translation. The study focuses on analysing the Spanish subtitles of the French series *Call My Agent*. The theoretical framework utilised is an adaptation of Pedersen's 2011 typology of Explicit Cultural References and their corresponding translation strategies in subtitling. **Geisy Labrada Hernández**'s study "Los antropónimos en la película cubana Los dioses rotos: su traducción al inglés y en el subtitulaje" analyses the fictional anthroponymy of the characters in the Cuban film *Los dioses rotos* (2008) and takes into account the English translation of these anthroponyms in the subtitles. The goal of **Eglė Aloseviciene**'s research, titled "Kulturbezüge in der Voice-over Übersetzung von multilingualen Filmen: Grenzen und Möglichkeiten der Übertragung", is to explore how cultural references can be effectively transferred when translating multilingual films into Lithuanian using voice-over techniques. The corpus for the study includes cultural references extracted from five multilingual films, systematically categorized according to the translation process.

The literary translation section starts with **Hiroko Inose**'s contribution "Transposition of a distorted universe: Cultural elements in *The Night is Short, Walk on Girl* by Morimi Tomihiko and its English translation". The author identifies various types of cultural elements present in the novel *The Night is Short, Walk on Girl* by Morimi Tomihiko, and investigates how they have been dealt with in the English translation. **Tiffane Levick**'s paper, "Translating sociolinguistic traces of urban youth culture in contemporary fiction", explores the interconnection between linguistic variety and cultural references in translation. The author postulates that both elements serve to situate a work of fiction in a specific temporal and geographical context, shedding light on the identities of its users. This notion is elucidated through a discussion introducing typologies for the translation of cultural references and slang. **Virginia Mattioli**'s contribution "Cultural awareness across time: a diachronic study of the use of cultural references in a corpus of translated novels" aims to provide a diachronic description of the use of cultural references used in a corpus of novels translated between 2000 and 2014. Considering the strict relationship between culture and language and the difficulties to recognize cultural references systematically highlighted in the previous literature, this study focuses on those cultural references representing linguistic culture. The goal of **Tanagua Barceló**'s contribution "Explotación didáctica del cómic en la formación de traductores: adquisición de las subcompetencias lingüística, extralingüística, de transferencia y estratégica a partir de las viñetas de Le Chat" is to showcase the usefulness of comic books in linguistic and cultural training of future translators in the French language classroom. Specifically, it analyses the peculiarities of the Belgian comic strip *Le Chat* and its didactic possibilities regarding the acquisition of linguistic, extralinguistic and translation knowledge. In the article "El taller de traducción teatral del C.R.E.C. o una experiencia de traducción colectiva de un sainete español", **Hélène Frison** and **Marie Salgues** introduce the translation workshop established by the Centre for Research on Contemporary Spain (Université Sorbonne Nouvelle) in 2006. The authors discuss the strategies guiding collective translation, using the 'sainete' *El amigo Melquíades* by Carlos Arniches as a case study and the challenges associated with translating its humour and cultural references. **Esmeralda Vicente Castañares**' work, titled "Propuesta de traducción de 'Un couteau dans la poche', de Philippe Delerm," presents a translation proposal for the short story *Un couteau dans la poche* (Gallimard, 1997) from Philippe Delerm's collection *La première gorgée de bière et autres plaisirs minuscules*. For the author, interculturality and adaptation remain a basic pillar of translation theory and practice. **Helena Aguilà Ruzola**'s research "'La Loba'" irrumpe: la presentación del personaje en algunas traducciones al español y al catalán del relato de Giovanni Verga. Reflexiones y una nueva propuesta" focuses on analysing the translation of various passages from Giovanni Verga's short story *La Lupa* (1880), specifically those that present challenges related to specific cultural references or unique semantic nuances that must be reconstructed based on the "Sicilianity" of the original text. **Elena Serrano Bertos'** contribution "Reigen y la traducción de los referentes culturales en teatro" addresses the translation of cultural references in dramatic literature from a double perspective: editorial translation and stage translation. The purpose of this study is to analyse to what extent these factors interfere in the treatment of cultural references for stage translation and editorial translation. For this aim, the author takes as a model the theatre play *Reigen (La Ronda)*, by the Austrian Arthur Schnitzler. **Maria Carreras i Goicoechea** paper titled "El trasvase de los referentes culturales y la fraseología en las versiones españolas de 'I Viceré'" explores the study of certain cultural references in I Viceré (Federico De Roberto), and their translation into Spanish. The researcher compiles and classifies examples to observe how cultural transfer is handled according to the date of translation or the translator. **Monica Savoca**'s contribution "La metamorfosis del «lirio» (y del «lilio»): de flor a símbolo" points to how the massive use of the floral metaphor throughout the Golden Age made these elements of nature become an integral part of the image that Spanish poetry delivered to the world. In the article "L'intercompréhension en contexte universitaire : traduction du *Petit Chaperon Rouge* de Charles Perrault dans différentes langues romanes", **Alexandra Marti** asks whether intercomprehension can be integrated into language teaching in the long term. To this end, she analyses intercomprehension as a means of achieving multilingualism and shares a pedagogical experience through Charles Perrault's *Le Petit Chaperon Rouge*, translated into several Romance languages. Finally, **María del Mar Jiménez-Cervantes Arnao**'s contribution, "La traducción al castellano de los culturemas de Le pays des autres", aims to identify the culturemes, classify the loanwords and moments of code-switching, and analyze the translation into Spanish of the novel *Le pays des autres* (Leïla Slimani), carried out by Malika Embarek López, to verify whether the linguistic and cultural richness of the original work has been retained.

Introducción

El presente volumen titulado *Aproximación a la traducción de referentes culturales en el ámbito audiovisual y literario* se compone de diecisiete artículos escritos por expertas en la traducción de culturemas en el contexto audiovisual y literario. La primera sección, dedicada a la traducción audiovisual, comienza con la contribución de **Verónica Arnáiz-Uzquiza** y **Paula Igareda**, titulada "Audiovisual translation & cultural references: May success lie at the roots?", donde se presentan los resultados de un estudio de la traducción de la sitcom *The Big Bang Theory* (Lorre & Prady, 2007–2008). El estudio realiza un análisis comparativo de las estrategias de traducción empleadas en las versiones de doblaje y subtitulado en francés, alemán y español, haciendo hincapié en la conservación de los aspectos más representativos de la versión original. Para las investigadoras, la calidad de sus traducciones resulta determinante para su expansión mundial, lo que la convierte en un tema digno de investigación académica. La contribución de **Jurgita Astrauskienė** y **Danguolė Satkauskaitė**, titulada "A translator's journey to the Land of the Dead and back: Rendition of culture-bound references in the Lithuanian-dubbed film 'Coco' (2017)", tiene como objetivo investigar la traducción de referencias culturales en la versión doblada al lituano de la película de animación *Coco* (2017). La importancia y la innovación de este trabajo radican en su modelo de análisis, que incorpora múltiples procedimientos. El artículo de **Enora Lessinger**, titulado "La receta del pistou: Referencias culturales francesas en la TAV," explora la traducción de referentes culturales en la traducción audiovisual. El estudio se centra en el análisis de los subtítulos en español de la serie francesa *Call My Agent*. El marco teórico utilizado es una adaptación de la tipología de referencias culturales explícitas de Pedersen (2011) y sus correspondientes estrategias de traducción en el subtitulado. El estudio de **Geisy Labrada Hernández**, "Los antropónimos en la película cubana Los dioses rotos: su traducción al inglés y en el subtitulaje," analiza la antroponimia ficcional de los personajes de la película cubana *Los dioses rotos* (2008) y tiene en cuenta la traducción de estos antropónimos al inglés en los subtítulos. El objetivo de la investigación de **Eglė Alosevičienė**, titulada "Kulturbezüge in der Voice-over Übersetzung von multilingualen Filmen: Grenzen und Möglichkeiten der Übertragung", es explorar cómo pueden transferirse eficazmente las referencias culturales al traducir al lituano películas multilingües utilizando técnicas de voz en *off*. El corpus del estudio incluye referencias culturales extraídas de cinco películas multilingües, clasificadas sistemáticamente según el proceso de traducción.

La sección de traducción literaria comienza con la contribución de **Hiroko Inose** "Transposition of a distorted universe: Cultural elements in *The Night is Short, Walk on Girl* de Morimi Tomihiko y su traducción al inglés". La autora identifica varios tipos de elementos culturales presentes en la novela *The Night is Short, Walk on Girl* de Morimi Tomihiko, e investiga cómo han sido tratados en la traducción inglesa. El trabajo de **Tiffane Levick**, "Translating sociolinguistic traces of urban youth culture in contemporary fiction", explora la interconexión que se establece entre la variedad lingüística y las referencias culturales en la traducción. La autora postula que ambos elementos sirven para situar una obra de ficción en un contexto temporal y geográfico específico, lo que permite arrojar luz sobre las identidades de sus usuarios. Esta noción se elucida mediante un debate en el que se introducen tipologías para la traducción de referencias culturales y argot. La contribución de **Virginia Mattioli**, "Cultural awareness across time: a diachronic study of the use of cultural references in a corpus of translated novels", ofrece una descripción diacrónica del uso de los referentes culturales empleados en un corpus de novelas traducidas entre 2000 y 2014. Teniendo en cuenta la estricta relación entre cultura y lengua y las dificultades para reconocer sistemáticamente las referencias culturales, este estudio se centra en aquellos referentes culturales que representan la cultura lingüística. El objetivo de la contribución de **Tanagua Barceló**, "Explotación didáctica del cómic en la formación de traductores: adquisición de las subcompetencias lingüística, extralingüística, de transferencia y estratégica a partir de las viñetas de Le Chat," es mostrar la utilidad del cómic en la formación lingüística y cultural de los futuros traductores en el aula de francés. En concreto, se analizan las peculiaridades del cómic belga *Le Chat* y sus posibilidades didácticas para la adquisición de conocimientos lingüísticos, extralingüísticos y traductológicos. En el artículo "El taller de traducción teatral del C.R.E.C. o una experiencia de traducción colectiva de un sainete español," **Hélène Frison** y **Marie Salgues** presentan el taller de traducción creado por el Centro de Investigación sobre la España Contemporánea (Université Sorbonne Nouvelle) en 2006. Las autoras abordan las estrategias que se utilizan en la traducción colectiva, tomando como caso de estudio el sainete *El amigo Melquíades*, de Carlos Arniches, y los retos asociados a la traducción de sus referentes humorísticos y culturales. El trabajo de **Esmeralda Vicente Castañares**, titulado "Propuesta de traducción de 'Un couteau dans la poche', de Philippe Delerm", presenta una propuesta de traducción del cuento *Un couteau dans la poche* (Gallimard, 1997) de la colección *La première gorgée de bière et autres plaisirs minuscules de* Philippe Delerm. Para la autora, la interculturalidad y la adaptación siguen siendo un pilar básico de la teoría y la práctica de la traducción. La investigación de **Helena**

Aguilà Ruzola "'La Loba' irrumpe: la presentación del personaje en algunas traducciones al español y al catalán del relato de Giovanni Verga. Reflexiones y una nueva propuesta" se centra en el análisis de la traducción de diversos pasajes del cuento *La Lupa* (1880) de Giovanni Verga, concretamente en aquellos que presentan retos relacionados con referentes culturales específicos o matices semánticos singulares que deben ser reconstruidos teniendo en cuenta la sicilianidad del texto original. La contribución de **Elena Serrano Bertos**, "Reigen y la traducción de los referentes culturales en teatro," aborda la traducción de los referentes culturales en la literatura dramática desde una doble perspectiva: la traducción editorial y la traducción escénica. El propósito de este estudio es analizar en qué medida estos factores interfieren en el tratamiento de los referentes culturales para la traducción escénica y la traducción editorial. Para ello, la autora toma como modelo la obra teatral *Reigen (La Ronda)*, del austriaco Arthur Schnitzler. El trabajo de **Maria Carreras i Goicoechea**, titulado "El trasvase de los referentes culturales y la fraseología en las versiones españolas de 'I Viceré'", explora el estudio de ciertos referentes culturales en I Viceré (Federico De Roberto), y su traducción al español. La investigadora recopila y clasifica ejemplos para observar cómo se trata el referente cultural en función de la fecha de traducción o del traductor. La contribución de **Mónica Savoca**, "La metamorfosis del "lirio" (y del "lilio"): de flor a símbolo," señala cómo el uso masivo de la metáfora floral a lo largo del Siglo de Oro hizo que estos elementos de la naturaleza se convirtieran en parte integrante de la imagen que la poesía española entregó al mundo. En el artículo "L'intercompréhension en contexte universitaire : traduction du *Petit Chaperon Rouge* de Charles Perrault dans différentes langues romanes", **Alexandra Marti** se pregunta si la intercomprensión puede integrarse a largo plazo en la enseñanza de idiomas. Para ello, analiza la intercomprensión como medio para alcanzar el multilingüismo y comparte una experiencia pedagógica a través de *Le Petit Chaperon Rouge de Charles Perrault*, traducido a varias lenguas romances. Por último, la contribución de **María del Mar Jiménez-Cervantes Arnao**, "La traducción al castellano de los culturemas de Le pays des autres", tiene por objeto identificar los culturemas, clasificar los préstamos y los momentos de cambio de código, y analizar la traducción al español de la novela *Le pays des autres* (Leïla Slimani), realizada por Malika Embarek López, para comprobar si se ha conservado la riqueza lingüística y cultural de la obra original.

Audiovisual translation & cultural references
May success lie at the roots?

Verónica Arnáiz-Uzquiza & Paula Igareda
Universidad de Valladolid | Universitat Pompeu Fabra

Technology and user demands have conditioned the products that are premiered today, forcing the audiovisual industry to consider the importance of translation. Products broadcast in small local contexts may become sought-after international hits, making their translations key to their expansion, and their quality, the object of study. This paper presents the results of a study of the sitcom *The Big Bang Theory* (Lorre & Prady, 2007–2008), focusing on one of the most representative aspects of the original version: cultural references. Following the classification designed by Igareda (2011), a comparative analysis is made of the translation strategies adopted in the French, German and Spanish dubbing and subtitling versions. The close conveyance of cultural references results in a limited combination of translation strategies that differ among languages and Audiovisual Translation modalities.

Keywords: cultural references, *The Big Bang Theory*, dubbing, subtitling, comparative analysis

1. Introduction

In recent years, the audiovisual industry has changed its economic models. Technique, technology, aesthetics and user demands, to name but a few, have conditioned the products that are broadcast, transmitted and premiered today: screens are no longer flat, static stages, but windows open to an ever-increasing number of possibilities; and rapidly evolving technologies ensure the production of hours of tailor-made, easily accessible material that are no longer instant, short-lived experiences that time the viewing habits of end viewers, but on-demand experiences that users can manage at will. But the technology has blown up not only the viewing experience for users, but also the quality of their experience.

This open and growing selection is forcing the audiovisual industry to consider the importance of translation processes, as products that were once broadcast in small local contexts have now become increasingly sought-after hits for international audiences. Their translation — and its immediacy — are currently the key to their expansion, making their quality the object of study and debate through many lenses: the growing expansion — the imposition — of traditionally minority modalities in certain contexts, the technological explosion that has burst into their technical, aesthetic and translatological development, and the high specialization of the audience, among others, mark the final result of the form. But what about the content? The audiovisual text remains the essence of the product, and its configuration the key to its success.

One of the most challenging aspects translators deal with when conveying these essential audiovisual texts is, to a great extent, cultural elements. In the present study we will focus on the analysis of these complex aspects when translated into other languages and cultures. The purpose of the present study is to analyse the cultural component of audiovisual texts, and the strategies adopted for their translation for different audiovisual translation modalities. To this aim, the study focuses on the US sitcom *The Big Bang Theory* (Lorre & Prady, 2007–2008), and its French, German and Spanish dubbed and subtitled versions.

2. Cultural references: Definition, classification and translation

In today's globalized world, talking about culture and cultural references is not always evident when the analysis departs from a text in English — as THE dominant language — confronted to another in a minority language — in terms of power, but not in terms of the number of speakers. Cultural references are, basically, a reflection of the language and worldview of a given culture. However, many of these cultural elements are becoming increasingly shared due to the aforementioned globalization, and most especially, due to the "contamination" of the audiovisual products that we consume on a daily basis. This is very much in line with what Pedersen (2011: 106) calls "transculturality", or the interconnection of cultural elements and their shared nature across cultures.

According to Santamaria (2001a: 237), cultural references are the objects and events created within a given culture with a distinctive cultural capital, intrinsic to the society as a whole. At about the same time, Olk (2001: 30) defined cultural references as

> [...] those lexical items in a source text which, at a given point in time, refer to objects or concepts which do not exist in a specific target culture or which deviate

in their textual function significantly in denotation or connotation from lexical equivalents available in the target culture.

However, it may be the definition provided by González-Davies & Scott-Tennent (2005:166) the one that presents a more detailed picture of what cultural references are, very much in line with the key aspects presented in the coming sections:

> Any kind of expression (textual, verbal, non-verbal or audiovisual) denoting any material, ecological, social, religious, linguistic or emotional manifestation that can be attributed to a particular community (geographic, socio-economic, professional, linguistic, religious, bilingual, etc.) and would be admitted as a trait of that community by those who consider themselves to be member of it. Such an expression may, on occasions, create a comprehension or a translation problem.

Nevertheless, besides the various definitions of cultural references existing, the most interesting aspect related to their nature may be the different proposals that have been presented for their classification.

2.1 Classification of cultural references

Newmark (1988) was one of the pioneers when it comes to classifying cultural references in translation studies. Relating to different lexical fields pertaining to a culture-specific lexicon, he adapted previous works by Nida (1945). Many subsequent studies are based on his initial classification, which is mainly divided into nine main categories: ecology, artifacts, social culture, organizations, customs, activities, gestures and habits.

Often addressed from specialized fields, from News to Tourism or Literary Translation, cultural references have also been a traditional field of research in Audiovisual Translation Studies, where different authors in the field have approached the classification of cultural references as a preliminary step for the study of their translation.

Nedergaard-Larsen (1993) makes the distinction between intralinguistic cultural references — speech acts, forms of address, grammatical categories, idiomatic expressions, etc. — and extralinguistic references, which are those aspects that refer to concrete things — institutions, place names, brand names, etc. For the latter, the author identifies four broad categories, with corresponding sub-categories: geography, history, society and culture. In this line, Pedersen (2005:2) coined the term Extralinguistic Cultural References (ECRs) to refer to any reference that is

> [...] attempted by means of any culture-bound linguistic expression, which refers to an extralinguistic entity or process, and which is assumed to have a discourse

referent that is identifiable to relevant audience as this referent is within the encyclopaedic knowledge of this audience.

Díaz-Cintas & Remael (2007: 221) introduce a detailed classification of cultural references, based on previous proposals, such as those of Nedergaard-Larsen (1993), Ramière (2004), or Vandeweghe (2005), and divide the references into three main groups, which in turn are subdivided: geographical references, ethnographic references, and socio-political references. Some years later, Pedersen (2011) includes twelve different domains: weights and measures; proper names; professional titles; food and beverages; literature; government; entertainment; education; sports; currency, technical material, and others.

Also addressing the classification of cultural references, special attention goes to the taxonomy proposed by Ranzato (2016: 64), who distinguishes between real-world and intertextual references; and points to the existence of verbal and non-verbal cultural references, and synchronous or asynchronous cultural references.

Taking into account most of the aforementioned works and the existing literature, Igareda (2011) also develops a methodological tool to categorize cultural references. The taxonomy proposed not only considers previous works in the field of Translation Studies that deal with the categorization of cultural references and their possible translation strategies, but also studies from other fields that provide an interdisciplinary and transmedial character, moving from anthropology, or psychology, to linguistics, literature, semiotics, or communication studies. The tool identifies nine main categories of cultural references also divided into different areas: Ecology, History, Social Structure, Cultural Institutions, Social Universe, Material Culture, and Humour & Linguistic & Cultural Elements.

But together with the various definitions and classifications of culture and cultural references, comes the importance of their translation, and the techniques and strategies adopted for their conveyance.

2.2 Translation of cultural references

Language is considered to be a reflection of culture, and so translation must consider the cultural distance between the original text and the target culture and audience. Thus, when we translate, an intercultural comparison is made between languages, cultures and societies, and the translator must have an in-depth knowledge of the sociocultural aspects of both sides, acting as a mediator between cultures (Igareda, 2011). This role of the translator as a mediator between cultures is shared by many specialists in the field of Translation Studies, just as well as its difficult and challenging nature (Snell-Hornby, 1988; Hatim & Mason, 1991; Agost, 1999; Castro-Paniagua, 2000; Bartrina, 2001; Santamaria, 2001b; Sellent,

2001; Bravo, 2004, Ramière 2004; Valdeón 2008; Fuentes-Luque & López, 2020; to name but a few).

A close look at the proposals for the translation of cultural references of authors such as Corteza (2005), Molina (2006), Pedersen (2011), Tringham (2014), Cómitre (2015), and Fuentes-Luque & López (2020), shows that most of them draw from previous studies by Newmark (1988), Leppihalme (1994), Nord (1990, 1997), Agost (1999), Gambier & Gottlieb (2001), Marco (2004) or Ruokonen (2010), among others.

As we move chronologically through the field, we see that, in many cases, many of these classifications are an extension or specialization of Newmark's (1988: 81–93, 103) — as already was the categorization of cultural references themselves — and his detailed set of eleven translation procedures.

2.2.1 Translation of cultural references in audiovisual texts

Already in 1996, Franco pointed out that the audiovisual translation of cultural elements depends on the overall strategy chosen, the mode of translation and the binding norms in the sociocultural environment for which they is translated. In this line, Ogea (2019: 334) states that, when dealing with cultural references,

> [...] the translator's responsibility is to identify any cultural feature within the original version and to determine whether they will be properly interpreted by the target audience, in order to deliver the information and cause the same impact on different socio-cultural environments.

Back in 1993, Nedergaard-Larsen defined film — and that could be extended to audiovisual texts — as a product created and framed in one culture, which will give rise to a number of difficulties of understanding if projected in a different culture.

Years later, and referring directly to the translation of cultural references in subtitling, Díaz-Cintas (2003: 247) identifies direct translation procedures (borrowing and calque), and oblique the translation procedures (explicitation, transposition, substitution, lexical recreation, compensation, omission and addition). Some years later, and also dealing with subtitling, Pedersen (2011) proposes a taxonomy of seven strategies including retention, direct translation, official equivalent, specification, generalization, substitution and omission.

With regards to dubbing, Chaume (2012: 145) points out how cultural references become an added obstacle for the translator, given that the linguistic code can interact with the acoustic and visual codes to create the full meaning of the scene. Fuentes-Luque & López González (2020) add that sometimes the opposite is the case: it is the acoustic and visual signs that facilitate the task of dubbing cultural references. Some of the strategies proposed by Chaume (2012: 145–146) for audiovisual texts also apply to other texts of various kinds, such as repetition (without translation), orthographic adaptation, literal translation, glosses, cultural adaptation or substitution, omission, or the creation of a new element.

Also created for dubbing, Ranzato's (2016) taxonomy outlines a detailed list of translation strategies: loan, official translation, calque, explicitation, generalization by hypernym, concretisation by hyponym, substitution, lexical recreation, compensation, elimination and creative addition.

In addition to the techniques / strategies / procedures proposed in the various taxonomies, there are aspects that must be taken into account when working with audiovisual texts, especially fiction — as in the case of our study — which Ogea (2019) rightly mentions, such as language density and speed, the expressive language with different levels of intensity, and the actors and actresses' personal way of speaking. In this line, recent research published by Alfaify & Ramos Pinto (2022: 112) defends that "the typologies resulting from those [AV] studies focus solely on verbal references and often ignore the multimodal meaning-making situation in which cultural references are construed or their non-verbal nature."

After such a quick overview of what cultural references are, how different taxonomies consider their classification, and some of the existing categorizations provided for the study of their translation, let's now focus on the practical section of our study.

3. Cultural references and translation in *The Big Bang Theory*

3.1 Corpus contextualization

In order to analyse, from a practical point of view, the role that cultural references play in the construction — and success — of audiovisual products, we set out to study a worldwide successful example of a long-running audiovisual product; that is the case of the US sitcom *The Big Bang Theory* (TBBT) (Lorre & Prady, 2007–2008). Over the course of 12 seasons and 279 episodes of 18–20 minutes, it presents the particular day-to-day of a group of young scientists in their social and occupational life, focusing mainly on their problems with human — and especially affective — relationships at all levels.

The marked personalities of the characters, the specific context that surrounds their social interrelations — *geek* culture in the United States — and the professional environment where part of the scenes take place — scientific labs — frame the series to a greater extent, together with the success that it progressively achieved internationally. This interesting combination made of such a product the perfect example to analyse to what extent cultural references define audiovisual products, and how their translation may extend their successful reception in third countries.

With this objective in mind, the analysis of season 1 was considered the most representative part of the series in order to provide more enriching results, given that, being the first contact of the product with the audience, it would present a greater concentration of cultural references, due to the need to construct the characters, their personalities, and the contexts that host the plot. Likewise, the study was aimed to combine English — the original language of the product — together with Spanish, French and German. The election of these languages was marked by the successful reception of this sitcom in the respective countries, where the product, in addition, was mainly consumed, in all cases, in its dubbed versions.

3.2 Cultural references in *The Big Bang Theory*

Once the product identified and the season selected, the study analysed the 17 episodes that build up THE season, with a total of 355 minutes. Adopting the taxonomy proposed by Igareda (2011), 1726 references were identified in the scripted texts, which, due to their complexity, became a total of 2759 cultural references in their original version, as we found, in many cases, examples of references with a double or even multiple classification (See Table 1).

Table 1. Example of cultural reference with a multiple classification

Time reference	Source text	Cultural references (Category. Area)
S01E01 (00:13:27,287 --> 00:13:31,222)	your Luke Skywalker no-more-tears shampoo	4.2 (Cultural Institutions. Arts) 4.5 (Cultural Institutions. Media) 6.3 (Material Culture. Cosmetics) 7.6 (Humour & Cultural & Linguistic Elements. Humour)

Although the number of cultural references per episode is, on average, 60 (± 20), special attention goes to episode two, where references almost double (110), possibly due to the fact that the pilot episode is traditionally conceived as a tentative test where no specific features — character constructions — are introduced. The second episode, on the contrary, tends to be where character definitions are traditionally presented: their way of speaking, tastes, background and sociological profile (especially their philias and phobias, in this case), among many other aspects. In this very same line, episodes 13, 14, 15 and 16 show a significant increase in the number of references with respect to the average figures previously mentioned — 171, 178, 207 and 173 respectively, as opposed to the 60 references on average — probably conditioned by the maturity of the series and the bond with the audience: the more familiar the audience is with the product, the more references are expected by end viewers, and so the product is built under those premises to meet the expectations.

Following Igareda's taxonomy, we proceeded to identify the profile of the references on the basis of the seven different categories defined by the author: Ecology, History, Social Structure, Cultural Institutions, Social Universe, Material Culture, and Humour & Linguistic & Cultural Elements.

According to the data collected, three main groups of cultural references were identified in the configuration of the original text with a significant prevalence over the other four groups, and that concentrated more than half — 53% — of the references in the corpus. These were the Social Universe — 18% of the total — Material Culture — 4% — and Humour & Linguistic & Cultural Elements — 21% of the total (see Figure 1).

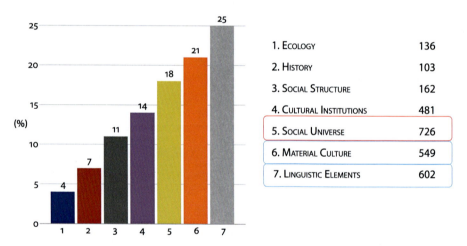

Figure 1. Cultural references in TBBT

In the case of the first four categories of the taxonomy — Ecology, History, Social Structure, and Cultural Institutions — it is also possible to identify areas that concentrate significantly the presence of references, as seen in Figure 2. Per areas, those related to human beings (level 1.4) stand out in the case of references in the category Ecology; those related to personalities (2.3) in History; references dealing with Social Organizations (3.2) in the case of Social Universe; and those related to Art (4.2) in the case of Cultural Institutions.

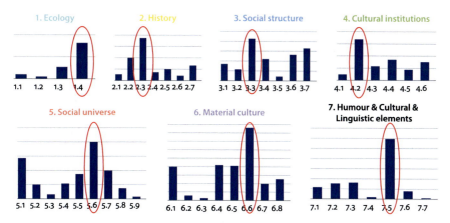

Figure 2. Prevalence of cultural references per group in TBBT

The dominant presence of references under all these areas is of particular interest, as they all serve to outline the plot structure, and help to construct and define the main characters of the series, by focusing on their tastes and hobbies (*geek* culture, with a special interest in cinema, comics and role-play games), their academic and/or professional dedication (doctors of physics or engineers) and their affective relationships (personal interactions, sentimental relationships, and family relationships, among others).

Nevertheless, and apart from the predominance of these areas in their different categories, the prevalence of the cultural references corresponding to the categories Social Universe, Material Culture, and Humour & Linguistic & Cultural Elements is significantly more important.

With regard to the first of the categories — Social Universe — 18% of the cultural references present in the series are concentrated here. References related to colloquial language abound, not surprisingly, given the nature of the series — sitcom — the age of the characters — young people — and the relationships between them — friendship. Similarly, the group of references dealing with social habits also stands out significantly (see Figure 3). This result is justified by the profile outlined for the different characters in the series: their complex personality and limitations for social relations, the impossibility of dealing with the female sex, the complicated maternal-filial relations of some characters, etc.

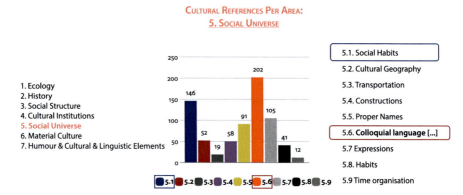

Figure 3. Cultural references per area in Social Universe in TBBT

The second category of references in terms of importance in the series — 21% of the references — is that of Material Culture. In this case, references grouped under the area Technology are significantly more used (See Figure 4). This important predominance is justified by the occupation of most of the main characters — and a large part of the secondary characters — and the settings where their interactions take place: physicists and engineers who work in a Caltech technology laboratory.

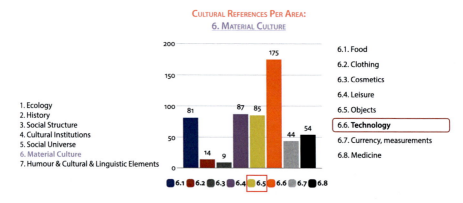

Figure 4. Cultural references per area in Material Culture in TBBT

The last of the main groups in the taxonomy, which encompasses linguistic and cultural elements and humour, is the most important one in terms of number of references per category, concentrating 25% of the total cultural references present in the series. In this case, it is puns the area with the most significant presence in the corpus (See Figure 5), with 50% of the total references used. There could be several reasons behind this prevalence: the characteristic humor (sitcom), the suspected disorder of one of the characters and his difficulty in deciphering double meanings, the recurrent presence of board games where puns play an important role, among others.

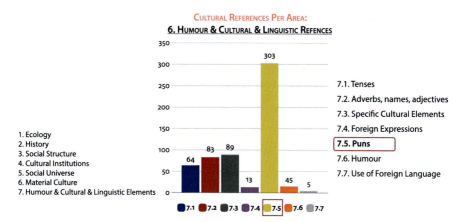

Figure 5. Cultural references per area in linguistic elements in TBBT

3.3 Translation of cultural references in *The Big Bang Theory*

Once all the cultural references were identified in the source text, it was time to focus on the translation process into French, Spanish and German, both for their dubbed and subtitled versions. For this part of the analysis, and considering the large volume of references present in the corpus, a preliminary study was conducted to determine whether a detailed or simplified translation taxonomy would better suit the aim of our study. As a result, attention was placed on the most recurrent translation strategies originally identified in the preliminary study: deletion, neutralization, adaptation, literal translation, and functional preservation. Nevertheless, this does not mean other strategies were not identified in the study. However, given their lesser presence in the corpus, they were discarded for the analysis.

As already advanced, we proceeded to identify the cultural references in the versions translated into French, Spanish and German both for their dubbed and subtitled versions. A first general analysis reveals that functional preservation is the most prevalent strategy in both modalities — dubbing and subtitling — and in all three languages — French, Spanish and German — as opposed to a minor presence of deletion (See Figure 6). In the case of both strategies — deletion and functional preservation — their presence in German is significantly more important, if compared to the results for both modalities in French and Spanish. By modalities, we observe that adaptation is the second strategy more frequently used in the

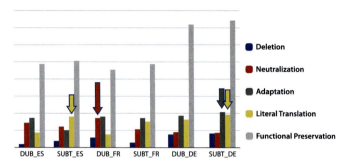

Figure 6. Main translation strategies per language and modality in TBBT

case of dubbing in all languages, closely followed by neutralization in French and Spanish, and literal translation in German. In the case of subtitling, on the other hand, there is a reversal in the solutions adopted: while literal translation is used to a greater extent in Spanish, both in French and German adaptation is again the predominant second-level strategy, closely followed by literal translation. It is interesting to note that the distribution between the strategies adopted in both modalities is very similar in German, whereas in Spanish and French there is a greater variety between the strategies adopted for either modality, although results are very similar for the two languages in the case of dubbing.

If we focus on the groups of cultural references with the most representative presence in the series, which, as we have seen, were those related to Social Universe (21%), Material Culture (18%) and Humour & Cultural & Linguistic Elements (14%), it is possible to identify an important difference in the patterns presented.

3.3.1 *Translation strategies in the category Social Universe*

Firstly, in the case of Social Universe (5), as already introduced in previous lines, the references are significantly concentrated in the area Colloquial Language (5.6) – 28% of the examples. In this case, the main strategy adopted for the translation in almost all the languages and modalities is adaptation. As presented in Figure 7, in the case of German dubbing, however, the set of strategies under the "Other" category includes practically all the references analysed. As far as the other languages and modalities are concerned, the strong presence of literal translation in the German and Spanish subtitled versions is also to remark, together with the use of functional preservation, this time, in all versions. In the case of the dubbed versions, on the other hand, in addition to the predominant adaptation, functional preservation stands out in second place, followed by neutralization in French, and deletion in Spanish. It is worth noting the important weight of this strategy –

functional preservation — in general terms, in the translation of colloquial language within Social Universe.

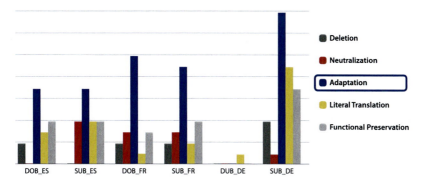

Figure 7. Main translation strategies per language and modality in the area Colloquial Language in TBBT

3.3.2 *Translation strategies in the category Material Culture*

As already presented in previous lines, with regard to Material Culture, that groups 18% of the references identified, Technology concentrates up to 32% of these references. In this case, and following the pattern already seen for the overall analysis of the strategies adopted for translation, functional preservation is the major strategy for all the languages and modalities, although there are differences by language. While in French and Spanish neutralization is the second most used strategy in both dubbed and subtitled versions, in German we find that adaptation IS more used in both dubbing and subtitling.

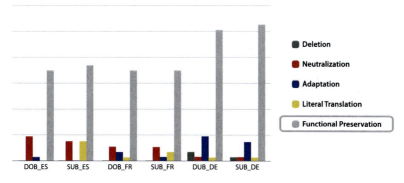

Figure 8. Main translation strategies per language and modality in the area Technology in TBBT

3.3.3 Translation strategies in the category Humour and Linguistic and Cultural Elements

The last group of cultural references — though first one in terms of relevance — in *The Big Bang Theory* is that that collects humour and cultural and linguistic elements, which represent 25% of the total. Of the seven areas that make up this category, puns are, by large, the most important group, amounting 50% of the total references in this category. As we can see in Figure 9, the results obtained in the analysis of the translation strategies for the different languages and modalities outlines, in this case, a totally changing scenario, where patterns differ among the three languages. The frequent strategy, in this case, for the translation of references in French and German, is adaptation, both for dubbing and subtitling. In the case of Spanish, on the contrary, we find that functional preservation is the predominant strategy in the case of dubbing, as opposed to literal translation, more predominant in subtitling. However different, nevertheless, both strategies — functional preservation and literal translation — are also significantly present in the German translations for both modalities, whereas a more balanced presence of all the main strategies is found in French. In this case, and much in line with the results obtained in the study of Colloquial language in the category Social Universe, the strong presence of deletion in German, mainly, and, to a lesser extent, in French, is noteworthy for both modalities.

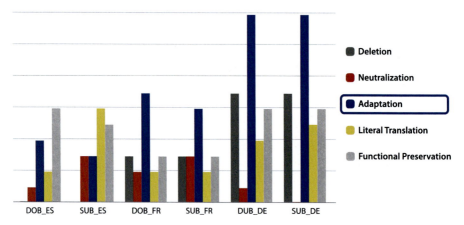

Figure 9. Main Translation strategies per language and modality in the area Puns in TBBT

4. Conclusions

A quick review of the different approaches adopted in the consideration of cultural references shows that definitions generally describe any element that serves to identify a certain aspect within a community. The classification of these references, as already presented, has also been the subject of a number of studies, both within and outside the Audiovisual Translation sphere, which have materialized in different taxonomies — more or less detailed — that deal with their classification according to their nature, in the aim of analysing the translation strategies adopted for their transfer.

The present study focuses on the identification of the cultural references in the successful US sitcom *The Big Bang Theory* (Lorre & Prady, 2007–2008), in order to analyse whether or not a characterization of the series is possible based on them, while analysing their translation into the French, Spanish and German versions both for dubbing and subtitling.

Adopting the classification of cultural references designed by Igareda (2011), the analysis of the 17 episodes that make up the first season has drawn the profile of the series on the basis of the seven categories that integrate the taxonomy. Although the number of references is significantly concentrated in the categories corresponding to Social Universe (18%), Material Culture (21%), and Humour & Linguistic and Cultural Elements (25%), it is worth noting the importance of the main areas — in terms of examples provided — in the rest of the categories: Human Being, in the case of Ecology; Personalities, in the case of History; Social Organization in Social Structure; and Art, as far as Cultural Institutions are concerned. This set of references serves to build the profile of the characters in the series — considering that this is the first season — marking their personality — manias, hypochondria, disorders, phobias, philias — and their relationship with others and with their environment. In the case of the categories with more references, the areas Colloquial Language, Technology and Word Games concentrate most of the examples, outlining character profile by the way the characters express themselves and the content of their interventions, and based on their characterization and interests — difficulties in understanding figurative language and double meanings, the recurrent presence of board games and role-play games, and interest in fantasy films, comics and science, among other aspects.

Once the cultural references identified in the original product, we proceeded to analyse the strategies used to translate them it into French, Spanish and German, both in their dubbed and subtitled versions. In this case, a reduced classification of strategies was adopted for the study in a preliminary test, taking into account not only — but mainly — the most recurrent strategies, such as omission, neutralization, adaptation, literal translation and functional preservation.

Back to the categories and areas of cultural references more present in the corpus, and focusing on the three major categories in terms of examples provided, we find that in the case of Social Universe, which accounts for 21% of the references, 28% of the examples are concentrated in colloquial language. We see then here that, apart from adaptation, which is the most common strategy, literal translation and functional preservation have an important role, especially in the version for German subtitles. This is not surprising if we consider that, in many cases, the texts of the subtitled versions come from translated templates, with the limitations this would entail.

In the case of Material Culture, Technology is the area with the biggest number of references: 32%. In this case, and in contrast to the previous category, functional preservation is the most common strategy for all the languages and modalities, followed by neutralization in Spanish and French, and adaptation in German.

The last of the categories analysed is Humour & Linguistic & Cultural Elements, which represents 25% of the cultural references, 50% of which are puns. Significant differences were identified in the three languages and both modalities when it comes to the study of the translation strategies identified in the study of this category. While in the case of translations into German and French, adaptation is the predominant strategy, the secondary strategy in the case of French is functional preservation, as opposed to omission in German. In contrast to this, in the case of the Spanish translations, functional preservation prevails in the dubbed version, while literal translation significantly predominates in subtitles.

The study of the strategies adopted by each language in each of the two modalities shows that, in general terms, functional preservation is the most recurrent strategy employed in all cases, somehow explaining the successful reception of the series in all three target cultures. Per languages, we find that the strategies adopted in Spanish and German for both modalities, although with subtle differences, coincide to a large extent, with adaptation in second place, followed by neutralization. In the case of French translation, however, although adaptation is also the second most important strategy in the dubbed version, literal translation is very present, becoming the second most important strategy in the case of subtitling.

The detailed analysis, first of the cultural references in the sitcom, and then of the translation strategies adopted by three of the main dubbing countries in Europe, shows that, for the most, the important load of references, and their marked nature condition, to a large extent, the success in the reception of audiovisual products, especially when it comes to transferring them into foreign languages. The close conveyance, not only of the content, but also of the aim of those references, is the result of a limited combination of translation strategies that differ among languages and Audiovisual Translation modalities.

References

Agost, Rosa. 1999. *Traducción y doblaje: palabras, voces e imágenes*. Barcelona: Ariel.
Alfaify, Abeer and Sara Ramos Pinto. 2022. "Cultural references in films: an audience reception study of subtitling into Arabic." *The Translator* 28(1): 112–131.
Bartrina, Francesca. 2001. "La investigación en traducción audiovisual: interdisciplinariedad y especificidad." In *¡Doble o nada! Actas de las I y II Jornadas de doblaje y subtitulación*, ed. by John D. Sanderson, 27–38. Alicante: Publicacions de la Universitat d'Alacant.
Bravo, Sonia. 2004. *La traducción en los sistemas culturales. Ensayos sobre traducción y literatura*. Las Palmas de Gran Canaria: Servicio de Publicaciones de la Universidad de Las Palmas de Gran Canaria.
Castro-Paniagua, Francisco. 2000. *English-Spanish Translation, Through a Cross-Cultural Interpretation Approach*. New York: University Press of America.
Chaume, Frederic. 2012. Audiovisual translation. *Dubbing*. Manchester: St. Jerome.
Cómitre, Isabel. 2015. Culture-bound aspects in subtitling of animated films. *Tales of the night of M. Ocelot*, 1–11. https://riuma.uma.es/xmlui/handle/10630/9798
Corteza, Assumpta. 2005. "El tractament dels referents culturals en la traducció catalana de Gabriela, cravo e canela." *Quaderns, Revista de Traducció* 12: 189–203.
Díaz-Cintas, Jorge. 2003. *Teoría y práctica de la subtitulación inglés/español*. Barcelona: Ariel.
Díaz-Cintas, Jorge and Aline Remael. 2007. *Audiovisual translation: subtitling*. Manchester: St. Jerome.
Franco, Javier. 1996. "Culture-specific items in translation." In *Translation, Power, Subversion*, ed. by Román Álvarez, Román and M. Carmen África Vidal, 52–78. Clevedon: Multilingual Matters.
Fuentes-Luque, Adrián and Rebeca Cristina López González. 2020. "Cine de animación made in Spain: doblaje y subtitulación de elementos culturales." *Íkala, Revista de Lenguaje y Cultura* 25(2): 495–511.
Gambier, Yves and Henrik Gottlieb. 2001. *(Multi) media translation: concepts, practices, and research*, Amsterdam: John Benjamins Publishing Company.
González Davis, María and Christopher Scott-Tennent. 2005. "A problem-solving and Student-Centred Approach to the Translation of Cultural References." *Meta* 50(1): 160–179.
Hatim, Basil and Ian Mason. 1991. *Discourse and the Translator*. London: Longman.
Igareda, Paula. 2011. "Categorización temática del análisis cultural: una propuesta para la traducción." *Ikala* 16(27): 11–32.
Leppihalme, Ritva. 1994. *Culture bumps. On the translation of allusions*. Helsinki: University of Helsinki, English Department Studies 2.
Marco, Josep. 2004. "Les tècniques de traducció (dels referents culturals): retorn per a quedarnos-hi." *Quaderns. Revista de traducció* 11: 129–149.
Molina, Lucía. 2006. El otoño del pingüino. Análisis descriptivo de la traducción de los culturemas. Castellón de la Plana: Publicacions de la Universitat Jaume I. Unpublished PhD thesis.
Nedergaard-Larsen, Birgit. 1993. "Culture-bound problems in subtitling." *Perspectives* 1(2): 207–242.

Newmark, Peter. 1988. *A Textbook of Translation*. London: Prentice-Hall.

Nida, Eugene. 1945. "Linguistics and ethnology in translation problems." *Word* 1(2): 194–208.

Nord, Christiane. 1990. "Zitate und Anspielungen als pragmatisches Übersetzungsproblem." *TEXTconTEXT* 5(1): 1–30.

Nord, Christiane. 1997. Translating as a Purposeful Activity. *Functionalist Approaches Explained*. Manchester: St Jerome.

Ogea, María del Mar. 2019. "Subtitling cultural humour in the Spanish comedy Paquita Salas." In *Translation in and for Society: Sociological and Cultural Approaches in Translation*, ed. by Beatriz Martínez Ojeda and María Luisa Rodríguez Muñoz, 330–349. Córdoba: Editorial UCOPress.

Olk, Harald Martin. 2001. The translation of cultural references: An empirical investigation into the translation of culture-specific lexis by degree-level language students. Canterbury: University of Kent. Unpublished PhD thesis.

Pedersen, Jan. 2005. "How Is Culture Rendered in Subtitles." In *MuTra 2005–Challenges of Multidimensional Translation: Conference Proceedings*, ed. by Heidrun Gerzymisch-Arbogast and Sandra Nauert, 1–18. https://riuma.uma.es/xmlui/handle/10630/9798

Pedersen, Jan. 2011. *Subtitling norms for television*. Amsterdam and Philadelphia: John Benjamins Publishing Company.

Ramière, Nathalie. 2004. "Comment le sous-titrage et le doublage peuvent modifier la perception d'un film. Analyse contrastive des versions sous-titrée et doublée en français du film d'Elia Kazan, A Streetcar Named Desire (1951)." *Meta* 49(1): 102–114.

Ranzato, Irene. 2016. *Translating Culture Specific References on Television: The Case of Dubbing*. New York: Routledge.

Ruokonen, Minna. 2010. Cultural and Textual Properties in the Translation and Interpretation of Allusions. *An Analysis of Allusions in Dorothy L. Sayers' Detective Novels translated into Finnish in the 1940s and 1980s*. Turku: University of Turku.

Santamaria, Laura. 2001a. Subtitulació i referents culturals. La traducció com a mitjà d'adquisició de representacions mentals. Barcelona: Universitat Autònoma de Barcelona. Unpublished PhD thesis.

Santamaria, Laura. 2001b. "Función y traducción de los referentes culturales en subtitulación." In *Traducción subordinada (II): el subtitulado*, ed. by Lourdes Lorenzo and Ana María Pereira, 237–248. Vigo: Publicacións da Universidade de Vigo.

Sellent, Joan. 2001. "Qualitat i recepció en el doblatge." In *La traducción en los medios audiovisuales*, ed. by Rosa Agost and Frederic Chaume, 119–122. Castellón de la Plana: Publicacions de la Universitat Jaume I.

Tringham, Damon. 2014. "Allusions and Cultural References: Translator Solutions in the Finnish Translation of Terry Pratchett's 'Reaper Man'". *MikaEL, Kääntämisen ja tulkkauksen tutkimuksen symposiumin verkkojulkaisu* 8: 170–183.

Snell-Hornby, Mary. 1988. *Translation Studies. An Integrated Approach*. Amsterdam and Philadelphia: John Benjamins Publishing Company.

Valdeón, Roberto A. 2008. "Alienation techniques in screen translation: The role of culture specifics in the reconstruction of target-culture discourse." *Languages in Contrast* 8(2): 208–234.

Vandeweghe, Willy. 2005. *Duoteksten. Inleiding tot vertaling en versaalstudie*. Gent: Academia Press.

Culture-bound references in the Lithuanian-dubbed "Coco"

Jurgita Astrauskienė & Danguolė Satkauskaitė
Vilnius University, Kaunas Faculty

The main objective of this study is to examine the translation of culture-bound references (CBRs) in the Lithuanian-dubbed film "Coco" (Unkrich and Molina 2017). Employing a three-step methodology, the research first identifies prevalent translation procedures for CBRs and their correlation with semantic categories. Subsequently, it assesses the factors influencing translator decisions and evaluates dubbing synchronization, exploring reasons behind specific translation choices. The analysis of "Coco" identified 451 distinct CBRs, with sociocultural references being the most prevalent. The majority of CBRs were preserved in the Lithuanian version of the film to maintain a rich representation of Mexican culture, as well as isochrony and lip synchronization when characters were seen on-screen.

Keywords: culture-bound references, dubbing, animation, translation procedures, synchronization

1. Introduction

Translating culture-bound references (CBRs) is a complex and multi-faceted task that requires a high level of intercultural and linguistic expertise. One of the major obstacles in translating CBRs is the lack of equivalence between languages and cultures. Another difficulty is the complexity of the multiple layers of meaning and context that CBRs often have. As highlighted by Ranzato (2020: 649), "culture-bound vocabulary [...] carries with it a whole world of images and associations". Several scholars have emphasized the difficulty in translating CBRs found in audiovisual products due to the unique constraints of each mode of audiovisual translation (AVT) (e.g., Pedersen 2011; Ranzato 2016; Díaz Pérez 2017; Alfaify and Ramos Pinto 2021). According to Chaume (2020: 109–110), cultural references belong to "[s]ociocultural constraints, or constraints inherent to the two cultural systems at play in any audiovisual transfer" (2020:110). The translation of CBRs, specifically for dubbing, is also influenced by various constraints such as professional, linguistic, formal and semiotic or iconic ones.

Previous research on CBRs in AVT has examined various aspects such as different classifications of CBRs into categories or domains (Díaz-Cintas and Remael 2007; Pedersen 2011; Ranzato 2016; Díaz-Cintas and Remael 2021). These categorizations not only assist in defining and identifying CBRs, but they may also be linked to the translation procedures, as highlighted by Pedersen (2011: 93, 157), Díaz-Cintas and Remael (2007: 203), and Ranzato 2016: 98). Another crucial aspect in the analysis of translating CBRs in audiovisual material is the selection and application of translation procedures or techniques such as those proposed by Vinay and Darbelnet (2002:128–137) and Díaz Cintas and Remael (2007:202–207). Furthermore, a significant area of investigation has been the various constraints that influence the translator's decision when rendering CBRs in AVT, as exemplified by Pedersen (2011) and Ranzato (2016).

This study aims to examine the prevalent translation procedures of different categories of CBRs in the Lithuanian-dubbed animated film "Coco". The objectives of the research are the following: to determine the number of CBRs and their distribution according to specific categories; to identify translation procedures applied in rendering CBRs from the SL into the TL; to identify the prevalent procedures used to render specific categories of CBRs; to disclose correlational tendencies of the translation procedures applied to render specific categories of CBRs, and to examine the ways how dubbing synchronies and other translation parameters affect the translation of CBRs. The study relies on a model specifically developed for the analysis of the translation of CBRs for dubbing.

2. Research material and methodology

The research material is the animated film "Coco" directed by Lee Unkrich and Adrian Molina, produced by Pixar Animation Studios, and released by Walt Disney Pictures in 2017. This film has been selected purposefully as it represents Mexican culture which is less familiar to the Lithuanian audience, especially to the younger generation. The film was dubbed into Lithuanian and first shown in Lithuania in January of 2018. "Coco" is an animated film that tells the story of Miguel, a young boy who dreams of becoming a musician despite his family's generations-old ban on music. When Miguel accidentally finds himself transported to the Land of the Dead, he embarks on a journey to find his great-great-grandfather, a legendary musician, in order to return to the living world and fulfil his dream. Along the way, he learns about the importance of family and tradition, as well as the power of music to bring people together.

The study relies the theoretical framework proposed in our previous publication (Astrauskienė & Satkauskaitė 2022) that was developed specifically for the analysis of the translation of CBRs for dubbing. Its revised version which includes translation parameters proposed by Pedersen (2011: 105) is presented in Figure 1.

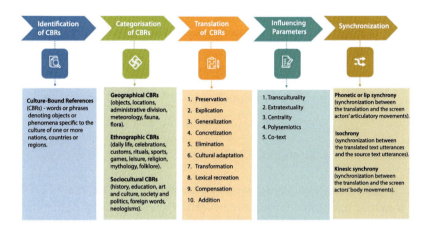

Figure 1. Model for the analysis of the translation of CBRs for dubbing

The model encompasses five main steps in analysing CBRs and their rendering for dubbing. The first step includes the identification of CBRs in the selected material. In our study we treated CBRs as words or phrases denoting objects or phenomena specific to the culture of one or more nations, countries, or regions. The second step is taken to determine the categories and subcategories of CBRs. Our model involves three main categories of CBRs, i.e., geographical, ethnographic, and sociocultural CBRs. As can be seen from Figure 1, each category is further subdivided into several subcategories of CBRs. The third step is to determine translation procedures that were applied when rendering CBRs into Lithuanian. We apply 10 CBR translation procedures that are listed in the model. The fourth step is based on the parameters proposed by Pedersen that influence the translator's decisions in rendering CBRs. The scholar distinguishes seven parameters, namely, (1) transculturality, (2) extratextuality, (3) centrality, (4) polysemiotics, (5) media-specific constraints, (6) co-text and (7) subtitling situation (Pedersen 2011: 105). The last parameter is related to subtitles and is thus not relevant to the analysis of dubbing. Regarding media-specific constraints, Pedersen's study also lists the requirements for subtitles; however, dubbing poses its own restrictions that influence the translation. One of the key constraints and requirements for quality in dubbing is synchronization. Therefore, instead of Pedersen's parameter of "media-specific constraints" our model distinguishes the fifth step based on the three types of synchronies as proposed by Chaume (2012): phonetic or lip synchrony, isochrony and kinesic synchrony. It should be noted that in the present study categorization of CBRs and their translation procedures were analyzed both quantitatively and qualitatively whereas the investigation of translation influencing parameters and synchronization was purely qualitative. It should also be highlighted that both, Chaume's synchronization and Pedersen's parameters, are closely intertwined thus it is almost impossible to analyse them separately. Both, parameters affecting the translator's choices and synchronization will be considered as much as it is relevant to the CBR under examination. We start the next section with an overview of the results of the quantitative analysis and then proceed to discuss the key observations from our findings of the qualitative analysis.

3. Quantitative analysis of CBRs in "Coco"

After extensive analysis of the selected film in the SL and TL, a total of 451 CBRs were identified and stored for further analysis. It should be clarified that the total number of CBRs includes repetitions of the same CBRs since it is possible that the same CBR might have been translated with a different translation procedure (this hypothesis was later confirmed). It should also be pointed out that we determined 439 CBRs in the SL material, while 12 newly-emerging CBRs were detected in the TL. These were completely new CBRs that were not present in the TL, but were added in the TL during the translation process. One more aspect that needs to be mentioned is multilingualism. The film, selected for the present study is an American one, but its narrative evolves in Mexican culture, therefore the creators also added some Spanish vocabulary. This means that the film is multilingual as it involves not only English but also some Spanish expressions. In relation to the film's multilingualism, it is important to clarify that we did not treat every Spanish word as a CBR, but only those words or phrases that conformed with the definition of CBRs and stood out as culture-bound segments.

3.1 Categories and types of culture-bound references in "Coco"

In the first stage of the analysis all CBRs that had been identified were divided into the three major categories, namely, geographical, ethnographic and sociocultural. The most productive category appears to be sociocultural CBRs comprising 82 percent[1] of all instances. This finding was anticipated as this category includes the subcategory of character names which comprises almost 67 percent (67 cases)

---

1. Number of instances of each category of CBRs is indicated in Figure 2.

of all CBRs in this film. Ethnographic CBRs were not as prominent and constituted 15 percent of all CBRs, while geographical category made up only 3 percent of all CBRs (see Figure 2).

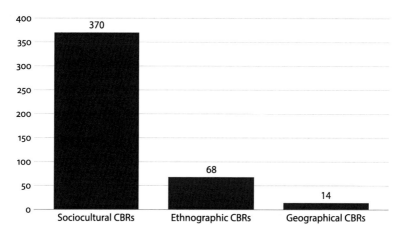

Figure 2. Distribution of the categories of CBRs in "Coco" (Unkrich and Molina 2017)

In the next stage of the analysis, the subcategories of each CBR were determined. The summary of the results and selected examples illustrating each category and sub-category of CBRs' are presented in Table 1.

Table 1 show all instances of CBRs including repetitions. For example, the name of the main protagonist Miguel was mentioned 83 times in the ST, including diminutives such as *Miguelito*. The subcategory of character names includes a wide variety of CBRs such as full names (*Ernesto de la Cruz*), words denoting kinship and first names (*Mamá Coco*), family names (*Rivera*), nicknames (*Cheech*), and pet names (*Dante*). However, we encountered some CBRs whose categories varied depending on the context of the film (see Table 1). Some scholars (e.g., Pedersen 2011: 60; Ranzato 2016: 61; Díaz-Cintas and Remael 2021: 204) highlight the inevitable overlap between the categories and our study showed a similar tendency. Hence, for example, in one context *chorizo* belonged was assigned to the subcategory of food as an ethnographic CBR since the characters were talking about it as a food item, but in a different context we assigned this same CBR to the subcategory of character names as a sociocultural CBR since *Chorizo* was also used as a nickname to refer to a character. In line with Pedersen (2011: 60) the most overlaps can be observed "between the proper names domain and some of the others". For instance, we determined CBR *Poco Loco* which was used as a title of the song in one segment of the film, but in another scene, it was used as a reference the main character Miguel as a nickname. In assigning each CBR to a specific category we relied on the context and its function in the film narrative.

Table 1. Examples of categories and types of CBRs in "Coco" (Unkrich and Molina 2017)

Category	Subcategory	No	Examples
Socio-cultural	Character name	301	Miguel, Mamá Coco, Ernesto de la Cruz, Héctor, Ceci, Tío Berto, Dante, Papá Julio, Tía Rosita, Rivera
	Intertextuality	23	Frida Kahlo, El Santo, Pedro Infante, Jorge Negrete
	Forms of address	18	Señor, señora, doña
	Titles	14	Remember Me, Los Chachalacos, Poco Loco, El Camino A Casa
	Nicknames	6	Chorizo, Chicharrón, Poco Loco
	Art	5	alebrije
	Music	3	mariachi
	Nation	1	Mexican
Ethnographic	Religion	43	Santa Maria, ofrenda, alebrijes, the Land of the Dead, a spirit guide
	Holidays	14	Día de los Muertos, The Day of the Dead,
	Food	4	tamales, churros, chorizo
	Footwear	2	huaraches, wingtips
	Work tools	1	lasso
	Sport	1	Luchadora
Geographical	Geogr. objects	5	Mariachi Plaza, the Plaza de la Cruz
	Geogr. locations	5	México, Santa Cecilia
	Flora	4	cempasúchil, papaya
	Fauna	1	Xolo dog

3.2 Translation procedures of culture-bound references in "Coco"

In terms of the translation procedures employed for the CBRs, almost 83 percent[2] of CBRs were translated using preservation (see Figure 3). Other translation procedures were distributed rather evenly: elimination, generalization, and cultural adaptation each constituted 3.10 percent, addition made up 2.66 percent, and transformation comprised 2.44 percent of the translation procedures. The least frequently applied translation procedures were concretization which constituted 1.55 percent, and explication with its share of 1.11 percent. From the 10 translation procedures listed in the analysis model (Figure 1) only lexical recreation and compensation were not applied in the Lithuanian-dubbed version of "Coco". As far as

---

2. Number of instances of application of each translation procedure is indicated in Figure 3.

compensation is concerned, perhaps the translator felt that they had added almost the same number of CBRs as they had eliminated, hence there was no need to compensate. However, we did not observe any correlation between eliminated and added CBRs which would indicate a compensatory intent on the part of the translator.

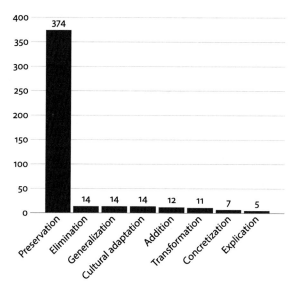

Figure 3. Distribution of CBRs' translation procedures in "Coco" (Unkrich and Molina 2017)

After analysing the distribution of CBRs' categories and translation procedures we proceeded to examine whether translation procedures applied for distinct categories of CBRs would significantly differ. The results of the correlational analysis are displayed in Figure 4.

The most frequent procedure of translating CBRs was preservation while the application of other translation procedures depended on the category. Addition, concretization and elimination were dominant for rendering sociocultural and ethnographic CBRs, generalization and explication were used to render geographical and ethnographic CBRs, transformation was mostly used to translate of ethnographic references, whereas no geographical CBRs were transformed, culturally adapted, concretized or added in the translation process.

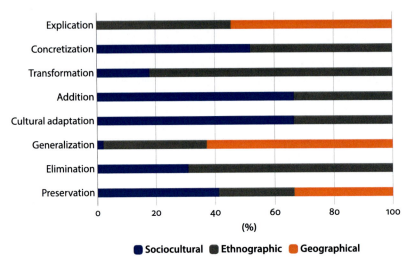

Figure 4. Correlation between CBRs' categories and translation procedures in "Coco" (Unkrich and Molina 2017)

4. Qualitative analysis of CBRs in "Coco"

This section is concerned with the fourth and fifth steps of the analysis model, i.e., with qualitative analysis of the translated CBRs focusing on the dubbing synchronies and translation parameters. The examples presented in this section are listed according to the distribution of the translation procedures. The last subsection is devoted to the discussion of CBRs which were rendered using different translation procedures throughout the film. All examples will be presented in tables with back translation from the Lithuanian in square brackets. We have also listed symbols (ON/OFF/VO)[3] to provide more information which is relevant to dubbing synchronisation.

4.1 Preservation of CBRs

As demonstrated in Figure 3, preservation was the most productive translation procedure in translating all categories of CBRs. This finding is quite reasonable since, as Chaume (2020:111) points out, "[f]idelity to the source film, through the preservation of its relevant features" is one of the key quality requirements in dubbing. In this study three types of preservation were distinguished: preserva-

---

[3]. ON means that the character is seen on the screen uttering the text, OFF refers to the opposite situation when the character is speaking while they are not seen, while VO denotes voice-over narration.

tion of form, preservation of content, and orthographic/morphological adaptation. Preservation of form was the least frequently applied procedure of the three since its application results in the transference of the same CBR from the SL into the TL without any changes to its form. As Lithuanian is a highly inflected language, this procedure is not used very often. Nonetheless, one such example from the analysed film is exemplified in Table 2.

Table 2. Examples of preservation of CBRs in "Coco" (Unkrich and Molina 2017)

Category	SL	TL
Ethnographic CBRs	MIGUEL: (VO) But my family still tells her story every year on Día de los Muertos...	Bet mūsų šeima prisimena ją kiekvienais metais per Día de los Muertos... (Preservation of form)
	ABUELITA: (ON) I asked if you would like more tamales.	Klausiau, ar tu dar nori tamalių? (Morphological adaptation)
Sociocultural CBRs	MIGUEL: (VO) My Abuelita?	Mano senelė. (Preservation of content)
Geographical CBRs	ABUELITA: (OFF) I found your son (ON) in Mariachi Plaza!	Pričiupau tavo sūnų Mariačių aikštėje (Orthographic/morphological adaptation)

The first example illustrates a rather intentional use of preservation of form and adheres to the concept of "centrality" as distinguished by Pedersen (2011: 2011–2013). In "Coco" the specific Mexican holiday, i.e., Day of the Dead or *Día de los Muertos* in its original form is central on the macro-level since it represents "the subject matter" (Pedersen 2011: 111) of the film. Thus, it was important to preserve this key ethnographic CBR in order to maintain the uniqueness of the Mexican culture as well as educate the TL viewers about this traditional holiday widely observed in Mexico and represented in this animated film. Naturally, the younger viewers are likely unfamiliar with this CBR, however, the visual cues as well as its translation into the *Day of the Dead* in the following sentence helps them grasp the idea of the festivity. As far as dubbing synchronies are concerned, the main character Miguel, who utters the CBR is not seen in this scene, therefore kinesic synchrony, isochrony and lip-sync are irrelevant.

The second example involves an ethnographic CBR *tamales*. Regarding Pedersen's parameter of transculturality, it is a monocultural one, meaning that the majority of TL viewers are likely unfamiliar with it. However, the other parameter, i.e., polysemiotics, facilitates the understanding of this CBR by TL audience since the information is delivered simultaneously through the acoustic and visual channels. Considering synchronization, as Abuelita is holding tamales while pronouncing the phrase in medium close-up frontal shot, the translator opted for the procedure of preservation. However, the CBR in the TL acquires the genitive inflection *-ių*. Hence, while isochrony is preserved, the lip-sync is not. Abuelita's lips are quite large and, as she insists that Miguel should eat more tamales, she repeats her question slowly and clearly. Her lips while pronouncing the last syllable *-les* are wide spread, but the last syllable of the translated CBR, i.e. *-ių* would require rounded and protruded position of her lips (according to classification of visemes by Koverienė 2015: 17–18), hence the utterance is not lip-synced. The results of the analysis have shown that the translator tended to use preservation when a certain CBR was uttered by the character shown on screen, while the image of the pronounced CBR was also portrayed in the scene. This was done to preserve the relation of verbal and visual content. As stressed by Chaume (2012:70), "translation must not only follow the written source text, but also the events on screen. In other words, it must be coherent with the communicative situation established on screen (context of situation)."

The analysis has revealed that preservation of content (or literal translation) was more prevalent in all categories of CBRs. The third example provided in Table 2 presents an interesting case, since the viewers can see Miguel in the scene, however, he is eating while the viewers can hear his voice uttering sociocultural CBR *Abuelita*. This Spanish CBR is used as a term of affection meaning *granny* as well as a character's name in the film. For this reason, it was transferred into Lithuanian literally as *senelė* (EN granny). As the viewers can only hear voice-over narration there is no need to address dubbing synchronies. Since Lithuanian is a highly inflected language, orthographic and/or morphological adaptation was applied quite often to render CBRs of all three categories. The fourth example illustrated in Table 2 involves a geographical CBR when Abuelita is pronouncing a phrase involving *Mariachi Plaza*. The scene begins with a long-shot framing of the Rivera's shoemaking shop as the camera reveals Abuelita. While uttering the CBR she is turned to her son, hence, her lips are not clearly visible and, as a result, lip-sync does not constrain the transfer for dubbing. Nonetheless, it should be noted that isochrony of the fragment of the sentence where Abuelita is visible in the scene was preserved in the translation into Lithuanian.

4.2 Generalization of CBRs

Some CBRs were preserved in the TL of the animated film to establish a traditional Mexican atmosphere, but others were generalized to make them more accessible and understandable for the younger target audience. Generalization was employed to all categories of CBRs (see Table 3).

Table 3. Examples of generalization of CBRs in "Coco" (Unkrich and Molina 2017)

Category	SL	TL
Sociocultural CBRs	ABUELITA: (OFF) You'll craft huaraches just like your Tía Victoria.	Meistrausi sandalus kaip tavo teta Viktorija. [You'll craft sandals just like your aunt Victoria].
Ethnographic CBRs	MIGUEL: (ON) And the winner is... Luchadora Coco!	Nugalėtoja yra.... nenugalimoji Koko. [The winner is... the invincible Coco].
Geographic CBRs	CLERK: (ON) Cempasúchil, cempasúchil.	Žiedlapis, žiedlapėlis. [Petal, little petal].

In the first example, the CBR *huaraches* was transferred into Lithuanian as sandals. The translator decided to use a more general and better-known term for the shoes since *huaraches* might be too difficult for children to understand. Moreover, the speaker, Abuelita, is not visible, hence the viewers can only hear her voice. The scene also introduces the audience to the *ofrenda*, i.e., home altar for offerings during the traditional Mexican Día de los Muertos celebration. While showing the ofrenda the camera focuses on Tía Victoria's photo and one shoe that is placed right next to it. As the speaker, Abuelita, is not visible on screen, isochrony and lip-sync are not limiting their choices. It was observed that when the image of a CBR is portrayed in a scene but the character speaking it is not visible, the translator tends to use domesticating translation procedures rather than preserving the CBR through foreignization. This contrast with the usual approach of preserving the CBR when both the speaker and the CBR are visible. It is possible that the visual cue of the speaker interacting with the CBR (e.g., holding or pointing to it) is considered more explicit than the CBR image alone.

However, the second example presents a case in which visual clues may be more confusing than helpful for viewers in the target culture (TC). At the start of the film, Miguel is shown playing with Coco, shouting the phrase *And the winner is... Luchadora Coco!* to her. The CBR *Luchadora* refers to a female professional wrestler in the sport of Lucha libre which is popular in Mexico since its introduction in the early 20th century. The wrestlers wear colorful costumes and masks that are significant to their identities and often represent various Mexican cultural symbols. The creators of the animated film acknowledge this; hence Miguel and Coco are seen wearing colourful masks in the scene under investigation. However, since this sport is not known in the TC, the target audience might associate such costumes with circus or some festivities. Possibly, due to this reason the translator may have decided not to preserve the SL CBR, but instead to generalise it by calling Coco *invincible*. Furthermore, dubbing synchronies also played a big part in the translator's decision making and choice of the translation procedure.

Miguel starts uttering the phrase *Luchadora Coco!* standing on the bed and is shot in a long-shot; however, he makes a pause and jumps from the bed towards Coco, at which point, he is shot at the medium shot. As a result, when he is pronouncing CBRs *Luchadora Coco!* his lips are clearly visible. Hence, the translator chose the Lithuanian word *nenugalimoji*, which is longer by two syllables, but its pronunciation is remarkably close to that of the original CBR. Indeed, the voice-talent utters the word quite fast, thus vowels /u/, /a/, and /o/ match perfectly and thus lip synchrony is maintained. In addition, the way CBRs were pronounced aided the voice-talent as Miguel is shouting the phrase as an announcer at the match, i.e., in a loud voice, excited manner, prolonging each word. After the phrase is heard, the camera swiftly shifts focus from Miguel to Coco. This turns out beneficial for the Lithuanian translation since the rendering of the CBR *Coco* is heard when the viewers cannot see Miguel, preventing any noticeable inconsistency in isochrony.

In the third example, a specific flower called *Cempasúchil* is mentioned as a geographical CBR. The official title of this flower in the TL is *serentis*, but this botanical term is rarely used in spoken Lithuanian. To fit the context of the film, the translator chose to use the more general term *petals* instead. This translation procedure fits the context of the film perfectly, since not the flowers or their blossoms but petals are used to lift the curse. In the scene, the petals of this flower are used to lift a curse and return Miguel from the Land of the Dead to the Land of the Living before sunrise, otherwise he will die. The Clerk is shown searching for a petal on the floor speaking the phrase. As he is presented in a long-shot in a bent body position with his head lowered and moving swiftly, his mouth is not visible for some of the phrase making lip-sync discrepancies less noticeable. Additionally, the TL phrase has the same number of syllables, preserving the isochrony. In this case, the use of the more general term *petal* is a reasonable choice since the focus is on the petals and not on the entire flower.

4.3 Elimination of CBRs

Though elimination might seem as the easiest choice for the translator when it comes to CBRs which do not have equivalents in the TL, deletion of the SL CBRs may change the original intent of the filmmakers by restricting the TL viewers from getting significant information which might be communicated specifically through the CBRs. Hence, the application of this procedure should be really calculated and rational. In the case of the selected film, only 14 instances of elimination have been observed. Consider two examples in Table 4.

It was observed that elimination was applied to the sociocultural and ethnographic CBRs, but no geographical CBRs were omitted in the process of translation. This translation decision is reasonable, as geographical references help to

Table 4. Examples of elimination of CBRs in "Coco" (Unkrich and Molina 2017)

Category	SL	TL
Sociocultural CBRs	MIGUEL: (ON) He loved you, Mamá Coco.	Jis tave labai labai mylėjo. [He loved you very much].
Sociocultural CBRs	TÍA VICTORIA: (ON) Find Héctor's photo.	Surast nuotrauką. [Find a photo].

establish the location and cultural background of the film. For example, in the selected film, the viewer is informed about the country (i.e., Mexico) and city (i.e., Santa Cecilia) where the action takes place and evolves. This information is significant to the viewer and, as a result, geographical CBRs were not eliminated. In regards to the other two categories, the translator eliminated the names of the main characters and one title of a musical band (e.g., Miguel (4), Héctor (3), Mamá Coco (1), Los Chachalacos (1)) in the sociocultural category. This decision was made because of the co-text parameter. The viewers are introduced to the characters at the beginning of the film, so they would be able to recognize them in their actions and interactions. For instance, in a scene where Miguel is talking to Coco, the translator eliminated Coco's name because the viewer can see that Miguel is saying the phrase while looking at Coco. However, in this scene Miguel is shown in a close-up, hence his lips are distinctly seen. Most probably the translator had to eliminate the name in order to maintain isochrony of the entire phrase. Additionally, the translator may have changed the order of words in the translation to better match Miguel's lip movements and maintain the isochrony of the phrase.

In the second example, the main character Héctor's name is eliminated to maintain isochrony, as translating the entire phrase would have made it considerably longer. In addition, the reference of a photo shown by aunt Victoria, which was already shown to the audience multiple times, is easily understood from the co-text. The scene is filmed in a low camera shot, with all members of the Rivera family in the Land of the Dead standing in a circle, discussing their tasks and actions. Although exact lip movements may not be visible, discrepancies in isochrony would still be noticeable. In the ethnographic category only one CBR *ofrenda* was eliminated four times. However, different translation procedures were used in translating this CBR, including elimination, so it will be addressed at the end of the section.

4.4 Cultural adaptation of CBRs

Naturally, there were some CBRs which needed to be adapted for the TL viewers. In the selected film, cultural adaptation was primarily utilized to ensure that the use of CBRs would sound more natural and less foreign to the TL viewers. Similar to the elimination procedure, cultural adaptation was not applied to geographical CBRs, likely in an effort to avoid distorting the original intent of the film's creator. Two instances of cultural adaptation are presented in the remaining categories (see Table 5).

Table 5. Examples of cultural adaptation of CBRs in "Coco" (Unkrich and Molina 2017)

Category	SL	TL
Sociocultural CBRs	HÉCTOR: (ON) I would move Heaven and Earth for you, mi amigo.	Dėl tavęs kalnus nuversčiau, mi amigo. [I would move mountains for you, mi amigo].
Ethnographic CBRs	ARRIVALS AGENT: (VO) Welcome back to the Land of the Dead.	Sveiki sugrįžę į Mirusiųjų pasaulį. [Welcome back to the World of the Dead].

The first example involves a phrase *to move Heaven and Earth* which is repeated several times by different characters during the film. This phrase is central on the macro-level as it serves to expose the duplicitous nature of the character Ernesto de la Cruz, who employs it as an intertextual reference in order to deceive and ultimately poison his friend. In the SL, the phrase denotes the earnest efforts that a true friend would undertake for another. However, in the TL, this phrase would sound confusing as a similar expression, namely *Heaven is intermixing with the Earth*, is commonly used to convey extreme weather conditions, e.g., the ones that emerge during a storm. To preserve the intended meaning while making it more relatable to the target audience, the translator employed the phrase *to move mountains* which would sound more familiar to the target audience, but at the same time would retain the initial idea of going to great lengths for a friend. In this specific scene the phrase is uttered by Héctor as he attempts to appeal to Ernesto de la Cruz by reminding him of his own words. The shot of Héctor in this scene is a long-short, thereby making his mouth movements less discernible. However, the use of cultural adaptation in translation ensures that the isochrony is maintained, as the number of syllables in the SL and the TL match.

The second example illustrates the application of cultural adaptation in the translation of an ethnographic CBR *Land of the Dead* into the *World of the Dead*. The creators of the film originally titled the realms in which the action takes place as the Land of the Living and the Land of the Dead, however, the translator chose to adapt the CBR to align with the target culture's established usage of similar terminology. This decision was likely influenced by the frequency of references to *the world of the dead* in Lithuanian culture, as it is commonly mentioned in prayers and religious funeral songs. Furthermore, the arriving agent is not depicted uttering this CBR, thus the constraints of dubbing synchronies were not an issue for the translator in this instance.

4.5 Transformation of CBRs

Upon conducting a thorough examination of the translation of CBRs in the Lithuanian dubbing, it was discovered that the majority of transformations occurred during scenes in which the characters speaking the dialogue were depicted in a long-shot or were not visible on screen at all. This is likely due to the fact that the translator had more latitude to improvise with the translation, as it was not constrained by the need to maintain dubbing synchrony. Additionally, it was observed that, similarly to previously noted procedures, geographical CBRs were not transformed (see Table 6).

Table 6. Examples of transformation of CBRs in "Coco" (Unkrich and Molina 2017)

Category	SL	TL
Sociocultural CBRs	DE LA CRUZ: (ON) Soon, the party will move across town for my "Sunrise Spectacular!".	Netrukus šventė persikels į mano "Saulėtekio fiestą". [Soon the festival will move to my Sunrise Fiesta].
Ethnographic CBRs	PAPÁ: (OFF) And wingtips, like your Papá Julio.	Ir kurpaites, kaip tėtis Chulijas. [And slippers, as father Julio].

In the first example, the character of Ernesto de la Cruz is depicted in a long-shot, with limited visibility of his lips when he utters the phrase. He expresses excitement as he invites Miguel to his performance titled *Sunrise Spectacular*. Notably, the translator chose to transform the title of the show to *Sunrise Fiesta*. This decision may have been influenced by the goal to preserve isochrony, as the SL phrase consists of six syllables, while the TL translation, if preserved, would have prolonged the phrase by at least two syllables (Sau-lė-te-kio Nuo-sta-bu-sis). Thus, by transforming the CBR, the translator was able to maintain isochrony while still preserving six syllables in the translation. Additionally, the term *fiesta* is fitting within the context of the film, as it is associated with celebration in Spain and Latin America. This transformation is foreignizing but also aligns with the Mexican culture depicted in the film. Furthermore, the translator's choice of *fiesta* sounds more natural in the TL, and thus adheres to one of the core quality requirements for dubbing, i.e., to produce "credible and natural dialogue" (Chaume 2020: 111). However, the second example is less successful. In this scene, Miguel's father explains to him that he is ready to learn how to make shoes on his own, like his late uncle Julio. Father mentions a specific type of shoe, wingtips, which are described as "strong leather shoes that fasten with laces and have an extra piece of leather with small holes in it over the toe" (Oxford Advanced Learner's Dictionary 2023).[4] As the phrase including CBR is spoken, viewers are not shown Miguel's father, but rather a photo of the uncle Julio with this specific type of shoe next to it. It is clear from the picture that this is a men's shoe, yet in the Lithuanian translation, *wingtips* were translated as *slippers*. In this scene, while isochrony or lip-synch are not relevant, multimodal coherence is particularly important and needs to be observed. Translating one type of shoe into another can cause viewers to interpret the dialogue differently. From Lithuanian translation, it seems that uncle Julio was making shoes for women. Additionally, the term *slippers* immediately evokes intertextual references to the Cinderella character which is not related to the film in any way. Thus, by transforming the CBR, the translator provides viewers with additional yet unnecessary information that might lead to confusion.

4.6 Addition of CBRs in the TL

The description of the model of CBR translation analysis above made mention of the fact that it is important to consider not only the SL but also the TL in order to determine the number of CBRs present in a film. This occurs because some CBRs that are not present in the original text may be added during the translation process to the TL. While not prevalent in audiovisual translation due to spatio-temporal constraints, the addition of CBRs may occur during the translation process into the TL, particularly in the case of dubbing. This is because, in dubbing, the SL is not heard by viewers, leaving them unaware of any CBRs that may have been eliminated or added to the TL. It was observed that such additions are typically applied in scenes where characters are not visible while speaking, or in other words, scenes that are not restricted by dubbing synchronies. Seven instances of such addition were distinguished. Additionally, in five instances, addition was applied where characters were portrayed in the scene in order to preserve dubbing synchronies. To provide examples of this usage of addition, two examples are presented in Table 7.

---

4. https://www.oxfordlearnersdictionaries.com/definition/english/wingtips

Table 7. Examples of addition of CBRs in "Coco" (Unkrich and Molina 2017)

Category	SL	TL
Sociocultural CBRs	CECILIA: (ON) Ya lo sabía, I gotta dress (OFF) forty dancers by sunrise and thanks to you, I'm one Frida short of an opening number!	O, šventas Abiza, turiu Saulėtekio teatre aprengti keturiasdešimt šokėjų, o dabar dėl tavęs man trūksta vienos Fridos. [Oh, saint Abiza, I gotta dress fourty dancers at the Sunrise theater and that's to you, I'm one Frida short].
Ethnographic CBRs	DE LA CRUZ (FILM CLIP): (OFF) You must have faith, sister.	Reikia tikėti, Cesilija. [You must have faith, Cecilia].

In the scene of the first example, Héctor and Miguel visit the studio of costume designer, Cecilia. However, upon their arrival, Héctor admits that he is unable to return Frida's costume to Cecilia. This revelation incites a furious response from Cecilia, who expresses her frustration through the use of raised vocal intonation and physical gestures, such as waving her hands in despair as she utters the sentence presented in first example of Table 9. At the beginning of the utterance Cecilia is portrayed in a middle close up over the shoulder shot. The filmmakers utilize the Spanish phrase *ya lo sabia* (EN *I knew it*) to add authenticity to the scene. As Cecilia's lip movement is clearly visible at the beginning of her utterance, the translator sought to retain lip-sync by addition of the CBR *saint Abiza* which sounds similar to the Spanish phrase in Lithuanian. However, it should be noted that there is no such saint Abiza in Lithuanian culture, and the use of this CBR serves solely for the purpose of maintaining lip-sync and potentially adding humor to the scene, as the unusual name may be perceived as humorous when spoken by an angry costume designer.

Interestingly enough, the second case of addition involves the name of Cecilia, which was added during the translation of a word sister. At first glance, addition seems an intriguing phenomenon that is difficult to explain. The character in question is not Cecilia, but rather a nun who appears in a short film clip featuring Ernesto de la Cruz dressed as a priest. The clip is shown on a large display at Ernesto de la Cruz's party and serves as inspiration for Miguel to sing in order to get Ernesto's attention. The clip is shown in a middle close-up, which allows for clear visibility of Ernesto's, or the priest's, lip movement. The translator may have added the name Cecilia in order to match the lip synchrony. The first syllable of the word *sister* in the SL uttered by the priest matches perfectly with the last syllable of the word *ti-kė-ti* (4 viseme) in the TL, while the second syllable of *sister* in the SL coincides with the first one in the name *Ce-ci-li-ja* (2 viseme). This suggests that visually similar phonemes were used in the TL to achieve lip synchrony in dubbing. It should be noted, however, that sometimes addition is used to compensate for the CBRs that are eliminated in translation. But in this specific case, no instances of compensation were determined.

4.7 Concretization of CBRs in the TL

There have been 7 instances (6 of which are classified as sociocultural and 1 ethnographic) in which the translator utilized the procedure of concretization. It was typically employed when CBRs may have been too obscure for the TL audience to understand (see Table 8).

Table 8. Examples of concretization of CBRs in "Coco" (Unkrich and Molina 2017)

Category	SL	TL
Sociocultural CBRs	MIGUEL: (OFF) That's my Mamá Coco. That's my Mamá Imelda.	Tai mano prosenelė Koko. Proprosenelė Imelda. [That's my great-grandmother Coco. Great-great-grandmother Imelda].

Though most of the character names were preserved in the translation, not all of them were translated using the same procedures throughout the film. For instance, the CBR *Mamá Imelda* was preserved in all the cases with the exception of the instance in which Miguel is conversing with Héctor. As Miguel is not yet aware of Héctor's familial relation to him (Héctor is his great-great-grandfather), he explains his relation to Mamá Imelda and Mamá Coco in a more specific manner. This concretization is necessary due to the fact that the Spanish term *Mamá* can refer to mother, grandmother, or even great-great-grandmother, whereas in Lithuanian it primarily refers to a mother. The filmmakers included explanations of the familial relationships at the beginning of the film through Miguel's voice-over narration, leading to the conclusion that they did not feel the need for further clarification later in the film. However, the Lithuanian translator sought to maintain consistency with the logic of the scene by having Miguel explain to Héctor that Mamá Coco is his great-grandmother and Mamá Imelda is his great-great-grandmother.

4.8 Explication of CBRs in the TL

The procedure of explication in dubbing is often problematic in dubbing mostly because it is applied in order to give the TL viewers more information about a certain CBR that might be too difficult to comprehend if rendered by preservation. However, this can result in prolonging the duration of the CBR and hindering isochrony. Despite these potential drawbacks, explication may be necessary for translation of monocultural CBRs.

Table 9. Examples of explication of CBRs in Coco (Unkrich and Molina 2017)

Category	SL	TL
Ethnographic CBRs	GUSTAVO: (ON) He choked on some chorizo!	Jis paspringo dešra čiorizo! [He choked on chorizo sausage].
Geographic CBRs	FRIDA: (ON) Oh, the mighty Xolo dog!	Juk čia beplaukis šuo. [But this is a hairless dog].

The first example in Table 9 involves the CBR *chorizo*. It is important to note that this specific CBR is classified as both a food item within the ethnographic category and as a nickname of the main character Héctor within the sociocultural category. As demonstrated in this example, the nickname *Chorizo* was given to Héctor due to the belief that he died after consuming this particular type of sausage. The CBR, as a nickname, is preserved in the translation, but only because it is explained right away why some characters call Héctor that way. This case serves as an exemplification of Pedersen's notion of co-text as one of the parameters that influence the translator's choices. Co-text means that CBR "is disambiguated or explained at some point earlier or later in the co-text" (Pedersen 2011: 114). In the fragment under analysis, explication is applied when *chorizo* as a food item is first mentioned. The character Gustavo who utters the CBR is depicted in a medium shot, making his facial expressions and body language clearly visible. Gustavo finds the reasoning behind the nickname amusing and, as such, moves closer to Héctor in a playful manner, elongating the pronunciation of the CBR *chorizo* at the end of the phrase and laughing loudly with the other characters in the background. As a result, his mouth movements are very distinctive. The translator, in turn, utilizes the elongation of the pronunciation to provide additional clarification to the TL viewers that *chorizo* refers to a type of sausage.

Analogous to the aforementioned scenario, a case of CBR involving the dog breed *Xolo* was observed. In the scene, Miguel inadvertently enters Frida's room with his dog, Dante, and Frida immediately recognizes that Dante is not an ordinary dog. She refers to him as *the mighty Xolo* dog while kneeling down to pet him. The viewer can see Frida in a medium close-up shot as she speaks. The translator could have retained the original of the breed's name, but instead chose to provide an explanation, referring to the dog as *a hairless dog*. This choice was likely made because in Lithuania, these dogs are commonly known as Mexican hairless dogs, hence providing an explanation that is more familiar to the target audience would be beneficial. Though such translation is one syllable shorter when the SL, at the end of the phrase the viewers can see Frida from her side, thus her lip movement is less distinct. Additionally, Frida expresses her excitement about the dog through her actions, such as touching his head lovingly and speaking slowly but proudly. The voice-talent, on the other hand, pronounces the phrase with enthusiasm and speed, which minimizes the discrepancies in dubbing synchrony. It should also be noted that the pronunciation of *Xolo* and the Lithuanian word for dog *šuo* match, which adds to the overall effectiveness of the translation. Therefore, it can be concluded that the translator carefully weighed the pros and cons of adding additional information and was able to achieve a balance between synchronization and explication of CBRs.

4.9 Different translation procedures for the same CBRs

One of the most intriguing cases in our corpus is the examination of the Spanish CBR *ofrenda* and its translation into the TL. This CBR has a high degree of centrality on the macro-level as it serves as the central leitmotif of the film under investigation. According to Pedersen (2011: 2011–2012), central references are most likely to be translated using retention or official equivalent strategies. However, in the chosen film, the translator employed a variety of translation procedures. Table 11 illustrates that various translation procedures were utilized to convey the CBR *ofrenda* into the TL. One potential explanation for this could be the transculturality parameter, which Pedersen (2011: 106) regards as the most significant from a communicative perspective. In terms of transculturality, the CBR *ofrenda* should be classified as a monocultural CBR. This means that it "causes a translation problem, which arises because the referent of an ECR [Extralinguistic Cultural Reference] can be assumed to be less identifiable to the majority of the relevant TT audience than it is to the relevant ST audience, owing to differences in encyclopaedic knowledge" (Pedersen 2011: 107). Therefore, the translation procedures suggested by Pedersen for the translation of central CBRs cannot be applied, as there are no official equivalents of *ofrenda* in the TL, nor is it possible to use retention, at least not using one equivalent TL word. Nevertheless, the application of different translation procedures assists in conveying the main semes of the word *ofrenda* from a semantic perspective. For example, it emphasizes that this specific altar belongs to a family and its purpose is to commemorate deceased relatives (see Table 10).

It is important to note that due to its centrality, this CBR is prominently featured throughout the film. To convey this concept, different translation procedures are employed to provide verbal explanations. Additionally, the meaning of the term *ofrenda* is not only conveyed through the acoustic verbal channel but also through visual nonverbal channel. In Pedersen's (2011: 113) terms, it shows "a

Table 10. Different translation procedures of the same CBR in "Coco" (Unkrich and Molina 2017)

SL	TL	Translation procedure
ABUELITA: (ON) We've put their photos on the ofrenda so their spirits can cross over.	Padedam jų nuotraukas ant altoriaus, kad jų sielos galėtų pereiti. [We've put their photos on the altar so their spirits can cross over].	Generalization (5)
DISTRESSED TRAVELER: (ON) We gotta get to a dozen ofrendas tonight…	Šiąnakt turim aplankyti krūvą giminių. [We gotta visit a lot of relatives tonight].	Transformation (4)
DEPARTURES AGENT: Your photo's on your dentist's ofrenda.	Jūsų nuotrauka — pas dantistą. [Your photo's at the dentist's].	Elimination (4)
MAMÁ IMELDA: (OFF) My family always… ALWAYS… puts my photo on the ofrenda!	Mano šeima visada, VISADA padeda nuotrauką ant atminimo altoriaus. [My family always, ALWAYS puts a photo on the remembrance altar].	Explication (3)
MAMÁ IMELDA: (ON) You took my photo off the ofrenda?!	Tu paėmei nuotrauką nuo šeimos altoriaus? [You took the photo off the family's altar?].	Concretisation (2)

high level of polysemiotic interplay", meaning that "there is a high level of interaction between the polysemiotic channels". But, differently from other CBRs, in the case of *ofrenda* TL viewers' comprehension was prioritized over dubbing synchronization. This decision may have been made due to the complexity of this particular CBRs in the film. It is also worth mentioning that no close-up shots were utilized in any of the examples presented.

Additionally, various translation procedures were utilized in the rendering of other CBRs, including generalization (as demonstrated in the translation of *at the Plaza de la Cruz* to *Kruzo aikštėje* (EN in the square of the Cruz)) and preservation (evidenced in the translation of *to the Plaza de la Cruz* to *į De la Kruzo aikštę*). Interestingly, the CBR *Frida* was rendered not only using preservation (occurring 8 times) and addition (occurring 4 times), potentially indicating that this particular CBRs was considered intercultural and more widely recognized among TL viewers. With regards to the categories and subcategories of CBRs, the greatest diversity of translation procedures was applied in the rendering of character names, which can be anticipated as these CBRs were utilized more frequently compared to other CBRs.

5. Concluding remarks

The analysis of the film "Coco" (Unkrich and Molina 2017) revealed a total of 451 CBRs, including repetitions and newly-emerging CBRs in the TL. The study found that the most productive category of CBRs was sociocultural, comprising 82 percent of all cases. Character names were the most representative subtype of CBRs, making up 67 percent of all CBRs. Ethnographic category of CBRs were less prominent and constituted 15 percent of all CBRs, while geographical CBRs occurred least frequently, constituting only 3 percent of all CBRs. The majority of CBRs in the Lithuanian-dubbed version of "Coco" were translated using preservation, with 83 percent of CBRs translated in this way. Other translation procedures were used more sparingly, with elimination, generalization, and cultural adaptation each accounting for 3.10 percent. The least frequently used translation procedures were concretization and explication, which made up 1.55 percent and 1.11 percent respectively. Lexical recreation and compensation were not applied in the translation of the selected film.

The study found that preservation was the most commonly used procedure among all three categories of CBRs, but the use of other procedures varied depending on the category. Addition, concretization, and elimination were dominant for sociocultural and ethnographic CBRs, particularly those with high centrality on the macro-level, such as character names and religious phenomena that are repeated multiple times. For geographical and ethnographic CBRs, which are mostly monocultural, generalization and explication were used since these CBRs are often unknown to the target audience and there may not be official equivalents in the TL. Transformation was mostly applied for ethnographic CBRs. Geographical CBRs, which typically refer to a specific place or object in the source culture, were mostly preserved and not adapted, concretized, or added in the translation process.

The analysis also revealed that the translator tended to use preservation when a character who was visible on the screen utters a CBR and the image of the CBR is also portrayed in the scene. This suggests that a high usage of the preservation procedure may be determined by isochrony, lip-sync as well as polysemiotics. However, when the image of the CBR was portrayed but the speaker was not visible, the translator tended to use translation procedures which are more domesticating such as cultural adaptation, transformation, rather than foreignizing (e.g., preservation, explication). This suggests that the presence of the speaker holding or pointing to a CBR is considered a more explicit visual cue than the image of the CBRs' alone.

Funding

This project has received funding from the European Social Fund (under the No 09.3.3-LMT-K-712 "Development of Competences of Scientists, other Researchers and Students through Practical Research Activities" measure). Project title "Translation of Culture-Specific Items in Contemporary Lithuanian-Dubbed Films" No 09.3.3-LMT-K-712-23-0178.

References

Alfaify, Abeer, and Sara Ramos Pinto. 2021. "Cultural References in Films: An Audience Reception Study of Subtitling into Arabic." *The Translator* 28 (1): 112–31.

Astrauskienė, Jurgita and Danguolė Satkauskaitė. 2022. "Kultūrinių realijų pavadinimų vertimas dubliažui: analizės modelis [Translation of culture-bound references for dubbing: a model for the analysis]." *Respectus Philologicus* 41: 193–206.

Chaume, Frederic. 2020. "Dubbing." In *The Palgrave Handbook of Audiovisual Translation and Media Accessibility*, ed. By Łukasz Bogucki, and Mikołaj Deckert, 103–132. Cham: Springer International Publishing AG.

Díaz Cintas, Jorge, and Aline Remael. 2021. *Subtitling: Concepts and Practices*. London, New York: Routledge.

Díaz Pérez, Francisco Javier. 2017. "The translation of humour based on culture-bound terms in Modern Family. A cognitive-pragmatic approach." *MonTI. Monographs in Translation and Interpreting* 9: 49–75.

Díaz-Cintas, Jorge, and Aline Remael. 2007. *Audiovisual Translation: Subtitling*. Manchester, Kinderhook: St. Jerome Publishing.

Koverienė, Indrė. 2015. Dubbing as an Audiovisual Translation Mode: English and Lithuanian Phonemic Inventories in the Context of Visual Phonetics. PhD diss. Vilnius University.

Oxford Advanced Learner's Dictionary. 2023. "Definition of wingtips" (https://www.oxfordlearnersdictionaries.com/definition/english/wingtips)

Pedersen, Jan. 2011. *Subtitling Norms for Television: An Exploration Focussing on Extralinguistic Cultural References*. Amsterdam, Philadelphia: John Benjamins.

Ranzato, Irene. 2016. *Translating Culture Specific References on Television: The Case of Dubbing*. New York, London: Routledge.

Ranzato, Irene. 2020. "The Problem with Culture." In *The Palgrave Handbook of Audiovisual Translation and Media Accessibility*, ed. By Łukasz Bogucki, and Mikołaj Deckert, 647–666. Cham: Springer International Publishing AG.

Unkrich, Lee, and Adrian Molina (Directors). 2017. Coco [Film]. Pixar Animation Studios, Walt Disney Pictures. 105 minutes.

"La receta del pistou"
Referencias culturales francesas en la TAV

Enora Lessinger
School of Education, Humanities and Languages, Oxford Brookes University

This article explores the translation of French cultural references in AVT by analysing the Spanish subtitles of the series *Dix pour cent* (*Call My Agent*). An adaptation of Pedersen's 2011 typology of extralinguistic cultural references (ECRs) and of their translation strategy in subtitling is used as a theoretical frame. The quantitative analysis shows that foreignisation is the dominant strategy, while a more detailed and qualitative analysis of the data reveals that this tendency is significantly more pronounced in ECRs thematically linked to France's strongest areas of soft power, such as luxury brand or food and drink.

Keywords: cultural references, translation, subtitles, French culture, AVT

1. Introducción

Desde el giro cultural que se observó en los años 80, la traducción de referencias culturales ha ocupado un lugar central cada vez más importante en los estudios de traducción. Unos 30 años después de la "intraducibilidad cultural" de Catford (1965), Venuti acuñaba los ya emblemáticos conceptos de "extranjerización" y "domesticación" como estrategias de traducción. Más recientemente aún, Zhang definía la traducción como un "acto comunicativo transcultural" (2013: 1919), ilustrando el papel clave de la cultura en el campo traductológico. Por lo tanto, no es de extrañar que la investigación producida en las últimas décadas diera lugar a una plétora de enfoques diferentes sobre las referencias culturales. Varios investigadores propusieron tipologías diferentes, intentando describir y clasificar los distintos tipos de referencias culturales con los que el traductor puede encontrarse, así como las mayores estrategias de traducción de tales referencias (Newmark 1988, Baker 1992, Aixelá 1996 y Davies 2003, entre otros).

Con la aparición de la traducción audiovisual (TAV) como subcampo de importancia creciente en los estudios de traducción a principios del siglo, aparecieron nuevas tipologías de referencias culturales y de sus correspondientes técnicas de traducción. Las categorizaciones propuestas por Díaz Cintas y Remael (2007) o Pedersen (2005, 2011), por ejemplo, se adaptan a la especificidad de los retos a los que se enfrentan los subtituladores cuando lidian con referencias culturales en el texto fuente. Esos retos están intrínsecamente relacionados con el carácter intersemiótico de la subtitulación y con las limitaciones espaciales, temporales y técnicas que conlleva. Por ejemplo, resulta imposible implementar notas a pie de página y glosas (Abdelaal 2019). Otras dificultades adicionales incluyen el hecho de que la subtitulación interlingüística representa un paso no solo de la forma oral a la escrita, sino también de una lengua a otra, lo que lleva a Gottlieb a describirla como "traducción diagonal" (1994).

En este corpus, que se compone de los subtítulos españoles de la serie francesa *Call My Agent*, la cuestión de las referencias culturales se hace aún más central debido a la propia temática de la serie. Esta gira en torno a una agencia de talentos artísticos en París, y durante cuatro temporadas, sigue la vida profesional y emocional de los agentes y de sus clientes, estrellas del cine francés tales como Charlotte Gainsbourg o Jean Dujardin, que actúan su propio papel en la pantalla.

Este artículo se propone investigar cómo se tratan las abundantes referencias culturales que salpican la serie en los subtítulos españoles, teniendo en cuenta el carácter central de la cultura francesa en el tema de la serie. De hecho, como demuestra Pedersen (2005:10), el carácter central de una referencia en contexto es uno de los parámetros más susceptibles de influir en la decisión de los subtituladores en la hora de traducir referencias culturales: cuanto más central una referencia en el macro- o micro-contexto, menos intervencionista es la estrategia de traducción.

En contraste con el corpus de Pedersen, que se compone antes todo de textos audiovisuales de lengua inglesa traducidos a idiomas escandinavos, aquí se analizan referencias culturales francesas traducidas al español. A pesar de la distancia lingüística relativamente corta entre los diferentes idiomas, tratándose únicamente de lenguas indoeuropeas, no se debe subestimar la importancia de la diferencia entre los dos corpus por razones más bien culturales. En los países escandinavos, la subtitulación ha sido históricamente el medio de traducción audiovisual preferido y dominante, mientras que tanto Francia como España tienen una larga tradición de preferencia por el doblaje (Díaz-Cintas y Remael 2007:17), aunque esta tendencia no se observe de la misma manera en los países de América latina.

Mientras los espectadores de textos audiovisuales doblados no tienen acceso al texto fuente, con subtítulos sí pueden oírlo, y a menudo entender o reconocerlo hasta cierto punto, especialmente en el caso de idiomas tan próximos como el francés y el español. En comparación con otros métodos de traducción, la subtitulación se presta entonces más naturalmente a estrategias de traducción de tipo extranjerizante. En otras palabras, en subtítulos, la tendencia es traer al espectador hacia la cultura fuente y su idioma (extranjerización), mientras que, en el doblaje, la tendencia es adaptarlos a la cultura meta (domesticación). Esta tendencia fue notada entre otros investigadores por Pedersen (2011).

Por lo tanto, resulta interesante comprobar cuál es la estrategia dominante adoptada por los subtituladores, puesto que, por un lado, traducen en idiomas vinculados a culturas con una fuerte tradición de doblaje (y por lo tanto de domesticación) pero, por otro lado, la cultura francesa ocupa temáticamente el primer plano en *Call My Agent*, lo que tiende a conducir a una estrategia extranjerizante.

2. Marco teórico

A fin de responder a las preguntas de investigación expuestas arriba, conviene inscribir este estudio en su contexto académico a través una reseña de estudios anteriores sobre el mismo tema, tanto en términos de metodología de investigación como de resultados.

Muchas tipologías de referentes culturales han sido propuestas por varios investigadores en traductología a lo largo de las últimas décadas, como Newmark (1988), Nedergaard-Larsen (1993), Leppihalme (1994), Davies (2003), Katan (2004), Díaz Cintas & Remael (2007), o Pedersen (2011). Algunas son mucho más detalladas que otras (por ejemplo, la de Nedergaard-Larsen se compone de cuatro categorías generales mientras que la de Pedersen consta de doce) pero aun así se evidencia la recurrencia de ciertos elementos, como referencias a la geografía y tipografía, a la cultura material (ropa, comida, etc.) o relacionadas con el campo político.

Esas clasificaciones de referencias culturales se acompañan típicamente de otra describiendo las maneras más comunes de traducir tales referencias. Aquí también, los nombres varían más que el contenido, lo cual no ha de extrañar dado que todas describen fenómenos similares. Leppihalme, por ejemplo, propone como categorías la retención, la adición, la explicitación, la substitución, la reformulación, y la recreación, y propone estrategias diferentes según el tipo de referente cultural — o "alusión", tal como lo llama (1994). Más recientemente, Díaz Cintas y Remael propusieron nueve estrategias de traducción diferentes: el préstamo, el calco, la explicitación, la sustitución, la transposición, la recreación lexical, la compensación, la adición y la omisión (2007: 202). Esta clasificación se diferencia de la precedente por haber sido cuñada específicamente para describir el tratamiento de referentes cultural en la subtitulación. Este tipo de traducción puede efectivamente influir en la estrategia de traducción por varias razones. Por una parte, las restricciones espaciales y temporales a menudo hacen imposible añadir explicaciones, y llevan, por el contrario, a condensar el texto. Por otra parte, los demás canales (audio y visual) pueden suplementar la pérdida de información que resulta de esta condensación, gracias a lo que Chaume (2004) describe como cohesión intersemiótica.

Otras categorizaciones específicas a la subtitulación incluyen la de Nedergaard-Larsen (1993), la de Aixelá (1994), la de Tomaszkiewicz (2001) y la de Pedersen (2011). Esta última, en la que se basa la presente investigación, distingue seis técnicas de subtitulación de referencias culturales, o tal como las llama Pedersen, "extralinguistic cultural references" (referencias culturales extralingüísticas, RCE).

Una de las ventajas de esta clasificación es que diferencia entre las técnicas de domesticación y de extranjerización. Esos conceptos fueron popularizados por Venuti (1995) pero la distinción proviene originalmente de Schleiermacher en el siglo XIX, en su descripción de los dos principales métodos de traducción: "Either the translator leaves the author in peace, as much as possible, and moves the reader towards him; or he leaves the reader in peace, as much as possible, and moves the author towards him" (in Lefevere, 1977: 74).

En la tipología de técnicas de traducción de Pedersen, las tres técnicas extranjerizantes son la retención, la traducción directa y la especificación, mientras que la generalización, la substitución y la omisión son clasificadas como domesticantes. Añade una séptima categoría, el equivalente oficial, que no cabe dentro del espectro domesticación/extranjerización, sino que corresponde a la traducción por defecto (de diccionario) de una ECR. Pedersen argumenta que los equivalentes oficiales siempre se basan en otra técnica que sí se puede clasificar como una u otra; sin embargo, admite que los casos donde mejor se percibe la estrategia de traducción de un texto se sitúa generalmente en otros sitios: "[o]ne of the most revealing translation crisis points is when some reference to the Source Culture is made, and there is no obvious official equivalent" (2005:1).

De manera general, estudios anteriores que examinan la subtitulación de referencias culturales tienden a concluir que predomina la extranjerización. Nedergaard-Larsen, por ejemplo, observa esta tendencia en su análisis de referencias culturales en un corpus escandinavo: "The analysis of specific examples showed a tendency, possibly norm-governed, to retain the local colour of the film and to remain faithful to the source language when this did not cause problems of comprehension" (1993: 238). Similarmente, Zojer nota una tendencia cada vez más pronunciada a no traducir referentes culturales (2011: 408), y Pedersen también observa una mayoría de técnicas de traducción extranjerizantes en su corpus audiovisual: "If all results from the Scandinavian Subtitles Corpus are taken into account, it must be said that source-orientation generally prevails.

This conclusion is also backed up by the studies of Orrevall (2004), who looked at ECRs in talk shows, and Steinholtz (2007), who looked at ECRs in a sitcom" (2011:193). Aunque algunos estudios encontraran resultados donde prevale la domesticación (por ejemplo, Fawcett 2003 o Validashti 2008), parece que la tendencia general observada sea una de extranjerización, sin que haya un vínculo claro con el par de idioma investigado o la dirección de traducción.

3. Método

El corpus de esta investigación incluye las cuatro temporadas de la serie francesa *Call My Agent*. El texto fuente corresponde al audio original en francés, y el texto meta consta de los subtítulos españoles accesibles en la plataforma de difusión Netflix. Varios ejemplos muestran que el texto de partida con el que trabajaron los subtituladores no consiste en los subtítulos franceses, y tampoco en los ingleses, sino en el audio francés. Por ejemplo, en el cuarto episodio de la cuarta y última temporada (T4E4), una de las protagonistas pregunta: "Elle est rentrée de Saint-Barth pour rien?" [Volvió de Saint-Barth en vano?]. En los subtítulos franceses, desaparece la referencia geográfica: "Elle est rentrée pour rien?" [¿Volvió en vano?], y en los subtítulos ingleses también: "She flew back for nothing?" [¿Volvió en avión para nada?]. En los españoles, al contrario, se mantiene la referencia geográfica: "Vino de Saint-Barth en vano?". Queda claro, entonces, que los traductores se basaron en el canal audio o en su transcripción para subtitular al español, y no en los subtítulos franceses o ingleses, como ocurre a veces.

En cada episodio, fueron notadas las ocurrencias de referencias culturales y clasificadas según el tipo de ECR. Las categorías utilizadas se basan en las de Pedersen (2011) pero con unos cambios que reflejan la realidad del corpus, y son las siguientes:

1. **Geografía**, p. ej. "Epinay-sur-Seine", "la côte d'Azur" o "le jardin des Plantes"
2. **Marcas**, p. ej. "Banania", "une étoile Michelin" o "La Poule d'Or"
3. **Comida**, p. ej. "les macarons", "un grand cru" o "le pistou"
4. **Gobierno**, p. ej. "l'Elysée", "Vigipirate" o "les Chirac"
5. **Entretenimiento**, p. ej. "*Gala*", "le théâtre du Rond-Point" o "Laure Manaudou"
6. **Educación**, p. ej. "bac", "collège" o "Polytechnique"
7. **Transportes**, p. ej. "un RER", "un VTC" o "Roissy".

Las referencias así clasificadas fueron entonces analizadas en términos de estrategia de traducción, que son las siguientes:

3.1   Estrategias domesticantes

a. **La retención** consiste en mantener la referencia como se da en la versión original, o simplemente con unas adaptaciones mínimas, por ejemplo, a través del uso de cursiva.

b. **La traducción directa** es una traducción literal donde las únicas diferencias con el texto fuente son las que son imprescindibles para que la traducción funcione en la lengua meta. Así, "le festival de Cannes" se traduce en la serie con "el festival de Cannes", y el premio cinematográfico "Un Certain Regard" con "Una Cierta Mirada".

c. **La especificación** es una técnica donde se añade más información en comparación con el texto fuente, sea por medio de completando un nombre o expresión (por ejemplo, "la Sécu" es traducido por "la Seguridad Social"), sea añadiendo información adicional. Así, un protagonista dice de otro que "il ne fait pas le Drucker" [no hace el Drucker], refiriéndose al presentador de un programa de televisión bien conocido en Francia, pero el subtítulo español dice que "no va al programa de Drucker" (T2E1 24:38), añadiendo la palabra explicativa "programa".

3.2   Estrategias extranjerizantes

a. **La generalización** es el opuesto de especificación: ocurre cuando se utiliza en la traducción un término más general que en el texto fuente, u otra forma de paráfrasis. Por ejemplo, uno de los agentes compara su vida con "faire le GR20 en tongs" [hacer el GR20 en chanclatas], el GR20 siendo una ruta de senderismo en la isla francesa de Córcega. En español, el subtítulo utiliza una formulación más general que no requiere que el espectador entienda la ECR: "Se siente como escalar en chanclatas" (T4E4 25:22).

b. **La sustitución** consiste en sustituir una ECR de la cultura fuente con otra de otra cultura, sea una referencia transcultural que se entiende en varias culturas, incluido en la cultura meta, sea con una de la misma cultura meta, aquí el mundo hispánico. Así, un protagonista comenta irónicamente "C'est pas les Experts" (T3E6 0:33), refiriéndose a un programa televisado de investigación criminal. En español, la referencia francesa se sustituye por otra americana, pero supuestamente percibida como transcultural: "esto no es *CSI*".

c. **La omisión**, a pesar de implicar la desaparición pura y simple de la referencia, sí puede ser una técnica de traducción apropiada, tal como lo demostró Toury

(1995:82), especialmente en un contexto de subtitulación donde el espacio es muy limitado. En la tercera temporada, un protagonista intenta adivinar por que otro está en el jardín botánico, que se encuentra cerca de la universidad de Jussieu en París, y supone que "il voit une étudiante de Jussieu" [está saliendo con una estudiante de Jussieu]. La referencia geográfica se omite en español, supuestamente porque no es central en contexto y no es indispensable para entender la escena: "Quizá tenga una cita con una estudiante" (T3E3 38:25).

4. Resultados y análisis

4.1 Visión global

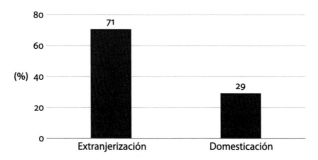

Figura 1. Resultados generales

El número total de referencias analizadas es de 140, y crece de la primera a la última temporada, con 24, 25, 33 y 58 ECRs respectivamente.

En la Figura 1 se puede observar que, en general, la extranjerización domina claramente como estrategia de traducción: unos 71% de las ECRs son subtituladas con una técnica de traducción extranjerizante. La evolución de temporada en temporada es mínima, con respectivamente 71%, 68%, 70% y 72% de extranjerización. Esas observaciones concuerdan con los resultados de estudios anteriores citados en la sección anterior. Zojer sugiere que la tendencia a extranjerizar referentes culturales se relaciona con una globalización en la que, por un lado, las referencias culturales originalmente propias a una cultura se vuelven conocidas más allá de esta cultura, y por otro lado esta forma de globalización resalta las diferencias culturales más de lo que las nivela (2011: 407).

4.2 Distribución por tipo de ECR

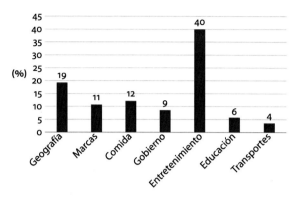

Figura 2. Distribución por tipo de ECR

En la Figura 2 se ve la distribución temática de las ECRs según la tipología expuesta arriba. Las referencias culturales vinculadas al entretenimiento representan unos 40% de todas las referencias. Esas referencias son las que se centran en el mundo del espectáculo (en particular el cine y la televisión), de la prensa y de la edición, y del deporte. En términos de centralidad temática, parece lógico que el entretenimiento sea la categoría de referencias culturales más representada en una serie sobre una agencia de estrellas del cine.

La segunda categoría que más predomina es la de referencias geografías, es decir a lugares o edificios específicos, con 18% de todas las ECRs. Esta omnipresencia de referencias geográficas concuerda con las observaciones de Ramière (2006) y Pedersen (2011) sobre la sobrerrepresentación de nombres propios en las ECRs: "[p]roper names of people, places and institutions make up the majority of ECRs one encounters" (Pedersen 2011: 48). Tal como observa Ramière, los nombres propios tienden naturalmente a ser traducidos de manera extranjerizante por tener un referente único; por lo tanto, se substrajeron todos los nombres propios del corpus para comprobar si alteraba la distribución de técnicas sobre el espectro domesticación – extranjerización, y apareció que la ratio no cambiaba de manera significativa.

La tercera y la cuarta categorías son las marcas y la comida, con el 12 y 11% respectivamente, mientras que las tres categorías restantes (referencias conectadas al gobierno, a la educación o al transporte) representan cada una menos del 10% del total.

4.3 Estrategia por tipo de ECR

Ahora nos proponemos examinar en mayor detalle la distribución de técnicas de traducción según el tipo de ECR. En vez de examinar cada categoría de ECR por separado, se repartieron en tres grupos distintos. El primero consiste en las referencias vinculadas con el entretenimiento, siendo esa la categoría más presente y la que constituye el tipo de referencia más estrechamente relacionado con el propio tema de la serie, además de ser un aspecto mundialmente conocido de la cultura francesa. A continuación, se analizan las referencias de geografía, marcas y comida: estas también figuran entre los aspectos de la cultura francesa más explotados por la industria del turismo, pero no son un tema central de la serie en sí mismo, lo cual permitirá comprobar qué aspecto influye más: centralidad temática en la serie o importancia simbólica en la representación de Francia al extranjero. Por último, se examinan las ECRs vinculadas a la vida cotidiana, y cuyo papel en la trama tanto como en el poder blando de Francia es menos central: educación, transporte y gobierno. Además, estas últimas tres categorías de ECR están menos presentes que las demás, y cada una consta de un número limitado de referencias (8 en educación, por ejemplo). Agrupar las tres categorías permite entonces que las estadísticas sean más significantes: este grupo representa aproximadamente el 20% de todas las referencias.

4.3.1 *Entretenimiento*

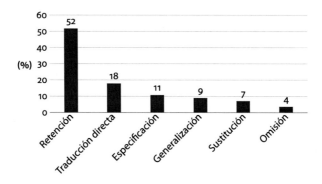

Figura 3. ECRs relacionadas con el entretenimiento

En la Figura 3 se observa la distribución de las técnicas de traducción utilizadas con las referencias al entretenimiento. 77% de las referencias son extranjerizadas, y las dos estrategias más extranjerizantes — retención y traducción directa — representan la gran mayoría de las técnicas utilizadas, con respectivamente el 43% y 30% de las 56 ECRs. En el campo cinematográfico, se nota por ejemplo la traducción de "la Palme d'Or", un prestigioso premio cinematográfico, con su equivalente oficial "y traducción directa": "la Palma de Oro" (T2E6 5:46).

Siguiendo en el ámbito del cine, se observan también muchos ejemplos de retención, como en la traducción de "une grande actriz de la Nouvelle Vague" [una gran actriz de la Nueva Ola] por "una gran actriz de la *Nouvelle Vague*" (T1E2 16:27), con solo el uso de cursiva para señalar el uso del francés. Esta elección de mantener la referencia en su idioma original puede atribuirse tanto a la importancia del tema del cinema en la trama narrativa de la serie como al prestigioso estatuto internacional del cinema francés, en particular gracias a la *Nouvelle Vague* en cuestión.

Sin embargo, se observa el mismo fenómeno con referencias menos conocidas. Así, cuando un personaje se refiere al papel de una actriz "dans *Un village français*" [en *Una aldea francesa*], el subtítulo dice: "habla de *Un village français*" (T3E6 35:15). Esta elección puede sorprender, dado que esta serie se tradujo al español, y se difundió en España sobre el nombre de *Un pueblo francés*. Además, este título es más corto que el francés, lo cual siempre es una ventaja en subtitulación. Una posible explicación puede ser el deseo de no traducir exclusivamente para un público español sino hispanohablante, y por lo tanto de evitar un equivalente oficial que lo sea solamente en España. También puede ser que la falta de tiempo haya sido el factor principal en la elección de usar retención, ya que cuanto menos intervencionista sea una estrategia, menos tiempo exige por parte del traductor.

Esta última observación puede explicar la elección de utilizar retención para traducir una ECR relativamente obscura para un público hispanohablante, una referencia a la editorial francesa Grasset. "Je raccroche avec Grasset" [Cuelgo con Grasset] se traduce con una retención: "Hablé con Grasset" (T4E4 21:31). La brevedad de la frase supone que se hubiera podido utilizar, por ejemplo, una generalización ("hablé con la editorial" o "con el editor") sin contravenir al número máximo de caracteres por línea, generalmente alrededor de 37.

De hecho, en otro episodio de la misma temporada, una referencia cultural al mundo editorial (el premio literario Goncourt) se traduce con una especificación, añadiendo información que clarifica la ECR para el espectador: "Déjeuner avec le dernier Goncourt" se traduce con "Almuerzo con el último ganador del Goncourt" (T4E2 8:35).

Sin embargo, se observan también ocurrencias de domesticación, en particular con referencias a aspectos menos conocidos del mundo del entretenimiento francés. Un ejemplo de ello es el uso de la generalización — el equivalente domesticante de la especificación — en el contexto de una referencia a la nadadora Laure Manaudou. En esta escena, el actor François Berléand se niega a entrar a una piscina para actuar su papel de Don Juan. Hablando con el director, se refiere a la nadadora olímpica de manera irónica:

"Si tu voulais Laure Manaudou, fallait prendre Laure Manaudou" [Si querías a Laure Manaudou, tenías que haber contratado a Laure Manaudou] (T1E6 37:09). Aquí, el referente específico importa menos que el carácter humorístico de la frase, que se pierde si los espectadores no entienden la referencia — lo cual sería bastante probable con una retención, dado que se trata de una referencia monocultural.[1] La traducción al español, sin embargo, permite retener tanto el humor como el sentido general, sin mantener la ECR tal cual: "Si querías a un nadador olímpico, haberlo llamado!".

4.3.2 *Geografía, marcas y comida*

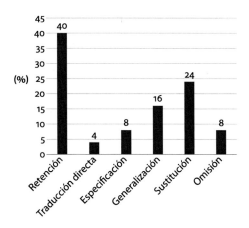

Figura 4. ECR relacionadas con geografía, marcas y comida

Como se ve en la Figura 4, este grupo representa un total de 42% de las referencias culturales en la serie. Eso puede indicar que los creadores de la serie tenían en mente un público internacional, ya que Francia es mundialmente conocida por sus sitios turísticos, su comida y sus vinos, y por su moda y marcas de lujo. Algunos ejemplos de retención que aparecen en la serie son "los Alpes" (T2E3 9:01), "los macarons" (T3E6 58:13) o "Vuitton" (T4E5 38:37).

Un examen más detallado del corpus muestra que los factores que más parecen influir en la elección de traducción de las ECRs en este grupo son el nivel de

---

1. Las referencias monoculturales son las que generalmente no se entienden fuera de su cultura de origen. Las tranculturales, al contrario, pueden provenir de la cultura meta o de una tercera cultura, y se entienden internacionalmente (cf. Pedersen 2011: 90).

cohesión intertextual e intersemiótica, cuán transcultural es la referencia, y cuál es su función textual.

Así, se observa que cuando el co-texto o la imagen ayudan los espectadores a entender de qué se trata, se utiliza generalmente la retención o la traducción directa, dos estrategias extranjerizantes. Por ejemplo, la referencia al Carlton, un hotel famoso en Cannes, se mantiene en español: "Logé au Carlton" [Alojado en el Carlton] pasa a ser "Habitación en el Carlton" (T1E3 14:28) — lo cual sugiere aún más claramente que el texto fuente que se trata de un hotel.

Aunque sea imposible saber si la retención se explica por la reputación internacional del hotel o porque la frase en la que aparece sugiere que es una forma de alojamiento, la misma estrategia se observa en el caso de ECRs menos emblemáticas de la cultura francesa. Así, la palabra "pistou" — que se refiere a una salsa del sur de Francia similar al mejor conocido pesto italiano — se mantiene en la traducción, supuestamente porque viene acompañado de la palabra "receta": "Et en plus, je lui ai filé une recette de pistou" [y encima, le pasé una receta de pistou] pasa a ser : "Además, le di la receta del pistou" (T1E3 8:50).

Sin embargo, los subtituladores no se apoyan siempre en el contexto, y se observan inconsistencias en las estrategias de traducción. En otro caso bastante parecido, donde la ECR es periférica y el contexto claramente sugiere que se habla de una forma de comida, los subtituladores españoles recurren a una generalización, traduciendo "calissons" — un dulce tradicional francés — con el hiperónimo "galleta". Así, "Hier, tellement je déprimais, j'ai mangé une boîte de calissons" [ayer, estaba tan deprimida que me comí una caja de calissons] se traduce por "Ayer estaba tan triste que me comí una caja de galletas." (T4E4 1:48)

Mientras el co-texto (es decir, el contexto lingüístico) proporciona tan solo pistas en cuanto al tipo de ECR, el canal visual permite a veces a los espectadores ver muy precisamente de qué se trata, aun tratándose de elementos de la cultura francesa que no existen en la cultura hispánica. Así, en la misma temporada, cuando una protagonista toma prestados los zapatos de marca de otra sin pedir permiso, esa le pregunta con indignación: "C'est mes Louboutin, ça?" [¿Son mis Louboutin, esos?] (T4E4 44:50), lo cual se traduce por "¿Esos son mis Louboutin?". La retención se puede explicar tanto por el hecho de que esta marca de zapatos de lujo francesa, siendo muy conocida internacionalmente, se pueda definir como referencia transcultural, como por el hecho de que se vea en la pantalla de qué se está hablando.

En el ejemplo siguiente, la referencia a "chouquettes" — otra especialidad dulce francesa — también se mantiene tal cual en la subtitulación, lo cual se puede atribuir principalmente a la aparición en la pantalla de los pequeños pasteles: "Bonjour à tous ! Chouquettes !" [Hola a todos! Chouquettes!]. La traducción española sólo señala el carácter extranjero del término mediante el uso de cursiva: "Hola a todos! Traigo *chouquettes*!" (T3E1 1:16)

Otro factor importante en la elección de la técnica de traducción es la función textual de la ECR, como se ve en la traducción diferente de la misma palabra "chouquette" cuando aparece en otro contexto. Cuando un jefe de la agencia está hablando de bajar todos los salarios para ahorrar dinero, y una de las asistentes dice que, si le bajan el salario, "je peux m'acheter une chouquette" [me puedo comprar una chouquette] (T2E1 10:21). La subtitulación al español es domesticante: "Me moriré de hambre." Esta traducción propone una paráfrasis del mensaje del original, enfocándose en la idea general — que no le quedará casi nada de dinero a la asistente, dado que ya gana muy poco. Aquí, la propia ECR cumple un papel principalmente ilustrativo y humorístico: el referente específico no importa tanto como el mensaje global, y fue lógicamente en este en el que se enfocaron los subtituladores.

El mismo fenómeno se observa con una referencia geográfica similarmente monocultural, y cuyo principal papel en contexto es expresar un mensaje de manera irónica. Aquí, un personaje se refiere al departamento de origen de su interlocutor, departamento conocido en Francia por sus barrios privilegiados: "Je sais que t'as grandi dans les Hauts-de-Seine, mais je suis pas en train de te racheter un marché public." [Sé que creciste en los Hauts-de-Seine, pero no estoy tratando de comprarte un mercado público] (T1E3 14:28). En la traducción española, no se mantiene la referencia a Hauts-de-Seine, ya que no se trata de una ECR transcultural comprensible en la cultura meta, sino que se utiliza otra paráfrasis: "Sé que eres de un entorno acomodado, pero no estoy negociando un contrato público".

El impacto de la función textual de una ECR es particularmente perceptible en otra escena donde aparecen tres referencias enseguida. Las dos primeras se tratan de indicaciones factuales de menor importancia contextual, y la última es una pregunta retórica con función humorística, que se refiere al jardín zoológico de Thoiry en las afueras de París. En esta escena, que se desarrolla de noche en un cementerio, un personaje se encuentra con un grupo de músicos y bailarines acompañados por un oso, y pregunta cómo llegaron hasta allí:

On a commencé par Le chat qui pêche, c'est un club de jazz rue de la Huchette. [...] On a fait un détour par le Paradis Latin. [Empezamos por El gato que pesca, es un club de jazz calle de la Huchette. [...] Tomamos un desvío por el Paraíso Latino]. Su interlocutor le pregunta entonces: "Et l'ours, là-bas ? C'est parce que vous êtes passés par Thoiry?" [¿Y ese oso de allí? ¿Fue porque pasasteis por Thoiry?]" En los subtítulos españoles, las diferentes referencias contenidas en la escena se tratan de maneras distintas: "- Empezamos en un club de jazz en la rue de la Huchette. [...] Fuimos al Paradis Latin. / — ¿Y el oso ese es porque pasaron por el zoológico?

La primera referencia desaparece completamente, probablemente tanto por falta de espacio como por menor importancia contextual, y su carácter infracultural[2] destacado por el hecho que la protagonista explica a sus compañeros parisienses de qué se trata. La segunda y la tercera se mantienen tal y como se daban en el original; ambas son sitios bastante conocidos de París, y se entiende por el contexto que se trata de lugares ya que la protagonista está describiendo su ruta. Además, la retención permite ahorrar caracteres en comparación con una traducción directa ("calle de la Huchette", "Paraíso Latino"). Sin embargo, la última referencia al zoo de Thoiry se traduce de manera domesticante, con una generalización que permite a los espectadores entender el vínculo entre la presencia del oso y la referencia a Thoiry: "el zoológico". Una vez más, los subtituladores dieron prioridad a la función textual de la referencia: su carácter humorístico.

Parece entonces que, con este grupo, lo que importa no es tanto el tema — por ejemplo, comida o marca — como el carácter mono- o transcultural de la ECR (cf. Pedersen 2011: 106), su función textual, y la presencia o ausencia de informaciones co-textuales e intersemióticas.

4.3.3   *Gobierno, educación y transporte*

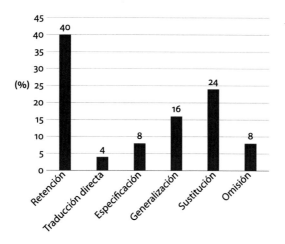

Figura 5. ECRs relacionadas con el gobierno, el transporte y la educación

---

2. Pedersen define las referencias infraculturales de la siguiente manera: "An Infracultural ECR is typically bound to the Source Culture, but it could *not* be assumed to be within the encyclopaedic knowledge of the ST nor the TT audience, as it is too specialized or too local to be known even by the majority of the relevant ST audience" (2011: 108).

Esas tres categorías tienen en común de ser las menos representadas (18% del total de ECRs) y de ser menos prominentes desde el punto de vista tanto de la trama narrativa como de la imagen de Francia en el extranjero. En cuanto a su subtitulación, este grupo también destaca porque el número de técnicas domesticantes en su traducción casi equivale al de técnicas extranjerizantes. La tendencia a la extranjerización que se encuentra en todas las demás categorías es entonces mucho menos pronunciada aquí (52%).

Además, incluso dentro de las técnicas extranjerizantes, se observan ejemplos de especificación, que es una técnica que se puede describir como cerca del límite entre orientación a la cultura fuente y a la cultura meta, ya que se trata de dejar la referencia no traducida, pero también de acompañarla de información adicional para ayudar la comprensión de los espectadores.

Así, en la última temporada, uno de los agentes entra en un taxi y le dice "Je vais à Roissy, s'il vous plaît" [Voy para Roissy, por favor], lo cual es traducido por "Aeropuerto Roissy, por favor" (T4E5 13:14). Esta adición se explica posiblemente por el hecho de que, a pesar de ser un aeropuerto internacional, "Roissy" se puede considerar como una referencia tan solo monocultural: no es el nombre oficial del aeropuerto (que es Paris-Charles-de-Gaulle), sino un sobrenombre basado en su proximidad con la ciudad de Roissy, en las afueras de París.

En el siguiente ejemplo se observa otro tipo de estrategia domesticante. Un personaje acusa otro de haber delatado la agencia a las autoridades fiscales por medio de una referencia monocultural relacionada con el gobierno francés: "Parce que tu nous as dénoncés au fisc. J'ai mes sources à Bercy." [Porque nos denunciaste al fisco. Tengo mis fuentes en Bercy]. En español, esta referencia se omite en el subtítulo: "Porque nos denunciaste al fisco. Tengo mis fuentes." (T2E2 43:01)

La ECR "Bercy" se refiere al Ministerio de Economía y Financias francés; aquí también, se trata de un sobrenombre debido a su localización en la calle de Bercy, en París. Aunque muy común en Francia, no se puede considerar como una referencia transcultural. La elección de omitirla en lugar de explicitarla se debe muy probablemente a factores técnicos. Por una parte, permite ahorrar bastante espacio y ayuda a que el subtítulo cabe dentro de los límites espaciales y temporales inherentes a este método de traducción. Por otra parte, permite también ahorrar tiempo, y entonces dinero: la retención y la omisión son las dos categorías que requieren menos tiempo por parte de los subtituladores, y se sabe que los plazos son a menudo muy ajustados y las tarifas bajas. Era posible también retener la ECR; sin embargo, fue omitida, una decisión que puede deberse a parámetros técnicos pero también a un deseo de no confundir al espectador, lo cual equivale a una estrategia domesticante.

Finalmente, cuando un personaje hace una referencia humorística a la prestigiosa escuela francesa Polytechnique de ingeniería para sugerir que se requiere mucho conocimiento técnico para utilizar cierto programa informático, se utiliza la tercera estrategia domesticante en el subtítulo: la substitución transcultural. "Vraiment il faut avoir fait Polytechnique…" [Realmente, hay que haber hecho Polytechnique…]: en español, la referencia al ámbito educativo es mantenida, pero la especificidad cultural desaparece. "¡Hay que hacer un master para esto!" (T1E5 25:41)

De manera general, las substituciones son la estrategia domesticante más utilizada en este grupo de ECRs, y es reseñable que ninguna de las sustituciones del corpus (incluido en otras categorías) corresponde a lo que Pedersen llama de "TC ECR" — una referencia cultural propia a la cultura meta, aquí la cultura hispánica. En vez de eso, las sustituciones son generalmente ECR anglófonas transculturales, como el "master".

Otro ejemplo notable de referencia anglófona se observa en la traducción de una referencia a la SPA (Sociedad de Protección de los Animales), una organización francesa bien conocida localmente pero poco internacionalizada. Una militante de los derechos animales pregunta a alguien a cuáles asociaciones pertenece, y ese le contesta: "La SPA, c'est la base" [La SPA, es lo fundamental] (S4E4 33:38). En español, sin embargo, se lee en el subtítulo: "La ASPCA, claro".

ASPCA significa "American Society for the Prevention of Cruelty to Animals", y aunque sea probablemente más conocida que la SPA francesa, tampoco se trata de una referencia muy transcultural. Por ejemplo, la página oficial de la organización no está localizada en otros idiomas, y su página Wikipedia no tiene traducción al español. El mantenimiento de una sigla en la traducción presenta la ventaja importante de ocupar muy poco espacio, pero también existen siglas para asociaciones parecidas en el mundo hispánico. El PACMA (Partido Animalista Con el Medio Ambiente) es una. La elección de no utilizar una referencia española, tratándose de una serie francesa, tampoco puede explicarse por motivos de credibilidad narrativa. De hecho, la referencia a la ASPCA utilizada también crea lo que Gottlieb llama un "problema de autenticidad" (1994: 51), dado que no tiene mucho sentido que el personaje describa esta asociación americana como la asociación por defecto para un activista francés.

Dos hipótesis parecen poder explicar que todas las sustituciones del corpus sean anglófonas. Es posible que los subtituladores quisieran evitar referencias perteneciendo a una parte u otra del mundo hispánico, tal vez para que la serie resulte atractiva para un público más amplio. También es posible que, a pesar de no ser el texto fuente, los subtítulos ingleses constituyeran una fuente de inspiración en los casos más problemáticos, y para ahorrar tiempo: en la mayoría de las sustituciones, la referencia anglófona de los subtítulos españoles también es la solución adoptada en los ingleses.

5. Conclusión

Este estudio mostró que en los subtítulos españoles de las referencias culturas francesas del corpus, la estrategia dominante es la extranjerización. Esta conclusión es consistente con los resultados de la mayoría de los estudios previos sobre la subtitulación de referencias culturales. Retención, en particular, es la técnica más representada aquí, lo cual no es de extrañar dado que es también una técnica muy económica en términos de espacio y de tiempo, siendo poco intervencionista.

La categoría de ECR más presente en la serie *Call My Agent* es la de entretenimiento, en particular las referencias vinculadas al mundo del espectáculo, que forma parte de la llamada alta cultura por la que Francia es bien conocida. La particularidad de esta categoría es entonces de ser central tanto temáticamente como en el poder blando de Francia. El examen detallado de las otras categorías temáticas y de sus estrategias de traducción sugiere que ambos factores desempeñan un papel clave a la hora de subtitular las ECRs, y llevan a una estrategia extranjerizante.

En particular, las referencias que más se traducen de manera extranjerizante son también las vinculadas a los aspectos más atractivos de la cultura francesa, desde el punto de vista del marketing de su imagen a escala internacional. Por el contrario, las referencias relacionadas a los aspectos más prosaicos de la cultura francesa, como los transportes — referencias que son mucho menos frecuentes — se traducen utilizando tanto técnicas domesticantes como extranjerizantes.

Las referencias temáticamente centrales a nivel macro- o micro-contextual también tienden a traducirse de manera extranjerizante, a excepción de las que tienen una función humorística, que se traducen de manera más domesticante, a menudo con una generalización. Sin embargo, independientemente de su función textual — y aun cuando tienen un papel humorístico, donde es crucial que los espectadores entiendan de qué se trata —, cuando se utilicen sustituciones en los subtítulos, las referencias utilizadas no provienen del mundo hispánico sino anglófono, posiblemente para no excluir a parte de los espectadores y/o para ahorrar tiempo.

References

 Abdelaal, Noureldin Mohamed. 2019. "Subtitling of culture-bound terms: strategies and quality assessment." *Heliyon* 8(4): 1–27.

Aixelá, Javier Franco. 1996. "Culture-specific items in translation." *Translation, power, subversion* 8: 52–78.

Baker, M. 1992. *In Other Words*. London and New York: Routledge.

Catford, John Cunnison. 1965. *A linguistic theory of translation*. London: Oxford University Press.

Chaume, Frederic. 2004. "Film studies and translation studies: Two disciplines at stake in audiovisual translation." *Meta: journal des traducteurs/Meta: Translators' Journal* 49(1): 12–24.

Davies, Eirlys. 2003. "A goblin or a dirty nose? The treatment of culture-specific references in translations of the Harry Potter books." *The Translator* 9(1): 65–100.

Díaz Cintas, Jorge & Aline Remael. 2007. *Audiovisual translation: subtitling*. Manchester & Kinderhook: St. Jerome.

Fawcett, Peter. 2003. *The manipulation of language and culture in film translation*. In *Apropos of ideology*, ed. by Calzada-Pérez, Maria, 141–163. Manchester: St. Jerome.

Gottlieb, Henrik. 1994. "Subtitling: diagonal translation." *Perspectives: studies in translatology* 2(1): 101–121.

Katan, David, and Mustapha Taibi. 2021. *Translating cultures: An introduction for translators, interpreters and mediators*. London and New York: Routledge.

Lefevere, André. 1977. *Translating literature: the German tradition from Luther to Rosenzweig*. Assen-Amsterdam: Rodopi.

Leppihalme, Ritva. 1994. "Translating Allusions: When Minimum Change Is Not Enough". *Target. International Journal of Translation Studies* 6(2): 177–193.

Nedergaard-Larsen, Birgit. 1993. "Culture-bound problems in subtitling." *Perspectives* 1(2): 207–240.

Newmark, Peter. 1988. *A Textbook of Translation*. New York: Prentice Hall.

Pedersen, Jan. 2005. "How is culture rendered in subtitles." *MuTra 2005–Challenges of Multidimensional Translation: Conference Proceedings* 18: 1–18.

Pedersen, Jan. 2011. *Subtitling norms for television*. Amsterdam/Philadelphia: John Benjamins.

Ramière, Nathalie. 2006. "Reaching a foreign audience: Cultural transfers in audiovisual translation." *The journal of specialised translation* 6: 152–166.

Tomaszkiewicz, Teresa. 2001. "Transfert des références culturelles dans les sous-titres filmiques." In *(Multi)media translation: Concepts, Practices, and Research*, ed. by Gambier, Yves and Henrik Gottlieb, 237–247. Amsterdam/Philadelphia: John Benjamins.

Validashti, Farzaneh. 2008. "Domestication, Foreignization and identity issues: A comparative study of translated novels." Unpublished MA Thesis, Islamic Azad University, Science and Research Branch, Iran.

Venuti, Lawrence. 1995. *The Translator's Invisibility: A History of Translation*. London and New York: Routledge.

Zhang, Baicheng. 2013. "Innovative Thinking in Translation Studies: The Paradigm of Bassnett's and Lefevere's 'Cultural Turn'". *Theory & Practice in Language Studies* 3(10): 1919–1924.

Zojer, Heidi. 2011. "Cultural references in subtitles: A measuring device for interculturality?" *Babel* 57(4): 394–413.

Los antropónimos en la película cubana *Los dioses rotos*
Su traducción al inglés en la subtitulación

Geisy Labrada Hernández
Departamento de Español, Universidad de Holguín

This paper examines the fictional anthroponymy of characters in the Cuban film *Los dioses rotos* (2008), considering the English translation of these anthroponyms in the subtitles. To achieve this, a thorough visualization (filmic, linguistic, and translational) of the film has been conducted, extracting all anthroponyms related to main and secondary characters, as well as those mentioned in the plot's dialogues. The close ties between characters and Afro-Cuban religion, along with the phonetic and mnemonic peculiarities of female anthroponyms in the realm of prostitution, are evident. In the subtitles, the decision to preserve Cuban characters' anthroponyms, respecting the orthography of the target language, is notable. The preference for using full names instead of diminutive names in subtitling, are highlighted.

Keywords: anthroponymy, fiction, audiovisual translation, subtitling

1. Introducción

La película cubana *Los dioses rotos* (Fallen Gods) fue estrenada en 2008 (Imagen 1). Tiene una duración de una hora y 37 minutos y su director es Ernesto Daranas Serrano. Se aproxima a uno de los temas más polémicos de la realidad cubana de todos los tiempos: la prostitución. Para ello toma como eje principal a Alberto Yarini Ponce de León, proxeneta muy conocido — y hasta venerado — que se hizo famoso en la primera década del siglo XX en La Habana.

Alberto Yarini nació el 5 de febrero de 1882 en una familia de élite y estudió Derecho en la Universidad de La Habana, pero abandonó sus estudios para dedicarse al negocio de la prostitución en el barrio rojo de San Isidro, donde se convirtió en el líder de los chulos cubanos que competían con los franceses por el control de las casas de tolerancia. Yarini era un hombre culto, educado, atractivo

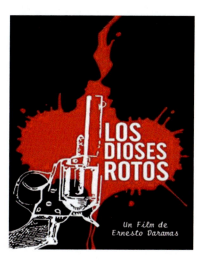

Imagen 1. Cartel de la película *Los dioses rotos*
Fuente: Tomada de Internet

y carismático, que se ganó el respeto y la admiración de muchos habaneros, especialmente de las mujeres que trabajaban para él. Como político y patriota apoyó las luchas por la independencia de Cuba y al Partido Liberal en las elecciones de 1908. Gracias a su labor perseverante logró que se instaurara el Día de la Madre en Cuba. Su vida terminó trágicamente el 22 de noviembre de 1910, cuando fue asesinado a balazos por Louis Lotot, un proxeneta francés que era su rival en el negocio del sexo.

Esta película, seleccionada en Cuba para aspirar a una candidatura en los Oscar, obtuvo varios premios como:

- Premio del Público en el 30 Festival de Nuevo Cine Latinoamericano de La Habana, 2008.
- Premios de la Crítica Cinematográfica y de la Crítica Cultural cubanas en el 30 Festival de Nuevo Cine Latinoamericano de La Habana, 2008.
- Premio de Cine en Construcción en el Festival de Cine de Gibara, 2008.
- Seleccionada por la Asociación Cubana de la Prensa Cinematográfica como la mejor película cubana del 2008.
- Premio de la Asociación Cubana de la Prensa Cinematográfica.

Así, la película se articula en torno a Laura, una profesora universitaria que está realizando una investigación para su tesis sobre Alberto Yarini. Esto la llevará a adentrarse en un mundo complejo, marcado por la inseguridad, la violencia y el dolor, por un lado; y por otro, repleto de argumentos y circunstancias que justifican, en cierta medida, la realidad de muchas de las prostitutas que ofrecen sus testimonios. Aun cuando algunas de ellas creen y aspiran a un futuro prometedor, libre de chulos y proxenetas, a través de *Los dioses rotos* se pone de manifiesto la vigencia del legendario Yarini — y de la prostitución — en Cuba.

En *Los dioses rotos* se entrelazan personajes de diferentes estratos sociales y se evidencia el fuerte vínculo de estos con la religión afrocubana. No debe obviarse, además, que este filme está inspirado en hechos reales y, en específico, en la vida y muerte de un personaje tan peculiar como Yarini. Debe subrayarse que, a su vez, en este filme confluyen dos épocas históricas y dos entornos socioculturales marcadamente diferenciados: los solares habaneros y la Universidad de La Habana. Por ende, el primer objetivo planteado en el estudio que aquí se presenta busca analizar la antroponimia ficcional de *Los dioses rotos*, con el interés de explicar los motivos que podrían incidir en la elección de los nombres de los personajes por parte del guionista en función de la trama.

Asimismo, a partir de una considerable variedad antroponímica, vista tanto de forma directa como indirecta, pues no son pocos los personajes históricos y religiosos que se mencionan en los diálogos, como segundo objetivo se ha considerado oportuno analizar, además, la traducción al inglés de dichos antropónimos en los subtítulos, en aras de ilustrar las estrategias principales y la correspondencia de estas con la variedad cubana de la lengua española, así como con el trasfondo cultural, religioso, histórico y social que sirve de base a la película.

2. Precisiones metodológicas

Para desarrollar el análisis que se presenta en el siguiente apartado se ha seguido una propuesta metodológica organizada en tres pasos fundamentales. En primer lugar, se ha llevado a cabo la visualización fílmica de la película, con el fin de comprender a fondo su trama y establecer una descripción de los personajes principales y secundarios. Luego, se puso en práctica una segunda visualización, de tipo lingüística, enfocada en el vaciado de todos los antropónimos directos e indirectos que, como se explicó antes, hacen alusión a los personajes que participan en el filme y a las personalidades políticas, históricas o religiosas que se mencionan en los diálogos.

Se incluyeron, además, los antropónimos que desempeñan una función anecdótica en la película, es decir, aquellos referidos en la trama como parte del testimonio experiencial de un determinado personaje. En esta etapa se fundamentaron, paralelamente, los principales motivos que podrían haber incidido en la elección de cada antropónimo por parte del guionista. Por último, con un fin traductológico específico, se realizó una tercera visualización, en la que se imbricaron, a su vez, los aspectos fílmicos y lingüísticos anteriores, con el fin de analizar las propuestas de traducción antroponímica en los subtítulos en estrecha relación con la función y el significado del nombre.

3. Análisis de los antropónimos y de su traducción

Para comenzar, se analizará la semántica, el valor onomástico y la traducción al inglés de los antropónimos directos, es decir, aquellos que corresponden a personajes protagónicos y secundarios de la película. Estos se recogen en la tabla que se muestra a continuación (Tabla 1):

Tabla 1. Antropónimos directos

Antropónimo	Papel del personaje	Traducción
Laura	Profesora universitaria. Es seducida y drogada por Alberto, bajo las órdenes de Rosendo.	Laura
Alberto Hipocorísticos: Albertico, Bertico.	Encarna al Yarini actual, aunque no es proxeneta, sino gigoló. Mantiene relaciones con Laura, Rosa, Isabel y Sandra, de quien está enamorado realmente. Es Licenciado en Lengua Inglesa y vivió varios años en Francia.	Alberto
Rosendo	Proxeneta. Guarda como reliquia el pañuelo con que secaron la sangre a Yarini el día de su muerte. Está perdidamente enamorado de Sandra.	Rosendo
Rosa	Arquitecta y empresaria. Hace negocios con Alberto y mantiene una relación amorosa con él. Le ofrece llevarlo a vivir a México.	Rosa
Isabel	Exprofesora universitaria, escritora (escribe una novela sobre Yarini). Mantiene una relación con Alberto, a quien le paga a cambio de sexo.	Isabel
Sandra Hipocorístico: Sandrita	Prostituta, salió recientemente de prisión. Mantiene una relación con Rosendo, pero está enamorada de Alberto.	Sandra
Carla o Karla	Prostituta	Karla
Adrián	Chulo	Adrian
Román	Expareja de Laura, profesor universitario.	Roman
Basilio	Amigo de Alberto y Rosendo. Chofer de este último y encargado de sus trabajos sucios.	Basilio
Lázaro	Es como un padre para Alberto. Santero.	Lazaro
Tony o Toni	Pareja de Laura. Ella lo engaña con Alberto.	Tony
Tamara	Exprostituta y amiga de Sandra.	Tamara
Bárbaro/Bárbara Hipocorístico: Baby	Transexual. Prostituta	Babby

Fuente: Elaboración propia

Como se resume en la Tabla 1, Alberto es el personaje que encarna al Yarini actual, o al menos a una versión con ciertos matices. Esto se debe a que, aun cuando Alberto es un hombre atractivo y que mantiene vínculos con el mundo de la prostitución, no es un proxeneta. Al contrario, es un gigoló que termina enamorado de otra prostituta. No debe obviarse que, durante la trama, además, mantiene relaciones con cuatro mujeres: Rosa, Laura, Isabel y Sandra. Si se tienen en cuenta estos elementos, unidos al hecho de que murió, como Yarini, asesinado por enamorarse de una de las prostitutas de un proxeneta — en su caso, Rosendo y, en el de Yarini, Louis Lotot — no es casualidad que el guionista haya decidido nombrar a este personaje así.

Por otro lado, no debe pasarse por alto que *Los dioses rotos* es una película basada en hechos reales, que parte de una figura real y conocida en Cuba. Al respecto, resulta evidente el parecido físico del actor que desempeña el papel de Alberto con Yarini, como se muestra en las Imágenes 2 y 3. Asimismo, en el propio guion se hace referencia al antropónimo Alberto Yarini Ponce de León, al decir que de esta figura llama la atención "desde la grandilocuencia de su nombre hasta su tumba (*from his boastful name to his grave*)". Debe mencionarse también que es Yarini la parte del antropónimo que permite identificar a este personaje, con lo que se advierte la pérdida del valor referencial del nombre de pila en favor del apellido.

Imagen 2. Alberto Yarini
Fuente: Tomada de Internet

Imagen 3. Carlos Ever Fonseca
Fuente: Tomada de Internet

Respecto a su traducción al inglés, como se aprecia en la Tabla 1, en los subtítulos se ha optado por conservar casi la totalidad de los antropónimos en español, adaptando su ortografía a la de la lengua meta. No obstante, debido a los requisitos técnicos de la subtitulación, sobre todo el relacionado con mantener, de manera general, hasta un máximo de 42 caracteres, en algunos casos se omite de los diálogos el hipocorístico *Albertico* o se emplea el nombre de pila como tal. No obstante, no siempre se debe a esto la preferencia de uso del nombre de pila en lugar del hipocorístico, tal y como se evidencia en fragmentos que no sobrepasan el número de caracteres permitidos: "Oye, Albertico (*Listen, Alberto*)". Esto trae consigo la pérdida del componente afectivo que transmiten los hipocorísticos, que, como apuntan RAE y ASALE (2010: 628), constituyen "formas diminutas, abreviadas o infantiles del nombre propio original que se emplean en lugar de este como designación cariñosa, familiar o eufemística".

En el caso de Isabel, exprofesora universitaria y escritora, quien inició a Alberto en el camino de la prostitución, aun con una notable diferencia de edad, cabe destacar que este coincide con el nombre de la actriz que da vida a este personaje: Isabel Santos. Se considera que Isabel, nombre con varios posibles orígenes, proviene del latín *Isis bella*, en honor a la diosa egipcia de la fecundidad Isis, cuyo culto era muy popular entre los soldados romanos, más el epíteto *bella*, lo que subraya su feminidad.

Por otra parte, en una película que lleva por título una alusión a la deidad, no es de extrañar la presencia de antropónimos con referentes hagiónimos. Tal es el caso de Lázaro, personaje que además encarna a un santero y es sumamente protector con Alberto. La imagen que se asocia en el sincretismo a San Lázaro es la de un mendigo leproso, repleto de llagas, harapiento, con muletas y acompañado por perros. El hecho de haber sido un santo que sufrió en carne propia el dolor y la enfermedad y al que se le atribuyen curaciones y sanaciones milagrosas, ha favorecido que el pueblo lo venere y siempre le pida por la salud.

Este antropónimo, como el resto, se ha mantenido en la traducción al inglés; no obstante, su ortografía se ha adaptado a la de la lengua meta y se ha eliminado la tilde de la palabra esdrújula en español. Sobre esto, es preciso subrayar que, al tratarse de una película basada en hechos reales con un fundamento histórico conocido, la decisión de mantener los antropónimos ha sido correcta.

Otro de los antropónimos más interesantes de la película es Bárbara, con el que se denomina a un personaje transexual — antes Bárbaro — que trabaja como prostituta. Al respecto, el propio personaje explica el origen y evolución de su nombre: "Ya tú ves, me pusieron Bárbaro para que saliera bien macho y ahora soy Baby. Baby, la Bárbara (*They named me Barbaro, to make me a real macho and you see, now I'm Babby. Babby, the tough one*)". Como se observa, la traducción del hipocorístico ha incluido una *b* adicional en Baby. Esto quizás se deba al interés por evitar confusiones entre *Baby* y *baby* (bebé), sobre todo en la última oración. "Babby, the tough one" abre un nuevo subtítulo y, por ende, se escribe con letra inicial mayúscula, lo que podría hacer pensar que, escrito con una sola *b*, se trata de *Baby* (bebé) como vocativo y forma de tratamiento.

Conviene apuntar, además, que Bárbara hace referencia también a la religión. Santa Bárbara se suele representar joven, bien con la palma del martirio, bien con plumas de pavo real, pues este animal es símbolo de la resurrección o la inmortalidad. El yugo paternal y autoritarismo hicieron de Santa Bárbara Bendita una joven muy infeliz, que vivió gran parte de su vida en cautiverio. Su padre pretendió casarla con un hombre de alto estatus social. Ante la negativa de su hija, decidió encerrarla en uno de sus castillos.

En el personaje de Baby se pone de relieve también a un joven infeliz que escondió su preferencia sexual, vivió así en el cautiverio de sus propios deseos. En Bárbara tiene lugar su resurrección, convertida en una mujer con excelentes habilidades para seducir a los hombres. Como más alto símbolo de feminidad no puede obviarse que la muñeca más famosa del mundo se llama Barbie, equivalente de Bárbara en inglés.

Para concluir el análisis de los antropónimos directos vale mencionar que todas las mujeres de la película, excepto Isabel, tienen nombres cortos terminados en -*a*. Casi la totalidad de estos personajes femeninos son prostitutas, de ahí la intención de utilizar antropónimos de poca complejidad fonética y con valor mnemotécnico, sobre todo si se toma en consideración el amplio número de personajes de este tipo que intervienen en la trama.

Mientras tanto, entre los antropónimos indirectos — aquellos que solo se mencionan en los diálogos pero que no forman parte del elenco — se encuentran algunos con *denotatum*[1] (Morris 1938) conocido o no conocido, opacos o transparentes, como se observa en la Tabla 2.

En la lista de antropónimos de esta tabla cabe destacar el caso de uno que, aunque no corresponde a una figura o personalidad reconocida, representa una tendencia de la antroponimia cubana. Se trata de Yanaisy/Yanaisi o Yanaysi, entre otras posibilidades de escritura. La Y es la cuarta inicial más utilizada a la hora de elegir nombres masculinos en Cuba, solo superada por la J, la A y la R. Por su parte, en las mujeres ocupa el primer puesto, con Yanet como el nombre más común. Otros, muy frecuentes en el caso de las mujeres son Yaima, Yadira, Yudeisi, Yuneisy, Yunisleydis, etc. Mientras, en los hombres aparecen Yoan, Yoel o Yasmani. De hecho, muchos famosos cubanos, sobre todo deportistas, son parte de este fenómeno: Yotuel (cantante), Yipsi Moreno (martillista), Yarisley Silva (pertiguista) y dos de los hermanos Gourriel, Yulieski y Yuniesky (famosos peloteros).

Al respecto, en la subtitulación al inglés de *Los dioses rotos* el antropónimo femenino Yanaisy no se traduce, se omite del diálogo: "Para no aburrirme los fines de semana me iba por ahí con Yanaisy (*I´d go out with a girl in my class who was already involved in this*)". Esto se debe quizás a que dicho personaje solo se menciona una vez en toda la trama y en el diálogo donde se alude a él el tema central es Carla y sus inicios en la prostitución. Por ende, Yanaisy solo tiene un valor referencial que nada aporta al argumento de la película.

A su vez, aun cuando la Generación Y cubana (todos los denominados con antropónimos con letra inicial Y) es bastante amplia y diversa, en la sociedad existen prejuicios hacia este grupo de antropónimos. En general, se advierte una tendencia a juzgar a las personas con estos nombres como muy comunes, sin grandes virtudes y de estratos sociales bajos. De hecho, a modo de burla, es frecuente sustituir el nombre de una mujer por Yumisisleydis o Yukasisleydis y utilizarlo como forma de tratamiento cuando se finge no recordar o conocer el nombre de la persona ("Oye, tú, Yukasisleydis") en programas de televisión, sobre todo humorísticos, para hacer referencia al exceso de creatividad de estos nombres cubanos o a la alta probabilidad de que el nombre de alguien comience con Y. Por ende, no es de extrañar que este antropónimo, por demás común, le haya sido atribuido a una prostituta y que, debido a la complejidad fonética, haya sido omitido también de la traducción.

---

1. De acuerdo con Morris (1938), por *denotatum* se entiende el conjunto de cosas realmente existentes, verificables de forma empírica, a las que aluden los signos.

Tabla 2. Antropónimos mencionados en los diálogos de los personajes

Antropónimo	Referencias	Traducción
Alberto Yarini Ponce de León Más frecuente: Yarini	Conocido por importar prostitutas de Francia y operar en San Isidro, entonces el barrio rojo de La Habana.	Alberto Yarini Ponce de Leon
Carpentier (Apellido)	Alejo Carpentier y Valmont (1904–1980). Escritor cubano y francés con gran influencia en la literatura latinoamericana.	Carpentier
Yanaisy, Yanaysi o Yanaisi	Denotatum desconocido. Amiga de Carla que la introdujo en la prostitución.	Se omite
Juana de Arco	Heroína de Francia. Símbolo de la Liga Católica y símbolo nacional de Francia.	Joan of Arc
Confucio	Uno de los pensadores más importantes de la historia de la humanidad, debido al gran impacto que ha tenido su filosofía tanto en China como en el mundo.	Confucius
Yemayá (Hagiónimo)	Divinidad de la fertilidad de la mitología yoruba, originalmente asociada al Mar.	Yemaya
Orula (Hagiónimo)	Divinidad de la adivinación y sabiduría en la religión yoruba.	Orula
Oggun (Hagiónimo)	Orisha de los herreros, de las guerras, de la tecnología, de los cirujanos, del ejército, los policías.	Oggun
Mariana	Mariana Grajales Cuello (1815–1893). Paradigma de mujer y madre cubana y progenitora de los Maceo, estirpe que simboliza toda la hidalguía y el valor del pueblo cubano.	Se omite
Maceo (Apellido)	Antonio de la Caridad Maceo y Grajales (1845–1896). Militar y político cubano, Mayor General y Lugarteniente General del Ejército Libertador.	Se omite
Louis Lotot	Francés afincado en Cuba que encabezaba el grupo de chulos de su país que tenían negocios en La Habana. Asesinó a Yarini.	Louis Lotot
Pepe Basterrechea	Amigo de Yarini que asesinó a Lotot.	Pepe Basterrechea
Juan Pablo II	Papa 264 de la Iglesia Católica y soberano de la Ciudad del Vaticano desde el 16 de octubre de 1978 hasta su muerte en 2005.	John Paul II

Tabla 2. *(continuación)*

Antropónimo	Referencias	Traducción
Dios (Hagiónimo)	Dios es el nombre que se le da en español a un ser supremo omnipotente, omnipresente, omnisciente y personal en religiones teístas y deístas (y otros sistemas de creencias). Concebido como el creador sobrenatural y supervisor del universo.	God
Changó o Shangó (Hagiónimo)	Orisha de la justicia, de los rayos, del trueno y del fuego.	Chango
Mahoma	Fundador del islam y considerado en la religión musulmana como el último de los profetas.	Se omite

Fuente: Elaboración propia

Por otra parte, la serie de hagiónimos que se mencionan en la película muestra la confluencia de las religiones católica y yoruba en Cuba. Debe subrayarse que el antropónimo, término más general, incluye también a aquellos nombres que "designan las divinidades y figuras religiosas (Alá, Apolo, Buda, Cristo, Dios)" (RAE y ASALE 2009: 218-219). Estos, cuyo origen se ubica en el mundo religioso cristiano, bíblico o santo, son conocidos como hagiónimos (Tabares 2020), donde se incluyen también los correspondientes a seres mitológicos legendarios o fantásticos (Hércules, Papá Noel, Pulgarcito).

En cuanto a su traducción, puede apreciarse en la Tabla 2 que, en su mayoría, junto a otras personalidades reconocidas del ámbito internacional, en los subtítulos se optó por emplear el equivalente acuñado. Sin embargo, aquellos hagiónimos correspondientes a la religión afrocubana fueron conservados, adaptando su ortografía a la lengua meta. Incluso, en algunos diálogos se cambian referencias yorubas por referencias cristianas: "El dueño de ese hierro no tenía ni los guerreros[2] (*The owner of this revolver didn´t believe in God*)".

Sobre los hagiónimos es interesante el caso de Mahoma, el cual es omitido de la traducción: "No creo ni en Mahoma (*I don´t believe in my shadow*)". Al buscar esta expresión —*no creer alguien ni en su sombra*—, que significa no temerle a nadie ni confiar, en internet aparecen 5.100 resultados. Ambas unidades fraseológicas, en español (*no creer alguien ni en Mahoma*) y en inglés (*I don´t believe in my shadow*), mantienen el mismo significado. No obstante, además de por contar con un equivalente inglés, quizás se haya optado por eliminar el referente de Mahoma para evitar conflictos religiosos.

---

2. Recibir los guerreros en la religión yoruba implica comenzar una nueva vida a través de una ceremonia de preparación para recibir a Elewá, Ochossi, Oshún y Oggún. Estas deidades —conocidos como los orishas guerreros Oddé— son otorgados a los creyentes para abrirles el camino hacia la tradición yoruba.

Finalmente, los antropónimos Maceo y Mariana, empleados también como parte de unidades fraseológicas, coincidiendo con Ghezzi (2012: 203), "expresan el grado superlativo de una cualidad a través de su comparación con un término prototípico o un estereotipo tangible". Antonio Maceo simboliza valentía e intransigencia para los cubanos, lo que también se extiende a varios miembros de la familia Maceo, entre los que se incluye, por supuesto, su madre, Mariana Grajales.

El apellido es "el nombre que las personas heredan de sus progenitores y mediante el cual queda establecida su filiación. No se trata de un atributo del individuo, sino de la familia a la que pertenece y, por tanto, no es susceptible de elección ni modificación arbitrarias" (RAE y ASALE 2010: 629). En el caso de la unidad fraseológica *tener más cojones/tenerlos más grandes que Maceo*, se advierte, de acuerdo con Labrada y Campo (2021: 40), la pérdida del valor referencial del nombre de pila en favor del apellido.

Estos antropónimos se emplean en la película en un diálogo entre Basilio y Alberto: "—¿Qué sabes tú de Sandra, Basilio? (*What the shit do you know about Sandra?*) —Que es estelar, que tiene los ovarios de Mariana, los cojones de Maceo (*She is a brave woman with balls as big as any man ́s*)".

Como se observa, en ambos casos se optó por eliminar el antropónimo en la subtitulación y, con ello, el valor fraseológico de la expresión cubana a partir del nombre de pila. No obstante, el equivalente *have balls* se ajusta al contexto de uso y mantiene el significado, aunque limita la expresividad de la unidad fraseológica y su contenido cultural particular.

4. A modo de conclusiones

De manera general y en consonancia con el primer objetivo planteado en este estudio, el análisis realizado ha permitido comprobar la presencia de elementos que denotan la intencionalidad del guionista a la hora de elegir los antropónimos del elenco de personajes. Esta se pone de manifiesto, sobre todo, en el interés de trazar analogías entre personajes actuales y otros con un reconocido fundamento histórico. Se evidencia, además, en la estrecha relación de los personajes con la religión afrocubana y, por otro lado, en las especificidades fonéticas y mnemotécnicas de los antropónimos femeninos del grupo de personajes que representan el mundo de la prostitución.

En cuanto a la traducción al inglés en los subtítulos, de acuerdo con el segundo objetivo expuesto, se advierte la decisión de conservar, respetando la ortografía de la lengua meta, los antropónimos de los personajes cubanos. A su vez, debe subrayarse la preferencia de uso del nombre de pila en lugar de los hipocorísticos en el subtitulado, en ocasiones por requisitos técnicos de la traducción audiovisual y, en otras, sin motivos aparentes. Se aprecia, además, el uso de equivalentes acuñados para hagiónimos de la religión católica y personalidades del ámbito internacional, lo que no ocurre con los hagiónimos pertenecientes a la religión yoruba. Hay que apuntar, también, la tendencia a eliminar los antropónimos que forman parte de expresiones con un significado fraseológico, donde se opta por emplear un equivalente o parafrasear la expresión.

Referencias bibliográficas

Ghezzi, Madalena. 2012. "Creación de una base de datos para el estudio de las comparaciones estereotipadas y su explotación en la enseñanza de E/LE". En *Unidades fraseológicas y TIC*, ed. por María I. González Rey, 203-216. Madrid: Instituto Cervantes (Centro Virtual Cervantes).

Labrada, Geisy, y Luis R. Campo. 2021. "¡De esos Marcos Pérez hay muchos en Buena Vista! Fraseología y antroponimia en Cuba". *Comunicación* 30 (2): 20-45.

Morris, Charles. 1998. "Foundations of the Theory of Signs". *International Enciclopedia of Unifid Science* 1 (2):1-59.

Real Academia de La Lengua Española (RAE) y Asociación de Academias de la Lengua Española (ASALE). 2009. *Gramática de la lengua española*. Madrid: Espasa Libros.

Real Academia de La Lengua Española (RAE) y Asociación de Academias de la Lengua Española (ASALE). 2010. *Ortografía de la lengua española*. Madrid: Espasa Libros.

Tabares, Encarnación. 2020. "Fraseología con nombre propio en el Diccionario de americanismos de la ASALE". *Revista de Filología Española (RFE)* 100 (2): 471-498.

Kulturbezüge in der Voice-Over-Übersetzung von multilingualen Filmen
Grenzen und Möglichkeiten der Übertragung

Eglė Aloseviciené
Institute of Languages, Literature and Translation Studies, Kaunas Faculty, Vilnius University

The aim of the study is to determine the transfer possibilities of cultural references in the voice-over translation of multilingual films into Lithuanian. The corpus consists of cultural references from five multilingual films, which were systematised according to the translation process. The comparative-descriptive combination of methods used in this qualitative pilot study leads to the following findings. Cultural references are generally described as either linguistic or extralinguistic. In relation to translation in film — as mono-, trans- or infracultural. An inconsistent rendering of multilingualism is observed. In dialogues with more than two languages, rare languages are neglected unless there are partial subtitles in a dominant language. Four translation procedures have proven to be predominant: the direct transfer of cultural references, omission, hyperonymic transfer and substitution.

Keywords: audiovisual translation, multilingualism, cultural references, translation strategies

1. Einleitung

Untersuchungen zu den Kulturbezügen in der Translation sind seit den 1980er Jahren ein populäres Thema geworden. In der audiovisuellen Übersetzung haben sie auch viel mit der Übertragung von Realienbezeichnungen zu tun. Kulturwörter bzw. Kulturbezüge als ein breites Spektrum umfassendes Phänomen dienen in diesem Beitrag als der Ausgangspunkt bzw. das Ziel des Forschungsinteresses, das einerseits Probleme der audiovisuellen Übersetzung von multilingualen Filmen in den Vordergrund stellt, andererseits aber auch die Grenzen bzw. Möglichkeiten der Übermittlung von Kulturbezügen zu behandeln versucht.

Um das formulierte Ziel zu erreichen, ergibt sich ein logischer Bedarf nach der Begriffsbestimmung von kulturell markierten Einheiten. Die Besonderheiten der Mehrsprachigkeit in der audiovisuellen Produktion je nach dem Übersetzungsmodus (Untertitelung, Synchronisation, Voice-Over) sind anschließend zu besprechen sowie die möglichen Übersetzungsverfahren und ihre Ursachen sind festzustellen.

In litauischen Kinos werden mit wenigen Ausnahmen nur Animationsfilme für Kinder synchronisiert; sonst herrscht üblicherweise die Untertitelung vor. Fernsehfilme und Serien werden dem Zuschauer im Voice-Over (als Nachvertonung) angeboten, was auch bei der Wiedergabe von Mehrsprachigkeit problematisch ist. Bei einem synchronisierten multilingualen Film geht der Zuschauer instinktiv davon aus, einen Film in seiner Muttersprache vor sich zu haben, denn die anderen Sprachen werden üblicherweise nicht irgendwie markiert. Bei der Untertitelung bleibt diese Authentizität erhalten. Die Voice-Over-Übersetzung, die am meisten mit der Übersetzung von Interviews und Dokumentarfilmen assoziiert wird, wird als eine Alternative zur Synchronisation angeboten, z. B. in Polen, Bulgarien und in den baltischen Staaten.

Bei der vorliegenden Analyse steht im Mittelpunkt die Voice-Over-Übersetzung ins Litauische als eine Art filmischer Übersetzung, wobei der gesprochene Originalton nicht komplett ersetzt wird, sondern es werden die eingesprochenen Übersetzungen über den Originalton gelegt, der im Hintergrund leise hörbar bleibt. Dieses Verfahren hat sicherlich beachtliche Nachteile: verzögerte Übersetzungstonspur, Überlappung der Originaltonspur von einer, zwei oder mehreren einsprechenden Stimmen, Unmöglichkeit der Wiedergabe von paraverbalen Elementen. Andererseits bietet das Voice-Over im Vergleich mit der Synchronisation weniger Raum für Manipulationen, eine scheinbare Authentizität, d. h. eine leichtere Identifikation mit den Figuren und ihren individuellen bzw. abweichenden Eigenschaften.

Der Hauptgrund für die Verwendung dieser Art von Übersetzung ist, dass sie im Gegensatz zur Synchronisierung in kurzer Zeit produziert werden kann, da die Stimmen nicht mit den Lippenbewegungen der Figur synchronisiert werden müssen. Wenn im Film eine Zeit lang nicht gesprochen wird, wird der Originalton aufgedreht (Bisbey 2019). Das bedeutet, dass die Isochronie im Voice-Over kaum eine Rolle spielt. Wichtig ist nur, dass die Nachvertonung in einzelne Aussagen passen muss. Es gibt darüber hinaus keine speziellen Anforderungen darauf, wie lange die Lücken vor und nach der Nachvertonung dauern müssen. In den mehrsprachigen Filmen erlaubt gerade das Voice-Over (wie auch die Untertitelung) den multilingualen Kontext zu identifizieren (Sepielak 2016: 79).

Das Korpus der vorliegenden Untersuchung bilden Kulturbezüge aus fünf mehrsprachigen Filmen, die je nach dem Übersetzungsverfahren systematisiert wurden. Die vergleichend-beschreibende Methodenkombination lässt im Rahmen dieser qualitativen Pilotstudie zu den vorläufigen Erkenntnissen gelangen, die eventuell mit Hilfe eines umfassenden Korpus überprüft werden können.

2. Kulturbezüge und ihre Typen

Kulturspezifische Elemente sind von der Geburt an Teil des menschlichen Lebens, deshalb prägen sie das Verhalten und das Weltbild. Dazu gehören nicht nur sprachliche Bezüge, sondern auch Zeichen, Gestik, Symbole, also nonverbale Elemente, die eine sprachliche Äußerung verstärken, ergänzen oder irgendwie anders modifizieren. Die zahlreichen Versuche, das viel diskutierte außersprachlich-sprachliche Phänomen zu bestimmen hat den Anfang in dem Artikel "Linguistic and Ethnology in Translation Problems" von Nida (1945: 194) genommen, der auf den kulturellen Kontrast von zwei Sprachgemeinschaften hinweist. Später sind in die Übersetzungswissenschaft die Termini "Realia" (Kade 1964, Vlakhov, Florin 1980) eingegangen, die präzisiert wurden, und zwar als "Realienbezeichnungen" (Drößiger 2010, Maksvytytė 2012). In anderen Untersuchungen wird die kulturelle Begriffskomponente hervorgehoben: "culture-specific items – CSI" (Franco Aixelà 1996), "culture bumps" (Leppihalme 1997), "culturally marked segments" (Mayoral Asensio, Muñoz Martín 1997), "extralinguistic cultural references – ECR" (Pedersen 2007), "culture-bound terms" (Díaz-Cintas, Remael 2009). Die Begriffe "Kulturspezifika" und "Realien" werden oft falsch als Synonyme verwendet. Zu den kulturspezifischen Elementen gehören außer Realien Toponyme, Eigennamen, Wortspiele, historische Ereignisse und Persönlichkeiten usw. Wenn von "Realien" die Rede ist, sind in der Regel außersprachliche kulturspezifische Elemente gemeint, d. h. sie beziehen sich direkt auf die Wirklichkeit außerhalb des Textes. In diesem Sinne versteht man darunter die spezifischen kulturellen Sachverhalte politischer, institutioneller, sozialer sowie geographischer Art und des dazugehörigen Wortschatzes. Auch alternative Versuche das Phänomen zu benennen, sind in der Fachliteratur zu finden: "Bezeichnungsexotismen" (Schippan 1984: 260 nach Drößiger 2010: 39), "lexikalische Lücke" (Hörmann 1994:109f. nach Drößiger 2015: 99), "äquivalentlose Lexik" (Kvašytė 2010).

Im Hinblick auf den Lebensbereich unterscheidet Newmark (2010: 173ff.) sechs Kategorien von Kulturspezifika, die folgende Bereiche vertreten: Ökologie: Geografie und Geologie (*Neapel, Fjord*); öffentliches Leben: Politik, Recht und Regierung (*Bundeskanzler, Sozialgesetzbuch*); gesellschaftliches Leben: Wirtschaft, Berufswelt, Bildung und Gesundheitswesen (*Stiftung Warentest, Assistenzarzt, Realschule, Versicherungskarte*); persönliches Leben: Kleidung, Haushalt,

Lebensmittel (*Kimono, Wok, Tagliatelle*); persönliche Vorlieben: Religion, Musik, Poesie (*Methodismus, Reggae, "Ein Sommernachtstraum"*), Feste, Bräuche und Tätigkeiten, darunter auch kulturabhängige Zeichen der Körpersprache, wie etwa Spucken über die Schulter, wenn eine schwarze Katze die Straße überquert, Kopfschütteln als Ausdruck der Zustimmung etc.

Die kulturspezifischen Elemente des Films können als sprachlich (linguistisch) oder außersprachlich (extralinguistisch) bezeichnet werden. Erstere beziehen sich beispielsweise auf Metaphern, Redewendungen, Wortspiele, Anspielungen, Sprachvarietäten etc. Zu den außersprachlichen Aspekten gehören in erster Linie visuelle Elemente (Gestik, Mimik), aber auch Musik, Klänge aus Geschichte, Geografie, Gesellschaft und Kultur sowie andere Komponente. Extralinguistische kulturelle Referenzen nehmen Bezug auf die reale Welt außerhalb des Sprachraums, z. B. auf Orte, Menschen, Institutionen, Bräuche, Speisen usw., die man vielleicht nicht kennt, auch wenn man die betreffende Sprache beherrscht.

Das Modell von Pedersen (2007) wurde speziell dazu entwickelt, um zu zeigen, wie Übersetzer bei der Untertitelung von Filmen und Fernsehsendungen mit außersprachlichen Kulturbezügen umgehen. Er griff auf eine Differenzierung zurück, um den Grad der Erkennung von Kulturbezügen und ihrer Wiedergabe zu betonen. Dementsprechend unterscheidet er monokulturelle Realien, die dem zielsprachlichen Zuschauer völlig unbekannt sind (*Volksschule, Tafelspitz, Frauenkirche*). Wenn es Erklärungen durch Kontext, Dialog oder andere Kommunikationskanäle wie Bilder im Film gibt, ist von infrakulturellen Realien die Rede. Dabei kann es sich z. B. um lokale geografische Namen oder Beschreibungen der technischen Ausrüstung bestimmter Berufsgruppen handeln. Transkulturelle Realien sind in einer anderen Kultur leicht zu erkennen und verursachen generell keine Übersetzungsprobleme (Pedersen 2011: 73f.).

Obwohl dieses Modell speziell für die Untertitelung entwickelt wurde, kann es auch für die Wiedergabe von Kulturbezügen bei den anderen Modi der audiovisuellen Übersetzung behilflich sein. So sind es beispielsweise transkulturelle Bezüge wie *DDR* oder *Salami* weltweit bekannt. Dennoch ergibt sich Fragen danach, warum sie inadäquat übertragen bzw. nicht übersetzt werden (s. Beispiele in den Tabellen 5 und 6).

3. Multilinguale Filme und die audiovisuelle Übersetzung

Die Übersetzung von Filmen ist fast so alt wie das Kino selbst. Seit Anfang 1900 wurden Zwischentitel in den Stummfilmen eingeführt und im Jahr 1926 erschien der erste Spielfilm "Don Juan", wenn auch nur mit Musik. Ein Jahr später wurde auf den Markt der Film "The Jazz Singer" gebracht, in dem schon einige Worte gesprochen werden (Wahl 2005:18). Danach folgten Versionen desselben Films für unterschiedliche Länder ("Versionenfilme" bzw. "Mehrsprachenversionen"), z. B. "Der blaue Engel" (1930) mit Marlene Dietrich und seine englische Version "The Blue Angel" (Wahl 2005:175ff.). Dieses Verfahren war besonders in den dreißiger und vierziger Jahren des 20. Jahrhunderts populär. Wann die ersten mehrsprachigen Filme erschienen sind, lässt sich genau nicht sagen. Bereits in den Stummfilmen finden sich beispielsweise Überblendungen mit einer Übersetzung ("The four Horsemen oft the Apocalypse", 1921). Vor allem aber in den Darstellungen des ersten Weltkriegs werden mehrere Sprachen eingesetzt, wie etwa in dem Film "Hell's Angels" aus dem Jahr 1930 (Kremer 2020:321).

3.1 Multilinguale Filme als Filmgattung

Multilinguale (auch: polyglotte) Filme zeichnen sich durch einen konsequenten Gebrauch bzw. durch eine Konfrontation von mehr als zwei Sprachen aus. Dieses kinematographische Genre erlaubt Sprecher- und Sprachenkontakte in einen konkreten kulturell markierten Kontext einzubinden sowie einen Einblick in lebendige Mehrsprachigkeit zu gewinnen. Ein polyglotter Film ist formal gesehen ein Genre, weil er "über ein immer wiederkehrendes Repertoire an Erzählmustern und Figuren verfügt" (Wahl 2005:145). Dennoch ist er im Hinblick auf die Intention keine Gattung im klassischen Sinne, weil die Filmmacher keine Absicht haben, ein mehrsprachiges Produkt zu schaffen. De Bonis (2015:52) behauptet, es sei zielgerechter von einem "Meta-Genre" zu sprechen. Ein mehrsprachiger Film als Vertreter einer kinematografischen Gattung wie etwa Komödie, Drama, Science-Fiction hat seine besondere Funktion in der Filmhandlung und dem Filmdiskurs.

Die Beiträge, die sich mit mehrsprachigen Filmen befassen, konzentrieren sich hauptsächlich auf Themen "Multikulturalismus" (wirtschaftliche und kulturelle Globalisierung), "Immigration" und "Krieg". Die Gegenüberstellung von Sprachen, Kulturen und Identitätsproblemen stehen dabei thematisch im Vordergrund. Aber auch Vorstellung der Charaktere oder Handlungsorte, Ausdruck von Ironie und Sozialkritik, Markierung des Kodewechsels bilden die wesentlichen funktionalen Kriterien.

Die Mehrsprachigkeit an sich wird in der Fachliteratur aus drei Hauptperspektiven untersucht: als narratives und ästhetisches Element eines Films, einschließlich Fragen der kulturellen Identität; unter dem Gesichtspunkt der Rezeption, insbesondere beim einsprachigen Publikum; und als spezifisches Problem für die Übersetzer, die verschiedene Strategien zur Lösung dieses Problems entwickeln. Gerade dieser Aspekt steht im Zentrum dieser Untersuchung.

3.2 Zur Wiedergabe des Multilingualismus im Filmkorpus

Synchronisation und Untertitelung sind in der Regel komplementäre audiovisuelle Übersetzungsstrategien, die in der Vergangenheit nicht oft in Kombination verwendet wurden. Dies ändert sich jetzt. Ein neuerer Trend besteht darin, sowohl die Synchronisation als auch die Untertitelung in die Übersetzung desselben Films einzubeziehen. Das ist eine nützliche Methode, um mehrsprachige Filme wiederzugeben, die für das Ausgangspublikum bereits teilweise untertitelt waren. Erfolgreich partiell untertitelte Filme enthalten laut O'Sullivan (2011: 107) in der Regel Untertitel für nur ein Viertel bis ein Drittel eines Filmdialogs. Diese partielle Untertitelung behindert den Erfolg eines Films nicht, d. h. sie wird nur für diejenigen Sprachen eingesetzt, die dem Zielpublikum unbekannt sind. Wenn aber mehrere Ausgangssprachen untertitelt werden müssen, dann ergibt sich die Frage nach ihrer Markierung. Daher entstehen auch Empfehlungen zu alternativen Verfahren wie etwa Einsatz von Farben, Schriftarten und -größen und sogar Länderflaggen in den Untertiteln (Beseghi 2017: 34, Bartoll 2006: 5, Mailhac 2000).

Im viersprachigen Film "Black Book" (2006) sind Niederländisch und Deutsch Hauptsprachen. Es wird auch gelegentlich Hebräisch und Englisch gesprochen. Das Hebräische wird ins Litauische genauso wie im Original nicht übertragen. Die Dialoge aus dem Englischen sind dagegen übersetzt, obwohl sie in der Originalfassung nicht übertragen werden. Die Originalsprache des dreisprachigen Films "Auf der anderen Seite" (2007) ist Deutsch, und für das deutsche Publikum wird untertitelt, sobald es Türkisch und Englisch gesprochen wird. Im litauischen Voice-Over bleibt auch die originelle partielle Untertitelung ins Deutsche vorhanden. In dem zweisprachigen Film "Anonyma – eine Frau in Berlin" (2008) wird im deutschen Original das Russische untertitelt. Im litauischen Voice-Over gibt es diese partiellen Untertitel nicht, beide Sprachen sind gleichwertig ins Litauische übertragen. Im englischen Original des dreisprachigen Films "Operation Finale" (2008) wird Spanisch mit partiellen Untertiteln wiedergegeben, Hebräisch dagegen – gar nicht übersetzt. Im litauischen Voice-Over wird das Spanische nachvertont, wobei man auch das partielle Untertiteln aus dem Spanischen sehen kann. Auch werden manche Aussagen aus dem Hebräischen übersetzt. "Berlin Syndrome" (2017) ist ein zweisprachiger Film auf Englisch und Deutsch. Diese beiden Sprachen werden ins Litauische übersetzt.

4. Zum Übertragungspotenzial von Kulturbezügen

4.1 Tendenzen in der audiovisuellen Übersetzung

Ein kulturell markierter Begriff enthält implizites kulturelles Wissen über die gesamte soziale Praxis und Kultur. "In solchen Fällen besteht die Herausforderung an Übersetzer nicht in der Wiedergabe des Schlüsselbegriffs selbst, sondern im Transfer sämtlicher diesem Begriff zugeordneter Signalstrukturen sprachlichen, außersprachlichen und sprachbegleitenden Verhaltens" (Schultze 2004: 929). Um diese Signalstrukturen dem Zuschauer in der Zielsprache bewusst zu machen, greift der Übersetzer zu bestimmten Verfahren wie etwa unveränderte Übernahme in die Zielsprache, Anpassung an die Zielkultur, Paraphrase etc. Während im Falle der Untertitelung (Nedergaard-Larsen 1993, Gottlieb 1997, Pedersen 2007) und der Synchronisation (Antonini 2007, Cuéllar Lázaro 2013) solche Übersetzungsverfahren mehr oder weniger eingehend untersucht wurden, wird die Übertragung von Kulturbezügen in der Voice-Over-Übersetzung von Spielfilmen, Serien und Animation im Fernsehen vernachlässigt.

Das Problem der Äquivalenz bzw. eines "lexikalisch-semantischen Defizites" (Drößiger 2015: 99) setzt nicht voraus, dass Kulturbezüge sich nur bedingt übertragen lassen. Vielmehr geht es in der audiovisuellen Übersetzung bei einer bewussten bzw. unbewussten übersetzerischen Entscheidung darum, das Potenzial der Zielsprache im Zusammenhang mit Bild auszunutzen. Die Kategorien der Anpassung und Verfremdung, der Freiheit und Treue sowie der Äquivalenz und Funktion werden vor allem dann berücksichtigt, wenn es um literaturbasierte, dialogorientierte Bewertungen von Film und Fernsehen geht. Im Bildschirmdiskurs werden diese Konzepte erst im größeren Zusammenhang erörtert, wobei das Seherlebnis, die Filmästhetik und die Multimodalität miteinbezogen sind (Wehn 2001: 70f. nach Dwyer 2017: 27).

In den ein- und mehrsprachigen Filmen entsteht das Problem vor allem aber dann, wenn ein kulturell markierter Begriff sowohl dem primären Publikum als auch dem Zielpublikum zugänglich gemacht werden muss oder aber auch, wenn derselbe Begriff in mehr als zwei Sprachen und Kulturen mit unterschiedlichem Inhalt besetzt wird, z. B. *mocha* im Türkischen und Italienischen, dt. *Professor* und en. *professor*, en. *Lieutenant* und dt. *Leutnant* etc.

Nedergaard-Larsen (1993: 224ff.) hat speziell für die Untertitelung folgende Übersetzungsverfahren ausgesondert:

- Transfer/Entlehnung/Exotismus: sp. *bolero* – dt. *Bolero*, en. *bolero*, lit. *bolero*,
- direkte Übersetzung/Lehnübersetzung: dt. *Realschule* – en. *middle/secondary school*,
- Explikation: en. *chihuahua* – dt. *Hunderasse*,

- Paraphrase: fr. *l'oral de l'ENA* — en. *exam in political science*,
- Imitation: en. *White House* — dt. *das Weiße Haus*,
- situative Adaptation: fr. *agrégé d'histoire* — en. *M.A. in History*,
- kulturelle Adaptation: dt. *F.A.Z* — en. *New York Times*, en. *Baseball* — dt. *Fußball*,
- Auslassung.

Bei der Synchronisation wird davon ausgegangen, dass sie näher an der Zielkultur ist. Daher werden Verweise auf die Ausgangskultur in der Regel durch Äquivalente der Zielkultur ersetzt, um die Rezeption der Übersetzung zu erleichtern. Anpassungen und Neutralisierungen fremder Inhalte sind hier häufig angewandte Mittel (Organ 2015: 51), z. B.:

- Ersetzung durch eine besser bekannte Referenz aus der ursprünglichen Kultur: *Mr. Potato Head* durch *E.T.* (der Alien aus dem amerikanischen Science-Fiction-Film "E.T. the Extra-Terrestrial" von Steven Spielberg, 1982) (Dore 2010: 20f.),
- Internationalisierung (Ersetzung einer kulturell besetzten Einheit durch eine international bekannte): en. *Fred and Ethel* (die Hauptfiguren der amerikanischen Seifenoper "I Love Lucy", 1951–1957) — sp. *Romeo and Juliet* (Lorenzo et al. 2003: 208 nach Dore 2010: 13),
- Kulturelle Kompensation: z. B. eine vielfältige Einstreuung einer Reihe von zeitgenössischen Referenzen in die Synchronisation von Disney-Filmen (di Giovanni 2003: 215f.).

Das Voice-Over sollte jedoch getreuer und näher an der Ausgangskultur sein. Im Falle der Voice-Over-Übersetzung gibt es wenig Untersuchungen, die sich mit kulturellen Referenzen, und zwar in den Spielfilmen, Serien bzw. in der Animation befassen (Newska 2011). Das liegt daran, dass dieser Übersetzungsmodus nur in einem kleinen Kultur- und Sprachraum für die Übertragung der Fernsehinhalte typisch ist. Entlehnung, Äquivalenz, Ökonomie (Konzentration, Straffung, Verknappung) und Erweiterung (Explizierung, Periphrase), Modulation sind die Verfahren, die Newska (2011) speziell für das Voice-Over zusammengefasst hat. Beim letzten Verfahren geht es darum, die Form des Textes durch die Einführung einer semantischen Änderung oder Perspektive zu modifizieren, z. B. fr. *dernier étage* — en. *top floor*, dt. *zweiter Stock* — lit. *trečias aukštas*.

Mailhac (2000), Herbst (1997) und Mera (1999) sind in ihren Untersuchungen zum Ergebnis gekommen, dass Untertitel häufig den Originaldialog um etwa 50% kürzen und daher weniger respektvoll und getreu sind als die Synchronisation (nach Dwyer 2017: 43). Gerade die Mehrsprachigkeit ist laut Dwyer (2017: 31) ein Bereich der akustischen Komplexität, der von Untertiteln regelmäßig ausgeblendet wird. Untertitel fungieren in Filmen, die eine subtile Darstellung der sprachlichen Vielfalt enthalten, als Nivellierungsmittel. Aber mindestens erlaubt die Untertitelung m. E. die Aufnahme von mehrsprachigen Inhalten, wenn auch nur akustisch. Es ist nicht selten im Film, wenn dem Zuschauer oder der handelnden Person das Verständnis fremdsprachlicher Äußerungen bewusst verschwiegen werden soll. In solchen Fällen zerstört sowohl die Untertitelung als auch die Synchronisation bzw. das Voice-Over die Intention des Filmemachers.

Tabelle 1. Übersetzung der eingeschobenen Aussage in der Fremdsprache

Film, Timecode	Originalsprache	Litauisches Voice-Over	Rückübersetzung
"Berlin Syndrome" (2017), 00:24:58–00:25:16	– What happens when you know someone? – *Man sieht die ganze Hässlichkeit.* – What did you just say? – I love your accent.	– Kas nutinka, kai žmogų pažįsti? – Matai visas jo ydas. – Ką pasakei? – Man patinka tavo akcentas.	– Was passiert, wenn man jemanden kennenlernt? – *Man sieht alle seine Laster.* – Was hast du gesagt? – Ich mag deinen Akzent.

In dem in der Tabelle 1 angeführten Beispielsatz auf Deutsch sollte dem potenziellen Opfer und eventuell auch dem Zuschauer, außer wenn er die deutsche Sprache beherrscht, immer noch kein Verdacht erzeugt werden, dass etwas mit der Hauptfigur nicht stimmt. Der Film handelt von dem Stockholm-Syndrom, das eine australische Backpackerin erleben muss, nachdem sie einen sympathischen Deutschen kennengelernt hat und von ihm als Geisel genommen wurde. Mit der Übersetzung im Voice-Over geht dieser Effekt verloren.

4.2 Übersetzungsverfahren am Beispiel der Voice-Over-Übersetzung mehrsprachiger Filme

Was die Übertragung von kulturell markierten Einheiten im analysierten Korpus angeht, so sind in den Filmen über den Krieg die mono- bzw. infrakulturellen Referenzen aus dem Militärbereich dominant, vor allem bei den Amtsbezeichnungen (*Kommandant, Hauptsturmführer*). Sie werden als direkter Transfer im Litauischen übernommen (*komendantas, hauptšturmfiureris*). Dieselbe Tendenz lässt sich auch bei den Referenzen aus dem persönlichen Bereich beobachten: türk. *rakı* – en. *raki*, lit. *rakija*, türk. *Bayramı* – dt. *Bayram*, lit. *bairamas* etc. Bild 1 veranschaulicht gerade die Präsenz der partiellen Untertitelung im Original mit der direkten Übernahme der Bezeichnung von einer Religionsfeier in der Türkei.

Die Beispiele in der Tabelle 2 illustrieren die Direktübernahme des ausgangssprachlichen Bezugs in die Zielsprache. Im zweiten Beispiel bedeutet *Kommandeur* "Befehlshaber eines größeren Truppenteils (vom Bataillon bis zur Division)" (Duden 2022). In Österreich und der Schweiz entspricht dies dem *Kommandanten*. Diese die sprachlichen Varietäten betreffende Nuance konnte im Litauischen nicht wiedergegeben werden.

Tabelle 2. Übersetzungsverfahren des direkten Transfers

Film, Timecode	Originalsprache	Litauisches Voice-Over	Rückübersetzung
"Black Book" (2006), 00:48:28–00:48:36	Herr *Obergruppenführer*, meine Damen, meine Herrschaften, ich habe die große Ehre Ellis de Vries anzukündigen. Sie wird uns jetzt etwas singen.	*Obergrupenfiureri*, ponios ir ponai, turiu garbės pristatyti jums Elizą de Frys. Ji mums padainuos.	Herr *Obergruppenführer*, meine Damen und Herren, ich habe die Ehre, Ihnen Eliza de Frys vorzustellen. Sie wird für uns singen.
"Anonyma – eine Frau in Berlin" (2008), 00:43:16	Der ist Bataillons*kommandeur*. Die haben keinen *Kommandanten*, sondern nur *Kommandeure*.	Jis bataljono *vadas*. Pas juos *komendantų* nėra, tik *vadai*.	Er ist Bataillons*kommandeur*. Hier gibt es keine *Kommandanten*, sondern nur *Kommandeure*.
"Berlin Syndrome" (2017), 00:10:03–00:10:16	– What did you … you said this [strawberries] was from a *schreber*…. – *Schreber*. I don't know the English word for it. These are small gardens. All together and all with German flags…	– Sakei, jos iš … *šrėbergarten*… – *Šrėbergarten*. Nežinau angliško žodžio. Tai nedideli sodai su Vokietijos vėliavom …	– Du hast gesagt, sie kommen aus … einem *Schrebergarten*… – *Schrebergarten*. Ich kenne das englische Wort nicht. Das sind kleine Gärten mit deutschen Fahnen …
"Auf der anderen Seite" (2007), 00:43:40	– *Bayramınız* kutlu olsun. – Teşekkürler, siz de.	– Laimingo *Bairamo*. – Ačiū, Jums irgi.	– Frohes *Bayram*. – Danke, Ihnen auch.

Die Bezeichnung "Schrebergarten" geht auf einen der Väter der Naturheilkunde D. G. M. Schreber (1808–1861) zurück. Er stellte fest, dass viele Kinder in der Großstadt an Haltungsschäden litten. Aber erst nach seinem Tod legte sein Schwiegersohn E. I. Hauschild eine Spielwiese in Leipzig an, auf der Kinder unter Betreuung toben und turnen konnten. Zu Ehren seines Schwiegervaters nannte Hauschild die Wiese "Schreberplatz". Allmählich entwickelte sich aus dem Schreberplatz eine richtige Kleingartenanlage, wo die Kinder ihre Beete angelegt haben, um aus bewegungstherapeutischer Sicht die Gartenarbeit zu erlernen. Doch bald machte die Gartenarbeit den Kindern keinen Spaß mehr und die Schrebergärten wurden von den Erwachsenen übernommen. Dieser Name gilt auch heute als alternative Bezeichnung für Kleingärten. Typisch hat man sie sich lange Zeit vorgestellt als einen Ort für spießige Rentner mit Gartenzwergen oder anderen Plastikfiguren (Hempel et al. 2020). Dieser Kulturbezug ist bewusst unübersetzt gelassen.

Bild 1. Partielle Untertitel mit einem Kulturbezug ("Auf der anderen Seite", 2007)

Aus der Tabelle 3 geht hervor, dass allen untersuchten Filmen Übersetzung von kulturellen Einheiten mittels einer Generalisierung durch eine hyperonymische Übertragung typisch ist. Die Bezeichnung der jeweiligen Referenz verliert somit das kulturell Einzigartige und wird durch einen allgemeinen Begriff wiedergegeben (türk. *börek* — lit. *pyragėliai*, hebr. *El Al* — lit. *Izraelio oro linijos*, sp. *pesos* — lit. *pinigai*, sp. *Fernet* — lit. *likeris*).

Partielle Untertitel im Bild 2, die Originalfassung des Films vorgesehen hat, geben dem ausgangssprachlichen Publikum die Aussage aus dem Spanischen mit einem entlehnten Kulturbezug wieder. Die Bezeichnung einer Likörsorte *Fernet* wird dagegen im Litauischen Voice-Over durch ein Hyperonym *likeris* übertragen.

Nach Pedersen (2005: 8) ist das Verfahren der Paraphrase, genauso wie das der Generalisierung, zieltextorientiert. Dieses Verfahren wird hauptsächlich zur Lösung von Problemen eingesetzt, die für eine Verallgemeinerung oder Spezifi-

Tabelle 3. Übersetzungsverfahren der hyperonymischen Übertragung

Film, Timecode	Originalsprache	Partielle Untertitel	Litauisches Voice-Over	Rückübersetzung
"Auf der anderen Seite" (2007), 00:23:13	*Bak, börek yaptım.*	Schau mal, ich habe Börek gemacht.	Iškepiau *pyragėlių*.	Ich habe *Brötchen* gemacht.
"Operation Finale" (2018), 00:21:48	I'm guessing *El Al* is not an option.	–	Turbūt *Izraelio oro linijos* irgi netinka?	Wahrscheinlich sind israelische *Fluggesellschaften* auch nicht geeignet?
"Operation Finale" (2018), 01:35:42	Tendré que llamar a un amigo para que traiga más *pesos*.	I'll need to call a friend to bring more *pesos*.	Turiu paskambint draugui. Jis atveš daugiau *pinigų*.	Ich muss einen Freund anrufen. Er wird mehr *Geld* bringen.
"Operation Finale" (2018), 01:43:39	Demasiado *Fernet*.	Too much *Fernet*.	Padaugino *likerio*.	Er hat zu viel *Likör* getrunken.

Bild 2. Partielle Untertitel mit einem Kulturbezug ("Operation Finale", 2018)

zierung zu komplex sind. Im analysierten Korpus gab es keine Beispiele, in denen eine Referenz spezifiziert würde, aber es findet sich ein einziges Beispiel zur Paraphrasierung des monokulturellen Inhalts, das in der Tabelle 4 angeführt ist.

Tabelle 4. Übersetzungsverfahren der Paraphrase

Film, Timecode	Originalsprache	Litauisches Voice-Over	Rückübersetzung
"Operation Finale" (2018), 01:38:45	General Müller asked me to check on the Einsatzgruppen.	Generolas Miuleris paprašė patikrinti vieną ten *dislokuotą mobilųjį žudymo batalioną*.	General Müller bat mich, ein dort *stationiertes mobiles Tötungsbataillon* zu überprüfen.

Tabelle 5. Übersetzungsverfahren der Auslassung

Film, Timecode	Originalsprache	Litauisches Voice-Over	Rückübersetzung
"Operation Finale" (2018), 00:33:18– 00:33:20	– *Yimakh shimo.* – *Yimakh shimo.* … May his name be obliterated, huh?	Vardas nebus pamirštas.	Der Name wird nicht vergessen.
"Berlin Syndrome" (2017), 00:38:41– 00:38:54	… als ob der Duft eines längst vergangenen Parfüms oder die Erwähnung einer Margarine *aus den DDR-Zeiten* der Figur in irgendeiner Weise Authentizität verleiht.	… lyg seniai pamirštų kvepalų aromatas ar margarino paminėjimas suteikia veikėjo gyvenimui autentiškumo.	… wie der Duft eines längst vergessenen Parfums oder die Erwähnung von Margarine dem Leben der Figur Authentizität verleiht.

Auslassung bzw. nicht Übertragung kann manchmal die einzige Option sein, aber dies sollte eine verantwortliche Entscheidung sein, die erst dann angemessen ist, wenn es keine Alternativen mehr gibt (Leppihalme 1994: 23 nach Pedersen 2005: 9). In den neuesten Studien wird der Vorrang gerade der Auslassung und der Direktübernahme (Boguzki 2020: 62) gegeben. In der Tabelle 5 zeigt das erste Beispiel aber die Nicht-Erkennung eines sprachlichen Kulturbezugs und seine Auslassung. Obwohl schon im Originaldialog eine Erklärung für diesen hebräischen Fluch vorhanden ist, der hinter den Namen bestimmter Feinde des jüdischen Volkes steht, gibt das litauische Voice-Over eine inkorrekte Interpretation wieder. Im zweiten Beispiel scheint im Film die Nicht-Übersetzung unmotiviert zu sein umso mehr, als an anderen Stellen die Bezeichnung *DDR* übertragen wird, und zwar mit einer litauischen Entsprechung in Form einer Lehnübersetzung: *VDR – Vokietijos Demokratinė Respublika (Deutsche Demokratische Republik)*.

Tabelle 6 illustriert die Ersetzungsstrategien beim Voice-Over. Im ersten Beispiel wird der Kulturbezug *SSD* bzw. *SD* (Sicherheitsdienst) aus der NS-Zeit durch einen dem litauischen Publikum mehr bekannten und hyperonymischen *SS* (Schutzstaffel) ersetzt. Der SD wurde 1931 auf Initiative des SS-Reichsführers Heinrich Himmler als ein Nachrichtendienst innerhalb der SS gegründet und erst 1943 aufgelöst (Scriba 2015, Mindler 2017). Im zweiten Beispiel gibt es eine eher unmotivierte Ersetzung eines transkulturellen Bezugs *Salami* durch lit. *salotos* (Salat).

Tabelle 6. Übersetzungsverfahren der Ersetzung

Film, Timecode	Originalsprache	Litauisches Voice-Over	Rückübersetzung
"Black Book" (2006), 01:42:25	Du, Optimist. Glaubst du wirklich, lässt man dich als *SSD-Offizier* ausreden?	Tu optimistas. Nejau manai, kad jie klausys *SS* karininko?	Du bist ein Optimist. Glaubst du, dass sie dich als einen *SS-Offizier* ausreden lassen?
"Operation Finale" (2018), 01:17:41-01:18:21	– Is it true you called the camps "liquidation machines"? – Mengele called you all kosher *salami*.	– Ar tiesa, kad lagerius vadindavai "utilizavimo mašinom"? – Mengelė jus vadindavo košerinėmis *salotomis*.	– Stimmt es, dass du die Lager "Verwertungsmaschinen" genannt hast? – Mengele hat euch kosheren *Salat* genannt.

5. Schlussfolgerungen

Die Übertragung von Bezeichnungen der kulturell markierten Einheiten ist immer noch ein wesentlicher Bestandteil des translatorischen Handelns. Die wissenschaftliche Diskussion umfasst nicht nur Aspekte der Äquivalenz bzw. möglichen Entsprechungen in der Zielsprache, sondern auch erhebt Fragen nach der Angemessenheit des jeweiligen Übersetzungsverfahrens im Hinblick auf den tradierten Übersetzungsmodus sowie situative Gegebenheiten.

Die Übertragung von Kulturbezügen wird in der audiovisuellen Übersetzung mithilfe von unterschiedlichen Techniken vorgenommen, die von dem Übersetzungsmodus abhängig sind. Schon die Übersetzung von mehrsprachigen Filmen verlangt nicht selten eine Kombination von Übersetzungsmodi wie etwa Synchronisation bzw. Voice-Over mit Untertitelung, die eventuell auch in der Originalfassung für eine konkrete Sprachgemeinschaft vorgesehen werden kann.

Im Zusammenhang mit der Übertragung von Kulturbezügen wird diese Diskussion umso wichtiger, als die durch die Sprache transportierte Eigenartigkeit sich im mehrsprachigen Raum bewegen muss. Die Synchronisierung unterschätzt das Publikum, eliminiert in vielen Fällen die Mehrsprachigkeit und gibt viel Raum für Interpretationen und Manipulationen (Sepielak 2016, 73). Bei dem Voice-Over handelt es sich wie auch bei der Untertitelung eher um eine sprachliche Addition in dem Sinne, dass die unübersetzte und übersetzte Sprache übereinander bestehen (Dwyer 2017: 28). Aber die Tatsache, dass man das Original und somit auch Mehrsprachigkeit im Hintergrund hören kann, verleiht dem Zuschauer mindestens einen Eindruck von Authentizität.

Anhand des untersuchten exemplarischen Korpus lässt sich generell eine inkonsequente bzw. sprachabhängige Wiedergabe der Mehrsprachigkeit im litauischen Voice-Over beobachten. Wenn es im Film nur zwei Sprachen vorherrschen, werden sie folgerichtig wiedergegeben. Wenn es Dialoge in mehr als zwei Sprachen vorkommen, werden seltene Sprachen vernachlässigt, es sei denn, dass es dafür partielle Untertitel in einer dominierenden Sprache gibt.

Vier Übersetzungsverfahren haben sich als vorherrschend herausgestellt: die unveränderte Übernahme eines kulturbezogenen Sprachmaterials in die Zielsprache (direkter Transfer), das Auslassen, die hyperonymische Übertragung und die Ersetzung. Es sollten jedoch am größeren Korpus die schon festgestellten bzw. alternativen Techniken überprüft werden, auf die ein Übersetzer gerade im Voice-Over zurückgreifen kann, wenn er kulturelle Bezüge vermitteln muss.

Literaturverzeichnis

Antonini, Rachele. 2007. "SAT, BLT, Spirit Biscuits, and the Third Amendment: What Italians Make of Cultural References in Dubbed Texts." In *Doubts and Directions in Translation Studies*, ed. by Yves Gambier, Miriam Shlesinger, and Radegundis Stolze, 153–167. Amsterdam: John Benjamins.

Bartoll, Eduard. 2006. "Subtitling Multilingual Films." Paper presented at the *Proceedings of the Marie Curie Euroconferences MuTra: Audiovisual Translation Scenarios*. [https://www.euroconferences.info/proceedings/2006_Proceedings/2006_Bartoll_Eduard.pdf]

Beseghi, Micol. 2017. *Multilingual Films in Translation. A Sociolinguistic and Intercultural Study of Diasporic Films*. Oxford: Peter Lang.

Bisbey, Bruce. 2019. "The Voice Over and Its Use in Film (In the Entertainment Industry)." [https://www.linkedin.com/pulse/voice-over-its-use-film-entertainment-industry-bruce-bisbey?trk=articles_directory]

Bogucki, Łukasz. 2020. *A Relevance-Theoretic Approach to Decision-Making in Subtitling*. Springer: Palgrave Macmillan.

Cuéllar Lázaro, Carmen. 2013. "Kulturspezifische Elemente und ihre Problematik bei der Filmsynchronisierung." *Journal of Arts and Humanities* 2 (6): 134–146.

De Bonis, Giuseppe. 2015. "Translating Multilingualism in Film: A Case Study on *Le concert*." *New Voices in Translation Studies* 12: 50–71. [https://www.academia.edu/13837637/Translating_multilingualism_in_film_A_case_study_on_Le_concert]

Di Giovanni, Elena. 2003. "Cultural Otherness and Global Communication in Walt Disney Films at the Turn of the Century." *The Translator* 9 (2): 207–223.

Díaz-Cintas, Jorge, and Remael, Aline. 2009. *Audiovisual Translation: Subtitling*. Manchester & Kinderhook: St. Jerome Publishing.

Dore, Margherita. 2010. "Manipulation of Humorous Culture-specific Allusions in AVT." *CTIS Occasional Papers* 6: 5–28.

Drößiger, Hans-Harry. 2010. "Zum Begriff und zu Problemen der Realien und ihrer Bezeichnungen." *Vertimo studijos* 3 (3): 36–52.

Drößiger, Hans-Harry. 2015. *Realienbezeichnungen in den Kinder- und Hausmärchen der Brüder Grimm. Intrakulturelle und interkulturelle Aspekte*. Hamburg: Dr. Kovač.

Duden. 2022. "Kommandeur". [https://www.duden.de/rechtschreibung/Kommandeur]

Dwyer, Tessa. 2017. *Speaking in Subtitles. Revaluing Screen Translation*. Edinburgh: Edinburgh University Press.

Franco Aixelá, Javier. 1996. "Culture-specific Items in Translation." In *Translation, Power, Subversion*, ed. by Román Álvarez, and M. Carmen-África Vidal, 52–78. Clevedon: Multilingual Matters.

Gottlieb, Henrik. 1997. *Subtitles, Translation & Idioms*. Copenhagen: University of Copenhagen.

Hempel, Silke, Muntermann, Natalie, and Eberhorn, Johannes. 2020. *Gartenkultur. Kleingärten und Schrebergärten*. [https://www.planet-wissen.de/natur/pflanzen/gartenkultur/pwiederkleingarten100.html#Wurzeln]

Herbst, Thomas. 1997. "Dubbing and the Dubbed Text — Style and Cohesion: Textual Characteristics of a Special Form of Translation." In *Text Typology and Translation*, ed. by Anna Trosborg. 291–308. Amsterdam and Philadelphia: John Benjamins.

Hörmann, Hans. 1994. *Meinen und Verstehen. Grundzüge einer psychologischen Semantik*. Frankfurt/Main: Suhrkamp.

Kade, Otto. 1964. "Ist alles übersetzbar?". *Fremdsprachen* 2: 84–99.

Kremer, Claude. 2020. "Film." In *Literatur und Mehrsprachigkeit. Ein Handbuch*, ed. by Till Dembeck, and Rolf Parr, 321–328. Tübingen: Narr Francke Attempto.

Kvašytė, Regina. 2010. "Pasvarstymai apie beekvivalentę leksiką arba latvių Joninės lietuviškai." *Gimtoji kalba* 10: 11–19. [https://www.llvs.lt/?recensions=658]

Leppihalme, Ritva. 1994. *Culture Bumps: On the Translation of Allusions*. Helsinki: University of Helsinki.

Leppihalme, Ritva. 1997. *Culture Bumps: An Empirical Approach to the Translation of Allusions*. Clevedon: Multilingual Matters.

Lorenzo, Lourdes, Pereira, Ana, and Xoubanova, María. 2003. "The Simpsons/Los Simpson. Analysis of an Audiovisual Translation." *The Translator*. 9(2): 269–291.

Mailhac, Jean-Pierre. 2000. "Subtitling and Dubbing, for Better or Worse? The English Video Versions of *Gazon Maudit*" In *On Translating French Literature and Film II*, ed. by Salama-Carr, Myriam, 129–54. Amsterdam and Atlanta: Rodopi.

Maksvytytė, Jūratė. 2012. "Sąvokų realija ir realijos pavadinimas apibrėžimo problema." *Studies about Languages* 21: 50–56.

Mayoral Asensio, Roberto, and Muñoz Martín, Ricardo. 1997. "Estrategias comunicativas en la traducción intercultural." In *Aproximaciones a los estudios de traducción*, ed. by Purificación Fernández Nistal, and José María Bravo Gozalo, 143–192. Universidad de Valladolid.

Mera, Miguel. 1999. "Read My Lips: Re-Evaluating Subtitling and Dubbing in Europe." *Links & Letters* 6: 73–85.

Mindler, Ursula. 2017. "Nationalsozialistischer Sicherheitsdienst und Gestapo". In *SIAK-Journal – Zeitschrift für Polizeiwissenschaft und polizeiliche Praxis* (4), 86–93.

Nedergaard-Larsen, Birgit. 1993. "Culture-Bound Problems in Subtitling." *Perspectives: Studies in Translatology* 1 (2): 207–240.

Newmark, Peter. 2010. "Translation and Culture." In *Meaning in Translation*, ed. by Barbara Lewandowska-Tomaszczyk, and Marcel Thelen, 171–182. Frankfurt: Peter Lang.

Newska, Joanna. 2011. Voice-Over-Übersetzungsverfahren am Beispiel der polnischen Übersetzung des Filmes "Das Leben der Anderen" von Florian Henckel von Donnersmarck. BA Thesis. Uniwersytet Warszawski.

Nida, Eugene Albert. 1945. "Linguistics and Ethnology in Translation-Problems." *WORD* 1 (2): 194–208.

Organ, Michał. 2015. "Dubbing versus Voice Over: Culture-Bound Jokes & References in the English-Italian-Polish Translation of Humour in Adult Animated Sitcoms." *Studia Anglica Resoviensia* 12: 50–60. [https://repozytorium.ur.edu.pl/server/api/core/bitstreams /f815b979-25bf-48dd-8686-e5e163282ad4/content]

O'Sullivan, Carol. 2011. *Translating Popular Film*. New York: Palgrave Macmillan.

Pedersen, Jan. 2005. "How is Culture Rendered in Subtitles?" *MuTra – Challenges of Multidimensional Translation Conference Proceedings*. [https://www.euroconferences.info /proceedings/2005_Proceedings/2005_Pedersen_Jan.pdf]

Pedersen, Jan. 2007. "Cultural Interchangeability: The Effects of Substituting Cultural References in Subtitling." *Perspectives* 15 (1): 30–48.

Pedersen, Jan. 2011. *Subtitling Norms for Television: An Exploration Focussing on Extralinguistic Cultural References*. Amsterdam & Philadelphia: John Benjamins.

Scriba, Arnulf. 2015. "Der Sicherheitsdienst (SD)" [https://www.dhm.de/lemo/kapitel/ns-regime/ns-organisationen/sicherheitsdienst.html]

Schippan, Thea. 1984. *Lexikologie der deutschen Gegenwartssprache*. Leipzig: Bibliographisches Institut.

Schultze, Brigitte. 2004. "Kulturelle Schlüsselbegriffe und Kulturwörter in Übersetzungen fiktionaler und weiterer Textsorten." In *Übersetzung. Translation. Traduction. Ein internationales Handbuch zur Übersetzungsforschung*, ed. by Harald Kittel, Armin Paul Frank, Norbert Greiner, Theo Hermans, Werner Koller, José Lambert, and Fritz Paul, vol. 1, 926–936. Berlin, New York: Walter de Gruyter.

Sepielak, Katarzyna. 2016. Voice-over in Multilingual Fiction Movies in Poland. PhD Thesis. Universitat Autònoma de Barcelona. [https://ddd.uab.cat/pub/tesis/2016/hdl_10803 _392684/ks1de3.pdf]
Vlakhov, Sergei, and Florin, Sider. 1980. *Neperevodimoe v perevode*. Moskva: Visšaja škola.
Wahl, Chris. 2005. *Das Sprechen des Spielfilms. Über die Auswirkungen von hörbaren Dialogen auf Produktion und Rezeption, Ästhetik und Internationalität der siebten Kunst*. Trier: Wissenschaftlicher Verlag.
Wehn, Karin. 2001. "About Remakes, Dubbing & Morphing: Some Comments on Visual Transformation Processes and their Relevance for Translation Theory." In *(Multi) Media Translation: Concepts, Practices, and Research*, ed. by Henrik Gottlieb and Yves Gambier. 65–72. Amsterdam and Philadelphia: John Benjamins.

Erwähnte und zitierte filme

Anonyma — eine Frau in Berlin (2008), Regie: Max Färberböck
Auf der anderen Seite (2007), Regie: Fatih Akin
Berlin Syndrome (2017), Regie: Cate Shortland
Black Book (2006, Originaltitel: Zwartboek), Regie: Paul Verhoeven
Der blaue Engel/The Blue Angel (1930), Regie: Josef von Sternberg
Don Juan (1926), Regie: Alan Crosland
E.T. the Extra-Terrestrial (1982), Regie: Steven Spielberg
Hell's Angels (1930), Regie: Howard Hughes
I Love Lucy (1951–1957), Produktion: Desi Arnaz, Jess Oppenheimer
Operation Finale (2008), Regie: Chris Weitz
The four Horsemen of the Apocalypse (1921), Regie: Rex Ingram
The Jazz Singer (1927), Regie: Alan Crosland

Transposition of a distorted universe

Cultural elements in *The night is short, walk on girl* by Morimi Tomihiko and its English translation

Hiroko Inose
Department of Japanese, Dalarna University

This paper identifies various types of cultural elements present in the novel *The Night is Short, Walk on Girl* by Morimi Tomihiko, and investigates how they have been dealt with in the English translation. The novel relies heavily on connotative elements in the Japanese language (*gokan*) which evoke culturally based associations in the minds of readers. While the translation accurately transmits the main meaning of the terms, many of the connotations have been lost, and, as a result, the translated text conveys much less information than the source text. The paper recommends that the translation of connotative cultural elements, which has been insufficiently studied, be the subject of more in-depth research.

Keywords: Morimi Tomihiko, translation of *gokan*, Japanese-English translation, connotative cultural elements, Japanese contemporary literature

1. Introduction: Reading experience as an encounter with a distinct universe

Reading a novel is to experience a distinct universe created on the basis of an "interaction between text and reader" (Iser 1980: ix). This universe contains various elements, one of which is the plot. The characters are another component, with yet another being the language used or writing style. The relative importance of each of these elements in the construction of a textual universe can vary from one novel to another.

The translation of a novel is an attempt to transpose this universe into a different language. However, when readers of the original and the translated version are imbued with very different bodies of cultural knowledge when interacting with the text, it would be difficult to claim that the reader of a target text (TT) and that of a source text (ST) experience the same — or very similar — textual universe. Clearly, a universe can be experienced differently by each reader even when the ST alone is read — however, the sharing of cultural knowledge between the author and the ST readers makes it possible for relatively common images and impressions to be conveyed. This shared body of cultural knowledge is what the author depends upon when s/he mentions certain material objects, customs, and institutions, among other things — which Newmark (1988: 95) calls cultural words that can cause translation problems. Indeed, the cultural knowledge required to share certain images and impressions with the author sometimes goes beyond merely knowing what these cultural references are. When the universe depicted in a novel relies heavily on the choice of language used — vocabulary, register, spelling (or different alphabets) and even verb and adjective conjugations — to evoke certain cultural associations, translation can become extremely difficult.

This paper analyses the novel, *Yoru wa mijikashi arukeyo otome,* by Morimi Tomihiko (2006), and its English version, *The Night is Short, Walk on Girl*, translated by Emily Balistrieri and published in 2019.[1] The focus is more on the ST, with an exploration of how readers are required to possess cultural knowledge at various levels in order to fully savour the universe depicted. After identifying different types of culturally loaded elements, we then determine the extent to which these can be translated into English, and, as a result, which aspects of the above-mentioned universe in the ST and TT might differ.

This novel was chosen for its heavy reliance on the use of a particular type of language which might sound obvious as all novels use language to convey meaning. I mean to say that the universe experienced by the reader is strongly influenced by cultural associations through the use of elements such as an unusual and distinctive vocabulary and register chosen by the author. Indeed, when one of his novels was to be made into an animated film, Morimi stated that:

> When I write, I write carefully and check the texture of each sentence. The images conveyed by each word are important, and the rhythm of the sentence is also important. From the accumulation of such sentences a distorted universe is created. This universe, whose distortion influences how the story develops, with its own particular rhythm, differs from the real world. Removing sentences from my novels would mean removing this distortion, and the story would cease to exist as such. I think this is the biggest problem when my novels are adapted for visual media.[2]   (Morimi 2017: 475)

---

1. In this paper, as is commonly the case in Japan, all Japanese names are preceded by the surname.

Although translation is clearly different from an adaptation of a novel to visual media such as an animated film, Morimi's comment above suggests how images, for example, evoked by a certain word, rather than its synonyms, can play an important role in the creation of a "distorted universe". This paper focuses on various cultural elements used in constructing this universe.

The paper consists of six sections. Following the introduction, the background of both the novel and the author is briefly presented. In the third section, some relevant concepts and previous studies are reviewed in order to define what can be considered as "cultural elements" in the ST. This is followed by an outline of the methodology used to collect and analyse examples of these elements and their translation. These examples are presented in the results and analysis section, which is followed by some considerations and conclusions.

2. Morimi Tomihiko and *Yoru wa mijikashi arukeyo otome*

The novel *Yoru wa mijikashi arukeyo otome* ('The night is short, walk on maiden', henceforth referred to as *Yoru wa mijikashi*) is by the author Morimi Tomihiko (born 1979) and was published in Japan in 2006. It is Morimi's highly successful second novel which has won several literary prizes and has been adapted into an animated film and for the theatre. Possibly due to the international success of the animated film, the novel was translated into English in 2019 by Emily Balistrieri.

The plot involves a romantic relationship between two university students in the city of Kyoto, the ancient capital of Japan. The male protagonist, whose name is not disclosed, attempts to get to know a younger female student with whom he is in love. The novel consists of four separate chapters, each featuring an event which takes place in Kyoto in locations such as a second-hand book market. The novel is mostly written in the first person, while the viewpoint alternates between the male protagonist and the female protagonist, whose voices are instantly distinguishable due to their very different speech styles. Although beyond the scope of this paper, it is worth noting that this distinctiveness is not only due to Japanese gender language, which uses elements such as different sentence-ending particles and personal pronouns, depending on the degree of masculinity and femininity expressed (e.g. see Nakamura 2013). Gender language markers, which are one of the characteristic features of spoken Japanese, can constitute a challenge for translators (e.g. see Furukawa 2013). However, apart from gender markers, Morimi's text is characterised by an abundant use of different types of cultural elements

---

2. Unless specified otherwise, citations from essays and other writings in Japanese have been translated by the author of this paper.

that are embedded in the Japanese language. With regard to the speech styles of his characters, Morimi has stated that "Characters in my novels never use Kyoto dialect and do not really speak in standard Japanese either. It is a language without a realistic feel, set in a highly artificial universe (Morimi 2017: 543)."

In many of his novels, including *Yoru wa mijikashi*, the story takes place in Kyoto. Morimi has defined the Kyoto portrayed in his novels as a product of his own fantasy and language, or "faux Kyoto" (Morimi 2017: 185), with its mix of realistic and fantastical elements. It transmits the feel of traditional Japanese culture which is mixed with aspects of contemporary popular culture such as *anime* and *manga*. This distinctive faux Kyoto, in addition to the novel's absurd characters, which, together, evoke "a highly artificial universe", are linguistically constructed through the use of numerous cultural elements, consisting of both so-called *realia* and elements embedded within the language itself. This paper aims to identify these cultural elements used in the ST which make the text, and thus the universe experienced by the reader, so original, and also to determine whether and how these elements are translated into English.

3. Culture and the problem of translation – relevant concepts

Culture has always been understood as one of the principal sources of translation problems. Newmark (1988: 95) has enumerated five different "cultural categories", including material culture and social culture, as well as a number of subcategories, such as food, and has also identified areas in which cultural words are bound to be present. Though often cited today, Newmark's all-encompassing categories are not always able to address what he calls "connotative problems" (98) with regard to the use of synonyms, both within a specific language and between different languages. For example, Newmark lists social culture terms such as "the people", "the common people", "the masses" and "the working class" in English (98). Differences in connotation could explain why the author of an ST chooses a specific word over other words from a group of synonyms. Clearly, such differences would be more difficult to replicate in a TT as compared to simpler cultural words such as those referring to traditional food. With regard to *Yoru wa mijikashi,* both cultural words and connotative differences abound. Numerous items, which are relevant to traditional Japanese culture such as *daruma* ("daruma-doll"), are used to create images of a faux Kyoto. However, the choice of certain terms based on their cultural connotations, such as obsolete expressions and conjugations, which make Morimi's text so original and distinctive, also plays an important role in the construction of his distorted universe.

Santamaria (2000) discusses mental representations developed by each reader from cultural references and how they are important for forming impressions about characters in fiction. She uses the term "cultural referents (CRs)" to refer only to cultural words relating to *realia* (cultural objects) and describes how values associated with such objects in the mind of readers can be used by the author of an ST in character descriptions (Santamaria 2000: 415). Thus, the focus is not on the cultural objects themselves in the ST, but on the value attached to these objects, a value that is meant to be shared between the author of the ST and the reader. In other words, the author of an ST relies upon associations shared with the reader which are part of common cultural knowledge. This appears to be very close to the concept of connotations, although Santamaria's study does not focus on connotative differences used as a basis for selecting certain words in the ST or on how this can pose a problem with regard to translation.

Due to its historical background and its flexible nature in relation to accepting loanwords, the Japanese language has many ways of writing a single word, as well as many synonyms. Theoretically, two phonetical alphabets, *hiragana* and *katakana*, as well as Chinese ideograms (*kanji*), can be used to write the same word. For example, the word *bara*, or rose, can be written in *hiragana, katakana* and *kanji* as ばら, バラ, and 薔薇, respectively, which evoke very different impressions in a reader; *hiragana,* with its rounded shape, evokes a softer impression, *katakana* sounds artificial or foreign, while *kanji* is more formal, dry, complex, and so on. Synonyms, which can include words of Chinese origin and other loanwords, are likely to have subtly different connotations that depend on a body of cultural knowledge shared by users of the language. Connotations or distinctive impressions conveyed by each word, as opposed to its synonyms, are referred to as *gokan* in Japanese. These are essential to facilitate the appreciation and translation of literary texts such as Morimi's, in which words are constantly chosen according to their *gokan* connotations. Nakamura (2010: 1171–1176) has attempted to systematically analyse and categorise different aspects of *gokan* in his *gokan* dictionary project, in which he describes three main categories: (1. the impression a word evokes about its user, 2. the background a word indicates in relation to its signified meaning — for example, certain adjectives are assumed to be used for women rather than men, and 3. the "aura" of a word), as well as 55 subcategories. These subcategories include features such as archaism, formality, association, impression, discriminatory tendency, as well as positive and negative images. *Gokan* connotations can play an important role in a single word or in a combination of words. Morimi often deliberately combines words with very different or even conflicting *gokan* connotations such as archaic words followed by informal and childish words (see Section 5), which resembles a foregrounding technique used to shock or surprise his readers (e.g. Douthwait, 2000).

Yet another culture-related concept that is relevant to an analysis of Morimi's texts is intertextuality. Miyazawa (2017) analyses the use of intertextuality in *Yoru wa mijikashi* which frequently refers to both Japanese and foreign literary works. This is directly relevant to a study by Kaźmierczak (2019), which focuses on intertextuality as a translation problem. The paper discusses intertextuality in the ST and the "problems connected with its translation *into* a stronger polysystem" (Kaźmierczak 2019: 370). Japanese literary works, songs, and so on, mentioned in *Yoru wa mijikashi*, have often not been translated into English and thus lack any officially recognised translation of their titles. Morimi often parodies these texts to achieve a humorous effect, which could make the task of translation even more problematic. Kaźmierczak states that "…intertextuality implies a dialogue and connection of a text with another text, other texts or types of texts — which is effected by means of quotations, allusions, by borrowing structures" and can occur in "text-text, text-genre, and text-reality" relationships (Kaźmierczak 2019: 364). For example, the use of exaggerated expressions to describe trivial matters observed in Morimi's text (see Section 5) suggests a strong influence of elements of popular culture such as *anime* and *manga*, which could be defined as a text-genre type of intertextuality.

Finally, the concept of cultural distance between the textual universe ('*mundo textual*') and the real world, as posited by Nord (2019: para.4), could be relevant when considering the role of cultural markers in the text. When cultural markers, such as the name of an actual street in Kyoto, that refer to the real world appear in the text, there is no cultural distance between the text and the reader, thus enabling the reader to identify or connect with the text. Morimi (2017: 296) has specifically emphasised the importance of using the names of various areas of Kyoto in the text: "Actually, novels have nothing to do with our daily life, our reality. (…) It is thanks to geographical names that a novel is anchored to the ground". However, this dimension might be diminished in translation, as readers are less familiar with these names. In other words, the cultural distance between the textual universe and the real world can change when the text in question is translated.

4. Methodology

As mentioned above, the purpose of this study is to analyse different types of cultural elements in the novel *Yoru wa mijikashi* and to determine whether these elements have been accurately transposed to the TT. In this section, we explain the methodology used to identify, categorise and compare these cultural elements in the ST and the TT.

4.1 Material

Certain parts of Chapter 1 of the novel *Yoru wa mijikashi arukeyo otome* by Morimi Tomihiko (2006) were used to identify cultural elements in the ST. Although the novel is written in the first person, the viewpoint alternates between the leading character, a male university student, and the female protagonist who are not named. As both characters have very different narrative voices, the parts of the novel narrated by the two protagonists were analysed separately. More specifically, the first part of the text narrated by the male protagonist (the "*He*" text, pp. 7–12), as well as the following part narrated by the female protagonist (the "*She*" text, pp. 12–20) in the ST, were used to identify the cultural elements (see Section 4.2. below). The corresponding parts in the English translation by Emily Balistrieri entitled *The Night is Short, Walk on Girl* (2019) were extracted to compare the translation of the cultural elements identified to the original text.

4.2 Methodology

The cultural elements from the *He* and *She* texts were identified through a close reading of the ST and were categorised as follows in Table 1 below.

Table 1. Types of cultural elements in the ST

	Type		
1	Cultural References (CRs) based on Newmark (1988)	Geography (place names), Material culture (artefacts), Social culture, Organisations/customs/activities/procedures/concepts, Gestures and habits
2	Intertextuality	References to other texts (literary works/songs), including parodies
3	Betrayal of expected connotations/*gokan*	Combinations of words with mismatching registers, partially changed idioms, use of inappropriate Japanese phonetical alphabets (*hiragana/katakana*), and so on.
4a	Pseudo-classical connotations/*gokan*	a. Archaic vocabulary (not conjugations), often associated with style used in modern Japanese literature (ca.1900).
4b		b. Archaic verb and adjective conjugations, often associated with style of modern Japanese literature (ca. 1900).
4c		c. Idioms written only in Chinese ideograms, including *yojijyukugo* (idioms written using four Chinese ideograms).
5	Exaggeration	Use of inappropriately exaggerated expressions to describe less significant matters, as commonly seen in elements of Japanese popular culture such as *manga* and *anime*.

The examples identified were listed and numbered in order of appearance, separately for the *He* and *She* texts. Each example was then compared to the corresponding part in the TT. If the cultural element was not omitted in the TT, we determined whether any of the effects listed above, such as exaggeration and pseudo-classical impressions, were transposed to the TT. As most of these effects are connotative (i.e. not the main meaning of a term) and are based on cultural knowledge, it is relatively easy to translate only the overall meaning of the term while leaving out these connotative effects. However, as argued above, for texts such as *Yoru wa mijikashi,* these effects are indispensable in creating the textual universe.

5. Results and analysis

The overall results and selected examples of each category, together with commentaries, are provided in this section.

5.1 Results

The number of cases identified, the frequency and the percentage of each type, as well as the occurrence of the examples in the TT, whose effects in the ST appear to have been transposed to some extent, are shown in Tables 2 and 3. Table 2 shows the results for the *He* text, while Table 3 shows those for the *She* text.

Table 2. *He* text

Type	Case	%	Effects maintained in the TT
1	9	12.3	8
2	3	4.1	1
3	7	9.6	5
4a	22	30.1	3
4b	13	17.8	4
4c	16	21.9	12
5	3	4.1	2
Total	73	100.0	35

A total of 73 examples were identified in the *He* text, while 69 cases were identified in the *She* text. However, rather than simply adding up the total number of examples, it is important to note the different distribution patterns observed in both texts. This partly explains why the voices of the two narrators (the male and female protagonists) sound so different.

Table 3. *She* text

Type	Case	%	Effects maintained in the TT
1	22	31.9	21
2	1	1.4	0
3	11	15.9	7
4a	18	26.1	5
4b	2	2.9	0
4c	7	10.1	4
5	8	11.6	6
Total	69	100.0	43

The reason why type 1 elements appear more often in the *She* text (31.9%) than in the *He* text (12.3%) is because geographical names, such as those of streets, areas and stations in Kyoto, are referred to more often in the *She* text. Another clear difference is the frequency of type 4 elements, which add a pseudo-classical tone to the text. In the *He* text, the occurrence of elements 4a, 4b and 4c reaches almost 70% (69.8%), as compared to roughly 40% (39.1%) for the *She* text. This means that the speech style of the male protagonist sounds more classical and literary than that of the female protagonist. By using such a classical-sounding style to describe trivial events, the author of the ST produces a humorous effect. In short, the male protagonist sounds overly serious as compared to the female protagonist. A breakdown of type 4 elements shows that this tendency is much more marked with regard to types 4b and 4c, rather than type 4a. Type 4b includes archaic verb and adjective conjugations, while 4c refers to idioms of Chinese origin. In other words, although pseudo-classical nouns appear in both texts, the male protagonist uses obsolete conjugations and intellectual turns of phrase much more often. However, this is not to say that the *She* text sounds less humorous. As Tables 2 and 3 above show, type 3 elements appear in both texts (7 and 11 examples, respectively). Type 3 highlights the playful use of *gokan* connotations which betray readers' expectations regarding the use of words and expressions. This is achieved, for example, by combining words with mismatching registers, such as the sudden appearance of baby language right after a highbrow-sounding Chinese idiom, or by changing part of an idiom. The *She* text also uses type 5 elements (8 examples) involving exaggeration, which include the use of inappropriate high-register words to describe insignificant matters, a technique commonly deployed in *manga* and *anime*. Unlike type 4 elements, type 5 exaggeration has a humorous effect on the reader, without however conveying an intellectual impression. Although type 2 intertextuality and its parodies are frequently used in the novel, not many examples appear in the parts of the text studied in this paper.

Only three cases — two in the *He* text and one in the *She* text — were completely omitted in the translation, all of which were examples of type 4a cultural elements. However, as shown in Tables 2 and 3, the translation of many of the terms did lose their *gokan* connotations. Type 1 cultural references were mostly translated intact, although the added explanation of a term sometimes changed its connotation in the ST. The pseudo-classical effect of type 4 elements seems to be much more difficult to transpose to the TT. The following section provides some examples of each type and their translations.

5.2 Analysis

5.2.1 *Type 1: Cultural references based on Newmark (1988)*

Most examples of type 1, which need to be translated intact, are proper nouns — streets, monuments, and institutions in Kyoto. In the TT, street names are transcribed, and official English translations are used for the names of institutions when they exist. As mentioned in Section 3, Morimi himself has commented on the special importance of the names of streets and areas in Kyoto, which connect the fantastical universe of his novels to reality, as expressed by the "cultural distance" between the textual universe and the reality in Nord (2019: para.5). Thus, it would seem appropriate to use official translations or transcriptions of these names in the TT, which fulfil a similar function to that in the ST.

(1) ST (p. 13): 「月面歩行」というバー
    "*Getsumenhokō*" to iu bā
    'A bar called Moon Walk'
    TT (p. 6): Bar Moon Walk

Interestingly, although the name of the actual bar in Kyoto, Bar Moon Walk, is in English, its name in the ST is translated into Japanese. In the TT, this is translated back to English, thus rendering the textual universe closer to the reality than in the ST.

Not all type 1 elements are proper names. In the novel, items that are closely related to old-style Japanese culture, such as *manekineko* (p. 1) — lucky cat — and *denki bran* (p. 19) — electric brandy — appear out of their usual context. In the ST, these items add a certain Japanese touch to the reader's mental representation of the textual universe. In the TT, as terms, such as "lucky cat" for *manekineko*, are translated in the customary manner, a similar effect might be expected if the reader is familiar with Japanese culture. However, sometimes cultural references need to be explained, which changes their function in the TT.

(2) ST (p. 10): お姫さま抱っこで
    ohimesamadakko de
    'in a princess-like hug'
    TT (p. 3): (...the bride) was scooped up into the groom's arms...

Ohimesamadakko, which is a relatively new cultural term, originates from popular culture, especially *shōjo* (girls) *manga*, in which the hero sweeps the heroine up in his arms when rescuing her from danger. By explaining the meaning of the term translated in the TT, its strong association in the ST with *shōjo manga* is lost, and thus also the humorous effect of the mismatched register, with the sudden appearance of a *shōjo manga* image generally rendered in a pseudo-classical writing style.

5.2.2 Type 2: Intertextuality and its parodies

As mentioned in Section 5.2, not many cases of intertextuality are present in the excerpt used for this study, even though the novel refers to a number of other texts, especially in the second chapter. It is worth mentioning, however, that the title of the novel itself parodies an old popular ballad from the Taishō era, entitled *Gondora no uta* ('A Song of Gondola'), which was released in 1915. A line in the original lyric, *Inochi mijikashi koiseyo otome* ('Life is short, fall in love, maiden'), is changed to *Yoru wa mijikashi, arukeyo otome* ('The night is short, walk on, maiden'). As the original lyrics are still well-known in Japan, the title of the novel is closely associated with the Taishō period (1912–1926). While the overall meaning of this line is rendered in the TT (although the term *otome* in the ST is closer in meaning to "maiden" than "girl"), the association with the Taishō period is clearly lost. As the TT does not include translator's notes, no explanation is provided. As with the title, intertextuality is often used in the novel to add a certain pseudo-classical feel to the text.

(3) ST (p. 7): 路傍の石ころ
    robō no ishikoro
    'a roadside pebble'
    TT (p. 1): '...a pebble by a wayside...'

This metaphor in the ST, which is used by the male protagonist to express his insignificant existence, is a parody of a famous unfinished novel by Yamamoto Yūzo, *Robō no ishi* ('Roadside Stone'), written between 1937 and 1940. The use of the term *ishikoro* (a pebble) rather than *ishi* (a stone) in the original text makes the register more colloquial, which produces a humorous effect. As Yamamoto's novel has not been translated into English, it would have been difficult to replicate the effect of the parody in the TT. Thus, although the meaning is translated accurately, the association is lost.

5.2.3 *Type 3: Betrayal of expected gokan connotations*

In the ST, type 3 elements are used in various ways to add a certain humorous touch to the text. As Tables 2 and 3 above demonstrate, this effect has been transposed to the TT relatively intact.

(4)   ST (p.16): 手に鰭をとって
te ni hire wo totte
'hand in fin'
TT (p.9):   …joined hand in fin…

One way to surprise readers and to betray their expectations is to change the second half of an idiom. The example given above is a parody of the idiom *te ni te wo totte* ('hand-in-hand'), when the female protagonist describes a koi fish farming business owned by one of the side characters as involving teamwork between the owner and the fish. A virtually identical idiom exists in English, which explains why the literal translation in the TT achieves the same effect.

(5)   ST (p.16): 終始ふくれっつらをした宇宙生物
shūshi fukurettsura wo shita uchū seibutsu
'extra-terrestrial organisms with permanently sulky expressions'
TT (p.9):   …sulky aliens…

This example illustrates another type 3 technique, which involves combining words with mismatched *gokan* connotations. When the female protagonist describes koi fish with blisters in the ST, the *wago* term *fukurettsura* ('sulky expression'), a Japanese-originated colloquial word, written in the *hiragana* alphabet, is combined with a *kango* word written in Chinese ideograms. This word *fukurettsura* from the spoken language is not used in more formal documents, while the term *uchū seibutsu* ('extra-terrestrial organisms') that follows, which is written using only Chinese ideograms, belongs more to the written language. Although the translation accurately transposes the meaning, a more academic term, such as "extra-terrestrial organism" rather than "alien" would have been more appropriate and closer to the original ST.

(6)   ST (p.20): オモチロイ
omochiroi
'much fun'
TT (p.11):   …funinteresting…

The ST uses baby language and mispronounces the word *omo*sh*iroi* ('interesting/fun') as *omo*ch*iroi*. The female protagonist, who normally uses a more formal language, suddenly employs this adjective with a mismatching register. It is also written in the *katakana* alphabet, which is normally used for foreign words, thus accentuating the feeling of a mismatch. This term also emphasises the cuteness of the female protagonist, whose voice suddenly sounds like that of a little child. The translation not only uses a neologism to convey the meaning of the term, but also provides nuance.

5.2.4 Type 4a: Pseudo-classical gokan connotation: Archaic vocabulary

Type 4a elements can be observed 22 and 18 times in the *He* and *She* texts, respectively. This is the most frequently used technique in the ST in order to add a pseudo-classical tone to the text, although this connotation is rarely transposed to the TT.

(7) ST (p. 8): 女たるもの
     Onna <u>tarumono</u>
     '<u>Being</u> a woman, (<u>one must</u>...)'
     TT (p. 2): A girl..

The expression *X tarumono* is virtually anachronistic when used at the beginning of a phrase, which is usually followed by a certain type of behaviour expected of that X, for example, a woman. Such expressions are frequently used in the ST to conjure up an old-fashioned atmosphere, which, however, cannot be transposed directly to the TT.

(8) ST (p. 11): 私め
     watakushi <u>me</u>
     'my <u>humble</u> self'
     TT (p. 5): Me

The male protagonist is imagining something he could say in order to ask the female protagonist out for a drink. Although the self-deprecatory expression *watakushi me* is used, in today's Japanese, *watakushi nado* would be more common. The connotation of the anachronistic expression used in the ST, which sounds exaggerated and comical, is lost in the TT.

(9) ST (p. 14): 殿方
     tonogata
     'a fine gentleman'
     TT (p. 7): ...man...

Tonogata is an extremely old-fashioned and respectful term to refer to a man/men, which was used by women either in formal conversations or in writing. The female protagonist uses a mismatched genteel archaic term to describe a middle-aged man encountered in a bar, who is portrayed as a rather shabby and miserable side character in the novel. The translation erases all these connotations, including a certain impression of the female protagonist: formal, strangely old-fashioned, and naïve character.

(10) ST (p. 16): ウヰスキー
        uiskii
        'whisky'
    TT (p. 8): ...whiskey..

Whiskey, pronounced *uiskii* in Japanese, is a word borrowed from English and therefore written in the *katakana* alphabet. The old spelling, using a *katakana* ヰ instead of イ, is used in the ST. ヰ, which is not used today, was used to express the "wi" sound, and イ to express the "i" sound. The old spelling, which is associated with old Japanese, can still be seen in company names, for example. Although its ability to produce an effect equivalent to that in the ST is unsure, the translator could have opted for the older, alternative spelling, which is "whisky" without e.

5.2.5 Type 4b: Pseudo-classical gokan connotation: Archaic verb and adjective conjugations

Not only the vocabulary, but also the grammar of Japanese, has changed greatly over time. The pseudo-classical style of Morimi's text is also created through the frequent use of archaic conjugations of verbs and adjectives. This gives the text a tone reminiscent of modern Japanese literature from the Taishō (1912–26) and early Shōwa (1926–89) periods, which is in stark contrast to the use of baby language and references to contemporary popular culture. Type 4b elements, which appear much more frequently in the *He* text than in the *She* text, make the male protagonist sound more out-moded, pedantic and sometimes ridiculous. These connotations are generally not transposed to the TT.

(11) ST (p. 8): やがて来たる混乱
        yagate <u>kitaru</u> konran
        '...ensuing confusion'
    TT (p. 2): ....ensuing confusion

The verb *kitaru* in the ST is conjugated according to classical Japanese grammar rather than to today's *kuru* ("to come"). The meaning of *kitaru* is similar to that of *kuru*, with the only difference being a *gokan* connotation from old Japanese. The verb "to ensue" was chosen for the English translation, which sounds more formal as compared to many of its synonyms, probably in order to replicate a similar connotation.

(12) ST (p. 10): 面白くなきところ
　　　　　　　　omoshirokunaki tokoro
　　　　　　　　'...that which is <u>unworthy of one's interest</u>...'
　　　TT (p. 3): ...uninteresting enough...

The negative form of the adjective *omoshiroi* ("interesting") in today's Japanese is *omoshirokunai*, although the classical conjugation *omoshirokunaki* is used in the ST. The only difference lies in the last syllable ("i" or "ki"), which changes the tone of the whole sentence, making it sound stiffer and more old-fashioned. Such nuance is difficult to replicate in the TT.

5.2.6 Type 4c: Pseudo-classical connotation or "gokan": Idioms written in Chinese ideograms

Though words from both the *kango* (Chinese-originated) and *wago* (Japanese-originated) lexis often appear in the same document, they have different *gokan* connotations. A *kango* word is written only in Chinese ideograms, whereas a *wago* word is normally partially written using the *hiragana* phonetical alphabet. Normally a *kango* word, which is chosen according to different *gokan* connotations, has synonyms in the *wago* lexis and vice versa. As briefly mentioned in Section 3, words written in Chinese ideograms convey a more formal, dry, classical and possibly intellectual impression. This is probably most apparent with idioms written using four Chinese ideograms (*yojijyukugo*). Such expressions are used more often in the *He* text in accordance with the impression conveyed by the male protagonist's character. Idioms are often used in the TT to translate type 4c elements, possibly to convey a somewhat equivalent connotation.

(13) ST (p. 9): 聖人君子
　　　　　　　　seijinkunshi
　　　　　　　　'men who are whiter than white'
　　　TT (p. 4): ...men of virtue...

(14) ST (p. 7): 読者諸賢
　　　　　　　　dokushashoken
　　　　　　　　'wise readers'
　　　TT (p. 1): Wise readers,

In both Examples 13 and 14 above, set phrases are used in the TT. For example, *dokushashoken* in Example 14 is an expression often used in modern Japanese literature but uncommon today, whose translation reproduces a classical tone.

5.2.7 Type 5: Exaggeration

This refers to an inappropriately exaggerated tone used to describe a trivial event, as can often be seen in genres of popular culture such as *anime* and *manga*. Both type 4 and type 5 examples add a comical tone to the text by using the inappropriate adjective or exaggerated expressions to describe insignificant matters. However, unlike in type 4 cases, the "inappropriate feeling" of type 5 cases is not dependant on the anachronism of vocabulary or verb/adjective conjugations. While examples of type 4 require readers to be familiar with old Japanese, examples of type 5 require more contemporary cultural knowledge.

(15) ST (p. 10): 黒焦げにした。
kurokoge ni shita.
'charred.'
TT (p. 3): …burned to a crisp.

In Example 15, the male protagonist is explaining how the unrestrained show of passionate love by the newlywed couple embarrassed the guests at the party. This exaggerated image of burning with embarrassment or extreme blushing, which is commonly used in *anime, manga,* and comics, can be literally translated while maintaining its effect.

(16) ST (p. 13): お財布への信頼に一抹の翳りある
osaifu e no shinrai ni ichimatsu no kageriaru
'those who experience a hint of darkness in trusting their wallets'
TT (p. 6): …those who can't feel very confident about the contents of their wallets…

In the example above, where the female protagonist is describing her financial circumstances, the meaning in the ST is translated accurately. However, expressions such as *ichimatsu no kageri aru* ('a hint of darkness'), which belong to literary language, are toned down to some extent.

6. Considerations and conclusions

This study aims to highlight the difficulty of translating cultural elements which are present in the ST at various levels in order to depict the novel's universe. The study focuses mainly on *gokan* connotations or nuances in the Japanese language. In this final section, some concluding remarks are made concerning issues that have arisen from analyses carried out during the study.

While the translation of more tangible cultural references such as material culture can be challenging, the transposition of associations or impressions based on readers' cultural knowledge can be next to impossible. Indeed, compared to type 1 cultural references, which mostly involve proper nouns and can be transposed in an unmodified form, the transposition of other types of cultural elements, whose *gokan* connotations and nuances play an important role in conveying subtle impressions, has proven to be much more difficult.

In this study, we focus on Morimi's "distorted universe" which is constructed through the accumulation of terms and expressions characterised by features such as archaic vocabulary, grammar, and peculiar spelling. The novel constantly uses such constructions and makes full use of their *gokan* connotations, a combination which underlies the pseudo-classicist tone of Morimi's universe. As Miyazawa (2017: 181) points out, this pseudo-classicism reminds readers of modern Japanese works of literature. As Section 5 of this paper shows, while it is difficult to transpose such connotations to the TT, it also depends on the types of ST expressions used. For example, idioms written only using Chinese ideograms, an integral part of the text's pseudo-classicism, often seem to be translated with somewhat similar connotations.

While the overall underlying tone of Morimi's text is that of a pseudo-classicism constructed through strictly chosen terms with certain *gokan* connotations, its other characteristic, humour, is achieved by sometimes deliberately breaking with this *leitmotif*. This is achieved by introducing mismatching *gokan* nuances such as baby language, references to contemporary popular culture, or items written in the *katakana* alphabet when normally written in Chinese ideograms. Alternatively, this is achieved by betraying readers' expectations, through devices such as the modification of the second half of idioms, parodies of intertextual references, and the use of exaggerated *gokan* connotations to describe trivial events. All of this adds a comical tone to the text, but it is also very difficult to translate into another language and to be appreciated by readers with a different set of cultural knowledge. However, the examples analysed in the previous section show that it is sometimes possible to transpose the effects evoked by contemporary popular culture references or modified idioms.

It is important to emphasise that this paper focuses, not on the core information or meaning conveyed by a word, but rather on its connotations. The core information is translated virtually without fail; as mentioned in Section 5.1, only three out of the total number of 142 examples identified were omitted in the TT. Thus, the information which is vital to follow the plot, including much of the humour, was found to remain intact. Nevertheless, by comparing the 142 examples identified in the ST with the corresponding parts in the TT, a certain amount of information is clearly lost. With this study's focus on the ST, it is not clear whether this loss is made up for by, for example, the use of archaic expressions in the TT when not present in the ST. It is also unclear whether it was considered necessary to compensate for this loss at all — for example, the TT does not contain any translator's notes to explain what could not be transposed from the ST. As this paper demonstrates, it is extremely difficult and often impossible to transpose connotations to the TT. Nevertheless, it is important to note that this consistent loss of information could alter the textual universe provided to readers of the TT.

This small-scale study is possibly one of the first attempts to identify the problems of translating certain types of cultural elements embedded in the Japanese language. Unlike gender markers, which are another cultural element embedded in Japanese, the complexities of translating *gokan* connotations are little understood. However, novels such as *Yoru wa mijkashi*, which relies heavily on *gokan* nuances, are now being translated into other languages, thus suggesting that further in-depth research is needed in this area. It is necessary to fine-tune the categorisation process in order to include different types of cultural elements embedded in the language, which would require research on a larger scale. A study of the same text used in this paper, but focused more on the TT, also needs to be carried out in order to identify possible translation strategies, such as the compensation approach, and to investigate in more depth the possibility of translating the cultural elements outlined above.

Funding

This research was funded by Åke Wibergs Stiftelse Foundation (Sweden).

References

Douthwait, John. 2000. *Towards a Linguistic Theory of Foregrounding*. Alessandria: Edizioni dell'Oso S.r.l.

Furukawa, Hiroko. 2013. "Women's language and Translation: Intra-Cultural Translation into the Feminine Ideal." *Interpreting and Translation Studies* 13: 1–23.

Iser, Wolfgang. 1980. *The Act of Reading*. Baltimore: Johns Hopkins University Press.

Kaźmierczak, Marta. 2019. "Intertextuality as Translation Problem: Explicitness, Recognisability and the Case of "Literatures of Smaller Nations"." *Russian Journal of Linguistics* 23(2): 362–382.

Miyazawa, Nana. 2017. "Morimi Tomihiko "Yoru wa mijkashi arukeyo otome" ni okeru senkō bungaku sakuhin jyuyō [Recipience of existing literary works in *Yoru wa mijkashi arukeyo otome* by Morimi Tomihiko]." *Toyama hikaku bungaku* 9: 172–199.

Morimi, Tomihiko. 2006. Yoru wa mijikashi, arukeyo otome [*The night is short, walk on maiden*]. Tokyo: Kadokawa Shoten

Morimi, Tomihiko 2019. *The Night is Short, Walk on Maiden*. Translated by Emily Balistrieri: New York: Yen On.

Morimi, Tomihiko. 2017. Taiyō to otome [*The sun and maiden*] (paperback edition). Tokyo: Shinchōsha.

Nakamura, Akira. 2010. Gokan no jiten [*Dicctionary of gokan connotations*]. Tokyo: Iwanami Shoten.

Nakamura, Momoko. 2013. Honyaku ga tsukuru nihongo: hiroin wa onna kotoba wo hanashituzukeru [*Japanese language created through translation: The heroine keeps on talking in female language*]. Tokyo: Hakutakusha.

Newmark, Peter. 1988. *A Textbook of Translation*. New York; London; Sydney: Prentice-Hall International.

Nord, Christiane. 2019. "La cortesía literaria en español e italiano: los tratamientos en la traducción de las novelas de Carlos Ruiz Zafón [Literary courtesy in Spanish and Italian: handlings in the translation of the novels of Carlos Ruiz Zafón]." *inTRAlinea* Special Issue: Le regioni del tradurre. Electric versión: https://www.intralinea.org/specials/article/2383

Santamaria, Laura. 2000. "Cultural References in Translation: Informative Contribution and Cognitive Values." In *Beyond the Western Tradition: Translation Perspectives XI*, ed. by Marilyn G. Rose, 415–426. Binghamton: Center for Research in Translation, State University of New York.

Translating sociolinguistic traces of urban youth culture in contemporary fiction

Tiffane Levick
Centre for Anglophone Studies, Université Toulouse - Jean Jaurès

This paper examines the links between linguistic variety and cultural references in translation, positing that both serve to anchor a work of fiction in a specific time and place, and to provide information about the identity of their users. This idea is borne out in a discussion presenting typologies for the translation of cultural references and of slang, demonstrating how drawing links between these two translation issues may allow us to understand better the functions of implicit and explicit signs of cultural affiliation in the source text. Providing examples from texts set in and around Paris featuring slang, it will comment on the repercussions of implementing various methods used to translate linguistic variety and cultural references.

Keywords: slang, linguistic variety, subcultures, functional theories, youth speech

1. Introduction

There is no shortage of papers exploring the links between culture and language written by scholars from a wide range of disciplines. With this reality in mind, and in an effort to offer an additional branch to the discussion, this paper will conceptualise the relationship between linguistic variety and cultural references. More specifically, it will adopt the prism of translation to assess how the use of linguistic variety can evoke various aspects of a person's identity, especially in terms of the culture/s with which they are affiliated. When incorporated in a work of fiction, linguistic variety and cultural references undoubtedly serve to anchor a story in a specific time and place, and to characterise the people who choose to use them. The presence of language so suggestive of identity and belonging in a work of fiction presents a distinct challenge to translators, who must grapple with the question of how to craft a linguistic network in the target text with extralinguistic significance akin to that of the original text, all the while using the tools of a different language.

To provide a framework within which to consider the complexities of the relationship between language and cultural affiliation, this paper will study the specific case of urban youth language and culture. It will begin with an overview of the functions and features of linguistic variety in general and of slang in particular, before demonstrating the links between the typologies of different strategies and techniques that one might use to translate linguistic variety and cultural references. The examples provided are taken from contemporary works of fiction featuring the voice of marginalised youth and translated from French into English. In this way, it will be possible to envisage urban youth culture as a subculture within the source culture, but also as a subculture that may transcend national borders and languages, and to see how this tension plays out in translation.

The notion of which extralinguistic suggestions embedded in the language used in the source text might be transferred into the target text is raised by Eirlys E. Davies in her 2003 article "A Goblin or a Dirty Nose?" dedicated to the translation of culture-specific references in the *Harry Potter* series:

> If we assume some kind of general culture of childhood, some universal properties of children's tastes and humour, then we might imagine that the child-friendly aspects of the books would perhaps cross linguistic and cultural barriers more easily than their specifically British cultural references. (Davies 2003: 66)

This idea of the relative transferability and universality of certain aspects of the source language, or linguistic variety, and culture, or subcultures, from the source text to the target text will serve as a key point of reference in the discussions that follow. Envisaging the process of translation in this manner allows us to recast the question of culture to examine the ties and tension between the multitude of aspects of an individual person's identity, and consider how language choices can be act as a means of communicating these facets of identity.

2. Defining youth language and culture

Before exploring the idea of youth language and culture in translation in more detail, it seems first pertinent to delineate the boundaries of what is understood by these concepts, and how they apply to works of fiction. When it comes to culture references, scholars seem to agree that the terms included in texts serve to refer to concepts, institutions and personnel which are specific to the source language culture (Harvey 2000: 358), and with which a person may not be familiar, even if they know the language in question (Pederson 2007: 30–31). Some scholars, in Pederson, differentiate between monocultural and transcultural references; in other words, references that are unique to one culture, and ones that are shared between or known across different cultures (ibid: 31). We might garner from these definitions that culture is shared by groups of people depending on where they live, but it is also evident that the idea of culture can be envisaged more broadly in terms of the predominate customs or behaviours that unite people in groups, both within and across geographical areas, because of their religion, job, age, habits, interests, etc.

The notion of the different strands binding people in groups can be extended to cover the concept of sociolinguistic variety, envisaged as a classification of people's linguistic habits and speech patterns based on a number of aspects of their background and identity. According to Françoise Gadet, sociolinguistic variety can be: regional, or diatopic (depending on where the person is from, or lives at the time of speaking); social, or diastratic (depending on the social class the person belongs to); demographic (depending on sex and/or gender, age, ethnicity, occupation, etc.); stylistic and situational, or diaphasic (depending on the communicative setting); temporal, or diachronic; or inherent (different ways of saying the same thing) (1997: 3–7).

It is clear that there is inevitable overlap between these categories, which makes the task of translating variety even more challenging and interesting, since we might wonder if the linguistic manifestations of specific aspects of a person's identity should be prioritised in translation, and if so, how. This question is intricately tied to that of the function of the text, both source and target, since it is relevant to consider why the author has decided to use the language they have, what kind of communicative meaning they are trying to convey, and how the role played by linguistic variety in the source text might be transferred into the target text.

When it comes to translation, we tend to talk about the process and result in fairly binary terms, considering source texts and target texts and involving the source language and culture on one hand and the target language and culture and the other. This would suggest that the language of the source text is tied up in or at least strongly linked to the source culture. But what if we shifted the focus slightly to conceive of the source culture and the target culture in the plural, envisaging the broader culture as being composed of a number of smaller cultures, of subcultures? In this way, we could identify links between distinct subgroups of the source culture and target culture, which may in turn use distinct "sublanguages" (i.e. forms of linguistic variety); links that transcend the source and target language, so that, despite the linguistic differences in the language that they are speaking based on their geographic space they occupy, we can draw parallels in terms of the symbolic space they occupy in society.

We might see marginalised youth in urban areas as having a lot in common with young people facing comparable issues and sharing comparable habits in other parts of the world, perhaps through hip-hop culture or other artistic subcultures, for instance. What might this mean for translation, where language is clearly at the heart of the matter? How might these ideas affect the ways in which translators go about rendering their voice as it is artistically transcribed in a fictional text into another language? And the ways in which we, as scholars of translation, attempt to understand and analyse the translation choices made? In what follows, reflections on translating cultural references and on translating linguistic variety will be raised and merged so as to open up a discussion around these questions.

2.1 Translating cultural references

The vast number of publications dedicated to the translation of cultural references pays testament to the fact that there are countless ways of translating these references, and, in turn, countless ways of classifying these choices. Typologies such as those put forward by Pederson (2007), Harvey (2000), Mailhac (1996), and Davies (2003) offer rich explorations of the reasons why translators may opt for certain techniques, and the repercussions of their implementation. The fact that each scholar provides a slightly different framework, with choices painted as more or less source- or target-oriented depending on the circumstances, also demonstrates the complexity of classifying choices: inevitably, no two translators will use the same words or turns of phrase to transfer a reference from one language and culture to another, and no two scholars will use exactly the same terms to label these choices in all cases. Bearing this in mind does not negate the necessity of numerous frameworks, rather, it celebrates the diversity of thought and acknowledges that the approach taken in this paper contributes to a broader debate.

For the sake of clarity, this paper will rely on Eirlys Davies' typology (2003) which proposes seven techniques to translate cultural references, based on her analysis of translations of the *Harry Potter* series. Firstly, preservation (1) occurs when a translator decides to "maintain the source text term in the translation" (ibid: 72), and so carry the term across without translating it. She does not specify if the term is highlighted as foreign through typographical choices (through the use of italics, for instance) or if the spelling of the term is altered to suit target-language norms, which would of course have an impact on the way in which the reader interprets the reference as foreign. Overall, however, it seems that the technique suggests that the translator considers there to be no convenient equivalent of the source-language reference and thus chooses to include the term in the target text. In cases where the translator deems it necessary or useful to assist the reader in deciphering the reference, the technique of addition (2) may be used.

Addition may be defined as an "augmented" form of preservation, accompanying the borrowed item from the source text with intra- or extra-textual explanatory notes to facilitate understanding (ibid: 77). Both these techniques are undoubtedly source-oriented, highlighting the foreign nature of the text, although the precise way in which they are implemented may yield to the perceived needs of the target audience.

When the translator decides, for whatever reason, that the cultural reference is not needed in the target text, perhaps because it is particularly opaque or ambiguous and does not play a significant enough role in the text to warrant its inclusion and potential explanation, we can talk of omission (3), which entails completely erasing the reference (ibid: 79). If the reference specific to the source culture is removed but replaced by a more general term which refers to a broader reality accessible to audiences from a range of cultural backgrounds, the translator has had recourse to the technique of globalisation (4). Davies does not specify if the globalised reference originates in the source or target culture, or beyond the borders of both, but it seems clear that the underlying goal of globalisation involves focussing on finding a balance between source and target realities to identify common ground between the two.

In stark opposition to the techniques or preservation and addition lies the adoption of localisation (5), a technique that seeks "to anchor a reference firmly in the culture of the target audience" (ibid: 84). Localisation results in an unequivocal erasure of the specificity of the source-culture reference in favour of a more readily accessible reference from the target culture, and necessarily involves risk-taking since there is an arguably a very fine line between passable and implausible localisation. Pedersen refers to this notion of plausibility when discussing the danger of the "credibility gap" (2007: 33), warning that a clash between the foreign setting of the text and the local reference may result in incredulity on the part of readers unable to reconcile the two. Overall, the use of localisation serves to neutralise the foreignness of the unfamiliar reference in favour of accessibility.

The final two techniques listed by Davies fall outside the realm of source- or target-oriented approaches, depending on the specific context in which they are used and on how one wishes to classify them. When it comes to transformation (6), the culture-bound term is "altered" or "distorted" in a way that does not correspond exactly to globalisation or localisation (ibid: 86). As such, the technique might be assigned to choices that do not fit neatly into any other category, but when the choices can be seen as corresponding to existing terms or norms. Finally, creation (7) involves the invention of a new culture-bound term that does not already exist in the source or target culture (ibid: 88). Although Davies does not venture into an exhaustive exploration of the various shapes that this technique might take outside of the examples presented, we might imagine creation taking inspiration from the linguistic form of the original reference, or involving the translator's creative impulses to propose a neologism.

Overall, Davies' work provides a practical port of entry into the analysis of countless choices made by translators depending on the role the reference in question is playing in the source text, and the role it plays outside of the text within the source culture, and especially on the extent to which it is deemed pertinent for readers of the target text. Her underlying goal of unravelling the reasons for and repercussion of the use of these seven techniques remains infinitely similar to the overarching objectives of this study, which seeks to show how language choices in a source text can suggest an individual's adherence to a specific subculture and how the way these language choices are carried across to the target text can contribute to accentuating the specificity of this subculture, to underscoring the parallels between this specific subculture and local subcultures, or to generalising the very concept of a subculture in hinting at the existence of the concept across the globe.

2.2 Translating slang

Before considering the implications of various possibilities for translating slang in particular and linguistic variety in general, it is useful to establish what exactly slang is. As with linguistic variety, slang constitutes a means of expressing diverse aspects of an individual's identity, and fits in with various branches of the framework, since it is influenced by a person's location, social class, and demographic, is used in specific situations among specific individuals, usually of the same subculture, and evolves over time. Slang also inevitably involves inherent variation, since no two users (or authors) will use language in exactly the same way, regardless of their potential shared adherence to a particular subculture.

The definition of slang advanced by the scholars who contributed to the 2014 collected volume *Global English Slang: Methodologies and Perspectives* underscores the suggestions of identity in slang use: "Slang is informal, non-technical language that often seems novel to the user and/or listener, and that challenges a social or linguistic norm. It can also imply complicity in value judgements and thus play a performative role in defining personal or group identity" (Coleman 2014: 30). As well as being playful and creative, slang is a form of language that deviates from the norm, and its use in a text clearly contributes to associating characters with a specific group. It is the contours of this group that interest us in translation, specifically the position of this group within the source culture, and within the global system of cultures.

When dealing with the presence of slang in a work of fiction, the translator is faced with a number of options. Their choices will necessarily be determined by the context in which they are translating, the type of text in question and the density and the role played by the slang in the source text. Although there is overlap between each of the three strategies and six techniques proposed below for the translation of slang, and the decision to describe choices with these labels may also vary depending slightly on personal judgements, as is the case with the typologies advanced for translating cultural references, sketching this framework allows for more careful examination of the potential reasons for and repercussions of different choices. The typology that follows is an updated version of that put forward in my doctoral thesis (Levick, 2018), established through the reading of theory and the analysis of texts set in and around Paris featuring the voice of marginalised youth and translated into English. It conceives of a strategy as being more general than a technique, constituting the concrete plan of how to go about translating a text on a more macroscopic level. These strategies are executed through the implementation of techniques, which represent the specific steps taken to translate a text on a more microscopic level, and which may also be used in conjunction to establish a new strategy. Though it concerned primarily with slang, the vast majority of the reflections put forward can be applied to other forms of linguistic variety.

The first of the strategies identified to translate slang is standardisation, which involves the non-standard language of the source text being brought closer to the standard variety of the target language. It goes (almost) without saying that this strategy should be envisaged as a spectrum, with choices being more or less standardising. The use of this strategy places emphasis on the clarity of content, prioritising audience comprehension over the communication of implicit information about characters' identity through language. Substitution is the second strategy identified to translate slang, whereby the slang of the source language is replaced by a slang in the target language when the two sets of slang users are seen to share sufficient similarities to warrant the fictional interchangeability of their voice. The third and final strategy advanced within this typology is that of register and/or orality, where features of casual, and usually spoken, language are exploited in the written text. In this way, the non-standard aspects of slang are brought closer to standard language, as with standardisation, but the language used retains an informal style, which is also not specific to a certain geographical group, as with substitution.

As part of these general strategies, a translator might choose to incorporate a number of techniques, in such a way that the strategy and techniques work in unison to forge a fictional style of writing to represent the voice of the foreign slang users in the target text. The first of these techniques is borrowing, essentially a form of non-translation, where the use of words or structures from the slang of the source text are transferred directly to the target text. The foreignness of the words and structures may be marked typographically through italics, and a definition or explanation may be provided through accompanying contextual or linguistic additions. Inventing new words or structures, perhaps based on the formal features seen in the source language slang, is the second technique included in the typology and can be seen as a means of harnessing the innovative and playful nature of slang, Thirdly, the inclusion of grammatically-deviant structures may serve to show distance from standard language, and may be combined with the fourth technique involving the addition of vulgarity, again marking deviation from standard forms. Finally, orthographic innovation may be incorporated into the translation to reflect speech (eye dialect) which involves manipulating the spelling of some words to indicate the speed of speech or suggest pronunciation (and therefore accent).

3. Translating (sub)culture and slang in practice: Case study

In order to illustrate more clearly the links between the two typologies and to allow for a more analytical consideration of the repercussions of various choices, the following section will incorporate brief examples taken from two contemporary works of fiction: the 2006 novel *Entre les murs*, written by François Bégaudeau, and the 1995 film *La Haine*, directed by Mathieu Kassovitz. These two texts are set in or around Paris and feature the voice of marginalised youth. They are both written and audiovisual texts, but in the case of audiovisual text it is the subtitles that will be analysed. Though the particular format of film texts has an impact on the way the slang is translated in a way that is not always relevant to purely written texts, it remains useful to include a film in the study since it allows us to consider how audiovisual elements of the text may affect translation choices.

The objective here is not to find complete correspondence between the two models, to have one fit neatly into the other, or to *translate* one into the other, but to establish a dialogue between the two to see how they might complement each other. In this way, the various procedures or techniques and strategies can be associated in terms of what seems to be prioritised in translation, the broader goal or *skopos* assigned to the translation project. It will become clear if the translator seems to place the emphasis on the allegiance to a specific subculture within the source culture, or if they seem to try to emphasise the foreign setting geographical of the text, or attempt to find a middle ground of sorts. More generally, this process will allow us to reframe the idea of the foreignness of the source text in terms of what exactly it is that is foreign to the target audience. Is it the geographical and cultural divide at the level of the entire source culture, unfamiliar to readers of the target text? Or is it perhaps the subculture being portrayed, and so similar to what is foreign to the source audience, since readers of fiction, in source or translated texts, are not always, and one might say rarely, members of the group being portrayed? By way of disclaimer, it is important to bear in mind that is all of course quite subjective, which is almost always the case when it comes to language used by marginalised groups. It is difficult to separate the use of language from societal and political issues, and audiences will engage with language in different ways depending on their own background, positioning and cultural affiliations.

3.1 Specificity of the subgroup within the source culture

Davies' concepts of preservation and addition can be linked to the technique of borrowing within the typology for translating slang, which covers both the direct transfer of terms from the source text into the target text with (*addition*) or without (*preservation*) accompanying clarification. All three techniques can be seen as focussing on the specificity of the subgroup within the source culture, reminding audiences of the overall foreign nature of the text and the non-target culture setting since there is emphasis placed on the geographic strand of the language used. In the case of cultural references, it could be argued that the process is more straightforward, since the terms to be transferred across from the source to the target text are already isolated from the rest of the text. When a text is written in non-standard language, however, the density of this non-standard language will necessarily influence the choice of words or expressions to carry across and the result will likely install in the target text a kind of hierarchy within the non-standard language. Indeed, unless entire sentences are carried across, which seems unlikely if the source text is written primarily in non-standard language, the translator will inevitably need to decide which words or clauses to transfer, which may result in break in cohesivity of the slang of the source text. An example of borrowing/preservation can be found in Linda Asher's translation of the novel *Entre les murs*, published in English in 2008 under the title *The Class*. The Arabic term "wesh" is commonly used as an interjection in urban French slang and its presence in the dialogue of the source text is carried across into the English text, highlighted through italics:

(1) a. *Wesh pourquoi tout à l'heure j'ai demandé un mot vous avez pas voulu écrire et maintenant vous écrivez ?* (Bégaudeau 2006, 81)
 b. *Wesh* how come before when I ask about a word you wouldden write it and now you writing one? (Bégaudeau, 2009 (trans. Asher), 73)

Through this translation technique, it is therefore an already borrowed term, lexicalised in French slang, that is included in the target text, and the internally foreign nature of the slang term that is stressed. Its exact meaning is not made clear in the translation through additional explanations, but this does not hinder the understanding of the segment since the role of the interjection is to punctuate the dialogue and not to contribute new information to the plot. The characterising role that the word "wesh" plays in the source text is partially apparent in the target text, since its inclusion in the students' dialogue makes it clear that the word is used by young people from marginalised groups of society and not by adults, such as the teachers of the novel, from dominant groups, though the connotations of the term cannot be fully appreciated by a reader of the target text unfamiliar with French slang.

Overall, the use of borrowing/preservation draws attention to the originally foreign nature of the target text and acts as a reminder of the uniqueness of the subculture being depicted, but does not necessarily allow for a clear demarcation of the subculture from other subcultures within the broader source culture in all cases, since the reader of the target text is not equipped with the exposure that would allow them to identify the undertones of the word or expression in question. Additionally, transferring some words and expressions rather than others requires translators to isolate items that the believe to be more relevant or useful in the context of the target text, which establishes a distinction between certain characteristics of slang not present in the source text.

3.2 Broadening the audience

The techniques of omission and globalisation used to translate cultural references may be aligned with the strategies of standardisation or register/orality used to translate slang. Drawing a parallel between omission and standardisation may be deemed plausible if one chooses to see standardisation as a complete flattening the specificity of the voice of the disenfranchised youth of the source text as synonymous with a symbolic erasure of the subculture in the target text, since signs of the linguistic manifestation of the subculture's voice are omitted. Since the use of informal register necessarily involves using language more akin to standard forms, the strategy of register/orality may also be associated with this overall effect of erasing deviation from standard language. However, it may also be argued that the strategies of register/orality and of standardisation may be more logically likened to the technique of globalisation, since their use results in rendering potentially challenging aspects of the source text accessible to a broader audience, breaking down the barriers between subgroups in society to make the language and the text available to readers from a range of background. Two versions of the subtitles of *La Haine* were provided in English, the first in 1995 and the second in 2005, and the second shows clear signs of standardisation:

(2) a. *Passer 48 heures au poste à se manger des grosses tartes dans ta gueule et rentrer à la maison pour que mes parents m'égorgent, je te dis franchement, mais franchement, je vois pas le chiffre cousin.* (Kassovitz, 1995)
   b. Tear gas, 2 nights in a cop shop, all the fists you can eat, getting hell at home, sorry cousin, but I ain't buyin'! (Kassovitz, 1995)
   c. Tear gas, two days being beaten up at the police station then back to face the music at home. I don't see the point. (Kassovitz, 2005)

In the first version of the subtitles, written by two American subtitlers, a more localised version of the slang of the French dialogue is proposed (see analysis below), whereas the subtitles produced by unknown British translators ten years later offer a cleaner, more immediately-understandable and broadly accessible translation. When it comes to film texts, it may also be argued that the multimodal aspects of the text act as a form of compensation when the language of the subtitles does not correspond to the playful, coded, or deviant functions of slang. Indeed, the tone of voice and body language of the actors, as well as the visual setting, may enable viewers to understand that the characters using slang belong to a distinct subculture. In all cases, it seems apparent that special attention is paid to clarity and accessibility, to enable all members of the target audience to follow the story of the target text, even if they are not granted access to the range of suggestions of deviance from dominant social groups implicit in the use of slang.

3.3 Parallels between subgroups

The strategy of substitution to translate slang seen in the above example from the subtitles of *La Haine*, as well as some instances of the technique of orthographic innovation, can be likened to the procedure Davies labels localisation. The connection between these methods is clear, since replacing the cultural reference from the source culture with one from the target culture is a very similar process to taking the slang of the source culture and replacing it with a slang from the target culture. The example from *La Haine* included in the above discussion of standardisation includes aspects of African American Vernacular English, with the contraction "ain't" and the noun "cousin" commonly used in urban youth slang in the United States. A second example below shows further signs of Americanisation in the subtitles with the two nouns "homeboy" and "gangsta" being used to translate the French back-slang term "caillera", which the 2005 version of the subtitles replaces with the typically British term "wanker":

(3) a. *Je vais pas me faire taper dessus pour une caillera que je connais pas.*
   b. I won't take hits for a homeboy gangsta I don't know. (Kassovitz, 1995)
   c. Why get hit for a wanker you don't know? (Kassovitz, 2005)

When it comes to orthographic innovation, if the spelling changes to reflect a specific accent, this also constitutes also a form of localisation, as in the examples below taken from the translation of *Entre les murs* Bégaudeau 2009 (trans. Asher):

(4) a. *J'peux m'lever m'sieur ?* (188)
 b. Kin I get up, m'sieur? (171)
 c. *Pfffh n'importe quoi celle-là.* (264)
 d. Pfffh oweys talkin bullshit that one. (241)
 e. *J'tai pas tipée j'm'en bats les yeuks de toi. Tsss.* (178)
 f. I din hiss you I don't give a fuck about you. Pffft. (162)

The spelling of "can" as "kin", of "always" as "oweys", and "didn't" as "din", deviate from standard spelling use and may evoke a specific accent to some readers, while for others may appear to constitute a means of bending the rules of standard language, without being suggestive of a specific subgroup (cf. techniques akin to transformation exposed below). In this way, orthographic innovation is a more subtle form of localisation since it is not as easily recognisable as the more frequent use of entire words or expressions taken from a substitute slang. Beyond the risks involved in implementing localising techniques in terms of the credibility gap cited above, as well as the ethical implications in suggesting that two subcultures from distinct broader cultural and geographic locations may be interchangeable, the focus seems to be placed on the demographics of the subculture, bringing to the fore the urban youth identity of slang users and drawing parallels between these subcultures within the two broader cultures, source and target.

3.4 Transforming the slang

The addition of vulgarity, the use of grammatically-deviant language, and some instances of orthographic innovation to translate slang may be associated with Davies' concept of transformation. In the examples below taken from the translation of *Entre les murs*, we can see how the translator has attempted to recreate the various functions of slang in a way not necessarily akin to standardisation or substitution, and in a way that does not explicitly call on the exact foreignness of the source text use of slang:

(5) a. **Student:** *C'est pas moi j'vous dis, je m'en bats les yeuks d'elle.*
 Teacher: *Tu t'en bas les quoi ?*
 Student: *J'm'en fous d'elle.* (Bégaudeau 2006, 54–55)
 b. **Student:** Wasn't me I'm telling you! I don't give a fuck about her.
 Teacher: You don't give what?
 Student: I don't care about her. (Bégaudeau 2009 (trans. Asher), 48)

c. *C'est n'importe quoi j'l'ai pas touchée j'm'en bas les couilles d'elle.*
   (Bégaudeau 2006, 264)
d. Talkin bullshit I never touch her I don give a shit about her.
   (Bégaudeau 2009 (trans. Asher), 241)
e. *Ceux-là qui z'ont dit ça ils ont juré sur leur vie.* (Bégaudeau 2006, 90)
f. Them people that say it, they swear on their life.
   (Bégaudeau 2009 (trans. Asher), 81)
g. *Vous vous êtes pas juge et vous vous vengez c'est tout.* (Bégaudeau 2006, 185)
h. You not a judge and you getting even that's all.
   (Bégaudeau 2009 (trans. Asher), 168)

The inclusion of grammatically deviant structures in the examples above, including the use of inaccurate determiners ("them" instead of "they"), incorrect tense ("touch" in the present instead of the required preterit), and the absence of auxiliary verbs ("you not a judge" and "you getting" without "are"), as well as the addition of vulgarity not present in the dialogue of the source text ("fuck" and "bullshit"), and the often absent punctuation to suggest run-on sentences, all contribute to signaling the students' language as non-standard. We can appreciate how the shift in translation brought about by these techniques seems to lie in a middle ground, suggesting a deviation from the norm in language without necessarily placing the focus on either the overall source culture or the subculture within that culture. We may be tempted to applaud this attempt to recreate some of the functions of slang in the target text, though may also wish to question the effectiveness of the suggestions made about the education, attitude or personality of the characters through these choices: the idea of bending the rules of language in slang here becomes synonymous with breaking the rules of language and may suggest a lack of education, and the addition of vulgarity could contribute to altering the tone of the speech. Regardless, these choices all constitute a form of transformation of the slang of the source text.

3.5 New slang

The final parallel to be drawn between the two typologies is in Davies' procedure of the creation of a new cultural reference which can be clearly aligned with the technique of invention to translate slang, since the idea is to take the functions of the slang and to recreate them linguistically in the target text. We could say that this technique isolates the demographics of youth subculture from its geographical roots, and places the emphasis on the playful use of language in general, rather than in a specific context within either broad culture, while acknowledging the potential for this technique to place the text in a kind of linguistic non-space.

4. Conclusions

This study constitutes an effort to understand the reasoning behind various choices to translate language that serves to communicate extralinguistic information about a character's identity and place in society. Drawing parallels between linguistic variety and cultural references offers the advantage of contextual considerations, allowing us to deepen understanding of the repercussions of different translation techniques and strategies. When we examine the function of the language used both in the source text and target text, we are better able to consider what aspect of the slang user's identity is emphasised in translation, and how this might affect the way in which readers conceive of the contours of the subgroup being depicted: if a picture of this subgroup is painted in the target text as being specific to the broader source culture and not having a direct equivalent in the target culture, as sharing sufficient similarities with a given group in the broader target culture to warrant comparison, or as belonging to a global network of subcultures. Overall, this paper has argued that it is useful to expand our often binary perception of the source and target language and culture, envisaging the two sets as being composed of subsets rather than as cohesive wholes. It therefore calls for a comprehensive and careful consideration of the reasons why a text producer might decide to use words and expressions as a means of implying identity, and how a translator might go about attempting to reproduce some of the strands of this identity in the target text.

References

Bégaudeau, François. 2006. *Entre les murs*. Paris: Gallimard.
Bégaudeau, François. 2009. *The Class*, trans. Linda Asher. New York: Seven Stories Press.
Coleman, Julie (ed.). 2014. *Global English Slang: Methodologies and Perspectives*. New York: Routledge.
Davies, Eirlys E. 2003. "A Goblin or a Dirty Nose?: The Treatment of Culture-Specific References in Translations of the Harry Potter Books." In *The Translator* 9 (1): 65–100.
Gadet, Françoise. 1997. *Le français ordinaire*. Paris: Armand Colin.
Harvey, Malcolm. 2000. "A Beginner's Course in Legal Translation: The Case of Culture-Bound Terms." In *ASTTI/ETI*: 357–69.
Kassovitz, Mathieu. 1995. *La Haine*. Paris: Lazennec & Associés.
Levick, Tiffane. 2018. *Orality and Universality: In Search of a Global Youth Speak in Translation*. Paris: Université Sorbonne Nouvelle.
Mailhac, Jean-Pierre. 1996. "Evaluating Criteria for the Translation of Cultural References." In *On Translating French Literature and Film* ed. by Geoffrey T. Harris. Amsterdam: Rodopi: 173–188.
Pederson, Jan. 2007. "Cultural Interchangeability: The Effects of Substituting Cultural References in Subtitling." *Perspectives Studies in Translatology* 15 (1): 30–48.

Cultural awareness across time
A diachronic study of the use of cultural references in a corpus of translated novels

Virginia Mattioli
Universidad de Cantabria

This paper aims to describe diachronically the use of foreign words as a specific type of cultural references representing linguistic culture in a corpus of novels translated between 2000 and 2014. The adopted corpus-based methodology consists in identifying foreign words of three semantic fields particularly related to culture, assessing their cultural impact, determining the translation techniques used for their transposition and the corresponding translators' behaviour (maintenance, loss or adaptation of the foreign items). The results show a peak of cultural awareness in the novels translated between 2005 and 2009, characterized by items with the greatest cultural impact mostly maintained during the translation process, offering interesting points of departure for further research from a conceptual and a methodological perspective.

Keywords: linguistic culture, foreign words, translated novels, translation techniques, corpus-based translation studies, cultural awareness, translators' behaviour, English-Italian translation

1. Introduction

The object of this paper is describing the use of cultural reference in Italian translated novels from a diachronic perspective. Actually, cultural references, as textual representations of a specific culture, highlight the existence of the foreignness by facing the readers to elements proper of a different culture and can be used as evidences of the degree of acceptance of the otherness. In this sense, a greater use of cultural references can be related to a greater acceptance of the otherness and of the foreignness, whereas, on the contrary, a preference for patrimonial words would represent a minor acceptance of the foreignness and a greater integration of the otherness within the target culture. As a consequence, observing the use of cultural references used in a set of English novels translated into Italian across fifteen years allows for assessing the tendency of Italian literary translators and, more generally, of Italian translated novels towards the acceptance of the otherness.

Several Translation Studies scholars have been focussing on cultural references in the last half century, describing and classifying them from different perspectives. Even if no agreement has been reached among the previous authors about the possible denominations and definitions of cultural references, the combination of their most commonly accepted proposals suggest that cultural references are characterized by three intrinsic and distinctive features: their specificity with respect to the original culture; their absence in the target culture; and their connotative value (see 2.1). Considering such features, cultural reference can be defined as the textual representation of the lack of equivalence between different cultures. However, how to determine systematically which elements effectively represent a specific culture in such a multicultural world where original cultures are always more frequently combined and cultural differences are increasingly disappearing due to the globalization, information generalization and population mobility (Fernández and Fernández Guerra 2010: 202)? Beyond the effort to denominate, define and classify cultural references, no one of the previous authors seems to explain clearly how to recognize and select cultural references within a text (Mattioli 2017: 191) and some authors even highlight the difficulties involved in their identification. Among these, Molina Martínez (2001: 90–91) underlines the dynamic character of cultural references, their unlimited growing over time, their existence only in those situations characterized by a linguistic and cultural transfer, such as the translational context, and the multiple interpretations of the same item according to the cultural context, a problem already considered also by Mayoral Asensio (1994). Similarly, Luque Nadal (2009) points out the indetermined number of cultural references which, in her opinions, change according to the society.

To avoid such problems and identify systematically the cultural references, this study assumes a linguistic perspective considering only a specific type of cultural references which, according to several authors (Molina Martínez 2001; Mangiron i Hevia 2006), represent the linguistic culture, that is foreign words. Actually, culture and language are strictly related and their relationship has been a central topic of several humanistic disciplines since the '50s. Among the many authors involved in the debate, Contreras (1952–1953: 177) defines the language as a cultural object, Coseriu (1981: 272–74) as a primary form of culture and human creativity and Kramsch (2003: 65) underlines its relationship with the culture and the cultural identity of the community in which it is spoken. Castillo Fadic (2002: 488) includes the social aspect in the debate and, considering language a cultural object, hence as a social manifestation, relates any change in the linguistic system with the changes in the linguistic community. If the use of foreign words is often determined by the need for new signifiers to designate new concepts (Castillo Fadic 2002: 478) and language is the "verbal culture of a society" where the "culture is the idea, while the language is the expression" (Rupini et al. 2021: 131), hence the absence of a word to define an object or concept in the target language denotes the absence of such an object or concept in the corresponding target culture. In this sense, foreign words can be considered textual representation of the lack of equivalence between the source and the target language and, as such, a specific type of cultural references.

With this aim, the paper is divided into three main blocks: a theoretical frame (Section 2), a methodological frame (Section 3) and a section dedicated to present and discuss the results (Section 4). Section 2 introduces the main studies about cultural references, summarizing previous proposals of their denomination, definition and classification, with a special attention for those cultural references related to the linguistic culture. This section also describes the techniques which can be used to overcome the problems produced during the translation of cultural references from a source to a target context (2.1). It follows a brief presentation of the foreign words and of the main factors responsible for their introduction into a target language (2.2). Methodological frame includes the description and distribution of the analysed material (3.1) and the corpus-based method adopted in the study (3.2), whereas the fourth section presents and discusses the results obtained from the analysis. Finally, some concluding remarks (Section 5) suggest the relevance of the obtained results for the development of the discipline and advance some proposals for further studies.

2. Theoretical frame

2.1 Cultural references

The first studies about cultural references date back to the 1960s, when several Translation Studies scholars, attracted by the challenge represented by the difficulties arisen from their translation, begin to propose differ denominations, definitions and classifications. Despite their efforts, no agreement has been reached yet about the name and nature of cultural references. The exponents of the Soviet or Slavic school (cf. Mayoral Asensio 1999) adopt the name "realia", considering their function of representation of a culture-specific reality; other scholars (Newmark 1988) denominate these lexical items "cultural words" for belonging to a "cultural language" representative of a specific culture; others refer to them with the expression "rich points" (Agar 1991), focussing on their origins related to situations of linguistic or cultural contact; and some others prefer the expression "cultural filters" (Hervey and Higgins 1992: 243; House 2006), pointing to the non-literal technique used to translate them. Among the most accepted denominations, Christiane Nord (1997) accepts Vermeer's proposal of "culturemes" defined as "social phenomenon of a culture X that is regarded as relevant by the members of this culture and, when compared with a corresponding social phenomenon to culture Y, is found to be specific to culture X" (Vermeer 1983: 8, as cited in Nord 1997: 32), a denomination and a definition later adopted by further authors, including Lucía Molina Martínez (2001) and Carme Mangiron i Hevia (2006). Baker (1992: 21) coins the expression "culture-specific items", whereas Mayoral Asensio (1994), Aixelá (1996) and Santamaria Guinot (2001) opt for the expression 'cultural references' (*referencias culturales*), highlighting their reference to the original culture that makes them impossible to be completely understood by the members of the target culture (Mayoral Asensio 1994: 76), evidencing their absence in the target language and culture (Aixelá 1996: 58) or underlining their distinctive and intrinsic cultural value (Santamaria Guinot 2001: 13).

The same lack of agreement arises from the attempt to classify the cultural references, which each scholar organizes in different classes and subclasses. Some authors classify them in few, very general categories, whereas others prefer very detailed taxonomies composed by several classes of cultural references. Among the firsts, Nida (1945), one of the first authors interested in the topic, distinguishes five categories including ecology, material culture, social culture, religious culture and linguistic culture, whereas Luque Nadal (2009: 98–101) distributes the cultural references across three main groups dividing the items related to the classical culture — including religion, history and traditions—, those ones related to national or supranational events, and those ones referred to archetypal situations or characters. Among the seconds, Mangiron i Hevia (2006) proposes a taxonomy compound of seven general categories divided in 25 subcategories further separated in very specific subclasses and Santamaria Guinot (2001) distinguishes six main classes further divided into 24 subclasses, including in her proposal those cultural references related to geography, meteorology, human beings, buildings, personalities, arts, social conditions and technology.

Regardless the number of classes and subclasses of their taxonomies, some authors give a particular importance to the language and, considering its relationship with culture, dedicate particular classes of cultural references to the language spoken by a certain community or to some specific linguistic forms. This is the case of Nida (1945: 196) who, already in 1945, distinguishes "linguistic culture" as a specific class of cultural references. The author is followed, in the next years, by Hervey and Higgins (1992: 243), who dedicate a category to the "linguistic filters", and by Molina Martínez (2001), who includes in her classification the categories of "linguistic culture" and adds a further group labelled "cultural interference", which the author defines as a phenomenon caused by the transference from a cultural context to another (Molina Martínez 2001: 95), containing false friends and cultural meddling. Both categories can be found also within the taxonomy proposed by Carme Mangiron i Hevia (2006): the class "linguistic culture" is divided in six further subclasses — writing systems; dialects; expressions, proverbs and idioms; word games; insults; and onomatopoeias —, whereas the second, called "cultural meddling", includes references to foreign languages, to cultural institutions and to historical events. Similarly, Seveborg (2016:2), describing cultural elements, includes in this group the lexis, the linguistic and the idiomatic habits used exclusively in a specific language, and Rupini et al. (2021: 134), in their study about Balinese folktales, conclude to have identified cultural references belonging to the class "linguistic culture".

The second issue faced by the Translation Studies scholars involves the techniques or strategies which can be used to transfer cultural references from the source to the target context in order to maintain the equivalence and avoid misunderstandings. The vocabulary referred to translation techniques, strategies and methods is still confused within the discipline (Mattioli 2018: 60) in the present study, the three terms will be used randomly. As fort the classification of translation techniques, previous proposals can be distinguished into two groups: the ones which classify them in discrete classes and the ones who, instead, organize them along a continuum which extremes represent foreignization (or the tendency towards the source context) and domestication (i.e., the tendency towards the target readers' context) (Venuti 1995), respectively. Both types of taxonomies have been developing and improving throughout the decades. The initial proposals are very simple, as the one advanced by Vinay and Darbelnet (1958[1995]: 31–40), who differentiate between direct and oblique translation techniques, Nida's (1964) classification, compounded by three basic classes — addition, omission and conversion —, or the proposal advanced by Hervey and Higgins (1992: 28), the first organised in a continuum and composed by just six translation techniques. More recent classifications, on the contrary, are very detailed and include many different types of techniques, such as the ones proposed by Newmark (1988: 103–104) or Molina Martínez (2006: 101–104) formed by 18 classes — adaptation, linguistic expansion, amplification, calque, compensation, linguistic compression, discursive creation, description, standard accepted translation, generalization, modulation, particularization, loan, reduction, substitution, literal translation, transposition and variation (Molina Martínez 2006: 101–104).

As for the choice of the proper translation strategies, the main complete contribution, accepted by several authors in the following years (Molina Martínez 2001; Santamaria Guinot 2001) seems to be the one advanced by Newmark

(1998:103). The author suggests to consider six factors to select the better translation technique for each occurrence: text finality, readers' motivation and cultural level, importance of the cultural reference in the original text, area of use, novelty and future of the term.

2.2 Foreign words

Before presenting a brief overview of the main causes of the introduction of foreign words, it seems necessary to clarify the definition of 'foreign word' adopted in this paper. Previous contributions about the topic do not present a terminological consistency and their authors opt to use the terms "foreign word", "transposition", "loan" or "borrowing" according to personal preferences or following very different criteria, such as the degree of adaptation of the term to the target language (Fernández and Fernández Guerra 2010) or its acceptance by the target language users (Degerstedt 2013). In this paper, the label "foreign word" is use to refer to any term which includes any feature not prescribed by the target language word formation rule, regardless its degree of adaptation.

As explained in 2.1, many Translation Studies scholars consider linguistic habits, including the linguistic meddling and the interference of other languages (i.e., the foreign words), as a part of the linguistic culture of a community. Actually, one of the main causes for the introduction of a foreign word in a target language is the cultural contact (Mattioli 2018:52). According to Castillo Fadic (2002:471), two or more cultures can experience a direct contact, through the coexistence of different population in the same area, or an indirect contact by means of social, economic and political relations. Indirect contact is particularly frequent when one of the languages involved presents a universal reach and, as a consequence, assumes a dominant position for social, political, economic, scientific or technological reasons (Castillo Fadic 2002:472).

In addition to cultural contact, other authors relate the introduction of foreign words to social phenomena, such as the immigration (Cece 2016:122), to translation (Payás 1996:403; Muñoz Martín and Valdivieso Blanco 2008:509) or to particular structural features of the target language, which, according to the principle of least effort, are substituted by the users with foreign items (Rodríguez González 2005:187). As a result, even if the foreign words originate prominently in situations of cultural contact, their introduction into a target language depends largely on non-cultural factors. To maintain the focus on culture and following the main aim of this paper, the present study will consider and assess the degree of cultural impact of the foreign words examined as a specific type of cultural elements representing linguistic culture.

3. Methodological frame

3.1 Analysed material

The study aims to describe diachronically the use of cultural references identified in a set of translated novels. To do that, the specific objective of the examination is to compare the use of foreign words as a specific type of cultural references identified in a set of English novels translated into Italian across three different time spans of five years each: 2000–2004, 2005–2009 and 2010–2014. Such population is represented by a set of three corpora. The corpus representing the first period (Corpus 2000–2004) is compound by five novels and includes 30,314 types and 338,182 tokens; the corpus representing the middle period (Corpus 2005–2009) includes five novels corresponding to 35,840 types 508,750 tokens; the corpus representing the third period (Corpus 2010–2014) is formed by three novels and includes 18,044 types and 144,251 tokens. The set of corpora was compiled following five criteria: representativeness, by selecting novels awarded with national and international literary prizes; variety, by choosing novels originally written by different authors in different varieties of English; selection of entire texts, as cultural references are distributed across the entire novels; and authenticity, as novels are authentic literary material.

The texts included in the corpora under analysis, listed at the end of this paper, were selected according to the research objectives of the present study from a greater corpus compiled for a previous study (Mattioli, 2018) which includes almost seventy awarded novels published between 2000 and 2014. As a result, the set of corpora examined in this study is not completely balanced in quantitative terms. To avoid the influence of the different sizes of the corpora on the results, each corpus is analysed separately and, at the end, the results expressed in percentage and the frequency calculated per million words (fpm) are compared across the three sets of texts. Actually, previous Translation Studies scholars advise of the necessity to modify the initial design of a corpus according to the availability of the material (The University of Manchester 2011: 29) and highlight that such modifications would not affect the outputs of the study if the distortions that they cause will be considered during the interpretation of the results (Zanettin 2011: 22).

3.2 Methodology

The analysis is developed by adopting a corpus-based method formed by four steps. Such method allows for identifying foreign words within each corpus (step 1), assessing their degree of cultural impact (step 2), analysing the strategies used to translate each occurrence from the source to the target language (step 3) and determining the translator's behaviour in terms of maintenance, adaptation or translation of the original form (step 4). In the following paragraphs, the methodology used to develop each one of these four steps will be detailed.

In the first step, foreign words, as a specific type of cultural references, are identified within each corpus in analysis. Not all the foreign words are considered for the study but only the most representative items from the qualitative and the quantitative perspective. Considering qualitative representativeness, only the foreign words of three semantic fields are selected: (1) Food and drink; (2) Clothing and body care; (3) Communication and transportation. These semantic fields are chosen for being particularly related to the cultural contact. Actually, food and clothes are elements common to any culture and, at the same time, very distinctive of each one of them, whereas communication and transportation allow for the displacement of ideas, individuals and material products. From a quantitative perspective, the sample includes only those foreign words presented at least in three novels out of the thirteen included in the entire archive of corpora and with a minimum frequency of ten occurrences (in the entire set of corpora). Such selection, on the one hand, allows for limiting the number of elements in analysis, consenting a more detailed examination of each one of them; on the other hand, choosing only the items with a certain frequency permits to exclude from the study those foreign words characteristic of specific novels or representing the personal style of an author or a translator, fostering the generalization of the results.

Once determined and limited the object of study, firstly, the corpora are semantically tagged by using the USAS Semantic Tagger (Piao et al. 2015); secondly, the tags corresponding to the three considered semantic fields are selected; and thirdly, each relevant tag is searched for in the concordance list provided by AntConc (Anthony 2022). The concordance list is a tool available in any corpus tools kits which allows for searching for an item and visualizing each resulting occurrence in its context. As a consequence, the search for each one of the semantic tags previously selected will return each occurrence immediately preceded by its corresponding words, as shown in the screenshot presented following Figure 1, where the searched tags appear in blue and the corresponding words in red.

From the results obtained from the search of each tag, only the foreign words are manually selected. According to the definition adopted in this study (see Section 2.2), only the items which do not follow the Italian word formation rule are considered, such as "whisky", including the letters "w", "k" and a "y" which do not belong to the Italian alphabet. Once retrieved all the foreign words from the three corpora, only the ones with a frequency equal or higher than ten occurrences and identified in three or more novels are considered for the analysis.

In the second step, each foreign word retrieved from the previous phase is classified according to its degree of cultural impact. To do that, a target perspec-

```
.1.1 L2 <NOM> gialle_O4.3 <ADJ> di_Z5 <PRE> curry_F1 <NOM> sulla_Z5 <PRE:det> tovaglia_H5 <NOM> ._Z9
> 1_N1 <NUM> lattina_F2 <NOM> di_Z5 <PRE> curry_F1 <NOM> in_Z5 <PRE> polvere_O1.1 B4 G3 <NOM> "_
> tavoli_O2 H5 <NOM> verdi_O4.3 L3 <ADJ> da_F1 <PRE>:3:2:1 picnic_F1 <NOM>:3:2:2 all\x92ombra_O4
:rela> fungeva_Z99 <VER:impf> anche_Z5 <ADV> da_F1 <PRE>:2:1 cucina_F1 <NOM>:2:2 e_Z5 <CON> due_N1
1.1.1 <NOM> di_Z5 <PRE> tavolo_O2 H5 <NOM> da_F1 <PRE>:2:1 cucina_F1 <NOM>:2:2 ._Z99 <PON> su_Z5
> il_Z5 <DET:def> tavolo_O2 H5 <NOM> da_F1 <PRE>:3:2:1 cucina_F1 <NOM> 3:2:2 del_Z5 <PRE:det
Z8m <PRO:poss> grembiule_B5 M3 <NOM> da_F1 <PRE>:4:2:1 cucina_F1 <NOM>:4:2:2 a_Z5 <PRE> fior
> vecchia_T3+ <ADJ> coperta_H5 O2 N5.2+ <NOM> da_F1 <PRE>:42:2:1 picnic_F1 <NOM>:42:2:2 che_Z8 <PRO:r
99 <SENT> I_Z5 <DET:def> coltelli_O2 <NOM> da_F1 <PRE>:2:2:1 cucina_F1 <NOM>:2:2:2 sono_A3+ <VER:p
5 <PRE> le_Z5 <DET:def> forbici_Z99 <NOM> da_F1 <PRE>:1:2:1 cucina_F1 <NOM>:1:2:2 ._Z99 <SENT> Ne
uno_N1 <DET:indef> sgabelloscaletta_Z99 <NOM> da_F1 <PRE> 11:2:1 cucina_F1 <NOM> 11:2:2 ._Z99 <PON> d
:pres> un_Z5 <DET:indef> mazzuolo_Z99 <NOM> da_F1 <PRE> 19:2:1 cucina_F1 <NOM> 19:2:2 ._Z99 <SENT>
W2 <NOM> di_Z5 <PRE> sciropposi_Z99 <ADJ> dessert_F1 <NOM> ._Z99 <SENT> Si_Z8f Z8m <PRO:
99 <PON> dopo_Z5 <PRE> il_Z5 <DET:def> dessert_F1 <NOM> usciva_M1 <VER:impf> per_Z5 <PRE> recarsi
:infi> davanti_M6 <PRE> al_Z5 <PRE:det> dessert_F1 <NOM> )_Z99 <PON> e_Z5 <CON> di_Z5 <PRE>
rano_X7+ <VER:pres> altri_N5+ <PRO:indef> dessert_F1 <NOM> ._Z99 <PON> offre_I1.1 A9+ I2.2 <VER:pres
> scelto_X7+ X6 <VER:pper> per_Z5 <PRE> dessert_F1 <NOM> -_Z99 <PON> La_Z5 <DET:def>
5 <PRE> caff\xE8_F2 <NOM> per_Z5 <PRE> dessert_F1 <NOM> ._Z99 <PON> avevamo_A9+ T1.3 C1 <VER:impf
99 <SENT> -_Z99 <PON> Basta_S6 <VER:pres> dessert_F1 <NOM> ._Z99 <SENT> -_Z99 <PON> È_A5.1 S7.1++ X3
.3+++ N5.1+++ A12- <NOM> inferiore_A5.1- <ADJ> di_F1 A4.2+ <PRE>:0:2:1 carne_F1 A4.2+ <NOM>:0:2:2 e_Z5
```

Figure 1. Fragment of the results obtained from the search for the tag F1, corresponding to "food", in the concordance list provided by AntConc (Anthony, 2022)

tive is taken into account and the selected foreign words are distinguished into three groups by considering the impression that their external origins provoke in the receptors:

a. Foreign words with echoes of cultural impact: terms included in the target language dictionary without any reference to its source language which origins are completely integrated within the target culture and totally unnoticed by the target language speakers (e.g., "jeans");
b. Foreign words with an explicitly accepted cultural impact: terms included in the target language dictionary and defined as loans or borrowings with an explicit reference to their source language and culture, which foreignness is evident for the target language speakers (e.g., "curry");
c. Foreign words with the highest cultural impact: terms not included in the target language dictionary that evoke a heavy sense of exoticism in the target language speakers (e.g., "parkway").

The idea of evaluating foreign words according to their exotic impact on the users has been previously considered also by Degerstedt (2013: 4). The author starts from the definition of foreign word as "a not assimilated borrowing with a scarce and restricted use" given by Gómez Capuz (2009, as cited in Degerstedt 2013: 4, my translation) to conclude that, if a borrowing is defined by its frequency of use and the frequency of use depends on the speakers' choices, hence the concept of borrowing is related to the speakers' perception of the foreign term.

In the third step, the strategies used to translate each occurrence from the source to the target language are analysed. With this aim, an *ad hoc* taxonomy is designed for the study, combining the previous proposals and including nine discrete classes of translation techniques ordered from the most exotic (i.e., transposition) to the most domestic (i.e., lack of equivalence) as shown in the Table 1 below. Each technique is presented with its definition and an example from the corpora in analysis — the terms considered in each example are underlined to favour their comparison between the source and the target language and, where necessary, an English translation of their Italian version is provided in parenthesis for a better comprehension.

Table 1. Taxonomy of translation techniques adopted in the study

Translation technique	Definition	Example
Transposition	Use of a foreign word not included in the target language dictionary	I turned onto Eastern Parkway > Svoltai in Eastern Parkway
Loan	Use of a foreign word included in the target language dictionary and defined as a term adopted from a foreign language	I never left the garage > non usciva mai dal garage
Naturalization	Adaptation of the foreign word to the target language phonetics and/or phonology	The school bus pulled up in front of the house > Lo scuolabus si fermò davanti alla casa
Literal translation	Use of the translation provided by the bilingual dictionary	...just walked into the Seventh Precinct station > ...appena entrato nella stazione del Settimo Distretto
Modulation	Generalization or specification of the original term	He comes flying into my taxi > Vola addosso alla mia macchina('car')
Addition	Addition of foreign word absent in the original text	He had to drive out well before dawn > Doveva prendere il camion e andare ben prima dell'alba ('truck')
Functional/cultural equivalent	Use of a different term which accomplishes the same structural or cultural function of the original one	No picnic those cells > Non erano una scampagnata quelle celle ('jaunt into the countryside')
Omission	Omission of the original term	A few coach passengers moaned > Qualche passeggero si lamentò
Lack of equivalence	Use of a translation not equivalent to the original	...down 110th Street > ...in fondo alla 10ª Strada

Once designed the adopted taxonomy, the original and the translated corpus are aligned and uploaded in the parallel corpus analysis toolkit AntPConc (Anthony, 2013). With this tool, a two-step search is realized: firstly, each selected foreign word is searched for in the target corpus to obtain the corresponding original words and the results are registered; secondly, each corresponding original word is searched for in the original corpus in order to identify the entire gamut of terms used to translate it, whether foreign or patrimonial words. Finally, the results of the first and the second search are added and each couple of terms (original and translated) are confronted and related to a specific translation technique of the adopted taxonomy.

In the last step, each couple of terms (original and translated) previously analysed is examined again and classified according to the translator's behaviour in terms of maintenance, adaptation or translation of the original form, following the classification depicted in Table 2 — as in the previous Table 1, the terms examined are underlined to favour their comparison between the source and the target language and, where needed for the understanding of the example, their Italian version is translated into English.

Table 2. Classification designed to determine the translators' behaviours

Translators' behaviour	Example
Adaptation	The school bus pulled up in front of the house > *Uno scuolabus si fermó davanti alla casa*
Addition from the language of the source text	He crossed Madison > *attraversó Madison street* ('street', from English)
Addition from a language different from the source text one	It was a double decker > *era un autobus a due piani* ('bus') ('autobus', from French)
Maintenance	Are there Corn Flakes? > *Ci sono dei Corn Flakes?*
Translation	...then country buses > *...poi corriere di campagna*
Omission	...to reserve a coach seat > *...per prenotare un posto*

The four steps are applied to each corpus separately and finally the results are compared as for the degree of cultural impact of the foreign words identified in each one of them, the translation techniques used in each case and the translators' behaviour in respect to the maintenance or the translation of the original terms.

4. Results and discussion

From a quantitative perspective, the comparison of the results show that the three corpora do not present great differences as for the quantity of foreign words — if considered that the Corpus 2010–2014 is smaller than the others —, as summarized in the following Table 3.

Table 3. Distribution of the foreign words across the corpora analysed

	Occurrences (fpm)
Corpus 2000–2004	1,318.8
Corpus 2005–2009	1,271.7
Corpus 2010–2014	1,081.4

However, the results assume a different relevance when considering the degree of cultural impact of the foreign words identified. In this case, the corpus representing the middle period (Corpus 2005–2009) presents a different pattern in respect to the other ones, showing less items with echoes of cultural impact but a greater quantity of terms with an explicitly accepted cultural impact and, particularly, with the greatest cultural impact. These results, which suggest a particular attention to the otherness and the foreign language and culture in the period between 2005 and 2009, are detailed in the graphic shown in the Figure 2 that follows.

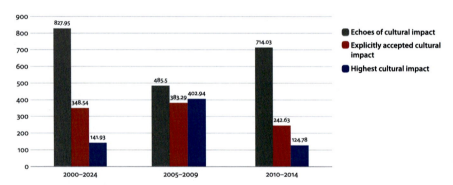

Figure 2. Degree of cultural impact of the foreign words identified in each corpus

The same outcomes arise from the comparison of the results related to the translation techniques used to transfer the terms in analysis from the source to the target text. In the three corpora, the most used translation techniques are transpositions, loans and literal translations. However, the corpus representing the period 2005–2009 shows a greater quantity of transpositions, that is of foreign words which are not included in the target language dictionary, (42% of the analysed occurrences) and less items transposed through literal translations (6%) than the other sets of texts (11% of transposition and 14% of literal translations in Corpus 2000–2004; 10% and 13%, respectively, in Corpus 2010–2014). These data, expressed in percentage in respect to the total number of occurrences analysed in each corpus (%) and in frequency per million words (fpm) in the Table 4 below, underlines the peak of awareness characterizing the novels translated between 2004 and 2009.

Table 4. Translation techniques most used in the three corpora analysed

Translation technique / Corpus	Transpositions %	fpm	Loans %	fpm	Literal translations %	fpm	Other techniques %	fpm
Corpus 2000–2004	11%	189.2	64%	1076.3	14%	236.5	10%	174.5
Corpus 2005–2009	42%	623.1	41%	601.5	6%	82.6	11%	155.3
Corpus 2010–2014	10%	145.6	63%	887.3	13%	180.2	14%	194.1

The comparison of the translators' behaviour across the three corpora confirms the same tendency and, again, translators seem to be particularly interest in maintaining the original foreign words, hence representing the source linguistic culture, between 2005 and 2009, as depicted in the following Table 5.

Table 5. Translators' behaviour during the transposition process of the analysed items in each corpus

Translators' behaviour / Corpus	Adaptation %	fpm	Addition %	fpm	Maintenance %	fpm	Translation %	fpm	Omission %	fpm
Corpus 2000–2004	1%	17.7	21%	354.8	60%	1008.3	13%	215.9	5%	76.9
Corpus 2005–2009	1%	9.8	22%	314.4	66%	963.1	7%	104.2	5%	72.7
Corpus 2010–2014	0%	0	27%	381.3	49%	686.3	18%	256.5	6%	90.1

In addition to support the previous results, the data obtained from the comparison of the translators' behaviour across the three corpora also show a change of tendency in the corpus representing the last five years of the study (2010–2014) in respect to the other two sets of texts. Actually, in Corpus 2010–2014, the tendency towards maintenance presented by the other corpora seems to decrease drastically in favour of translations (18%) and additions of foreign words absent in the original texts (27%), such as in "Simon's building on Franklin" > *il palazzo di Simon, su Franklin Street*, where in the Italian translation the (optional) English word "street" was added. If the preference for translation can be interpreted as a form of integration of the otherness vis-à-vis the use of foreign words, which use, on the contrary, represents the linguistic culture of the source context, the tendency to add foreign words absent in the original text remains unexplained and calls for further research.

The data related to the two types of addition considered in this study, addition from the language of the source text and addition from a language different from the source text one, show that in the period between 2010 and 2014 translators opt to add to the target texts more foreign words proceeding from a language different from the one of the source texts, as evidenced by the greater difference between the percentage of occurrences of the two types of addition in this period (see Table 6).

Table 6. Frequency of additions in each corpus analysed

Translation technique / Corpus	Addition from the language of the source text %	Addition from the language of the source text fpm	Addition from a language different from the source text one %	Addition from a language different from the source text one fpm	Total additions %	Total additions fpm
Corpus 2000–2004	12%	195.2	10%	159.7	21%	354.8
Corpus 2005–2009	6%	94.3	15%	220.1	22%	314.4
Corpus 2010–2014	9%	124.8	18%	256.5	27%	381.3

Finally, Table 6 also shows that the Corpus 2005–2009 presents the minor percentage of additions from the source language of the text (6%). Such results could originate controversial interpretations: on the one hand, such a small percentage of additions from the same source language of the original texts could be thought to contrast with the translators' tendency to maintain the foreign words used in the source text, hence to show a greater acceptance of the source language and culture; on the other, these data could be related to a translators' inclination to remain faithful to the original text, by maintaining the original material and avoiding to add any other term proceeding from the same language but absent in the source text. Whichever the reason, this study does not offer enough data to examinate the issue, which remains just an idea for further research.

5. Conclusions

The aim of the present study was describing the use of cultural references in a sets of corpora representing novels translated from English into Italian between 2000 and 2014 from a diachronic perspective. Actually, the use of cultural references can be interpreted as an evidence of the acceptance or the integration of the otherness which can offer an overview of the translators' attitude towards the foreignness and, more in general, a snapshot of the posture represented by the Italian translated novels as for the relationship with the otherness.

With this objective, foreign words, a specific type of cultural references systematically recognizable from their particular linguistic features, have been identified in three sets of novels translated from English into Italian and representing three periods of five years each: 2000–2004, 2005–2009 and 2010–2014. By using a corpus-based method and specific corpus tools, foreign words of three specific semantic fields particularly related with culture have been identified and classified as for their cultural impact; then, the translation techniques used to transpose them from the source to the target texts have been determined and related to a translator's behaviour in term of maintenance, adaptation or translation of the original elements. Finally, the results have been compared across the tree sets of texts.

The outcomes indicate a peak of cultural awareness in the period between 2005 and 2009, which shows a preference for the foreign words with the greatest cultural impact and for the translation technique of transposition, through the maintenance of certain terms in the source text language despite their absence in the target language dictionary. Such results suggest at least two directions to follow up the present study. On the one hand, the causes of the particular awareness for the foreign culture identified in the middle period (between 2005 and 2009) could be analysed from a sociolinguistic perspective, considering that the cultural contact that originates the introduction of foreign words in a target language is fostered by social, economic, political and technological factors. On the other hand, starting from Castillo Fadic's (2002: 488) contribution about the existence of a correlation between linguistic and social changes, the results suggest to searched for possible social consequences related to the exotic tendency identified between 2005 and 2009 in the years following to the examined periods and examine them from a (socio)linguistic perspective.

The study can also be an interesting point of departure for further studies from different perspectives. Translators' preference for additions of foreign words which arises from the analysis of the Corpus 2010–2014 suggests to investigate what are the source languages and/or the semantic fields of the terms added by the translators or if there is any relationship between translators' behaviour and the social, political and economic events of the period in exam. Similarly, once corroborated the results with further examinations, other research questions could arise from the evidence of the translators' tendency to avoid additions from the source texts language in the Corpus 2005–2009: Is this tendency related to any non-cultural, stylistic factor? How could it be interpretated in relation to the current prestige of the English language? Such questions, among many other which could be suggested by the outcomes of the present study, represent original research proposals to be developed in the frame of the sociological, cultural and literary branches of Translation Studies, or to be examined from the perspective of different linguistic disciplines. Finally, from the methodological point of view, the study offers a replicable corpus-based methodology, which, once improved and adapted to other language pairs or other lexical elements, could be used in further research.

References

Agar, Michael. 1991. "The Biculture in Bilingual." *Language in Society* 20 (2): 167–82.

Aixelá, Javier Franco. 1996. "Culture-specific items in translation." In *Translation, Power, Subversion. Topics in Translation Series*, ed. by Román Álvarez Rodríguez, and María Carmen África Vidal Claramonte, 52–78. Clevedon, Philadelphia, Adelaide: Multilingual Matters.

Anthony, Lawrence. 2022. *AntConc (Version 4.1.4) [Computer Software]*. Tokyo, Japan: Waseda University. ⟨https://www.laurenceanthony.net/software⟩.

Anthony, Lawrence. 2013. *AntPConc (Version 1.0.3) [Computer Software]*. Tokyo, Japan: Waseda University. ⟨http://www.laurenceanthony.net/⟩.

Baker, Mona. 1992. *In other words: A coursebook on translation*. London: Routledge.

Castillo Fadic, M. Natalia. 2002. "El préstamo léxico y su adaptación: un problema lingüístico y cultural." *Onomázein*, 7: 469–496.

Cece, Angelo. 2016. El impacto de la globalización económica y del anglicismo léxico en el sociolecto económico de los diarios y suplementos de Italia y España. Alicante: Universitat d'Alacant-Universidad de Alicante. Unpublish PhD thesis. ⟨http://hdl.handle.net/10045/58645⟩.

Contreras, Lidia. 1952–1953. "Anglicismos en el lenguaje deportivo chileno." *Separata del Boletín de Filología Universidad de Chile tomo VII (1952–1953)*: 177–341.

Coseriu, Eugene. 1981. *Lecciones de lingüística general*. Madrid: Gredos.

Degerstedt, Andrea. 2013. *Guardar o no guardar, una cuestión de prestar: Un estudio de neologismos y préstamos y su inclusión en el Diccionario de la Real Academia Española*. Uppsala: Uppsala Universitet. Unpublished bachelor degree project. ⟨https://www.diva-portal.org/smash/record.jsf?pid=diva2%3A627929&dswid=-1386⟩.

Fernández, Francisco and Ana Belén Fernández Guerra. 2010. "Transparencia en la teoría, translucidez en la práctica: a vueltas con la traducción de los elementos culturales." In *Lengua, traducción, recepción: en honor de Julio César Santoyo*, coord. by Rosa Rabadán, Marisa Fernández López, and Trinidad Guzmán González, 199–230. León: Universidad de León, Área de publicaciones, vol. 1

Gómez Capuz, J. (2009). "El tratamiento del préstamo lingüístico y el calco en los libros de texto de bachillerato y en las obras divulgativas." *Revista electrónica de estudios filológicos 7*. Electronic version <http://www.um.es/tonosdigital/znum17/secciones/tritonos-1-librosdetexto.htm>

Hervey, Sandor and Ian Higgins. 1992. *Thinking translation. A course in translation method: French to English*. London and New York: Routledge.

House, Juliane. 2006. "Covert Translation, Language Contact, Variation and Change." *Synaps*, 19: 25–47.

Kramsch, Claire. 2003. *Language and culture*. Oxford: Oxford University Press.

Luque Nadal, Lucía. 2009. "Los culturemas: ¿unidades lingüísticas, ideológicas o culturales?" *Language Design: journal of theoretical and experimental linguistics*. Secial issue (2009): 93–120.

Mangiron i Hevia, Carme. 2006. El tractament dels referents culturals a les traduccions de la novel·la Botxan: la interacció entre els elements textuals i extratextuals. Barcelona: Universitat Autònoma de Barcelona. Unpublished PhD thesis. ⟨http://hdl.handle.net/10803/5270⟩.

Mattioli, Virginia. 2017. "La creatividad del traductor en la transposición de elementos culturales: un estudio de corpus." *Quaderns de Filologia-Estudis Lingüístics* 22(22): 187–213.

Mattioli, Virginia. 2018. Los extranjerismos como referentes culturales en la literatura traducida y la literatura de viajes: propuesta metodológica y análisis traductológico basado en corpus. Castellón de la Plana: Universitat Jaume I. Unpublished PhD thesis. ⟨https://www.tdx.cat/handle/10803/587106⟩.

Mayoral Asensio, Roberto. 1994. "La explicitación de la información en la traducción intercultural." In *Estudis sobre la traducció*, ed. by Albir Hurtado, 73–96. Castellón de la Plana: Publicacions de la Universitat Jaume I

Mayoral Asensio, Roberto. 1999. "La traducción de referencias culturales." *Sendebar: Revista de la facultad de Traducción e Interpretación*, 10: 67–88.

Molina Martínez, Lucía. 2001. Análisis descriptivo de la traducción de los culturemas árabe-español. Barcelona: Universitat Autònoma de Barcelona. Unpublished PhD thesis. ⟨http://hdl.handle.net/10803/5263⟩.

Molina Martínez, Lucía. 2006. *El otoño del pingüino*. Castellón de la Plana: Publicacions de la Universitat Jaume I.

Muñoz Martín, Javier and María Valdivieso Blanco. 2008. "Interferencia lingüística y traducción. ¿Pierde el traductor su papel o ha perdido los papeles?" In *Traducción, contacto y contagio: Actas del III Congreso 'El español, lengua de traducción' 12 a 14 de julio, 2006 Puebla (México)*, coord. by Luis González and Pollux Hernúñez, 495–513. Bruxelles: El Español, Lengua de Traducción (ESLEtRA).

Newmark, Peter. 1988. *A textbook of translation*. New York: Prentice Hall.

Nida, Eugene Albert. 1945. "Linguistics and Ethnology in Translation Problems." *Word*, 1: 194–208.

Nida, Eugene Albert. 1964. *Toward a Science of Translating: With Special Reference to Principles and Procedures Involved in Bible Translating*. Leiden: Brill Archive.

Nord, Christiane. 1997. *Translating as a purposeful activity*. Manchester: St Jerome.

Payás, Gertrudis. 1996. "La responsabilidad del traductor ante la lengua: préstamos, 'lavado' y liberalismo lingüístico." *Estudios de Lingüística Aplicada*, 23/24: 400–407.

Piao, Scott, Francesca Bianchi, Carmen Dayrell, Angela D'egidio, and Paul Rayson. 2015. "Development of the multilingual semantic annotation system." In *The 2015 Conference of the North American Chapter of the Association for Computational Linguistics: Human Language Technologies (NAACL HLT 2015), Denver, Colorado, May 31 – June 5, 2015*, 1268–1274 The Association for Computational Linguistics.

Rodríguez González, Felix. 2005. "Calcos y traducciones del inglés en el español actual." In *Lengua y sociedad: investigaciones recientes en lingüística aplicada: Cursos de Invierno 2004 "los últimos 10 años"*, coord. by Pedro Antonio Fuertes Olivera, 177–191. Valladolid: Universidad de Valladolid, Secretariado de Publicaciones e Intercambio Editorial.

Rupini, Luh Nitya Dewi; Sedeng, I. Nyoman, and Indrawati, Ni Luh Ketut Mas. 2021. "The Translation of Cultural Terms in The Balinese Folktales." *Linguistika: Buletin Ilmiah*, 28(2): 130–135.

Santamaria Guinot, Laura. 2001. Subtitulació i referents culturals. La traducció com a mitjà d'adquisició de representacions mentals. Barcelona: Universitat Autònoma de Barcelona. Unpublished PhD thesis. (http://hdl.handle.net/10803/5249).

Seveborg, A. (2016). «"Me agarro del cuello" y otras expresiones suecas traducidas al español: Un análisis de la traducción al español de las expresiones idiomáticas y refranes en la novela Cirkeln de Mats Strandberg y Sara Bergmark Elfgren». Electronic version <http://www.diva-portal.org/smash/record.jsf?pid=diva2%3A934817&dswid=-9090>

The University of Manchester. 2011. "The Translational English Corpus: A practical approach to corpus building". Electronic version (https://artisinitiative.files.wordpress.com/2014/05/the-translational-english-corpus1.pptx).

Venuti, Lawrence. 1995. *The Translator's Invisibility*. London and New York: Routledge.

Vinay, Jean-Paul & Jean Darbelnet. [1958] 1995. *Comparative stylistics of French and English: a methodology for translation*. Amsterdam: John Benjamins.

Zanettin, Federico. 2011. "Translation and corpus design." *SYNAPS – A Journal of Professional Communication* 26:2011, pp. 14–23.

Analysed novels

Corpus 2000–2004

Atwood, Margaret. 2003. *Oryx and Crake*. New York, London, Toronto, Sydney, and Auckland: Doubleday [Nan A. Talese].

Atwood, Margaret. 2003. *L'ultimo degli uomini*. Transl. by Belletti, Raffaella. Milano: Ponte alle grazie.

Coetzee, Jhon Maxwell. 2003. *Elizabeth Costello*. London: Secker and Warburg.

Coetzee, Jhon Maxwell. 2004. *Elizabeth Costello*. Transl. by Baiocchi, Maria. Torino: Einaudi.

De Lillo, Don. 2003. *Cosmopolis*. New York, London, Toronto, Sydney, and Singapore: Scribner.

De Lillo, Don. 2003. Cosmopolis. Transl. by Pareschi, Silvia. Torino: Einaudi.

Potok, Chaim. 2001. *Old men at midnight*. New York: Random House, Ballantine Books.
Potok, Chaim. 2002. *Vecchi a mezzanotte*. Transl. by Muzzarelli, Mara. Milano: Garzanti.
Naipaul, Vidiadhar Surajprasad. 2001. *Half a life*. London, Picador.
Naipaul, Vidiadhar Surajprasad. 2002. *La metà di una vita*. Transl. by Cavagnoli, Franca. Milano: Adelphi.

Corpus 2005–2009

Auster, Paul. 2005. *The Brooklyn follies*. London: Faber & Faber.
Auster, Paul. 2005. *Le follie di Brooklyn*. Transl. by Bocchiola, Massimo. Torino: Einaudi.
Banville, John. 2006. *The sea*. New York: Vintage International.
Banville, John. 2006. *Il mare*. Transl. by Kampmann, Eva. Parma: Guanda.
Cunningham, Michael. 2005. *Specimen days*. New York: Harper Perennial.
Cunningham, Michael. 2005. *Giorni memorabili*. Transl. by Cotroneo, Ivan. Milano: Bompiani.
Ghosh, Amitav. 2005. *The hungry tide*. Toronto: Penguin Group (Canada).
Ghosh, Amitav. 2005. *Il paese delle maree*. Transl. by Nadotti, Anna. Vicenza: Neri Pozza.
Roth, Philip. 2004. *The plot against America*. New York: Vintage International.
Roth, Philip. 2005. *Il complotto contro l'America*. Transl. by Mantovani, Vincenzo. Torino: Einaudi.

Corpus 2010–2014

Desai, Anita. 2011. *The artist of disappearance: Three Novellas*. Boston: Houghton Mifflin Harcourt.
Desai, Anita. 2013. *L'artista della sparizione*. Transl. by Nadotti, Anna. Torino: Einaudi.
Lessing, Doris. 2008. *Alfred and Emily*. New York: Harper-Collins.
Lessing, Doris. 2010. *Alfred e Emily*. Transl. by Pareschi, Monica. Milano: Feltrinelli
Morrison, Toni. 2012. *Home*. New York and Toronto: Alfred A. Knopf.
Morrison, Toni. 2012. *A casa*. Transl. by Fornasiero, Silvia. Piacenza: Frassinelli.

Explotación didáctica del cómic en la formación de traductores
Adquisición de las subcompetencias lingüística, extralingüística, de transferencia y estratégica a partir de las viñetas de *Le Chat*

Tanagua Barceló Martínez
Departamento de Traducción e Interpretación, Universidad de Málaga

Besides being undoubtedly a challenge when translated, comic books are a text genre which, due to its characteristics, is ideal as a didactic tool in foreign language and culture teaching, since its use can help in the acquisition of skills attached to translation competence. The goal of this paper is, therefore, to showcase its usefulness in linguistic and cultural training of future translators in the French language classroom. Specifically, it aims to analyse the peculiarities of the Belgian comic strip *Le Chat* and its didactic possibilities regarding the acquisition of linguistic, extralinguistic and translation knowledge. To this end, this study will stem from a linguistic corpus composed of several strips that have a significant number of cultural references in order to verify what knowledge and skills can be worked on. To sum up, it seeks to demonstrate the beneficial use of a ludic resource for training purposes in the field of Translation Studies.

Keywords: comic translation, *Le Chat*, French language and culture, translation competence, FLE

1. Introducción

La enseñanza de lenguas extranjeras puede, y debe, adoptar formas muy diversas en función del fin perseguido. Es lo que conocemos bajo la denominación de enseñanza de lenguas para fines específicos, concepto surgido a finales de la década de los sesenta del pasado siglo en conjunción con la aparición del enfoque comunicativo.

Según el Instituto Cervantes,

> la enseñanza de la lengua para fines específicos se centra en los procesos de enseñanza-aprendizaje que facilitan el dominio de la comunicación especializada, esto es, la lengua que utilizan [...] los expertos que desarrollan su actividad en una disciplina académica concreta.

Ello nos permite hablar del español de los negocios, el francés del turismo o el inglés jurídico, entre otros. De forma algo más específica, la misma institución afirma que se trata de "una enseñanza dirigida a potenciar una habilidad concreta, la que solicita el aprendiente". Entre dichas habilidades menciona "la comprensión lectora de textos técnicos, la capacidad para mantener conversaciones con fines comerciales, la comprensión y expresión orales en usos académicos, etc." En el contexto que nos ocupa, el fin perseguido es traducir, lo que implica la adquisición de la denominada competencia traductora.[1] En ese sentido, y retomando las palabras de Clouet (2010: 29), podemos hablar de una lengua

> aplicada a la traducción como una realidad que presenta sus propias especificidades y que ha de ser definida para construir, a partir de ella, el sentido y la orientación de la actividad docente.

Traducir exige unos conocimientos lingüísticos muy profundos de las lenguas de trabajo, lo que implica un excelente manejo de las reglas gramaticales, ortográficas, sintácticas y estilísticas, a lo que hay que sumar unos amplios conocimientos extralingüísticos que faciliten la perfecta comprensión de los textos, así como las habilidades necesarias para su posterior traslación a la lengua meta mediante la adquisición de las destrezas necesarias. En palabras de Clouet (*ibid.*:14), "un traductor o un intérprete serán tanto más competentes en sus tareas cuanto mejor conozcan los sistemas de las lenguas con las que trabajan".

La enseñanza de lenguas extranjeras en este escenario se presenta, pues, como un auténtico reto para docentes y aprendientes, ya que esta debe abarcar, en la medida de lo posible, todas las esferas (lingüísticas y no lingüísticas) relacionadas con las distintas formas de expresión. Esto configura un panorama en el que dicha enseñanza debe adaptarse y adecuarse a las necesidades, y que exige el diseño y la puesta en marcha de metodologías específicas y el empleo de los materiales adecuados con el objeto de que los estudiantes "sean capaces de crear textos coherentes que [...] cumplan con eficacia la misma función que el texto original" y tengan a su disposición los "instrumentos para solucionar cualquier problema relacionado con la construcción de textos en la lengua término". Siempre según el autor,

---

1. Según el Grupo PACTE, esta incluye las subcompetencias lingüística, extralingüística, instrumental/profesional, psicofisiológica, de transferencia y estratégica.

esto "implica, además del dominio de la especificidad cultural de la comunidad a la que se dirige el texto traducido, el conocimiento del instrumento lingüístico" (*ibid.*:29).

En este trabajo, nos centraremos en la explotación del cómic en el aula de lengua y cultura francesas aplicadas a la traducción y la interpretación por considerar que se trata de un género textual de una gran riqueza y variedad lingüístico-cultural que permite, desde un enfoque lúdico, abordar diferentes aspectos conducentes a la adquisición de la competencia traductora. A nuestro entender, este género se perfila como una herramienta muy completa que permite poner en práctica una amplia gama de actividades. En esta ocasión, nos basamos en el cómic belga *Le Chat*, de Philippe Geluck, por las razones que más adelante expondremos, y partimos de una experiencia docente concreta que también detallaremos y cuyos resultados nos han llevado, en un primer momento, a reflexionar acerca de las necesidades de nuestros estudiantes y, a continuación, a intentar diseñar tareas y actividades destinadas a trabajar determinados aspectos lingüístico-culturales aplicados a la combinación francés-español. Se trata, específicamente, de mostrar cómo dicho cómic permite trabajar con tres subcompetencias en concreto: la competencia lingüística; la competencia extralingüística; y aquellas directamente relacionadas con el proceso traductor, esto es, la competencia de transferencia y la competencia estratégica.

2. Antecedentes

Son numerosos los estudios realizados acerca del cómic desde el punto de vista de sus orígenes, desarrollo histórico, rasgos definitorios, así como desde el punto de vista de su traducción como género dentro de la traducción literaria, en general, o de la denominada traducción subordinada, en particular. Tal es el caso de Valero Garcés (2000) o Mayor Ortega (2021), entre otros. Sin embargo, y tal y como ya se ha anunciado, el objeto del presente trabajo es abordar el cómic como herramienta didáctica para la enseñanza-aprendizaje del francés aplicado a la traducción. En este sentido, existen trabajos que abordan el uso del cómic en el aula de lenguas extranjeras, como los de Alonso Abal (2010), Bongaerts (2017), Del Rey Cabero (2013), Escudero Medina (2007), Flores Acuña (2008) o García Martínez (2013), y, específicamente en la enseñanza-aprendizaje del francés como lengua extranjera, destacan los trabajos de Bannier (2014), Paré (2016) o Soto Cano (2019). Estos últimos autores subrayan la importancia de usar este tipo de material para enseñar el francés y la cultura francófona y presentan modelos didácticos basados en el uso del cómic en el aula de francés lengua extranjera (FLE). Por otra parte, destacamos los estudios de Ramos Caro (2015) o Estalayo Vega (2005), quienes recalcan la importancia del cómic como herramienta didáctica en el aula de traducción, o el de Kamal Zaghloul (2010), que presenta una unidad didáctica para la clase de traducción general basada en el uso de este género textual como material para la adquisición de la competencia traductora.

Por último, cabe señalar que el presente trabajo tiene varios precedentes en el uso del cómic de *Le Chat* como material de análisis. Es el caso de los trabajos académicos de Herce Lorente (2020) y de Maldonado Taza (2019) que, si bien se han servido de esta obra para analizar aspectos relacionados con las dificultades de traducción, ninguno se ha basado en este cómic con el objetivo que aquí nos marcamos.

3. Caracterización del cómic

De forma previa a la presentación de nuestra propuesta, resulta necesario realizar una breve aproximación al objeto de estudio, esto es, al cómic. Conviene, no obstante, subrayar que dicha caracterización no conforma el núcleo de este trabajo, por lo que nos limitaremos a ofrecer una definición y a enumerar las características generales de este género textual con el mero objeto de contextualizar nuestro estudio.

3.1 Qué es un cómic

En español, existen diferentes denominaciones para referirse a nuestro objeto de estudio, como *cómic, historieta* o *tebeo*, pero ¿son sinónimas? Soto Cano (2019: 142) se hace eco de esta variedad y afirma que "resulta especialmente interesante observar cómo la forma de denominar este concepto de expresión literaria tampoco es unánime". En esta ocasión, y por ser el término más frecuentemente utilizado en el ámbito de la traducción, emplearemos el vocablo *cómic*, préstamo del inglés aceptado y adaptado a nuestra lengua y definido por el *Diccionario de la lengua española* (*DLE*) como "serie o secuencia de viñetas que cuenta una historia" y, por extensión, "libro o revista que contiene cómics". Soto Cano, por su parte (*loc. cit.*), señala que el cómic presenta "una secuencia de imágenes consecutivas que articulan el relato en torno a un personaje estable que prolonga el hilo argumentativo de la historia". Esto, tal y como la autora afirma, "representa un rasgo distintivo a la vez que definitorio del cómic". Nos acogemos, además, a la definición de Arango Johnson, Gómez Salazar y Gómez Hernández (2009: 21) por incluir el aspecto cultural. Así, para estos autores, el cómic es un mensaje secuencial diacrónico, narrativo o descriptivo, en el que predomina la acción; construido por medio de viñetas y otros signos verbo-icónicos, que siguen una línea de indicación y conforman códigos sistematizados hacia un sentido determinado. Es un producto cultural creado para entretener, concebido como medio masivo de comunicación. Desde el punto de vista semiótico el cómic connota, y conduce a un sistema icónico, y denota la presencia de un sistema político y social, que expresa su pedagogía.

3.2 Características generales del cómic

Es innegable que el rasgo distintivo del cómic es el uso que hace de la imagen como elemento de comunicación, en combinación con el lenguaje escrito. Brandimonte (2012: 156) señala que:

> [e]l cómic manifiesta su especificidad empleando convenciones artísticas y narrativas propias donde la comunicación se realiza a través de dos códigos distintos: el texto, en su aspecto verbal, y la imagen, en su aspecto visual.

El cómic, sus características y su tipología han evolucionado con el paso del tiempo. El interés en traducir este género ha estado siempre presente, puesto que supone un gran reto tanto por su contenido lingüístico y extralingüístico como por su peculiar formato y sus características tan singulares. Podemos, pues, afirmar que la cultura y la lengua actúan de forma imbricada en este género. El hecho de que el cómic represente un desafío traductológico ha provocado que su uso como herramienta en la enseñanza-aprendizaje de lenguas extranjeras sea igualmente interesante.

Ramos Caro (2015: 767) subraya que, debido a la variedad de formatos, estilos y temáticas que podemos encontrar en los cómics, resulta complejo establecer un patrón común para describir sus características y, por ende, los "problemas lingüísticos, culturales y comunicativos a los que nos enfrentaremos a la hora de enfrentarnos a su traducción". Son precisamente estos problemas los que hacen que este género textual resulte tan atractivo para la enseñanza de lenguas extranjeras. Tal y como indica Cáceres Würsig (1995), la naturaleza lúdica y coloquial de los cómics propicia la abundancia de ciertos rasgos que diferencian este tipo de texto — y su traducción — de otros. De acuerdo con la caracterización del cómic realizada por Eisner (2002), Ramos Caro (2015) y Jaime (2022), podríamos afirmar que entre sus principales características destacan las siguientes:

1. Suelen ser historias breves con una temática y un público variados.
2. Presenta un espacio limitado, con una estructura definida y elementos específicos como viñetas o globos.

3. Predominan las oraciones simples y las elipsis sintagmáticas y se hace un uso del lenguaje verbo-icónico. Abundan las metáforas visuales, oraciones exclamativas, abreviaturas, diminutivos y aumentativos, fraseología, diferentes registros y variedades lingüísticas o insultos.
4. Emplea multitud de recursos lingüísticos: chistes, juegos de palabras, onomatopeyas, interjecciones, etc.
5. Destaca la presencia (y la combinación) de factores lingüísticos y extralingüísticos.
6. Presenta intenciones o fines muy variados: entretener, informar, educar, criticar, ironizar, etc.
7. Incluye numerosas referencias culturales, no solo a través del texto, sino también con (o a veces únicamente) la imagen.

A esto cabría añadir las ventajas que ofrece y que, en palabras de García Martínez (2013: 15), son las que siguen:

1. Permite trabajar diferentes contenidos: fonético-fonológicos, lingüísticos o gramaticales, léxico-semánticos, funcionales y comunicativos, culturales o estratégicos.
2. Permite trabajar las cinco destrezas: comprensión escrita y oral, interacción oral, expresión oral y escrita.
3. Es un material auténtico, no manipulado ni adaptado.
4. Es un recurso dinamizador, comunicativo y familiar para el alumnado que favorece el trabajo cooperativo.
5. Su componente lúdico favorece el proceso de enseñanza-aprendizaje a través del juego, lo que le convierte en un recurso atractivo para el alumnado joven.

En apoyo al uso didáctico del cómic, el Marco Común Europeo de Referencia para las Lenguas propone las tiras cómicas como tipo de texto escrito explotable y recomendable en el aula de lenguas extranjeras (2002:93).

4. *Le Chat*, de Philippe Geluck

El autor de *Le Chat* es Philippe Geluck, actor, escritor, pintor y escultor nacido en Bruselas en 1954. Hijo de artistas, con solo diecisiete años publicó sus primeros dibujos en el diario humorístico *L'œuf*. Su carácter polifacético y su extensa obra se hacen visibles en la definición que el propio Geluck hizo de él mismo en una entrevista: "Je fuis systématiquement l'étiquetage et cela m'arrange bien qu'on ne puisse pas me caser dans un casier particulier". Sin embargo, pese a su multitud de actividades, Geluck se dio a conocer internacionalmente gracias a *Le Chat*, un cómic sobre un gato vestido de traje y corbata. La primera aparición pública de este personaje tuvo lugar el 22 de marzo de 1983. A petición del periodista Luc Honorez, *Le Chat* aparece por primera vez en las páginas del diario belga *Le Soir* y se convierte rápidamente en la "mascota" del periódico, traspasando posteriormente las fronteras de su país de origen y del mundo francófono.

Tras la primera aparición de este personaje, Geluck sigue colaborando con el periódico belga. Sin embargo, unos años después, en octubre de 1986, Geluck y la editorial Casterman se unen para publicar el primer álbum, de 80 páginas. Tras este ejemplar vendrán otros 6 de la misma extensión, aunque en el año 2002 se reeditarán pasando a 48 páginas. Actualmente, la obra escrita de *Le Chat* está compuesta por 24 tomos. Asimismo, destacan otras 6 obras que recopilan las mejores viñetas de otras recopilaciones, versiones de este cómic adaptadas a un público infantil, así como otras obras relacionadas con este personaje, como *Le fils du Chat*.

Cabe destacar que estas obras publicadas no son temáticas, no siguen ningún patrón o historia, sino que recogen viñetas creadas por el autor sobre temas muy diversos, lo que lo hace más interesante para el objetivo perseguido. En lo que respecta a la organización o composición de estos tomos, suelen predominar las viñetas individuales, aunque el autor también hace uso de tiras de tres viñetas y, con menor frecuencia, una página entera (con varias viñetas). A pesar de que la mayoría de las viñetas contiene algún fragmento, más o menos extenso, de texto, también las hay que tan solo contienen una imagen. El propio autor, a través de su carismático personaje, define así su obra en su página web oficial:[2] "Je suis né en 1983 dans le journal *Le Soir*. Mon métier consiste à faire des gags à propos des grands problèmes du monde pour amuser mes concitoyens". Geluck subraya así la principal intención del cómic: la crítica y el análisis del mundo a través del humor o la ironía. También nos muestra las principales características de este personaje y, por tanto, de su obra: es un gato con gustos muy exquisitos que realiza actividades propias de los humanos (ir al bistró o conducir un coche), aunque mantenga su naturaleza felina (cazar o comer ratones); su discurso tiene un componente de humor e ironía, siempre con el objetivo de hacer pensar al lector; tiene familia y, aunque en la mayoría de viñetas será él el protagonista, habrá otros personajes como su mujer, sus hijos, sus sobrinos, etc. También habrá otros personajes como Roger, el barman, el propio autor, su psicólogo, etc. El personaje es, a todas luces, el *alter ego* del autor.

---

2. Para más información, véase: https://lechat.com/lechatdeambule/lechat/.

4.1 Características de Le Chat

En lo relativo al formato del cómic, Geluck, a pesar de ligeras evoluciones en su obra, ha seguido siempre un mismo estilo, sencillo y eficaz, aunque muy rico en contenido y matices. Con el objetivo de que su discurso tuviera mayor importancia e impacto en el lector, el dibujo ha sido calificado por el propio autor como sobrio y limpio. Las líneas son precisas y los colores muy variados, aunque planos. En cuanto a la escritura, esta es manuscrita. La representación típica del personaje suele ser de pie, inmóvil, mirando al frente, levantando la mano izquierda y, en especial, el dedo índice, mientras habla o se dirige al lector. No obstante, hay ocasiones en las que el personaje suele hacer algún otro gesto o el autor hace que haga un movimiento más rápido, como correr. Su indumentaria suele ser la misma: un abrigo cerrado, en su mayoría en los mismos tonos (naranja, verde, azul marino o amarillo), con una corbata que contrasta con el color del resto de su ropa. Rara vez usa zapatos.

Con respecto al contenido, conviene señalar que *Le Chat* puede resultar una obra "engañosa", por lo que es necesario leer mucho a este personaje para entender y saber que Geluck, a través de *Le Chat*, realiza una caricatura. *A priori*, podemos leer viñetas de este antihéroe y pensar que es machista, xenófobo, racista, etc. Nada más lejos de la realidad. En los cómics de *Le Chat* se abordan muy diversos temas, como la relación entre países en conflicto; la relación de Bélgica (su país de origen) con el mundo (especialmente con Francia); el mundo y los países francófonos; el deporte; la gastronomía; la religión; el sexo; la política; el machismo; etc. Geluck también se refiere a personajes concretos pertenecientes a ámbitos muy diversos que están o han estado de actualidad en un momento determinado.

Para abordar estos temas y mostrar numerosos aspectos culturales, el autor utiliza diferentes recursos estilísticos, lingüísticos o extralingüísticos, siempre a través del humor y la ironía, entre los que destacan especialmente los juegos de palabras, los dobles sentidos, la polisemia, la sinonimia, la homonimia, las onomatopeyas y los referentes culturales en todas sus variantes, para lo que Geluck se sirve de refranes, canciones, expresiones, frases hechas, así como de la intertextualidad, jugando especialmente con la imagen.

Todo lo antedicho muestra que la perfecta comprensión de la obra y del mensaje de su autor (así como su traducción, dado el caso) exige al lector poseer conocimientos lingüísticos y extralingüísticos muy profundos. Por ello, consideramos que el uso de este cómic para la enseñanza-aprendizaje del francés con vistas a la traducción y, por tanto, para la adquisición de la correspondiente competencia traductora, puede resultar un recurso formativo muy completo y explotable a varios niveles.

5. Explotación didáctica de *Le Chat*

Además de lo ya expuesto, en el caso concreto del francés cabría cuestionarse acerca de "la relevancia y la pertinencia del uso del cómic en el aula no sólo como herramienta pedagógica, sino también como fuente de transmisión cultural", ya que se perfila como un "género literario que atraviesa las fronteras geográficas del hexágono y que nos permite observar un amplio abanico sociocultural cuyo nexo de unión es la lengua francesa" (Soto Cano, 2019: 141), de ahí nuestro interés.

Las propuestas de explotación del cómic de *Le Chat* que aquí se incluyen se derivan de las observaciones realizadas en el aula y de las conclusiones extraídas a partir de un pequeño "experimento" didáctico. Para ello, se seleccionaron 12 viñetas extraídas de diferentes álbumes de *Le Chat* y escogidas en función de su contenido y de su adecuación para trabajar determinados aspectos y habilidades (subcompetencias). Las viñetas se enviaron a alumnos de todos los cursos del Grado en Traducción e Interpretación de la Universidad de Málaga que tuviesen el francés como primera lengua extranjera, así como al profesorado que imparte docencia en dicha lengua, ya sea en asignaturas de lengua y cultura o de traducción, procedentes de diferentes universidades españolas. Además de responder a las preguntas a las que a continuación nos referiremos, a los alumnos también se les pedía (aunque de forma voluntaria) que propusiesen una traducción para cada una de las viñetas. Conviene subrayar que el objetivo no consistía tanto en obtener la traducción ideal sino en comprobar, a partir de sus propuestas, el grado de comprensión de todos los elementos de las viñetas y las estrategias empleadas para trasladarlos a la lengua meta (el español en este caso).

Las viñetas seleccionadas fueron las siguientes (véase Tabla 1).

Tabla 1. Viñetas de *Le Chat* seleccionadas

Tabla 1. (*continuación*)

Con el objeto de comprobar hasta qué punto la idea de la que partíamos era compartida, se pidió a cada uno de los encuestados que, a partir de cada viñeta, respondiese a las siguientes preguntas:

1. ¿En qué grado (siendo 0 el nivel más bajo y 5 el más alto) consideras que esta viñeta sirve para adquirir (o trabajar con) conocimientos lingüísticos?
2. ¿En qué grado (siendo 0 el nivel más bajo y 5 el más alto) consideras que esta viñeta sirve para adquirir (o trabajar con) conocimientos temáticos o extralingüísticos?
3. ¿En qué grado (siendo 0 el nivel más bajo y 5 el más alto) consideras que esta viñeta sirve para desarrollar habilidades traductológicas?

Los datos obtenidos resultaron especialmente interesantes, a la par que curiosos, por su diversidad. En ese sentido, podríamos afirmar, de forma general, que el profesorado, al que se le presupone unos conocimientos muy profundos de la lengua francesa, priorizó el aspecto traductológico, consciente de la enorme dificultad que la traducción del cómic reviste. Para el alumnado, sin embargo, la traducción resultó ser relativamente asequible, aunque reconocían dificultades lingüísticas y extralingüísticas, lo cual no resulta del todo coherente, sobre todo si se analizan las propuestas de traducción ofrecidas, malogradas en su práctica mayoría. En cualquier caso, las respuestas fueron dispares y difícilmente podríamos ofrecer datos concluyentes homogéneos. Lo que sí quedó patente fue, por un lado, las lagunas de los estudiantes a varios niveles y, por otro, las posibilidades de explotación didáctica tanto de las viñetas elegidas como de otras o de los cómics en general, tal y como se mencionaba anteriormente.

Las siguientes tablas (véanse Tablas 2 a 5) incluyen las propuestas de traducción de los alumnos para 4 de las 12 viñetas, así como los datos de la encuesta relativos a dichas viñetas y algunas ideas de explotación didáctica del cómic objeto de estudio.

Tabla 2. Viñeta 1

Viñeta 1	
	– Desde arriba – El mapa mundi – El corte global – Corte internacional – De corte mundial – El corte del mundo – El corte de la copa del mundo – El pico del mundo – A ras de tierra, por favor – La copa del mundo
Encuesta a alumnos	Encuesta a docentes

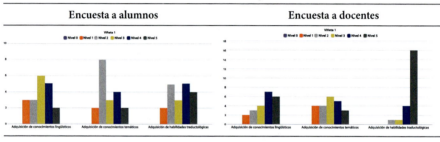

Comentarios y explotación didáctica

La elección de esta viñeta se justifica por varios motivos. Primero, permite trabajar con la polisemia a partir del término *coupe* (*). Segundo, sirve para introducir temas culturales en el aula (**). Y, tercero, muestra claramente la importancia de la combinación del texto con la imagen para poder entender la intencionalidad del autor (***).

(*) Los equivalentes más comunes de *coupe* en español podrían ser *corte* o *copa* (además de otros como *tala*). Ello daría pie a trabajar en el aula con la polisemia de forma bidireccional con las lenguas implicadas y a mostrar la importancia del contexto al elegir el equivalente adecuado, ya que, en español, el término *corte*, por ejemplo, podría trasladarse al francés como *coupe* o como *cour* (refiriéndose a un organismo judicial o al conjunto de la familia y acompañantes de un rey). De igual modo, el término *cour* también puede tener como equivalente en español el vocablo *patio*. Esto permite crear actividades de traducción de pequeñas oraciones, además de presentar al alumnado expresiones hechas construidas en las lenguas de trabajo a partir de cada uno de los términos aludidos. Esto permite la adquisición de vocabulario de un modo más ameno y atractivo.

(**) La expresión *coupe du monde* remite directamente al ámbito deportivo, en general, y, más concretamente, al fútbol (una simple búsqueda en internet nos ofrece millones de resultados en este sentido). Esto podría dar pie a hablar del deporte en el ámbito francófono. Para ello, podrían explotarse textos y vídeos con el objeto de trabajar la comprensión lectora y auditiva. También se podría proponer un trabajo a los alumnos que consistiese en la presentación de algún deporte, utilizando expresiones propias de la especialidad elegida. Por otro lado, y teniendo en cuenta la doble intencionalidad del autor de la viñeta, por una parte, y el hecho de que las guías docentes de las asignaturas de lengua y cultura suelen incluir el tema de las profesiones, se podría abordar el

Tabla 2. *(continuación)*

Viñeta 1
ámbito de la peluquería y la estética.
(***) La imagen que acompaña al texto de la viñeta permite, para todo aquel que posea los conocimientos lingüísticos necesarios, detectar el "juego" del autor y, por lo tanto, entender su intención, actos indispensables de cara a una posible futura traducción con la misma intención que el original.
Otra actividad interesante sería comentar, analizar y valorar con el estudiantado las propuestas de traducción de sus compañeros, poniendo de relieve los aciertos y las debilidades e intentando buscar las causas de las propuestas menos acertadas. Esta puesta en común permitiría retomar los aspectos lingüístico-culturales mencionados, así como empezar a concienciar a los traductores en formación de la importancia de poseer conocimientos amplios y profundos de las lenguas y culturas de trabajo, además de introducir conceptos como la adaptación, la modulación o incluso la imposibilidad de trasladar un determinado contenido con la misma intención y en las mismas condiciones en las que fue creado originalmente. Ello podría dar pie a comentar las respuestas de las encuestas y a destacar la relativa facilidad traductológica referida por los alumnos frente a la enorme dificultad expresada por el profesorado.

Tabla 3. Viñeta 2

Viñeta 2
   – Vuelven los vertidos de Río Tinto – El nuevo Beaujolais está de vuelta – El Beaujolais Nouveau se fue de nuevo – El Rioja se ha ido – El Rioja mudó de cielo – El Rioja enrojece

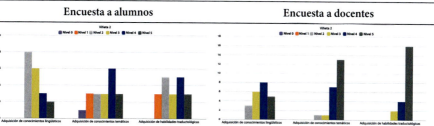

Comentarios y explotación didáctica
Si la viñeta 1 permitía trabajar más con aspectos lingüísticos, la viñeta 2 se centra, fundamentalmente, en el aspecto cultural (*). Facilita, además, trabajar con los usos y significados

Tabla 3. *(continuación)*

Viñeta 2

del verbo *repartir* (**) y muestra la importancia de la cultura general para traducir (***). Además, muestra la importancia de la combinación del texto con la imagen para poder entender la intencionalidad del autor (****).

(*) Esta viñeta hace alusión a un tema relacionado con la gastronomía, más concretamente, con el vino, industria de gran importancia en Francia. Beaujolais es una zona de la región francesa de Borgoña, muy conocida por la producción vinícola. En esta zona se elabora principalmente el Beaujolais. El Beaujolais nouveau es el primer vino de la nueva cosecha, que sale a la venta cada año el tercer jueves de noviembre. Para promocionar su vino en todo el mundo, a principios de los años 50 del pasado siglo se lanzó una campaña de marketing que todavía perdura y que tuvo por eslogan "Le Beaujolais nouveau est arrivé !" (lo que da sentido a la viñeta). La festividad, que se celebra desde hace más de medio siglo, ha traspasado fronteras y ya está presente en más de 100 países de todo el mundo. Este aspecto cultural y la explicación de dicho fenómeno servirían para introducir el tema de la gastronomía francesa o francófona, en general, y de la industria del vino, en particular. La clase podría organizarse en grupos a los que se les adjudicaría una región de Francia o de otro país francófono y el objetivo sería que buscasen un plato típico del que posteriormente deberían hablar al resto del grupo. Sería particularmente interesante que pudiesen vincular dichos platos a alguna tradición o festividad de la zona en cuestión. Posteriormente, podría establecerse un pequeño debate. De forma paralela, el docente podría elaborar material léxico relacionado con la gastronomía, desde términos básicos hasta expresiones hechas a partir de conceptos culinarios.

(**) Desde un punto de vista lingüístico, esta viñeta permite reflexionar sobre el uso del verbo *repartir* en francés y sus posibles equivalentes en español, además de analizar los sentidos que los verbos *ir* y *venir* pueden adoptar y las dificultades que todo ello podría conllevar de cara a la traducción en una u otra dirección. Los equivalentes de *repartir* en español válidos para la correcta interpretación y posible traducción de esta viñeta podrían ser *irse, volver a irse, volver a partir, marcharse* o incluso *desaparecer*. Asimismo, en francés existen otros verbos con sentidos cercanos, como son *revenir, retourner* o *rentrer*. Esto permitiría trabajar con todos estos verbos, para lo cual los alumnos podrían construir frases, observar hasta qué punto los verbos son intercambiables en un mismo contexto y proponer traducciones.

(***) En relación con los dos primeros aspectos abordados, se podría mostrar a los alumnos la importancia de la cultura general para traducir. Para entender y traducir correctamente esta viñeta, el alumnado debe detectar el aspecto cultural y no solo saber que el Beaujolais es un vino, sino que se trata de un juego de palabras que el autor de la viñeta ha hecho a partir del eslogan "Le Beaujolais nouveau est arrivé !", "jugando" así con los verbos *arrivé* (empleado cuando el nuevo vino sale a la venta cada año) y *reparti* (empleado en esta ocasión por el autor para indicar que el vino "se ha ido", "ha desaparecido"). La imagen aporta, además, información acerca de la causa de dicha "desaparición", que se debe a que *Le Chat* se ha bebido el vino.

(****) Tal y como se ha mencionado, la imagen que acompaña al texto de la viñeta permite, para todo aquel que posea los conocimientos temáticos necesarios, detectar el "juego" del autor y, por lo tanto, entender su intención, actos indispensables de cara a una posible futura traducción.

Las propuestas de traducción ofrecidas por los estudiantes permitirían, en esta ocasión, debatir

Tabla 3. *(continuación)*

Viñeta 2
acerca de los límites de la libertad del traductor y de la domesticación o la adaptación como estrategias traslativas. Como puede observarse, muchos han optado por emplear referentes culturales propios de la cultura española (como el vino Rioja o los vertidos de Río Tinto) y otros han preferido intentar ser más fieles al original mediante una traducción literal. Así, a partir de las propuestas "El Beaujolais Nouveau se fue de nuevo" y "El Rioja enrojece" (seleccionadas por ser, tal vez, las más "extremas" y opuestas entre sí) cabría preguntarse: ¿cuál de las dos opciones es más acertada y por qué?; la opción "El Beaujolais Nouveau se fue de nuevo", que responde fielmente al contenido del original, ¿cumple la misma función que el texto original?, ¿es culturalmente comprensible para el lector español sin conocimientos de la cultura francesa?, ¿tendría "sentido" su aparición en una publicación en español? Con respecto a la segunda propuesta, ¿sería infiel al original y la intención del autor?

Tabla 4. Viñeta 3

Viñeta 3
 — ¿De dónde saldrá el Tour de Francia? Se echa a suertes. — Francia apuesta por nuevos criterios de vacunación. "De perdidos, al río". — Próxima vacuna. — ¿Por dónde comenzará el tour de Francia? Por el tiro de salida. — El punto de partida del Tour de Francia se determinará por sorteo. ¡A ver dónde cae! — ¿De dónde saldrá el Tour de Francia? Es por pito pito gorgorito. Se echa a los dardos. A dos ping de saberlo.

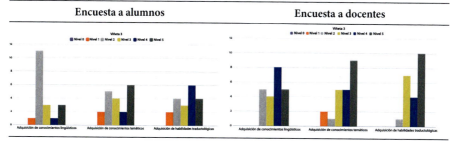

Tabla 4. *(continuación)*

Viñeta 3
Comentarios y explotación didáctica

La elección de esta viñeta se justifica por varias razones. Primero porque, aunque contenga aspectos lingüísticos, se centra, fundamentalmente, en aspectos extralingüísticos o culturales (*). Segundo, porque muestra la importancia de la cultura general para entender los textos y traducirlos de forma adecuada (**). Tercero, porque muestra la importancia de la combinación del texto con la imagen para poder entender la intencionalidad del autor (***). Y cuarto, porque permite trabajar aspectos léxicos en el aula, así como la comprensión oral y escrita (****).

(*)(**) La viñeta 3 hace alusión a un tema relacionado con el ciclismo, deporte de gran importancia en Francia, y a su competición por excelencia: el Tour de Francia, que se celebra cada año en el mes de julio en territorio francés. En la viñeta aparece el personaje principal, *Le Chat*, frente a un mapa de Francia y se puede deducir que está simulando jugar a los dardos, adoptando estos la forma de jeringuillas, y donde el mapa de Francia sirve como diana. Todos estos elementos hacen claramente referencia al tema del dopaje en el ciclismo, en general, y a los casos concretos que se han producido en los últimos tiempos en el Tour de Francia, en particular. Tan solo el conocimiento de esta realidad (relacionada con la cultura general) puede llevar a la correcta comprensión de la viñeta. La presentación de esta viñeta en el aula podría suscitar un debate acerca del dopaje, con el fin de trabajar la expresión oral, así como la capacidad de argumentación del estudiantado.

(***) La imagen, y más concretamente, el uso de dardos en forma de jeringuillas apuntando al mapa de Francia, es lo que realmente da sentido al texto de la viñeta. Este hecho debería ponerse de relieve en el aula y daría pie a comentar, además, algunas de las propuestas de traducción de los estudiantes que han relacionado las jeringuillas con un tema más actual y cercano para ellos: la vacunación ("Francia apuesta por nuevos criterios de vacunación. De perdidos, al río"; "Próxima vacuna"). Esto permitiría poner de relieve la importancia de poseer una cultura general amplia en el tiempo y no centrada en el momento actual.

(****) Parte del léxico relacionado con el deporte, en general, y con el ciclismo, en particular (al igual que ocurre con casi cualquier ámbito de especialidad), pasa a la lengua general y es de aplicación en contextos "similares" al de origen, pero relativos al día a día de la sociedad. Por ello, una actividad interesante podría ser proponer a los alumnos que trabajasen a partir de un léxico específico dado[*] con el objeto de buscar los equivalentes en español y ver los usos dentro y fuera del ámbito del ciclismo en ambas lenguas/culturas. Cabría también diseñar actividades de comprensión a partir de elementos escritos[**] y sonoros.[***]

Con respecto a la traducción de la viñeta, cabe subrayar que una traducción literal del texto (por la que, con variantes, ha optado la mayoría) que aparece en la imagen (*"D'où partira le Tour de France ? C'est tiré au sort"*) sería "válida" ("¿Desde dónde saldrá el Tour de Francia? Se echa a suertes"). Sin embargo, esto no demuestra que los alumnos hayan captado todas las connotaciones del original. Por ello, sería interesante comentar todas las propuestas en el aula y preparar actividades encaminadas a comentar, analizar y valorar con el estudiantado las propuestas de traducción de sus compañeros, poniendo de relieve los aciertos y las debilidades. Esta puesta en común permitiría retomar los aspectos culturales mencionados, así como empezar a concienciar a los traductores en

Tabla 4. *(continuación)*

Viñeta 3
formación de la importancia de poseer conocimientos muy amplios y profundos de las lenguas y culturas de trabajo.
* https://www.tf1info.fr/sport/tour-de-france-2020-vocabulaire-chasse-patate-sucer-la-roue-frotter-le-lexique-des-fans-de-cyclisme-2057059.html ** https://www.radiofrance.fr/franceculture/podcasts/la-question-du-jour/un-tour-de-france-sans-dopage-est-ce-possible-3939478?at_medium=Adwords&at_campaign=france_culture_search_thematiques&gclid=EAIaIQobChMIjuCDxa-__AIV3410CR2viwxcEAMYASAAEgJpjfD_BwE *** https://www.dailymotion.com/video/x11xq0d

Tabla 5. Viñeta 4

Viñeta 4

– A mi derecha, un halcón con un Nikon; a mi izquierda, un verdadero estúpido con un cañón.
– Foto de Nikon: un halcón con un pico. Foto de Canon, un cañón con un marrano.
– A mi derecha, un halcón y una Nikon; a mi izquierda, un soberano imbécil con un cañón.
– La guerra
– A mi derecha, un ave alado con una Nikon; a mi izquierda un alelado con un cañón.
– A mi derecha... majestuoso halcón. A mi izquierda... un capullo y un cañón.

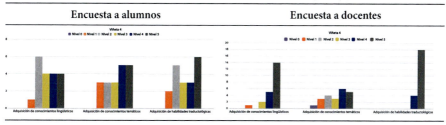

Encuesta a alumnos	Encuesta a docentes

Comentarios y explotación didáctica

Por sus características, esta viñeta debería explotarse en un nivel algo más avanzado, tal vez en asignaturas de lengua y cultura de segundo curso, que es cuando los alumnos tienen sus primeros contactos con la traducción propiamente dicha en las asignaturas de traducción general.
En el análisis conjunto que cabría hacer de la viñeta en el aula habría que destacar:
– El juego de palabras empleado por el autor: *faucon* (= halcón) frente a *faux con* (= falso idiota), lo que se opone al resto del texto, en el que se habla de *vrai con* (= verdadero/auténtico idiota).

Tabla 5. *(continuación)*

Viñeta 4

- La importancia de las imágenes que conforman la viñeta: la foto del halcón, que da sentido al juego de palabras antes mencionado, por un lado, y la foto del soldado al lado del cañón, que muestra la crítica a lo bélico mediante la expresión *vrai con*, por otro.
- El componente cultural relacionado con el ámbito de la fotografía, al emplear los vocablos Nikon (conocida marca de material fotográfico) y *canon*, empleado en minúscula por referirse en francés tanto a otra marca de material fotográfico (Canon) como al objeto que aparece en la fotografía y que se corresponde con un *canon* (cañón).

Al trasladar el contenido al español, encontramos un obstáculo importante relacionado con los juegos de palabras, aparentemente imposibles de reflejar del mismo modo en español. Estos juegos de palabras, además, no solo se refieren a la lengua, sino que, además, pueden relacionarse con elementos culturales, lo que complica aún más la situación (aunque, en este caso, se trata de referentes universales por ser Nikon y Canon marcas mundialmente conocidas). Una vez analizados todos estos elementos, sería interesante comentar los aciertos y los errores de cada una de las propuestas de traducción incluidas en la tabla. Así, por ejemplo, algunos de los comentarios sobre algunas propuestas podrían ser:

- "A mi derecha, un halcón con un Nikon; a mi izquierda, un verdadero estúpido con un cañón": se pierde el juego de palabras del original con respecto a *faucon/faux con*; se pierde el juego de palabras del original con respecto a C/*canon*, así como la contraposición entre lo positivo (*faux con*) y lo negativo (*vrai con*).
- "Foto de Nikon: un halcón con un pico. Foto de Canon, un cañón con un marrano": en esta ocasión, y a pesar de que también se pierde la contraposición positivo/negativo señalada, el autor ha retomado los dos elementos culturales a los que el original hace alusión (Nikon y Canon) y se ha atrevido con el uso de la rima, lo que es signo de creatividad y da lugar a una propuesta acertada o, cuando menos, digna de elogio.
- "La guerra": se trata, sin duda, de una propuesta arriesgada cuya justificación solo podría entenderse con la explicación de su autor. Podría dar pie a hablar sobre los "peligros" que puede conllevar alejarse tanto del original.
- "A mi derecha, un ave alado con una Nikon; a mi izquierda un alelado con un cañón": en esta ocasión, el autor ha querido hacer un juego de palabras relativamente acertado (aunque debería ser "ave alada" que, por otro lado, es redundante, pues una de las características de las aves es que tienen alas, es decir, que son aladas) y, además, retoma la crítica hacia quien se sitúa al lado del cañón. Sin embargo, el hecho de que solo se retome una de las marcas fotográficas hace que se cree un cierto desequilibrio y, por lo tanto, cierta incomprensión, por parte del lector.

La Tabla 6 contiene el resto de las viñetas objeto de la encuesta e incluye, sin ser exhaustivos, algunos de los aspectos que se podrían trabajar a partir de ellas.

Tabla 6. Explotación didáctica de las 8 viñetas restantes

	– Juego de palabras – Revisión de las cifras – Léxico sobre animales
	– Juegos de palabras – Léxico sobre gastronomía – Puesta en común de propuestas de traducción
	– Cultura general: ¿quién es Yann Arthus-Bertrand?, ¿qué es La Terre vue du ciel?
	– Cultura general: cuentos infantiles – Léxico del cuerpo humano (dedos de la mano) – Lectura del cuento *Le petit poucet* (ejercicios de comprensión, léxico, traducción, etc.) – Propuestas de traducción en el aula
	– Cultura general: Bélgica y las patatas fritas; "guiño" a la cultura gastronómica japonesa – Léxico de la gastronomía – Ortografía de topónimos

Tabla 6. *(continuación)*

– Cultura general: Bélgica y su relación con Francia
– Referentes culturales: Torre Eiffel, patatas fritas

– Juego de palabras
– Uso de anglicismos en francés y español
– Léxico sobre deportes
– Puesta en común de propuestas de traducción

6. Reflexión final

Tras la presentación de parte de un trabajo de campo más amplio que, por motivos de espacio, no podemos incluir aquí en su totalidad, estamos en disposición de reafirmar la idea, ya enunciada y trabajada por numerosos autores, de que el cómic es un género textual cuya explotación puede ayudar a cubrir diferentes esferas indispensables en la formación de traductores. Sus numerosas características y su propia naturaleza lo convierten en un recurso atractivo, en consonancia con los estudios de ludificación del aprendizaje de los últimos años (Olvera Lobo, 2018; Brousse Lamoureux y García Luque, 2020; Montesdeoca Santana, 2020; Ortiz Correa; 2021), que permite múltiples aplicaciones. En el caso concreto de la combinación lingüístico-cultural Francia-España, esta afirmación cobra, si cabe, un interés añadido por la importancia y la repercusión del cómic en Francia, en general, y en los países francófonos, en particular. La variedad, pues, de tiras cómicas se extiende a diferentes ámbitos temáticos, así como a un público extenso y variado. En este contexto, *Le Chat* reúne las características necesarias para potenciar de forma notable y desde una óptica más lúdica la adquisición de las subcompetencias lingüística, extralingüística, estratégica y de transferencia, y permite diseñar una amplia gama de actividades en la formación de traductores, tal y como hemos tratado de mostrar, de forma resumida, en el presente trabajo. Este género textual destaca también por su transversalidad, ya que permite su uso en asignaturas de lengua, cultura o traducción.

Por otro lado, tanto las respuestas a la encuesta realizada como las propuestas de traducción de los alumnos nos llevan a reflexionar acerca de la realidad del estudiantado de los grados en traducción e interpretación. En ese sentido, podríamos afirmar que carecen de la "experiencia vital" necesaria para llevar a cabo la labor traductora con éxito. Teniendo en cuenta que se trata de traductores en formación, este hecho es, hasta cierto punto, normal y aceptable. Sin embargo, suele ir aparejado a una falta de interés o a la falsa creencia de que traducir no es tan complicado y de que el uso de las tecnologías puede solucionar satisfactoria y rápidamente cualquier dificultad o problema traductológico. Las traducciones presentadas denotan, sobre todo: falta de conocimientos temáticos (culturales); falta de recursos/conocimientos lingüísticos a todos los niveles; habilidades traductológicas deficientes; habilidades documentales deficientes; se ha obviado el carácter subordinado del cómic y la importancia de la imagen. Nos preguntamos, además, si nuestros alumnos son plenamente conscientes de la responsabilidad que implica traducir. Esto debería conllevar un análisis y un debate conjunto de la situación con el objeto de adoptar las medidas necesarias.

Referencias

Alonso Abal, Marina. 2010. "El cómic en la clase de ELE: una propuesta didáctica". *Trabajo de Fin de Máster*, Universidad de Nebrija.

Arango Jonhson, Jorge Alberto; Luz Elena Gómez Salazar y Mónica María Gómez Hernández. 2009. "El cómic es cosa seria. El cómic como mediación para la enseñanza en la educación superior". *Anagramas: Rumbos y sentidos de la comunicación* 7(14), 13–32.

Bannier, Augustin. 2014. "La bande dessinée en classe de FLE. Pourquoi n'est-elle pas étudiée pour elle-même?" *Trabajo Fin de Máster*, Université d'Angers.

Bongaerts, Hanne. 2017. "Actividades interculturales mediante historietas para la clase de español como lengua extranjera en Argentina". Tesis Doctoral, Universidad de Salamanca.

Brandimonte, Giovanni. 2012. "La traducción de cómics: algunas reflexiones sobre el contenido lingüístico y no lingüístico en el proceso traductor". En *Metalinguaggi e metatesti. Lingua, letteratura, traduzione, XXIV Congresso AISPI (Padova, 23–26 maggio 2007)* ed. por Alessandro Cassol, Augusto Guarino, Giovanna Mapelli, Francisco Matte Bon y Pietro Tavavacci, 151–168. Roma: AISPI Edizioni.

Brousse Lamoureux, France y Francisca García Luque. 2020. "Juguemos en serio para aprender divirtiéndonos. La gamificación aplicada al aprendizaje de la lengua y la cultura francófonas". En *Metodologías innovadoras en la enseñanza-aprendizaje de lenguas extranjeras para traductores e intérpretes*, ed. por Tanagua Barceló Martínez, 70–81. Granada: Comares.

Cáceres Würsig, Ingrid. 1995. "Un ejemplo perfecto de traducción cultural: la historieta gráfica". En *V encuentros complutenses entorno a la traducción*, ed. por Rafael Martín-Gaitero, 527–538. Madrid: Editorial Complutense.

Clouet, Richard. 2010. *Lengua inglesa aplicada a la traducción: una propuesta curricular adaptada al Espacio Europeo de Educación Superior*. Granada: Comares.

Consejo de Europa. 2002. *Marco común europeo de referencia para las lenguas: aprendizaje, enseñanza, evaluación*. Madrid: Instituto Cervantes y Anaya.

Del Rey Cabero, Enrique. 2013. "El cómic como material en el aula de E/LE: justificación de uso y recomendaciones para una correcta explotación". *Revista española de lingüística aplicada* 26: 177–196.

Eisner, Will. 2002. *El cómic y el arte secuencial*. Barcelona: Norma Editorial.

Escudero Medina, Consuelo. 2007. "Un nuevo enfoque para la explotación del cómic en E/LE". *Foro de profesores de E/LE* 3: 59–68.

Estalayo Vega, María. 2005. "El uso de cómics en la clase de traducción general japonés-español: la traducción de aspectos pragmáticos de comunicación interpersonal". En *Actas del II Congreso Internacional de la Asociación Ibérica de Estudios de Traducción e Interpretación*, ed. por María Luisa Romana García, 44–57. Madrid: AIETI.

Flores Acuña, Estefanía. 2008. "El cómic en la clase de italiano como segunda lengua: posibilidad de explotación didáctica". *Didáctica. Lengua y literatura* 20: 89–116.

García Martínez, Isabel. 2013. "El cómic como recurso didáctico en el aula de español como lengua extranjera". *Trabajo de Fin de Máster*, Universidad de Cantabria.

Herce Lorente, Belén. 2022. "Traducción comentada del cómic Le chat est parmi nous (Philippe Geluck, 2020)". *Trabajo Fin de Grado*, Universidad de Valladolid.

Jaime, Alejandra. 2015. "El cómic: qué es, sus características, elementos y relación con la ideología". *¿Y ahora qué? Aleesota*.

Kamal Zaghloul, Ahmed. 2010. "Adquisición de la competencia traductológica: propuesta de una unidad didáctica de traducción general". *Didáctica. Lengua y Literatura* 22: 185–197.

Maldonado Taza, Javier. 2019. "De la (in)traducibilidad del componente cultural en el cómic belga *Le Chat*". *Trabajo Fin de Grado inédito*, Universidad de Málaga.

Mayor Ortega, Carlos. 2021. "Reflexiones sobre el proceso de traducción de un cómic a partir de la nueva edición de *Persépolis*". *Estudios de traducción* 11: 11–20.

Montesdeoca Santana, Pino María. 2020. "El juego como herramienta aplicada en el aprendizaje del francés como lengua extranjera". *Trabajo Fin de Máster*, Universidad de La Laguna.

Olvera Lobo, María Dolores. 2018. *GAMificación en el grado de TRADucción e Interpretación: una nueva perspectiva metodológica en el aula (GAMTRADI). Memoria de Innovación Docente*. Granada: Universidad de Granada.

Ortiz Correa, Haribian. 2021. "El juego como recurso didáctico y empleo de las TIC en FLE". *Trabajo Fin de Máster*, Universidad de La Laguna.

Paré, Charlène. 2016. "Diseño, aplicación y evaluación de un modelo didáctico basado en el cómic francófono para el aula de francés, lengua extranjera de Educación Primaria". Tesis Doctoral, Universidad de Murcia.

Ramos Caro, Marina. 2015. "Los cómics como herramienta didáctica en el aula de traducción". *Opción* 31(5): 763–777.

Soto Cano, Ana Belén. 2019. "El uso del cómic en el aula de francés como lengua extranjera (FLE)". *Tendencias pedagógicas* 34, 139–152.

Valero Garcés, Carmen. 2000. "La traducción del cómic: retos, estrategias y resultados". *TRANS. Revista de Traductología* 4: 75–88.

Varios autores (Instituto Cervantes). 2023. "Diccionario de términos clave de ELE: Enseñanza de la lengua para fines específicos".

El taller de traducción teatral del C.R.E.C. o una experiencia de traducción colectiva de un sainete español

Hélène Frison & Marie Salgues
Université Paris 13 Sorbonne Paris Nord – Pléiade (UR 7338) | Centre de Recherche sur l'Espagne Contemporaine (EA 2292) / CRAL-UMR 8566 CNRS-EHESS, Université Sorbonne Nouvelle

The translation workshop of the Centre de recherche sur l'Espagne contemporaine (CREC EA 2292 – Université Sorbonne Nouvelle) has chosen to translate a *sainete* (*El amigo Melquíades o por la boca muere el pez* by Carlos Arniches) because this specific form of Spanish drama combines several difficulties, including omnipresent humor. A collective translation was advocated, insisting on the staging and voice of the text.

Experience shows that translating humor is always possible, accepting that translation is not limited to strict literalism. By using transpositions, shifting certain comic effects, respecting the intentions of the text, it is possible to achieve a faithful translation that will make audiences laugh a century later.

Keywords: collective translation, the translation of humor, Spanish drama, global translation, Carlos Arniches

1. Introducción

En un artículo de 1987, el catedrático Julio César Santoyo (1987: 11–18) afirmaba que las piezas cómicas españolas — de las que Arniches sería un representante emblemático — no se habían traducido nunca porque eran intraducibles.[1] Y, añadía, en caso de que se hiciera, no sería traducción, sino adaptación. Partiendo de la opinión de dicho especialista de la traducción e insistiendo en la traducción del

---

[1] Si bien hay que matizar ligeramente esta afirmación. En francés, existe una única traducción de Carlos Arniches, la de *Es mi hombre*. Solo son fragmentos, destinados a la radiodifusión y la traducción de Juan Ignacio Murcia quedó manuscrita después de la difusión en 1959 (cf. Horn-Monval 1961: 23).

humor, intentaremos presentar la experiencia de traducción colectiva de una obra cómica de Arniches que presenta las mismas características que, según Santoyo, la hacen intraducible.

Entre abril de 2019 y abril de 2022, los miembros del taller de traducción teatral del CREC tradujeron el sainete de Carlos Arniches, *El amigo Melquíades o por la boca muere el pez* (1914). El taller se inserta en el grupo de investigación del CREC (*Centre de Recherche sur l'Espagne Contemporaine* EA-2292) de la Universidad de la Sorbonne Nouvelle, un grupo que se dedica al estudio de la España de los siglos XVIII a XXI, desde el enfoque de la historia cultural. Concebimos la historia cultural como un trabajo sobre las representaciones a través de las cuales podemos acceder al conocimiento de la sociedad española o un trabajo sobre las representaciones que se dan de dicha sociedad. Semejante estudio de las representaciones conlleva la interdisciplinariedad y una vocación pluridisciplinar (entre literatura, iconografía, música, cine, prensa, etc.) así como un interés por las transferencias y los intercambios (de un campo a otro, de un país a otro, etc.). Como consecuencia, la traducción se contempla como transferencia, de un sistema a otro, y no como una mera transposición o reproducción, de un idioma a otro. Por ello el nuevo sistema creado por el proceso de traducción obedece a su propia lógica, importando más el sentido global que el detalle puntual, sin que se pierda de vista la necesaria fidelidad del traductor, evidentemente.

Por otra parte, trabajar sobre las representaciones supone un cambio de enfoque en cuanto a los objetos estudiados: ya no se trata tanto del canon (excepto en su construcción de un horizonte de expectativas para los miembros de la sociedad) sino de la revalorización de lo que constituye la cultura de masas — o lo que se le suele asociar —. El interés del estudioso se ve desplazado de lo cualitativo hacia lo cuantitativo, de los grandes nombres de la literatura universal hacia aquellos autores que más éxito tuvieron en su época, pero se quedaron fuera de las posteriores antologías.

2. El taller de traducción teatral

2.1 Los objetivos del taller

Enmarcándose en estas pautas, el taller de traducción teatral reúne a investigadores especializados en el teatro, los espectáculos y la escena. Fue creado en 2006 reivindicando la misma dimensión globalizante que la de la historia cultural en su manera de concebir la traducción teatral. Consideramos que el texto teatral tiene otro fin más allá de sí mismo, que es el de la representación teatral; o sea, que está destinado a ponerse en voz y en escena. Por lo tanto, la única traducción aceptable es una traducción global o total, que dé cuenta del conjunto de los efectos producidos por el texto de partida. Resulta, pues, imposible limitar la traducción de un texto de teatro al mero traspaso del sentido. En efecto, cada una de las palabras se eligió, cada una de las frases se fraguó y se encadenó pensando en la puesta en escena y su pronunciación. Se hace imposible pensar el lenguaje únicamente en su dimensión semántica; al contrario, hace falta concebirlo como un conjunto orgánico, constituido por diferentes elementos. Podríamos encontrar en las palabras que Efim Etkind dedica a la traducción poética un símil para la tarea del traductor teatral. En efecto, escribe (1982:XI):

> Si un poema fuera una suma aritmética de ideas y sonidos, uno podría, al perder una parte, conservar la otra. Pero no nos enfrentamos a una suma, nos enfrentamos a un organismo: si perdemos una parte, lo perdemos todo. Cuando uno cree que solo está sacrificando la forma, también está matando el fondo. Un hombre al que le han cortado la cabeza no es, simplemente, un hombre midiendo una cabeza menos; ha dejado de existir.[2]

En un texto teatral, las palabras han sido pensadas como signos, como portadoras de significación y tienen una realidad física (trasparentada en el sonido, el ritmo o el silencio, llegado el caso); son significado y significante. Por otra parte, las palabras solo constituyen uno de los elementos, además de la entonación, la gestualidad, la puesta en escena, etc., que participan en la significación total de la obra. Fue esta concepción de la obra teatral "total" la que guio nuestra elección a la hora de seleccionar los textos para el taller, buscando obras en las que se asumiera claramente esta importancia dada al significante. De ahí que, en 2006, empezamos traduciendo *El hombre deshabitado* de Rafael Alberti (Alberti 2020), un texto que bebe de su poemario *Sobre los ángeles* y está plagado de efectos rítmicos, prosódicos y sonoros.

La metodología de trabajo del taller también ostenta el carácter pluridisciplinar que caracteriza la historia cultural en que se funda.

2.2 La metodología del taller

Repasando las definiciones que da el diccionario francés de la palabra taller, nos detendremos en dos acepciones. Primero, la que define el taller como un "lugar en el que se hacen manualidades, en que se practican trabajos manuales en el

---

2. 'Si un poème était une somme arithmétique d'idées et de sons, on pourrait, perdant une partie, conserver l'autre. Mais on n'a pas affaire à une somme, on a affaire à un organisme : si on perd une partie, on perd le tout. En croyant ne sacrifier que la forme, on exécute aussi le fond : un homme dont on a coupé la tête n'est pas simplement plus court d'une tête, il cesse d'exister'. (Traducción nuestra).

ámbito del arte o del ocio y, por extensión, un lugar donde se elabora una obra".[3] Esta primera definición corresponde al taller en la medida en que no nos ceñimos a una teoría de traductología precisa, al considerar que no existe una fórmula que permita tomar en cuenta el conjunto de los efectos de un texto.[4] Por ello, nuestra labor se parece a un trabajo de terreno en el que los problemas surgen a medida que vamos avanzando y donde encontramos soluciones adaptadas a cada situación, andando a tientas, sin conceptualización previa. A veces, la solución no termina de satisfacernos, o se considera un mal menor, a la espera de ajustes posteriores que se impongan a medida que la significación profunda del texto y su funcionamiento se vayan revelando. En el caso del sainete de Arniches, el nombre de los personajes constituyó un tema de debate hasta el final. Las soluciones evolucionaron a medida que fuimos conociendo mejor cada personaje y se vieron influidas por los juegos de palabra que salpican el texto — o por la vis cómica que el conjunto del papel le da a tal o cual personaje —. Volveremos sobre ello. La idea es la de una praxis de la que, quizá, a posteriori, surja una teorización, o elementos de teorización.

Siguiendo con la definición de taller, esta permite asimilar el trabajo de traducción llevado a cabo en el taller a un arte: así como el intérprete, el actor o el director de escena crean una de las posibles realizaciones/concreciones de la obra, también lo hace la traducción. Recuerda Robert Vivier que (Etkind 1982: XV):

> la traducción no es una técnica de reproducción sino un arte, es decir, una actividad que crea una cosa a partir de otra cosa (...). ¿Acaso el mismo poeta no fue ya, del mismo modo, el pintor de su propia aventura mental? La puso en palabras (...), unió la verdad emotiva con una belleza verbal. A su vez, el traductor intentará pintar esta pintura, transponiéndola a un colorido nuevo en el que se esfuerce por conservar las relaciones y el efecto general de la obra primitiva.[5]

---

3. https://www.cnrtl.fr/lexicographie/atelier ('Lieu où s'exécutent des travaux manuels, où se pratiquent des activités manuelles d'art ou de loisir ; par extension, lieu où s'élabore une œuvre'. (Traducción nuestra).

4. Más allá de reivindicar, como Anne-Françoise Benhamou, el lenguaje del teatro como "la lengua traductora reina" que, según Antoine Berman, preside a toda gran traducción (cf. Benhamou 1990). Si la oralidad del texto teatral es un componente que tener en cuenta en la traducción, seguimos a Susan Bassnett (1991: 99-111) cuando considera que el texto teatral escrito es un texto completo, que no está amputado de una *"performability"* que habría que traducir.

5. 'la traduction n'est pas une technique de reproduction mais un art, c'est-à-dire une activité qui crée une chose à partir d'une autre (...). Le poète lui-même n'avait-il pas été déjà de la même manière le peintre de sa propre aventure mentale ? Il l'avait mise en mot (...) il avait uni la vérité d'émotion à une beauté verbale. Le traducteur tentera à son tour une peinture de cette peinture en la transposant dans un coloris nouveau où il s'efforcera de conserver les relations et l'effet général de l'œuvre primitive'. (Traducción nuestra).

Si la traducción no es reproducción sino trasposición, la cuestión de la fidelidad al texto ya no se plantea de la misma manera, y nos permite rebatir, ya, la imposibilidad defendida por Santoyo.

Volviendo al diccionario, la segunda acepción presenta el taller como un "lugar en el que unos obreros ejecutan en común una serie de trabajos similares o conexos".[6] De hecho, la traducción elaborada es una obra conjunta en la que participan todos los miembros del taller (unas 7 u 8 personas), independientemente de su estatuto (reciben el mismo trato el catedrático emérito y el doctorando más novato). Antes de cada sesión, uno de los miembros (nos vamos turnando) traduce un fragmento que manda al grupo. Nos reunimos luego con esta propuesta en mano y vamos corrigiendo, modificando, retomando esa primera traducción, frase por frase, teniendo en cuenta los comentarios y las objeciones de todos y cada uno. Así la propuesta de uno sufre la prueba de la oralidad y del oído de los demás. De este modo, cada miembro traduce y se enfrenta al texto, siendo el texto final una elaboración conjunta. En caso de desacuerdo, gana la mayoría.

Al tratarse de un trabajo que se desarrolla en periodos largos (con una sesión al mes durante varios años), resulta posible observar y asimilar las especificidades de cada texto, ateniéndonos tanto a la exactitud gramatical, como a la fidelidad al texto español, los efectos prosódicos, el sentido global, etc. En este sentido, la traducción se vuelve global por la voluntad común de tener en cuenta el conjunto de los parámetros del texto, gracias a las fuerzas aunadas en el colectivo, un colectivo que aprendió a trabajar al alimón, lo cual disminuye el riesgo de lo accidental o contingente.

2.3 La elección del texto

Después de la traducción de la obra de Alberti ya mencionada, nos pareció que *El amigo Melquíades*, de Carlos Arniches, cumplía con todos los requisitos.

En cuanto dramaturgo reiteradamente puesto en escena en la primera mitad del siglo XX, Arniches formaba parte del horizonte de expectativas de los espectadores españoles, si bien hoy día no figura en muchas de las historias de la literatura española que prefieren enfocar a autores poco representados en su época pero que constituyeron hitos en la historia del teatro (García Lorca, Valle-Inclán, etc.) Cuando lo citan, casi siempre es por la crítica que encierran algunas obras suyas, sobre todo sus últimas producciones, como por ejemplo *Los Caciques*. Sin embargo, C. Serrano y S. Salaün lo consideran como uno de los tres renovadores del teatro español (2002: 171–172).[7]

---

6. https://www.cnrtl.fr/lexicographie/atelier : 'Lieu où des ouvriers exécutent en commun des travaux similaires ou connexes'. (Traducción nuestra).

7. Junto con los ya citados García Lorca y Valle-Inclán.

Se trata de un dramaturgo cuya modernidad estriba en un idioma desbordante; en términos de registros de lengua, humor, ritmo, constituye un caso fuera de norma. Arniches, en una especie de recuperación de la herencia simbolista, concibe el lenguaje como un fin, en ruptura completa con la concepción naturalista y realista del teatro burgués español cuya lengua es, antes que nada, divertimiento y/o información. Arniches crea un idioma que va más allá de la mera función designativa verbal, que supera el mensaje conceptual y cognitivo. El lenguaje pasa a ser un fin en sí mismo, un objeto de gozo como ya subrayara García Lorca apuntando la

> aptitud de Arniches a trabajar con y sobre la lengua, a reanudar con todas las potencialidades y las materialidades de la palabra, a crear significación a partir de mecanismos sensibles, físicos, mucho más que mentales o morales.
> (Salaün 1994: 27)

Así, pues, las palabras parecen escogidas por su significante, su materialidad, su proximidad sonora con otras, su extrañeza. S. Salaün (1994: 31) habla de «jerga, jerigonza, verborrea, garrulería desarticulada».

Además, en *El amigo Melquíades*, hay cantables que plantean la cuestión del ritmo y de la rima, un problema que se agudiza por la diferencia entre la lengua española, acentual, y el francés, que no lo es. Las múltiples complicaciones que suponen estos cantables no entran aquí en nuestro tema, si bien fueron un argumento en favor de la elección de la obra. Tampoco hablaremos aquí de la historicidad de la lengua. Si bien queda evidente que Arniches no reprodujo, de una manera "naturalista" o "realista", frases escuchadas en las calles madrileñas de la época, sino que creó una lengua propia que condensa, ejemplifica, magnifica también, la jerga madrileña de entonces, este idioma se enmarca en el Madrid de las clases populares de principios del siglo XX, tal como lo escribía P. Salinas caracterizando el sainete (Arniches 1978: 20):

> Las obras del *género chico* traen un teatro de costumbres, de inspiración directa de la realidad ambiente, de transcripción fácil y elemental de sus datos. Modos de vivir y de hablar, tipos, inclinaciones de las gentes, usos y amaneramientos sociales, desfilan por esas obrillas. La sociedad como modelo de arte es lo que se propone el género.

Ello nos llevó a tener que decidir si queríamos una traducción que restituyera el texto en su estado antiguo, marcando la distancia temporal (y provocando en los espectadores franceses la misma extrañeza que la que siente el español de hoy ante ciertos giros de Arniches) o si optábamos por una traducción actualizadora, con el riesgo de una caducidad más rápida. Aparte de los términos ya "clásicos" de este debate (Topia 1990: 45-61), la importancia del humor zanjó el tema. En efecto, la cuestión del humor es central en la obra y va cobrando múltiples formas, participando en la estructuración misma de la obra. Desde juegos de palabras, proximidad sonora, frases encadenadas en una dinámica asociativa, hasta alusiones, polisemias y desplazamientos, las estrategias son variadas y se suceden casi sin interrupción.

3. La traducción del humor

3.1 De cómo las dificultades nos abrieron la senda

La dificultad para el traductor, como recuerdan numerosos estudiosos, es que el humor constituye una práctica eminentemente cultural, basada en un patrimonio compartido (que acarrea una connivencia intracultural).[8] El humor se construye por y en un idioma preciso, pero también sobre un carácter cultural. La primera dificultad, como recuerda Laurian (1989: 5-14) es la de la "significación" de las bromas; "¿qué significa "significación" tratándose de humor? ¿Existen juegos de palabras "gratuitos"?"[9]

La segunda dificultad, sigue Laurian, es la de las connotaciones y referencias que permiten crear una connivencia entre autor y espectador, entre actor y público. Aquí entran en juego la suma de conocimientos (históricos, políticos, literarios, culturales, morales, religiosos, etc.) comunes y adquiridos por los nativos continuamente inmersos en su medio. Esta suma cambia de un lugar a otro, de un idioma a otro, suponiendo un obstáculo intercultural.[10] Frente a este problema, no existe ninguna solución teórica previa, ninguna fórmula aplicable una vez para todas. Lo único que hay es una imposibilidad: la de la nota de pie de página para explicar (un juego de palabras supuestamente intraducible o una connotación cultural muy específica) por tratarse de un texto teatral puesto en escena y no destinado a la lectura. La traducción del humor tiene que ver con la transposición y la traducción "global", puesto que contempla el texto como un movimiento de conjunto. La traducción debe encerrar tanto valor añadido como el texto de par-

---

8. Cualquier acto de comunicación, para funcionar, supone un "patrimonio" común entre los interlocutores. Quizá podamos postular que este requisito esencial, que funciona *a minima* en un acto básico de comunicación, constituye el centro mismo del proceso tratándose de humor.
9. '[O]ù est le sens ? Quelle est la signification de "sens" lorsqu'il s'agit d'humour ? Y a-t-il des jeux "gratuits" avec les mots ?' (Traducción nuestra).
10. Esta unión estrecha entre un idioma y todas sus connotaciones culturales constituye, a nuestro parecer, la primera dificultad en cualquier traducción, si bien se ve como llevada al cuadrado en el caso de un texto humorístico que condensa cualquier efecto.

tida, aunque no necesariamente el mismo (Vandaele 2001: 32; Henry 2003: 290),[11] ni situado en el mismo lugar (Wecksteen 2008: 116 y siguientes).

Las obras de Arniches intentan cautivar al público desde principio hasta fin, entre otros métodos gracias a un ritmo desenfrenado, rápidos cambios de tempo, etc. El humor forma parte de los medios que permiten mantener la atención del público y conservarla (a veces más, incluso, que el argumento mismo). El texto ha sido concebido para divertir y mover a risa, así como para captar y fijar la atención del espectador. Por lo tanto, la recepción es un elemento fundamental a la hora de elaborar el texto porque si la atención se suspende, entonces la historia se interrumpe y falla el efecto. Importa pues mantener este elemento a la hora de traducir: se privilegió sistemáticamente el oído del espectador que acude, lo mismo que el del Madrid de 1910, para reírse. Es él, el espectador deseoso de divertirse (y no el especialista) quien siempre se lleva la última palabra, es quien oye (y no quien escribe o lee). En este sentido, el humor debe funcionar según los resortes de un público vivo que comparte con "el destinatario un imaginario etno-socio-cultural" (Laurian; Szende 2001: 2) y, por consecuencia, según los resortes de un público actual. Llegados a este punto, se habían impuesto dos exigencias: "traducir por y para el oído", como preconiza Chevalier pero también traducir por y "para un oído de hoy día" (Chevalier 1997: 11). Se respeta al texto que debe oírse, y no al texto escrito. Ahora bien, la preponderancia concedida al receptor no induce la desaparición sistemática de la distancia temporal, dado que esta distancia está inscrita en la escritura, pero también en las situaciones, los temas, las relaciones de los personajes entre sí, etc.

3.2 Los ejemplos concretos

3.2.1 *Paronimia y antanaclasis*

En esta escena, Avelino, un chico muy buena persona, con poca instrucción, pero al que le gusta utilizar palabras cultas — o intentarlo — está saltando a la comba.

En español, se encadenan dos bromas, una basada en una paronimia (la semejanza entre dos palabras provoca una confusión), la otra en una antanaclasis (la repetición de una misma palabra, pero utilizada con dos de sus acepciones distintas, si bien en sentido propio ambas). Al principio, la proximidad sonora entre récord (una palabra de origen inglés que constituye un préstamo léxico) y rencor

---

11. Mecanismo recordado por Jeroen Vandaele que lo llama "effet semblable". Jacqueline Henry habla de "traduction homomorphe" cuando el tipo de juego es el mismo, aunque con otras palabras, otro sentido literal. Y llama "traduction hétéromorphe" el hecho de traducir un juego de palabras por un procedimiento distinto al del original, buscándose un equivalente "natural" que "respete las características del idioma".

Cuadro 1. I, escena primera

Zoila — Pero ¿qué furia te ha entrao de saltar, demonio?	Zoila — Qu'est-ce qui t'prend de sauter comme ça, bon dieu?
Avelino (…) — No, ¿sabe usté? Es que le estoy batiendo a un amigo el *rencor* de la hora, en el salto a comba. Ya le he batido el *rencor* de la media.	Avelino (…) — Vous ne savez pas? Je veux battre le Ricard de l'heure d'un copain à la corde à sauter. J'ai déjà battu le Ricard de la demie.
Zoila (…) — ¿De la media? ¿Y por qué no te subes el calcetín?	Zoila — T'as descendu un Ricard? Remonte plutôt ton falzar!
Avelino — ¡Ah, es verdad! (*Se sube el que se le está cayendo.*)	Avelino — Ah oui, c'est vrai. (*Il remonte son pantalon qui tombe.*)

lleva a Avelino a confundirlas. Luego, habla de media en el sentido de 30 minutos, mientras Zoila lo repite, pero con la significación de calcetín. En francés, conseguimos mantener una paronimia entre el record y una bebida alcoholizada, muy popular, el Ricard. Al no conseguir encontrar ningún tipo de antanaclasis sobre "media", y ya que estábamos limitados por la acotación escénica, buscamos una rima divertida (Ricard / falzar), con una palabra que, por pertenecer a un registro popular, ya crea algún desfase en comparación con "pantalones". Subrayemos que la antanaclasis no ha desaparecido del todo ya que se adivina el juego sobre los dos sentidos de 'descendre' (beberse un vaso / caerse sus pantalones) para explicar lo de "remonte plutôt ton falzar".

Aprovechemos este ejemplo para hacer una puntualización. En su obra, Arniches elige señalar gráficamente unas marcas de oralidad que remiten al "pueblo" o, en todo caso, a una pronunciación que nos aleja de la cuidadosa lengua escrita y que participa en la atmósfera distendida, amable, que se crea. En francés, intentamos conservar dichos efectos, de nuevo en un nivel global, sin reproducirlos necesariamente en las mismas palabras que en español. Además, algunas grafías no cambian realmente la pronunciación; en el caso de "usté" por ejemplo, solo impide una versión excesivamente culta del pronombre, con una D oíble. De ahí que no se hayan sistematizado estas señales de oralidad, aunque solo fuera para evitar una lengua artificial.

3.2.2 *Encadenamiento de frases y adaptación*

El siguiente juego de palabras tiene lugar en una escena en que Serafín está intentando seducir a Nieves. El piropo de Serafín estriba en el doble sentido que le confiere a la palabra nieves, como nombre propio de la chica y como sustantivo que designa un fenómeno meteorológico. Al referirse a la Sierra de Guadarrama y a las nieves que aún perduran en primavera, introduce esta referencia meteorológica que le permite establecer una conexión entre ellos dos. Hay que esperar el final de la quinta frase para entender el juego de palabras. En francés, surgió primero una traducción que permitía guardar algo parecido, pero que obligaba a traducir los nombres.

Cuadro 2. I, escena 4

Serafín — Daría la metá de mi existencia por ser el Guadarrama.	Ange — Je donnerais la moitié de ma vie pour être le sommet du Mont Blanc.
Nieves — ¿Pa qué?	Olympe — Pourquoi ?
Serafín — Pa verme rodeao de "nieves" por todas partes.	Ange — Pour être plus près de l'Olympe.
Nieves — Iba usté a tener mucho frío.	Olympe — Vous auriez très froid.
Serafín — ¡Quiá! Nieves usté y primavera yo, a la media hora el deshielo.	Ange — Bah ! Vous, Olympe et moi, Ange, en un rien de temps, l'ambiance serait divine.
Nieves — ¡Pamplinas!	Olympe — Balivernes !

La cuestión de la traducción, o no, de los nombres de los personajes, se planteó y nos obligó a reflexionar sobre sus implicaciones (Ballard 2001). Pero no fue lo que nos llevó a rechazar esta propuesta. En efecto, se consideró que el nombre Olympe (pijo, excesivamente fino) no convenía para el personaje de Nieves, al tiempo que resultaba tan poco corriente como Nieves sí lo era. Preferimos esquivar, de cierto modo, el problema, acudiendo a una traducción que no nos obligaba a traducir los nombres.

Cuadro 3. I, escena 4

Serafín — Daría la metá de mi existencia por ser el Guadarrama.	Séraphin — Je pourrais passer ma vie en plein cagnard.
Nieves — ¿Pa qué?	Blanche — Pourquoi ?
Serafín — Pa verme rodeao de "nieves" por todas partes.	Séraphin — Parce que t'es mon soleil.
Nieves — Iba usté a tener mucho frío.	Blanche — Vous auriez trop chaud.
Serafín — ¡Quiá! Nieves usté y primavera yo, a la media hora el deshielo.	Séraphin — C'est bien simple, quand j'te regarde, je bronze.
Nieves — ¡Pamplinas!	Blanche — Balivernes !

Nuestra traducción parte de un piropo malo, cuando se quiere seducir a una mujer: «t'es belle comme un soleil, quand je te regarde, je bronze» (Luces como un sol, solo con mirarte, me pongo moreno). Con ello, podíamos recuperar la alusión meteorológica. A partir de ahí, remontamos el diálogo, para introducir el campo léxico del sol ('cagnard', una palabra popular para un sol que arde). Al final, desplazamos el carácter un poco hortera del cumplido, recuperando en francés un piropo que pertenece a la cultura popular e introduciendo una palabra de registro popular. Este ejemplo muestra que, a veces, la fidelidad no se sitúa en la conservación de una palabra exacta, en la traducción literal de un juego de palabras, sino en mantener el espíritu de la obra, los efectos buscados por el autor.[12]

3.2.3 Encadenamiento de frases y traducción de los apellidos

En el fragmento siguiente, Avelino se acerca a Benita con un cuchillo, y después de darle un susto de muerte, le pregunta lo siguiente:

Cuadro 4. I, escena 6

Avelino — (...) ¿Cómo se llama usté?	Avelino — (...) Comment vous appelez-vous ?
Benita — ¡Ah !, pero, ¿es el padrón?	Benita — Ah, c'est pour le recensement ?
Avelino — Es otra cosa más de adorno. ¿Cómo se llama usté?	Avelino — C'est autre chose, plus décoratif. Comment vous appelez-vous ?
Benita — Benita.	Benita — Benita.
Avelino — Digo de apellido.	Avelino — Non, votre nom de famille.
Benita — Baranda.	Benita — Barrière.
Avelino — (*Sonriendo.*) ¡Baranda! ¡Hombre, qué casualidad! Usté Baranda y yo, Escalera! ¡Nos completamos! (*Mirándola con arrobamiento.*) ¡Baranda! (*Muy meloso.*) ¡Con qué gusto me asomaría!	Avelino — (*Il sourit.*) Barrière ! Comme le monde est bien fait ! Vous Barrière, et moi Dujardin ! On se complète bien. (*Il la regarde avec ravissement.*) Barrière ! (*Tout mielleux.*) Comme j'aimerais l'ouvrir !
Benita — ¿Dónde?	Benita — Quoi ?
Avelino — Nada, nada; es una cosa pa mí solo. De forma que las iniciales de usté son B. B.	Avelino — Rien, rien ; je me parlais à moi-même. De sorte que vos initiales sont B. B.
Benita — Creo que sí; B. B.	Benita — Je crois, oui, B. B.
Avelino — Pues, la voy a hacer a usté un B. B. entrelazao, en el tronco de un árbol, con letra de adorno, que se va usté a quedar "visueja". (...)	Avelino — Bon, je vais vous faire un B. B. entrelacé, sur le tronc d'un arbre, avec de belles lettres, que vous allez en avoir la berlue. (...)

---

12. Terminamos por traducir el nombre Nieves en Blanche, considerando que las connotaciones de cierta inocencia, rayana en ingenuidad, tenían mucha importancia.

Cuadro 4. *(continuación)*

Avelino — Y debajo de su enlace pondré mis iniciales: Avelino Escalera Jordán. A. E. J. (*Muy fino.*) ¿Me permitirá usted que por lo menos toque la J en su enlace?	Avelino — Et sous vos initiales, je mettrai les miennes : Avelino Dujardin Normand, A. D. N. (*Avec délicatesse.*) M'autoriseriez-vous à mettre mon A. D. N., au moins en partie, dans votre B.B. ?
Benita — Como si quiere usted tocar la muñeira.	Benita — Mettez-le où vous voulez, je m'en fiche.
Avelino — Ni una palabra más. Lo grabo en aquella encina (…)	Avelino — Alors c'est dit. Je le grave sur ce chêne (…)

El diálogo está enfocado al juego de palabras final sobre la jota, y encierra la idea de un matrimonio, de Avelino con Benita, aunque él no se menciona a sí mismo, pero ha dejado bien claro que está muy enamorado: sus comentarios sobre sus respectivos apellidos evocan una suerte de complementariedad arquitectural, así como sugieren una posible primera proximidad física. El comentario sobre las iniciales hace hincapié en dicha proximidad, pero esta vez en tono más pícaro. Una vez comprobada la imposibilidad de una traducción literal del juego de palabras, nos pareció que lo importante era jugar con las iniciales y desembocar en un juego de palabras que aludiera a la posible relación amorosa entre ambos. Suponía cambiar los apellidos (es el único momento en la obra en que se mencionan), lo que hicimos. Ya que eran significantes, a la fuerza tuvimos que traducir y darles apellidos franceses, para que se entendiera el juego de palabras.

4. Conclusión

El trabajo colectivo en la duración permite un verdadero aprendizaje. Con la repetición, la materia se domestica, se domina. Lo mismo que en una orquesta, cada uno ocupa su lugar sin, probablemente, tener la misma función. Pero todos tendemos hacia una misma meta, cuyo resultado es la traducción que nace de la colaboración. A la hora de sacar conclusiones traductológicas de esta experiencia, podemos volver a la imposibilidad, apuntada por Santoyo, de traducir a Arniches. El texto existe, hemos completado la traducción,[13] lo cual no permite saber, aún, si hemos conseguido traducir a Arniches. Como bien subrayaba Santoyo al final de su artículo, la prueba última sería la de la representación. Si se ríen los espectadores como se reían en el Madrid de 1910, entonces sí que podremos con-

---

13. La traducción está por publicar en la editorial UGA de Grenoble.

siderar nuestra empresa como victoriosa. A la espera de un montaje, tan deseable como lejano, podemos insistir en la idea que ya destacara Vandaele (2001: 37–38): cuando se plantea la cuestión de "¿cómo traducir el humor?", en realidad, estamos volviendo a la cuestión de "¿qué llamamos traducción?" Y, añadimos nosotras, renunciar a intentarlo, pensando que en vez de traducción, estamos haciendo una adaptación, es condenar al silencio a demasiados textos.

Bibliografía

Arniches, Carlos. 1978. *Del Madrid castizo: sainetes*. [Edición de José Montero Padilla]. Madrid: Cátedra.

Ballard, Michel. 2001. *Le nom propre en traduction*. Paris: Ophrys.

Bassnett, Susan. 1991. "Translating for the Theatre: The Case Against Performability". *TTR (Traduction, Terminologie, Rédaction* 4 (1): 99–111.

Benhamou, Anne-Françoise. 1990. "Quel langage pour le théâtre? (À propos de quelques traductions d'*Othello*)". *Palimpsestes* 4. http://journals.openedition.org/palimpsestes/599)

Chevalier, Jean-Claude. 1997. "Préface." En *El Ingenioso hidalgo Don Quixote de la Mancha*, de Miguel de Cervantes. 1605. Madrid: Juan de la Cuesta. Citado por la traducción francesa *L'Ingénieux Hidalgo Don Quichotte de la Manche*, 1, de Aline Schulman, 7–14. Paris: Seuil.

Etkind, Efim. 1983. Кризис одного искусства. Опыт поэтики поэтического перевода. Lausanne. Citado por la traducción francesa *Un art en crise: essai de poétique de la traduction poétique*, de Wladimir Troubetzkoy. 1982. Lausanne: L'Âge d'Homme.

Henry, Jacqueline. 2003. *La traduction des jeux de mots*. Paris: Presses de la Sorbonne Nouvelle.

Horn-Monval, Madeleine. 1961. *Traductions et adaptations françaises du théâtre étranger du XVe siècle à nos jours*, T. 4, Paris: CNRS.

Laurian, Anne-Marie. 1989. "Humour et traduction au contact des cultures". *Meta* 34 (1): 5–14.

Laurian, Anne-Marie, y Thomas Szende (eds). 2001. *Les mots du rire: comment les traduire? Essais de lexicologie contrastive*. Bern, Berlin: Peter Lang.

Salaün, Serge. 1994. "Carlos Arniches o la difícil modernidad teatral". En *Estudios sobre Carlos Arniches*, coord. por Juan Antonio Ríos Carratalá, 21–33. Alicante: Diputación provincial de Alicante, Instituto Alicantino de Cultura Juan Gil-Albert.

Salgues, Marie, y Évelyne Ricci (dirs.). 2020. *L'Homme déshabité. (Mystère en un prologue, un acte et un épilogue) 1930*. Grenoble: UGA Éditions. Citado por la traducción colectiva de Rafael Alberti. 1930. *El hombre deshabitado: (auto en un prólogo, un acto y un epílogo)*. Madrid: Gama.

Santoyo, Julio César. 1987. "Translatable and Untranslatable Comedy: The Case of English and Spanish". *Estudios Humanísticos Filología* 9: 11–18.

Serrano, Carlos y Serge Salaün. 2002. *Temps de crise et "années folles". Les années 20 en Espagne*. Paris: Presses de l'Université de Paris-Sorbonne.

Topia, André. 1990. "*Finnegans Wake*: la traduction parasitée". *Palimpsestes* 4: 45–61. http://journals.openedition.org/palimpsestes/602.

Vandaele, Jeroen. 2001. "Si sérieux, s'abstenir. Le discours sur l'humour traduit". *Target* 13 (1): 29–44.

Wecksteen, Corinne. 2008. "Connotations et double jeu des mots, ou comment ne pas perdre le(s) sens de l'humour en traduction". *Équivalences* 35 (1–2): 103–125. https://www.persee.fr/doc/equiv_0751-9532_2008_num_35_1_1433)

Propuesta de traducción de «Un couteau dans la poche»

Esmeralda Vicente Castañares
Departamento de Lenguas Modernas y Literaturas Comparadas,
Universidad de Extremadura

> This work undertakes a proposal of translation into Spanish of the short story "Un couteau dans la poche" of Philippe Delerm's book *La première gorgée de bière et autres plaisirs minuscules*, (Gallimard, 1997). We consider Javier Albiñana's 1998 translation while contemplating an option of translation prioritising Cultural Competence (Neubert, 2000). We contrast both translations in order to contribute to highlight P. Delerm's work in Spanish and Latin American Literary Systems. We update the status of the issue about interculturality and adaptation. We conclude finding interesting that revision of J. Albiñana's translation will contribute to the OT temporary adaptation.
>
> **Keywords:** interculturality, translation strategies, adaptation, literary translation, French literature

1. Introducción

Planteamos en este estudio una propuesta de traducción sobre un relato corto del libro de relatos de Philipe Delerm ya mencionado, que entendemos no ha tenido la trascendencia que merecería a nivel de reescritura, adaptación, retraducción, ya que no ha sido traducido desde 1978 en que se realizó la primera traducción por parte de Javier Albiñana. Ello nos llevará a revisar algunas de las corrientes y escuelas de traducción más relevantes en los últimos tiempos, sus enfoques respecto a la relación canon-traducción, así como a intentar poder dilucidar el porqué de este limitado interés de la Institución y el Mercado (véase Even-Zohar, 1979 y 1990) en el Sistema Literario español y latinoamericano por esta obra de Philipe Delerm. De igual modo, consideraremos los planteamientos de otros autores en materia de interculturalidad, interpretación textual, adaptación y competencia traductora, para de este modo poder abordar la mencionada propuesta

https://doi.org/10.1075/ivitra.45.11cas
© 2025 John Benjamins Publishing Company

como un ejercicio traductológico sujeto a mejora, del mismo modo que nosotros expondremos nuestras propias observaciones sobre la traducción anterior de Javier Albiñana.

2. Traducción literaria, canon, interculturalidad y adaptación

En lo relativo al estado de la cuestión de la traducción literaria en relación con el canon, la interculturalidad, la competencia traductora y adaptación, así como la necesaria implicación de todas ellas en la tarea traductora, rexaminaremos algunos autores de entre aquellos que nos han servido como referencia para establecer nuestras propias conclusiones al respecto. Ana Mª González Álvarez (2012) hace un recorrido por las distintas escuelas que han investigado en los diversos ámbitos relacionados con el proceso traductor, sus campos de influencia y sus resultados, de entre los que destacamos, por acercarse más a nuestros tiempos, y tener una especial preponderancia en los estudios posteriores la Escuela de la Manipulación, la Escuela de Göttingen, los estudios cognitivos y la introducción de la TAO en el siglo XX y XXI:

> En los años setenta, las investigaciones de índole descriptiva de la Escuela de la Manipulación tomarán en cuenta los factores comunicativos, normativos y sociológicos implicados en la traducción literaria a lo largo de la historia, mediante el estudio comparado de traducciones con sus respectivos textos originales. Ello nos ha encaminado a cuestionar algunos conceptos tradicionales teóricos e ideológicos que han impregnado la concepción de la traducción literaria, como la noción de autoría, equivalencia, traducibilidad o norma. [...] Los trabajos posteriores de la Escuela, principalmente los que transcurren en los años 90 y basados en el estudio del mecenazgo y las instituciones implicadas en la traducción literaria y su lectura canónica, son de relevancia para el desarrollo de la competencia social del traductor en el aula en relación con el mercado y su diálogo con los otros actantes del proceso (cf. Lefevere, 1992). Paralelamente a estos trabajos descriptivos, cabe destacar las investigaciones sobre traducción literaria realizadas por la Escuela de Göttingen (cf. Schulze, 1987, entre otros autores), las cuales pueden igualmente aportar indicios interesantes sobre las normas y recepción histórica de algunas traducciones literarias. A finales de los 80, Lörscher critica la tendencia generalizada de que la mayoría de los modelos metodológicos no dan cuenta de la realidad psicológica de la traducción [...] (1989,64), [...]. Por ello, urge la necesidad de incorporar métodos y modelos procedentes de la psicología cognitiva que describan adecuadamente la relación entre mente-traducción. La técnica del método de pensar en voz alta ha sido, de hecho, el método inductivo empírico-experimental más usado durante la década de los 90 para el estudio de dicha relación mente-traducción. [...] En consecuencia, se ha introducido tam-

bién el ordenador en la presente década. Su función consiste en medir ciertas variables procedimentales y temporales. [...] El grupo PACTE de Barcelona, por ejemplo, utiliza el Proxy para analizar también el comportamiento traductor y estudiar con mayor detalle la competencia traductora. [...] Existen ya bastantes trabajos que estudian con bastante viabilidad la conciencia humana (cf. Damasio, 2010), que investigan los distintos tipos de conocimientos implicados en la adquisición de la metacognición sobre una determinada actividad (Mateos, 2001; Pozo, 2006) o que aportan herramientas metodológicas interesantes para estudiar la manera como pensamos e imaginamos (cf. Fauconnier & Turner, 2002). Estas investigaciones aún no han sido incorporadas en profundidad al estudio del proceso de la traducción y, mucho menos, al estudio del proceso específico de la traducción literaria.
(González Álvarez 2012: 47–50)

Así mismo, nos ha resultado de gran interés la visión del canon expuesta por Francisco Lafarga, y en especial la referida a la influencia de las obras traducidas en el canon de un determinado Sistema Literario (véase Even-Zohar, 1979 y 1990). Precisamente, teniendo en cuenta que el auge de los estudios dedicados a la traducción toma un destacado impulso entre las décadas de los 70 y los 90, con los enfoques dados por las distintas escuelas, nos parece lógico que existiesen ciertas lagunas al respecto del estudio del canon combinado con la traducción hasta que irrumpen en la escena editorial las publicaciones de Zohar, Toury y Lefevere, entre otros autores que ponen el punto de mira en la considerable influencia que pueden ejercer las obras traducidas, adaptadas, reescritas en el canon de los Sistemas Literarios que las reciben:

El canon, [...] es una cuestión enormemente debatida en los años 1980 y 1990. [...] Menor atención crítica ha recibido la combinación canon-traducción. [...] preciso es mencionar el libro de André Lefevere Translation, Rewriting, and the Manipulation of Literary Fame, de 1992. [...] El entronque [de la denominada «teoría del polisistema» (véase Even-Zohar, 1979 y 1990)] con la idea del canon estriba en la apreciación que la literatura traducida es una literatura importada que, en determinadas circunstancias, puede llegar a imponerse o a desbancar a la literatura propia («original» o tradicional), convirtiéndose así en canónica o modélica [unido a] la idea del papel de la institución — o del poder — en la regulación de los trasvases literarios y culturales, sobre el que insistió el citado Lefevere, está en relación con algunos mecanismos de canonización en los que se halla presente la traducción. [Por ejemplo] [...] la presencia de la cultura francesa en España en el siglo XVIII [...], que va más allá de lo literario, [...] fue constante en la segunda mitad del citado siglo y primeros años del siguiente [...]. Obviamente, la traducción y las traducciones contribuyeron eficazmente a la difusión y el asentamiento (lo que Iriarte denominó «connaturalización») en España de autores, obras y géneros literarios llegados de Francia. Aceptando, pues, que esa notable presencia existe, preciso será demostrar cómo la traducción contribuyó poderosamente a afianzar modelos canónicos en la época, mientras que — paralelamente — dejó de contribuir a la fijación de otros modelos.

(Lafarga 2017: 904-906)

Evidentemente, en tanto que traductores, hemos de admitir a su vez, que no siempre vamos a tener la suerte de abordar un texto en el que la experiencia vital pueda suponer un plus que nos ayude a sumergirnos por completo en la *supuesta otra cultura*. En esos múltiples casos, habremos de estar ciertamente atentos a nuestro espectro conocido y desconocido del amplio margen de estudio que abarca la interculturalidad, es decir a nuestra propia competencia en materia teórica de interculturalidad y adaptación aplicable a la traducción. Para ello, sí puede resultarnos de utilidad tener en cuenta reflexiones como las expresadas por Albrecht Neubert quien ya en el 2000 incluye la Competencia Cultural en la Competencia Traductora:

> There are roughly five parameters of translational competence, viz. (1) language competence, (2) textual competence, (3) subject competence, (4) cultural competence, and, last but not least, (5) transfer competence. It is precisely the interplay of these kinds of competence that distinguishes translation from other areas of communication. (Neubert 2000: 6)

Si lo que buscamos es cómo conjugar interculturalidad y traducción, las palabras de Fernando Limón Aguirre al respecto, en su artículo «Interculturalidad y traducción. Retos al entendimiento y la comunicación», nos dan una idea de lo que podría suponer esta fusión para los traductores convertida en *experiencia utópica*:

> Al interesarse uno en la temática de la interculturalidad y mayormente al pretender involucrarse en una actividad tendente a realizarla, debe uno primero pensar y reconocer cuál es su propia experiencia, su conocimiento, su imaginario y sus deseos al respecto. ¿Cómo ha estado constelada mi experiencia al respecto: cuáles han sido mis convivencias con otras culturas, qué conflictos o dificultades personales o sociales han marcado esta experiencia, qué reglas y leyes la intentan orientar y contener, qué mensajes se transmiten en los medios, qué formación se me ha dado y qué cotidianeidad de relaciones multiculturales alimento?

(Limón Aguirre 2013: 93)

Así como Philippe Delerm, el autor del TO que presentamos en este estudio, habla en su texto de la mera satisfacción que produce tocar una navaja, abrirla y cerrarla, porque esa acción automáticamente evoca un pasado contemplativo, feliz y despreocupado de la infancia; el abordar esta traducción estaría muy cerca para nosotros de lo que Paul Ricoeur define como traducción intercultural: «una noción del traducir que se vincula con la felicidad que procura la posibilidad de comunicación con el otro», (Ricoeur 2005: 10).

En uno de sus epígrafes, dedicado a «Los problemas de recepción de las obras literarias traducidas.», Salud María Jarilla Bravo expone, al tratar la adaptación, las reescrituras y la recepción de las obras literarias, algunos de los condicionantes a que éstas suelen verse expuestas tanto en sus Sistemas Literarios (véase Even-Zohar, 1979 y 1990) de origen como de llegada, que nos remiten a la reivindicación que quisiéramos hacer con este artículo, sobre el olvido por parte de los Sistemas Literarios español y latinoamericano de las reescrituras del libro de relatos de Philippe Delerm, *La première gorgée de bière et autres plaisirs minuscules* (Gallimard, 1997):

> Así pues, generalmente, las normas y las reglas impuestas por el momento histórico y el sistema literario, en el cuál ha quedado incrustada una traducción, han sido determinantes y concluyentes a la hora de encumbrar o condenar un determinado trabajo […]
> Ahora bien, la mayoría de las veces, cuando encontramos una obra denominada canónica, lo que realmente apreciamos y valoramos es su trasgresión a la norma, al horizonte de expectativas. La mayoría de las veces estamos frente a obras que rompieron con la normativa vigente y generaron nuevos modelos de referencia.
> (Jarilla Bravo 2021: 150–151)

Por ello, al toparnos en su día con este relato «Un couteau dans la poche» (1997) de Philippe Delerm, sobre el que trabajamos en este artículo, y al retomar ahora su lectura y reescritura con nuestra propuesta de traducción, quisiéramos que otros críticos, investigadores, y todo el gran entramado que forman los Sistemas Literarios español y latinoamericano viese de nuevo en este libro de relatos un potencial del canon literario de las reescrituras en español, digno de ocupar la parte central de los mencionados Sistemas.

3. Corpus

Componen nuestro corpus el texto original ya mencionado *La première gorgée de bière et autres plaisirs minuscules*, de Philippe Delerm, publicado por Gallimard en 1997, en la colección L'arpenteur, y concretamente su primer relato: «Un couteau dans la poche», su traducción del original francés al español, realizada en 1998 por Javier Albiñana, publicada por Tusquets, e igualmente mencionada con el título «Una navaja en el bolsillo», así como la propuesta de traducción de dicho relato que presentamos aquí con idéntico título: «Una navaja en el bolsillo» (2023).

4. Motivaciones para retraducir «Un couteau dans la poche»

¿Qué razones nos mueven a retraducir el relato corto «Un couteau dans la poche» de Philippe Delerm? En nuestro caso no se ha producido ningún encargo editorial que haya movilizado tal tarea. Sin embargo, sí confluyen en la decisión misma de acometerla otros dos móviles que entendemos la justifican: por un lado, la distancia temporal hallada entre la única traducción al castellano existente hasta la fecha del libro completo de Philippe Delerm : *La première gorgée de bière et autres plaisirs minuscules*, realizada por Javier Albiñana en 1998, con el título *El primer trago de cerveza y otros pequeños placeres de la vida* (1998, Tusquets Editores) «Una navaja en el bolsillo», por otro lado, un móvil únicamente personal de admiración y atracción por esta obra, y, más concretamente, por el relato corto en cuestión, al realizar nuestra primera lectura del texto original, que consigue llevarnos a una infancia rural conocida, en la que encontramos una destacada cercanía cultural con el narrador del relato.

5. Procedimiento y metodología seguidos

Tras aquella primera lectura que nos descubre tanto al autor como la fascinación por esta obra, hemos realizado, posteriormente, varias lecturas sosegadas del texto original. A continuación, hemos desarrollado una Propuesta de traducción en la que, como receptores, hemos valorado posibles interpretaciones del relato, teniendo en cuenta que nos enfrentamos a una lectura culturalmente diacrónica: ¿atenderíamos a un texto que narra una historia vivida por el autor?, ¿querría P. Delerm describir un posible tándem abuelo-nieto de la época?, ¿podría tratarse de un homenaje al abuelo Opinel (de la marca de cuchillos y navajas Opinel) así como a los creadores e impulsores de la marca Laguiole? O... ¿se trataría de una posible combinación de todas estas hipótesis? Así, siguiendo a Gadamer, «*El comprender debe pensarse menos como una acción de la subjetividad que como un desplazarse uno mismo hacia un acontecer de la tradición, en el que el pasado y el presente se hallan en continua mediación*» (Gadamer, Agud Aparicio, de Agapito 1977:360). Hemos querido dejarnos sumergir con este relato por unos instantes en ese pasado rememorado en el relato de Delerm para contribuir a traerlo al presente de otros posibles receptores. Seguidamente, hemos pasado a una confrontación analítica en tabla comparativa de los tres textos. Es en este momento cuando nos vamos a la traducción de Javier Albiñana. En una primera fase, a hacer una primera lectura de su traducción. Seguidamente, a observar cómo ha resuelto él los propios problemas con que nosotros nos hemos encontrado, así como a leer sus propios comentarios a su propia traducción y la crítica publicada sobre la misma. A continuación, establecemos comparaciones y tratamos de determinar cuáles de sus soluciones nos han parecido más adecuadas que aquellas por las que nosotros hemos optado y viceversa. Hemos vuelto a releer nuestra traducción haciéndonos un replanteamiento de la misma observando de nuevo los tres textos. Hemos adoptado algunas expresiones que hemos considerado interesantes de la traducción realizada por Albiñana y hemos continuado puliendo nuestra propia versión. Tras lo cual hemos expresado las conclusiones presentadas en el artículo.

6. La traducción de Javier Albiñana, *El primer trago de cerveza y otros pequeños placeres de la vida* (1998, Tusquets Editores)

Indudablemente, toda vez que decidimos acometer la reescritura de un texto se nos imponen diversas tareas. Una de ellas es tratar de conocer las posibles traducciones, en este caso en castellano, realizadas hasta la fecha, de la obra que nos proponemos traducir. Tras leer la traducción de Albiñana ya aludida, hemos consultado los siguientes trabajos críticos: reseña de Alejandra Montoro y Amelia Ros, «El primer trago de cerveza», publicada en la revista *Hieronymus Complutensis*, (Montoro, Ros s.f.: 147–148), así como los comentarios del propio Javier Albiñana sobre su labor traductora en el relato de Philippe Delerm, publicados en la revista *Vasos comunicantes: revista de ACE Traductores*, vol. 12,: «El primer trago de cerveza, la traducción y otros pequeños placeres de la vida» (Albiñana Serain 1998–1999: 110, 112).

Ofreceremos nuestro propio parecer al respecto de la traducción de Javier Albiñana integrado en la confrontación de los tres textos que presentamos en este estudio.

7. Propuesta de traducción (2022) «Un couteau dans la poche» (1997) de Philippe Delerm y análisis comparativo con la traducción de J. Albiñana (1998)

En este análisis comparativo entre los tres textos presentados nos centraremos directamente en secciones del relato en que hemos podido encontrar mayores divergencias entre los distintos escritos. Además, para ordenar nuestro trabajo y favorecer así mismo el acceso directo al cotejo de cada texto seguiremos estas pautas nominativas: (TO) para referirnos al relato de Philippe Delerm, (T3) para nuestra propuesta de traducción del (TO), y (T2) para nombrar la traducción de Javier Albiñana.

La posición en que aparecen los textos en las tablas que siguen, obedece al método establecido para el tratamiento de las obras, ya expuesto en el apartado dedicado a la metodología. Por ello, encontramos primero el (TO), seguido de nuestra propuesta de traducción (T3) y finalmente la traducción de Javier Albiñana (T2). Porque como comentábamos en el procedimiento utilizado para abordarlos, aparecen aquí en el orden en que nosotros mismos hemos accedido a ellos como lectores o traductores de los mismos.

El relato escogido para esta propuesta de traducción y su cotejo con la traducción de Javier Albiñana es el primero del libro *La première gorgée de bière et autres plaisirs minuscules*, de Philippe Delerm. El autor probablemente rememora una infancia feliz a través de la figura de un abuelo y su omnipresente navaja. A continuación, presentamos varias tablas comparativas con los tres textos, tras las cuales abordaremos el estudio de los mismos.

Tabla 1. Análisis comparativo: (TO), (T3), (T2)

	(TO) de Philippe Delerm: *La première gorgée de bière et autres plaisirs minuscules* (1997, Gallimard) «Un couteau dans la poche»	(T3) Nuestra propuesta de traducción: «Una navaja en el bolsillo» (2023)	(T2) Traducción de Javier Albiñana: *El primer trago de cerveza y otros pequeños placeres de la vida* (1998, Tusquets Editores) «Una navaja en el bolsillo»
Opción A	*Pas un couteau de cuisine, évidemment, ni un couteau de voyou à cran d'arrêt. Mais pas non plus un canif. Disons, un opinel nº 6, ou un laguiole. Un couteau qui aurait pu être celui d'un hypothétique et parfait grand-père.*	*No un cuchillo de cocina, evidentemente, ni una navaja de bandido. Pero tampoco una sirla. Digamos una opinel nº6 o una laguiole. Una navaja que habría podido ser la de un hipotético y perfecto abuelo.*	*Está claro que ni es un cuchillo de cocina, ni un quitapenas de golfo. Pero tampoco una navajita. Pongamos que un Opinel del 6, o un Laguiole. Una navaja que perfectamente hubiera podido ser la de un hipotético y cabal abuelo,*

Nada más empezar a leer el texto de Albiñana, nos sorprende la amplificación que ha hecho de la oración inicial con la expresión aclaratoria que entendemos innecesaria (T2) *está claro que*. Para la época en que se fecha su traducción, 1998, es decir, hace 24 años, entendemos que casan bien el término (T2) *quitapenas*, asociado, además, al de (T2) *golfo*. En la segunda oración ya traduce (TO) *un canif* por (T2) *navajita*. No entendemos, entonces, por qué en la tercera oración ha utilizado el género gramatical masculino para seguir y decir (T2) *un Opinel del 6* y (T2) *un Laguiole*. En la primera oración del texto, nos puede parecer comprensible que use el género gramatical masculino, ya que Philippe Delerm en el texto original quiere dejar claro desde la primera línea que no va a hablar de un cuchillo. De hecho, nos parece que Javier Albinaña en esta primera oración ha encajado de manera interesante la concordancia con el género gramatical masculino introducido por el término (T2) *cuchillo de cocina* al usar la expresión (T2) *quitapenas de golfo* continuando en esta oración con el género gramatical masculino. Ahora bien, una vez que Philippe Delerm ha dejado claro en el (TO) que no se trata de un cuchillo sino de una navaja, no entendemos por qué en la tercera oración, Javier Albiñana no usa ya directamente el término *navaja*, y sigue, sin embargo, aferrándose al vocablo *cuchillo*. Máxime cuando en la cuarta oración, él mismo va a venir ya a utilizar finalmente el término navaja.

Sí nos parece factible el que J. Albiñana (T2) haya nombrado las navajas en mayúscula, aunque en el (TO) vengan en minúscula. Nosotros (T3) también hemos usado la minúscula, entendiendo que si en lo que el autor quiere centrarse es en tratar de acercar a los lectores a un contexto de la niñez, merced al niño/a grande que supuestamente relata recuerdos de la infancia, es quizá más probable que su evocación sea de observación visual de los movimientos del abuelo con las navajas más que de la denominación de las navajas per se. Así, estos recuerdos atenderían con mayor probabilidad al carácter oral que al escrito, por lo que el uso de la mayúscula no habría sido relevante para escribir un relato que se centraría, en gran parte, en la expresión corporal y en lo que los objetos en sí transmiten como remembranza.

Nos parece interesante la traducción de *parfait* (TO) por *cabal*, en lugar de la literal (T3) *perfecto* que habíamos utilizado nosotros en principio, y nos planteamos incorporarla a nuestra traducción. La ampliación (T2) *perfectamente* que quizá busca darle mayor verosimilitud a la historia nos parece aceptable.

Para la oración del (TO) *Un couteau qu'il aurait tiré de sa poche à l'heure du déjeuner*, en nuestra traducción hemos optado por la omisión del pronombre sujeto. Omisión frecuente tanto en la lengua hablada como escrita en castellano, (T3) *Una navaja (*) que habría sacado del bolsillo*, ya que hay suficiente contexto anterior que permite esa omisión, y en español sonaría redundante. Mientras que Albiñana ha optado por la ampliación al sintagma nominal (T2) *el abuelo*, que vemos como una posible opción. En el caso del (TO) *à l'heure du déjeuner*, nosotros hemos optado por reducir la expresión a (T3) *a mediodía*, en cambio Albiñana ha preferido mantener el calco (T2) *a la hora de la comida*.

Para el (TO) *piquant les tranches de saucisson avec la pointe, pelant sa pomme lentement*, en el caso del gerundio (TO) *piquant*, nosotros hemos optado por usar el infinitivo (T3) *para pinchar / pelar*, que es más corriente que el gerundio, que sí se usa más frecuentemente en francés, tanto para el ejemplo del salchichón como para el de la manzana. Por el contrario, Albiñana prefiere mantener el gerundio (T2) *hincando / pelando*. En este fragmento hemos omitido una coma que hemos

Tabla 2. Análisis comparativo: (TO), (T3), (T2)

	(TO) de Philippe Delerm : *La première gorgée de bière et autres plaisirs minuscules* (1997, Gallimard) « Un couteau dans la poche »	(T3) Nuestra propuesta de traducción: «Una navaja en el bolsillo» (2023)	(T2) Traducción de Javier Albiñana: *El primer trago de cerveza y otros pequeños placeres de la vida* (1998, Tusquets Editores) «Una navaja en el bolsillo»
Opción A	*Un couteau qu'il* aurait glissé dans un pantalon de velours chocolat à larges côtes. Un couteau qu'il aurait tiré de sa poche *à l'heure du déjeuner, piquant* les tranches de saucisson avec la pointe, *pelant* sa pomme lentement, le poing *replié à même la lame.*	Una navaja que *él* habría deslizado en un pantalón marrón de pana gorda y patera ancha. Una navaja que (*) habría sacado del bolsillo a mediodía, *para pinchar* las lonchas de salchichón con la punta (*) *y pelar* tranquilamente una manzana, con el puño replegado *sobre el propio filo.*	(*) *Que éste* se hubiera metido en el pantalón de pana de canalillo ancho color chocolate. Una navaja que *el abuelo* se hubiera sacado del bolsillo *a la hora de la comida, hincando* la punta en las rodajas de salchichón, *pelando* lentamente una manzana, *con* el puño replegado *sobre la hoja.*

sustituido por el conector copulativo *y*. Sustituimos así mismo el posesivo francés *sa* por el determinante artículo del objeto: *la/una manzana*: (T3) (*) *y pelar tranquilamente una manzana*.

Con el (TO) *le poing replié à même la lame*, en esta ocasión, tanto Albiñana como nosotros hemos ampliado la estructura con la preposición *con* al inicio: (T2) *con el puño replegado sobre la hoja //* (T3) *con el puño replegado sobre el propio filo*, sin la cual, entendemos que el extracto quedaría en cierta forma incompleto en español. Además, en nuestro caso, hemos interpretado el (TO) *replié à même la lame* como (T3) *sobre el propio filo*.

El empleo de la palabra (T2) *ademán*, en el texto de Albiñana, que haciendo uso de la variación le imprime un registro formal realzado por la inversión (T2) *con amplio y ceremonioso ademán*, que le da un carácter poético, nos parece excesivamente culto para reescribir este texto que entendemos se circunscribe, más bien, en un registro estándar.

Este relato da una relevancia suma a la expresión corporal y vivencias del abuelo. La forma de beber el café es uno de esos ejemplos. Muchos cafeteros, al acudir al bar o a la cafetería, eligen el café *bebido en vaso*. Esta forma de tomarlo es en sí misma un ritual. No lo saborean igual si no está servido así. Nosotros usamos, por tanto, esta expresión (T3) *café bebido en* (*) *vaso*, omitiendo el pronombre indefinido *un*, ya que entendemos que en un registro estándar correspondiente al utilizado en el (TO), no sería necesario, por tanto, el uso de este pronombre.

Tabla 3. Análisis comparativo: (TO), (T3), (T2)

	(TO) de Philippe Delerm : *La première gorgée de bière et autres plaisirs minuscules* (1997, Gallimard) « Un couteau dans la poche »	(T3) Nuestra propuesta de traducción: «Una navaja en el bolsillo» (2023)	(T2) Traducción de Javier Albiñana: *El primer trago de cerveza y otros pequeños placeres de la vida* (1998, Tusquets Editores) «Una navaja en el bolsillo»
Opción A	Un couteau qu'il aurait refermé d'un geste ample et cérémonieux, après le café bu dans un verre -et cela aurait signifié pour chacun qu'il fallait reprendre le travail.	Una navaja que habría vuelto a cerrar con un gesto amplio y ceremonioso, después del *café bebido en vaso* -y eso *sería la señal de que* había que volver al trabajo.	Una navaja que hubiera cerrado *con amplio y ceremonioso ademán*, tras *tomarse el café en un vaso* — y eso hubiera significado *para los allí presentes* que había que volver al trabajo.

Para el extracto del (TO) -*et cela aurait signifié pour chacun qu'il fallait reprendre le travail,* nosotros hemos empleado la omisión (T3) -*y eso sería la señal (*) de que,* porque comprendemos que está implícito en el mensaje evocado por el extracto completo lo que Albiñana explicita en su traducción con la amplificación (T2) *para los allí presentes.*

Tabla 4. Análisis comparativo: (TO), (T3), (T2)

	(TO) de Philippe Delerm : *La première gorgée de bière et autres plaisirs minuscules* (1997, Gallimard) « Un couteau dans la poche »	(T3) Nuestra propuesta de traducción: «Una navaja en el bolsillo» (2023)	(T2) Traducción de Javier Albiñana: *El primer trago de cerveza y otros pequeños placeres de la vida* (1998, Tusquets Editores) «Una navaja en el bolsillo»
Opción A	Un couteau que *l'on* aurait trouvé merveilleux si *l'on était enfant* : un couteau pour l'arc et les flèches, pour *façonner* l'épée de bois, la *garde* sculptée dans l'écorce — le couteau que vos parents trouvaient trop dangereux quand vous étiez *enfant*.	Una navaja que *nos* habría parecido maravillosa *siendo niños*: una navaja para el arco y las flechas, para *tallar* la espada de madera, *la guarnición* esculpida en la corteza — la navaja que nuestros padres juzgaban demasiado peligrosa cuando éramos *críos*.	Una navaja que para *un niño* hubiera sido maravillosa: una navaja para *confeccionar* el arco y las flechas, para *tallar* la espada de madera, *la empuñadura* esculpida en la corteza — la navaja que a nuestros padres les parecía demasiado peligrosa cuando éramos *críos*.

Para traducir *on*, en el (TO) *Un couteau que l'on aurait trouvé merveilleux si l'on était enfant*, en (T3) mantenemos la coherencia con el resto de nuestra propuesta, utilizando el plural, como hemos hecho en lo que precede de traducción. En el caso de Albiñana, observamos que en esta ocasión usa el singular (T2) *un niño*.

En el extracto del (TO) *un couteau pour l'arc et les flèches*, nosotros hemos decidido mantener una traducción literal (T3) *una navaja para el arco y las flechas*, mientras que Albiñana ha preferido ampliarlo insertando el verbo (T2) *confeccionar*, que no vemos necesario, pues nuevamente, dicho acto va implícito en el mensaje.

Nos parece del todo pertinente el empleo de (T2) *tallar* utilizado por Albiñana para (TO) *façonner*, que hemos incluido en nuestra traducción, que habíamos elaborado en un principio como (T3) *dar forma a*.

Sin embargo, hemos encontrado un posible error de Albiñana al traducir (TO) *la garde sculptée dans l'écorce* por (T2) *la empuñadura esculpida en la corteza*. Ya que (TO) *garde* se referiría a (T3) *guarnición*, que es la parte de la espada que protege la mano: *partie entre manche et lame* (https://www.wordreference.com/fres/garde). Dado que, los niños y niñas no podrían hacer una empuñadura con la corteza, al ser demasiado blanda para este fin. Aunque sí podría servirles en sus juegos de espada, utilizada como tal, sin manipulación alguna, para simular una guarnición protectora de la mano, una vez han empuñado la espada, que como nos dice el autor está hecha de madera. Al igual que comentamos con respecto al uso del verbo *tallar* por parte de Albiñana, en el caso de la traducción de (TO) *quand vous étiez enfant.*, por (T2) *cuando éramos críos.*, nos parece que refleja bastante bien ese posible momento de la infancia, y que está acorde con el registro del (TO) y, por ello, la adoptamos también para nuestra traducción, en la que habíamos optado, en un principio, por el vocablo común *niños*.

Con respecto a la estructura del (TO) *l'on n'est plus… l'on n'est plus*, nosotros (T3) hemos mantenido el calco, mientras que Albiñana ha preferido la fórmula (T2) *ni estamos… ni somos ya*. Nosotros (T3) mantenemos coherentemente el uso del plural como en apariciones anteriores del pronombre *on*, mientras que Albiñana (T2), que en otras ocasiones ha preferido el uso del singular, esta vez también se decanta por el plural.

En el siguiente fragmento, Philippe Delerm quiere recalcar el carácter imprescindible de la navaja como herramienta de trabajo, tal como lo fue y sigue siéndolo en ciertos contextos, como, por ejemplo: la agricultura y ganadería de alta montaña y minifundio, la pesca, etc.

Tanto Albiñana como nosotros, al traducir del (TO) *-Mais si, ça peut servir à plein de choses*, hemos omitido el pronombre sujeto *eso* que no es imprescindible en castellano, mientras que sí lo es en francés: (T3) *-Pero sí, (*) //* (T2) *-Pues claro,*

Tabla 5. Análisis comparativo: (TO), (T3), (T2)

	(TO) de Philippe Delerm : *La première gorgée de bière et autres plaisirs minuscules* (1997, Gallimard) « Un couteau dans la poche »	(T3) Nuestra propuesta de traducción: «Una navaja en el bolsillo» (2023)	(T2) Traducción de Javier Albiñana: *El primer trago de cerveza y otros pequeños placeres de la vida* (1998, Tusquets Editores) «Una navaja en el bolsillo»
Opción A	Mais un couteau pour quoi ? Car *l'on n'est plus* au temps de ce grand-père, *et l'on n'est plus enfant*. Un couteau virtuel, alors, et cet alibi dérisoire :	¿Pero una navaja para qué? porque *ya no estamos* en la época de aquel abuelo, *y ya no somos niños*. Una navaja virtual, entonces, y esa excusa ridícula:	Pero una navaja ¿para qué? Porque *ni estamos* en los tiempos de ese abuelo, *ni somos ya niños*. Una navaja virtual, entonces, con esta irrisoria coartada:

Tabla 6. Análisis comparativo: (TO), (T3), (T2)

	(TO) de Philippe Delerm : *La première gorgée de bière et autres plaisirs minuscules* (1997, Gallimard) « Un couteau dans la poche »	(T3) Nuestra propuesta de traducción: «Una navaja en el bolsillo» (2023)	(T2) Traducción de Javier Albiñana: *El primer trago de cerveza y otros pequeños placeres de la vida* (1998, Tusquets Editores) «Una navaja en el bolsillo»
Opción A	- *Mais si*, ça peut servir à plein de choses, *en promenade, en pique-nique,* même pour bricoler quand on n'a pas d'outil...	- Pero sí, (*) puede servir para muchas cosas, de paseo, *de picnic*, incluso para hacer bricolaje cuando no se tienen herramientas...	*Pues claro, (*) si* puede servir *para la tira de cosas, para un paseo, una excursión al campo,* hasta para hacer un apaño cuando no tienes a mano otra herramienta...

(*) si. Sin embargo, la diferencia entre ambas traducciones estriba en que Albiñana ha querido subrayar la afirmación presente en el énfasis inicial introducido en el (TO) -*Mais si*, amplificando además con (T2) *(*) si puede servir para la tira de cosas*.

En (T3) Hemos utilizado el préstamo *pícnic*, del inglés *picnic* por estar ya muy introducido en nuestra lengua y cultura.

Para traducir el fragmento del (TO) *on le sent bien*, Albiñana ha optado por omitir el pronombre sujeto (T2) *(*) No servirá*. Por otro lado, ha hecho una traducción más formal que nosotros del (TO) *on le sent bien*, que además ha ampliado con el uso del conector copulativo *y*, (T2) *y nos consta*. Nosotros,

Tabla 7. Análisis comparativo: (TO), (T3), (T2)

	(TO) de Philippe Delerm : *La première gorgée de bière et autres plaisirs minuscules* (1997, Gallimard) « Un couteau dans la poche »	(T3) Nuestra propuesta de traducción: «Una navaja en el bolsillo» (2023)	(T2) Traducción de Javier Albiñana: *El primer trago de cerveza y otros pequeños placeres de la vida* (1998, Tusquets Editores) «Una navaja en el bolsillo»
Opción A	Ça ne servira pas, on le sent bien. Le plaisir n'est pas là. Plaisir absolu d'égoïsme : une belle chose inutile de bois chaud ou bien de nacre lisse, avec le signe cabalistique sur la lame qui fait les vrais initiés : une main couronnée, un parapluie, un rossignol, l'abeille sur le manche.	Eso no servirá, lo sabemos de sobra. El placer no está ahí. Es un placer puramente egoísta: una bonita cosa inútil de madera cálida o bien de nácar liso, con el signo cabalístico sobre el filo propio de auténticos iniciados: una mano coronada, un paraguas, un ruiseñor, la abeja sobre el mango.	(*) No servirá, y nos consta. El placer que le vemos no es ése. Se trata de un placer pura y absolutamente egoísta: un hermoso objeto inútil de cálida madera o de liso nácar, con ese signo cabalístico en la hoja que marca la impronta de los auténticos iniciados: una mano con corona, un paraguas, un ruiseñor, la abeja en el mango.

siguiendo la coherencia de mantener un registro sencillo, hemos utilizado la expresión (T3) *lo sabemos de sobra*.

En el caso del fragmento del (TO) *Le plaisir n'est pas là*, nosotros hemos utilizado el calco (T3) *El placer no está ahí*, mientras que Albiñana ha amplificado este fragmento con la expresión (T2) *que le vemos*, dándole, nuevamente, un tono más formal al relato.

Para el siguiente fragmento, si Delerm utiliza una nominalización (TO) *Plaisir absolu d'égoïsme*, nosotros, si bien, en principio habíamos optado por el calco (T3) *Placer absoluto de egoísmo*, finalmente, en (T3) hemos ampliado la expresión con el verbo *ser* y el pronombre indefinido *un*, pues entendíamos que podía ayudar a la comprensión textual: (T3) *es un placer puramente egoísta*.

No vemos necesaria la primera amplificación de Albiñana (T2) *Se trata de*. La segunda amplificación (T2) *pura y absolutamente egoísta*, nos resulta un poco larga, aunque interesante, si bien le da un tono más formal que el que entendemos muestra el (TO). Por ello decidimos tomar el adverbio y utilizar una transposición en nuestra propuesta, aunque siendo más conservadores que Albiñana, cambiamos únicamente el adjetivo por un adverbio: (T3) *es un placer puramente egoísta*.

En este complicado extracto del (TO) *une belle chose inutile de bois chaud ou bien de nacre lisse*, Albiñana decide volver a aplicar dos inversiones (T2) *un hermoso objeto inútil de cálida madera o de liso nácar*, que le dan un tono poético y formal que entendemos no tiene el (TO) aunque reconocemos resuelve el galimatías presente en la expresión.

Al final, nuestra versión de esta expresión del (TO) *une belle chose inutile de bois chaud ou bien de nacre lisse*, quedaría como: (T3) *un trasto pulido de madera cálida o bien de nácar liso*.

Philippe Delerm nos acaba de dar los primeros indicios de los tipos de navajas a los que se refiere, si bien será en el fragmento que ahora pasamos a comentar donde ya entre más de lleno en materia con la expresión (TO) *avec le signe cabalistique sur la lame qui fait les vrais initiés*. Nosotros hemos resuelto el extracto (TO) *qui fait*, con la expresión breve (T3) *propio de*. Nuevamente, Albiñana ha preferido una amplificación utilizando (T2) *que marca la impronta de*.

En el fragmento que sigue, el autor desvela, por fin, completamente, cuáles son esos signos cabalísticos que nos confirmarán que se trata de navajas Opinel y Laguiole: (TO) *une main couronnée, un parapluie, un rossignol, l'abeille sur le manche*.

Tabla 8. Análisis comparativo: (TO), (T3), (T2)

	(TO) de Philippe Delerm: *La première gorgée de bière et autres plaisirs minuscules* (1997, Gallimard) «Un couteau dans la poche»	(T3) Nuestra propuesta de traducción: «Una navaja en el bolsillo» (2023)	(T2) Traducción de Javier Albiñana: *El primer trago de cerveza y otros pequeños placeres de la vida* (1998, Tusquets Editores) «Una navaja en el bolsillo»
Opción A	Ah oui, le snobisme est savoureux quand il s'attache à ce symbole de vie simple. A l'époque du fax, *c'est le luxe rustique. Un objet tout à fait à soi*, qui gonfle inutilement la poche, et que *l'on sort* de temps en temps, jamais pour *s'en servir*, mais pour le toucher, le regarder, pour la satisfaction benoîte de l'ouvrir et de le refermer.	Oh sí, el esnobismo es atractivo cuando va ligado a este símbolo de vida sencilla. En la época del fax, *es el lujo rústico. Un objeto propio*, que abulta inútilmente el bolsillo, y que *sacamos* de cuando en cuando, nunca para utilizarlo, sino para tocarlo, mirarlo, por la plácida satisfacción de abrirlo y cerrarlo.	Sí, el esnobismo resulta atractivo cuando va ligado a ese símbolo de *la* vida sencilla. En la época del fax, *es un lujo rústico. Un objeto totalmente personal*, que abulta inútilmente el bolsillo, y que sacamos de cuando en cuando, nunca para utilizarlo, sino para tocarlo, mirarlo, por la bobalicona satisfacción de abrirlo y cerrarlo.

En este caso, Albiñana elide el intensificador presente en el (TO) *Ah oui,* reduciendo a (T2) *Sí,*. Mientras que en el caso del (TO) *ce symbole de vie simple,* prefiere añadir el artículo determinado *la*: (T2) *ese símbolo de la vida sencilla.*

Nosotros entendemos que cuando Delerm usa en el (TO) el determinante artículo *le* para referirse a *luxe rustique* es porque quiere concretar. Por ejemplo, si poseer un *Ferrari* o un *Masserati* va socialmente asociado a un lujo *chic*, en el relato, el autor querría presentarnos la contraposición a ese lujo *chic*, que según su concepción de la vida sería el lujo *rústico*. Por ende, ser poseedor de una Opinel o una Laguiole, no es que sea para él *un lujo rústico*, es que es, nada más y nada menos, que *el lujo rústico* per se. Esta valoración de este fragmento del (TO) es la que nos lleva a nosotros a mantener en nuestra propuesta de traducción el artículo determinado *el* para: (T3) *el lujo rústico*.

Una vez presentadas las navajas, Delerm va imprimiéndole al relato *un plus d'attachement à l'objet* y a lo que representa: (TO) *Un objet tout à fait à soi,* que nosotros hemos vertido como (T3) *Un objeto propio,* y Albiñana (T2) *Un objeto totalmente personal.*

Volvemos a utilizar coherentemente el plural para *on* (T3) *y que sacamos de cuando en cuando.* En el caso de la última parte de este fragmento del (TO) *jamais pour s'en servir, mais pour le toucher, le regarder, pour la satisfaction benoîte de l'ouvrir et de le refermer,* tanto nosotros como Albiñana, hemos decidido invertir el adjetivo calificativo que acompaña a *satisfaction* al ser más usado en este orden en la Lengua Meta: (T3) *por la plácida satisfacción de abrirlo y cerrarlo*// (T2) *por la bobalicona satisfacción de abrirlo y cerrarlo.*

Albiñana habría decidido darle cierto aura poético al invertir el verbo y el sujeto en este primer fragmento (T2) *En ese presente gratuito duerme el pasado.* Una inversión que no está presente en el original y que nosotros hemos trasladado con un calco.

Creemos que la expresión del (TO) *Dans ce présent gratuit le passé dort,* nos invita a vivir ese *présent gratuit,* y que, por ello, no deberíamos dejarlo escapar -como creemos que hace Albiñana traduciendo el (TO) *Quelques secondes* por (T2) *A los pocos segundos,* sino más bien, aprovechar el instante en que Delerm nos sumerge en la memoria con (T3) *Durante unos segundos.*

Para trasladar este extracto del (TO) *Quelques secondes on se sent à la fois le grand-père bucolique à moustache blanche et l'enfant près de l'eau dans l'odeur du sureau,* en (T3) si por coherencia semántica mantenemos el plural para la traducción de *on* usamos también el plural para *abuelos bucólicos* y tenemos la opción de dejar en singular *bigote blanco* pero decidimos usar también el plural para *enfant*: (T3) *Durante unos segundos nos sentimos a la vez abuelos bucólicos con bigote blanco y niños cerca del agua oliendo el saúco.* Para verter al castellano el sintagma preposicional (TO) *dans l'odeur du sureau,* que, ciertamente, se nos

Tabla 9. Análisis comparativo: (TO), (T3), (T2)

	(TO) de Philippe Delerm : *La première gorgée de bière et autres plaisirs minuscules* (1997, Gallimard) « Un couteau dans la poche »	(T3) Nuestra propuesta de traducción: «Una navaja en el bolsillo» (2023)	(T2) Traducción de Javier Albiñana: *El primer trago de cerveza y otros pequeños placeres de la vida* (1998, Tusquets Editores) «Una navaja en el bolsillo»
Opción A	Dans ce présent gratuit le passé dort. *Quelques secondes* on se sent à la fois le grand-père bucolique à moustache blanche et l'enfant près de l'eau *dans l'odeur du sureau.*	En ese presente gratuito el pasado duerme. Durante unos segundos nos sentimos a la vez abuelos bucólicos con bigote blanco y niños cerca del agua oliendo el saúco. El tiempo de abrir y volver a cerrar la hoja, ya no estamos entre dos épocas, sino que somos dos épocas -ése es el secreto de la navaja.	En ese presente gratuito duerme el pasado. *A los pocos segundos* nos sentimos a un tiempo el bucólico abuelo de blancos mostachos y el niño que juega junto al agua en medio de un olor a saúco.

resistía, lo hemos transpuesto en un sintagma verbal (T3) *oliendo el saúco*. En este caso hemos recurrido a sustituir la estructura preposicional *dans l'odeur* por el gerundio *oliendo*, para intentar escenificar esa envoltura ambiental que entendemos quiere reflejar Delerm con la expresión (TO) *dans l'odeur du sureau*, dándonos como resultado la expresión (T3) *oliendo el saúco*.

En este caso, dada la dificultad que encontramos para trasladar el ambiente que evoca la expresión (TO) *dans l'odeur du sureau*, vemos muy adecuada la solución encontrada por Albiñana con la amplificación (T2) *en medio de un olor a saúco*.

Llegamos así al final del relato, y apenas en media docena de palabras, la mínima reducción de un haiku, se nos desvela en ese *presente gratuito*: *le secret du couteau*. Si hemos alcanzado a sumergir nuestra memoria en esos *quelques secondes* del fragmento anterior… entonces ya hemos atravesado la barrera mental del secreto.

Una vez más, en (T3) mantenemos la coherencia con el resto de nuestra propuesta de traducción utilizando el plural para traducir *on* en (TO) *on n'est plus* por (T3) *ya no estamos*. Así mismo, nos parece importante mantener el calco (T3) *El tiempo*, para (TO) *Le temps*, porque como acabamos de evocar en la presentación de este último fragmento, aquellos *quelques secondes*, mencionados en el fragmento anterior, entendemos que guardan una relación estrecha con esta otra expresión *le temps*, y con la siguiente que aparece aquí: (TO) *on n'est plus entre deux âges, mais à la fois deux âges -c'est ça, le secret du couteau.*

Tabla 10. Análisis comparativo: (TO), (T3), (T2)

	(TO) de Philippe Delerm : *La première gorgée de bière et autres plaisirs minuscules* (1997, Gallimard) « Un couteau dans la poche »	(T3) Nuestra propuesta de traducción: «Una navaja en el bolsillo» (2023)	(T2) Traducción de Javier Albiñana: *El primer trago de cerveza y otros pequeños placeres de la vida* (1998, Tusquets Editores) «Una navaja en el bolsillo»
Opción A	*Le temps* d'ouvrir et refermer la lame, *on n'est plus entre deux âges, mais à la fois deux âges -c'est ça*, le secret du couteau.	*El tiempo* de abrir y volver a cerrar la hoja, *ya no estamos entre dos épocas, sino que somos dos épocas — ése es* el secreto de la navaja.	*Con sólo* abrir y cerrar la hoja, *no somos ya de mediana edad sino que tenemos dos edades a la vez: en eso radica* el secreto de la navaja

En (T2) Albiñana vuelve a recurrir a la amplificación con la expresión *en eso radica*, que no vemos necesaria para explicar el contexto, que queda ya bastante claro si se observa el resto del contexto. Vuelve a darle al relato un tono más formal que, como ya hemos comentado anteriormente, no vemos que tenga el (TO).

8. Conclusiones

Si la novela lleva siglos estando en la cresta de la ola de los cánones literarios de los Sistemas Literarios de medio mundo, no deberíamos olvidar a pioneros y pioneras del relato corto que terminaron abriendo la llave al género de la novela. Sin embargo, en tiempos del hipertexto, pensamos que la literatura canónica, y géneros como el relato corto, dejados por un tiempo a un lado tras el fulminante éxito de las novelas por entregas hasta ocupar el género novela en su conjunto un reinado canónico casi absoluto a lo largo del siglo XX, ha llegado el momento de darle a las creaciones de relatos cortos el esplendor que merecen en el canon, si los Sistemas Literarios quieren mantenerse en pie frente a la fulminante oferta del hipertexto, en ese misterioso y paradójico monstruo de creación y destrucción masiva que es Internet. Al proyectar la propuesta de traducción presentada en este trabajo, hemos sido conscientes de la escasa repercusión del libro de relatos de Philippe Delerm, *La première gorgée de bière et autres plaisirs minuscules* (Gallimard, 1997) como reescritura en el Sistema Literario español, hecho que quisiéramos poner de manifiesto, y que esperamos este estudio contribuya a revelarlo.

En lo que respecta al tratamiento dado por cada una de las traducciones presentadas, exponemos, en resumen, lo observado a lo largo del análisis realizado. Creemos que resulta forzado darle un tono poético a golpe de sintaxis a un fragmento cuando no lo tiene, del mismo modo que resulta sumamente importante intentar captar su esencia poética cuando sí la tiene. Entendemos que esta esencia poética que Albiñana intenta imprimir al relato en buena parte de su traducción no siempre está presente en el (TO). Sin embargo, sí la vemos necesaria en la parte final, como ya hemos comentado con la relación poético-temporal existente a partir del fragmento: *dans ce présent gratuit le passé dort*. En (T3) procuramos mantener a lo largo de nuestra propuesta de traducción una coherencia con el uso de *on* manteniéndonos en el uso del plural. Utilizamos un registro menos formal y creemos que más cercano al (TO). En (T2), Albiñana, practica cierto vaivén con el uso de *on*. Utiliza un registro más formal que el (TO), con técnicas recurrentes de amplificación, ampliación, inversión.

Funding

Este estudio ha recibido una ayuda del Fondo Europeo de Desarrollo Regional Una manera de hacer Europa, Junta de Extremadura, Consejería de Economía, Ciencia y Agenda Digital. Grupo de Investigación HUM008 – CILEM.

Referencias

Albiñana Serain, Javier. 1998–1999. «El primer trago de cerveza, la traducción y otros pequeños placeres de la vida.» *Vasos comunicantes: revista de ACE Traductores*, Talleres: Francés-castellano 12:110–112.

Delerm, Philippe. 1997. *La première gorgée de bière et autres plaisirs minuscules*. Paris: Gallimard.

Delerm, Philippe. 1998. *El primer trago de cerveza y otros pequeños placeres de la vida*. Translation from French of Javier Albiñana. Barcelona: Tusquets.

Even-Zohar, Itamar. 1979. «Polysystem Theory.» *Poetics Today* 1: 287–310.

Even-Zohar, Itamar. 1990. «Polysystem Studies.» *Poetics Today* 11:1.

Gadamer, Hans-Georg. 1977. *Wahrheit und Methode: Grundzüge einer philosophischen Hermeneutik*, Tübingen: J.C.B. Mohr (Paul Siebeck), 1960. *Verdad y método: fundamentos de una hermenéutica filosófica*. Translation to Spanish of Ana Agud Aparicio and Rafael de Agapito. Salamanca: Sígueme.

González Álvarez, Ana María. 2012. «La didáctica de la traducción literaria, estado de la cuestión.» *Teoría de la Educación. Educación y cultura en la sociedad de la información* 13 (1): 40–89. Electronic version: ⟨https://www.redalyc.org/articulo.oa?id=201024387003⟩

Jarilla Bravo, Salud María. 2021. Adaptación y reescritura. La traducción literaria en español. Gabriele d'Annunzio y el Triunfo de la muerte. Madrid: UAM. Departamento de Filología Española. Unpublished doctoral thesis. Electronic version: ⟨http://hdl.handle.net/10486/684143⟩

Lafarga, Francisco. 2017. «La traducción, impulso y freno del canon: España, Francia y el siglo XVIII.» *Arte Nuevo. Revista De Estudios Áureos* 4: 903–920

Limón Aguirre, Fernando. 2013. «Interculturalidad y traducción. Retos al entendimiento y la comunicación.» *TINKUY*, Section d'Études hispaniques 20:92–100.

Montoro, Alejandra; Ros, Amelia. n.d. «El primer trago de cerveza», reseña, *Hieronymus Complutensis* Centro Virtual Cervantes 8:147–148.

Neubert, A. 2000. «Competence in language, languages, and in translation.» In *Developing translation competence*, ed. by Christina Schäffner, and Beverly Adab, 3–18. Birmingham: Aston University.

Ricoeur, Paul. 2005. *Sobre la traducción*. Translation and prologue of Patricia Wilson. Buenos Aires: Paidós.

Vicente Castañares, Esmeralda. 2023. Propuesta de traducción: «Una navaja en el bolsillo.» (2022) de Philippe Delerm : *La première gorgée de bière et autres plaisirs minuscules* (1997, Gallimard) « Un couteau dans la poche ». Unpublished translation.

"La Loba" irrumpe
La presentación del personaje en algunas traducciones al español y al catalán del relato de Giovanni Verga. Reflexiones y una nueva propuesta

Helena Aguilà Ruzola
Universitat Autònoma de Barcelona

The present paper focuses on the analysis of the translation of various excerpts of Giovanni Verga's short story "La Lupa" (1880), concerning the introduction of the protagonist. These specific fragments imply difficulties due to the knowledge of specific cultural references or peculiar semantic loads which have to be reconstructed starting with the "Sicilianity" of the original text. The translations under investigation are those of José Abad Baena (2011) and those of Paloma Alonso (2017), both into Spanish, and the translation into Catalan by Rosa M. Pérez Fuster and Xavier Lloveras (1990). Moreover, this study provides a new proposal for a Spanish translation, which will be concluded by the end of 2024.

Keywords: Verga, La Lupa, literary translation, Sicilian, *verismo*

1. "La Loba" en su campo entre Italia y España

El cuento "La Lupa" forma parte de la recopilación de relatos de Giovanni Verga (Catania, 1840-1922) *Vita dei campi*, publicada en 1880 por la editorial milanesa Treves y cuyo rasgo más destacado es, como indica el mismo título, la ruralidad, que incluye una honda y genuina sicilianidad presente en los entornos descritos y en el carácter y la conducta de los personajes, así como en determinados aspectos lingüísticos. Las tramas de los relatos son siempre el reflejo de grandes pasiones, grandes vicios encarnados por los protagonistas, víctimas o verdugos en un contexto y una realidad social cuyos errores e injusticias se muestran de un modo pesimista, descarnado, fatalista. Todos estos elementos se adscriben a la corriente literaria italiana del *verismo*, deudora del naturalismo francés, de la que Verga fue uno de los máximos exponentes a partir de la publicación del mencionado volumen. Característico de dicho movimiento es también el uso de un estilo indirecto libre regido por el principio de impersonalidad que persigue el narrador, quien desea contar los hechos con objetividad y dejar que sea el lector quien juzgue por sí mismo (cf. Guglielminetti 2007). Con el mismo fin, el narrador emplea lo que ha dado en llamarse el "artificio de la regresión", técnica mediante la cual prescinde del registro culto que le es propio con el objeto de desaparecer tras un registro coloquial y popular, dentro del cual salpica la lengua italiana de vocablos, giros y proverbios sicilianos que pretenden ser un fiel reflejo del habla de sus personajes, aunque a menudo los italianiza para facilitar su comprensión, o los transforma ligeramente para adaptarlos a su relato (cf. Bottari 2020).

Es fácil intuir que los rasgos descritos han de plantear algún que otro quebradero de cabeza a todo traductor que se proponga trasladar a su lengua materna cualquiera de las narraciones del libro, y el caso de la que nos ocupa no es una excepción. Las traducciones que he elegido como objeto de estudio del presente trabajo son la de José Abad Baena (2011) y la de Paloma Alonso (2017), ambas al español, así como la traducción al catalán de Rosa M. Pérez Fuster y Xavier Lloveras (1990). En las tres, "La Loba", o "La Lloba", forma parte de una recopilación de relatos que no corresponde a la totalidad de la original, *Vita dei campi*.[1] Sus respectivos títulos y cubiertas dan pistas relevantes sobre la recepción de la obra verguiana en España que sugieren: el título del volumen de Abad Baena, *Cavalleria rusticana*, en lengua original, corresponde en realidad a uno de los relatos y, sin duda, es utilizado como reclamo por resultar familiar al lector español gracias a la ópera del mismo nombre; lo sigue un subtítulo, "y otros cuentos sicilianos", que, unido a la imagen de la cubierta, un mapa de la isla, subraya el carácter sículo del libro. El título de la traducción de Alonso, que reza simplemente *Historias sicilianas* y va acompañado de la imagen de un paisaje isleño, resalta la misma idea. Ya he aludido a la profunda sicilianidad de los relatos; sin embargo, cuando se trata del texto traducido, el hecho de remarcar dicho carácter aun antes de abrir el volumen parece responder a una voluntad de avisar a los lectores de que van a adentrarse en un contexto ajeno, en unas páginas ambientadas en Sicilia, y de pedirles que realicen un esfuerzo de contextualización. No sé hasta qué punto tal prevención puede ser un acierto, pues deja entrever una interpretación en exceso local y limitada de los textos de Verga, que no por ser muy sicilianos dejan de plasmar conflictos, personajes y sentimientos de alcance universal. Limitada es también, en el sentido de parcial, como he dicho, la traducción que ambos libros ofrecen

---

1. Un cuadro completo de las traducciones al español y al catalán de la obra en el catálogo de traducciones españolas de obras italianas hasta 1939 del *Proyecto Boscán*. Las traslaciones posteriores a esa fecha pueden localizarse en la *Base de datos de libros editados en España*.

de *Vita dei campi*, y otro tanto puede decirse de la versión catalana, si bien en esta aparece el vocablo *selecció* entre paréntesis en la cubierta, mediante el cual se indica con claridad que se trata de una antología de la obra original. Además, el título catalán, *Vida dels camps*, es el único de los aquí examinados que ofrece una traducción literal del italiano.

A continuación, cotejaré algunos pasajes emblemáticos del TO con las tres traslaciones citadas, a lo cual añadiré una nueva propuesta de traducción, resultado de un proyecto compartido con la colega Giorgia Marangon, de la Universidad de Córdoba, que verá la luz próximamente y que consiste en la traducción íntegra, con introducción y notas, de *Vita dei campi*. Una iniciativa surgida de la intención y necesidad de ofrecer al lector hispanófono un TM más acorde a la forma y el contenido del original, reescrito con criterios modernos, fruto de prolongadas reflexiones y de una mirada al TO en la que prime el rigor filológico sin renunciar a transmitir en la medida de lo posible la frescura, la sensibilidad y la poética de la narrativa verguiana. Una tarea compleja en la que hemos procurado aunar nuestros conocimientos teóricos y prácticos en el ámbito de la traducción, la filología, la literatura y la crítica con el fin de conseguir un resultado que aporte herramientas para una recepción nueva, más comprensible y comprendida, de la obra de Verga en España.

2. La mujer bestia entra en escena

"La Lupa" es un cuento basado en un suceso de crónica negra que el autor conoció a través del gran teórico del *verismo* Luigi Capuana, quien le contó la historia de una "sciagurata madre adultera" de su pueblo cuyos tintes trágicos Verga creyó percibir luego, durante un baile en aquellos parajes, cuando tuvo la sensación de ver como si las tuviera delante "le fosche figure di quel dramma fosco" (Verga 1991: 8–9). A partir de esos hechos, ideó y construyó una narración breve que cosechó un gran éxito desde el principio, lo cual propició que años más tarde la convirtiera en una pieza teatral del mismo título, estrenada en 1896. Y lo cierto es que el cuento ha seguido suscitando interés y siendo objeto de adaptaciones teatrales y cinematográficas hasta nuestros días (cf. La Magna 2010). El relato incluido en *Vita dei campi* se caracteriza por un ritmo veloz y esencial, con una alternancia entre la recreación en detalles elocuentes e ilustrativos y el recurso a elipsis sumamente efectivas, pues, como afirmaba el propio Verga en la famosa dedicatoria a Salvatore Farina que abre "L'amante di Gramigna", otro cuento del mismo libro, no es necesario explicitarlo todo; por eso habla sólo de "il punto di partenza e quello d'arrivo, e per te basterà, e un giorno forse basterà per tutti" (Verga 1996: 202). Con su técnica innovadora, el autor aspira a que su obra parezca "*essersi fatta da sé*, aver maturato ed esser sorta spontanea come un fatto naturale, senza serbare alcun punto di contatto col suo autore" (Verga 1996: 203). Así, el relato, cuyo trasfondo cada vez más teñido de negro hace presagiar lo peor, avanza deprisa a lo largo de sus cuatro secuencias narrativas, que, como señala Marangon (2019: 224), son: "il ritratto iniziale della Lupa, l'innamoramento, l'amore incestuoso tra genero e suocera, la morte/sacrificio che ristabilisce l'ordine delle cose".

A continuación, entramos en la parte más sustancial del presente trabajo, dedicada al cotejo entre algunos pasajes centrados en la presentación de la protagonista en el TO y en los TM seleccionados. Y, como no podía ser de otro modo, en primer lugar, nos detendremos en el inicio de la primera secuencia, el célebre *incipit* que constituye el retrato de la Loba, un personaje icónico, que desafía los cánones. Su descripción física, que incluye rasgos de la personalidad de una mujer peligrosa, inmoral, que tiene algo de bruja, que pertenece al lado de lo demoníaco, lo bestial, corresponde a cuanto piensan y dicen de ella los vecinos de la aldea, constituidos en una especie de voz coral, de expresión del sentir de una sociedad que la rechaza.

> Era alta, magra, aveva soltanto un seno fermo e vigoroso da bruna e pure non era più giovane; era pallida come se avesse sempre addosso la malaria, e su quel pallore due occhi grandi così, e delle labbra fresche e rosse che vi mangiavano.
> (Verga 1996: 197)

El texto posee un tono coloquial, expresivo, colorido, es armonioso y eufónico. Tomemos en consideración la primera frase, hasta el punto y coma. Abad Baena la traslada así:

> TRAD. JOSÉ ABAD BAENA (JAB): Era alta, delgada, y no tenía más que un pecho firme y vigoroso de mujer morena. Ni siquiera era joven.

Una especie de hipertraducción, diría yo, en la que se añade el sustantivo "mujer", innecesario y de pobre efecto, y en la que una cualidad física de la protagonista, que tenía el pecho firme pese a no ser joven, pasa a ser la única cualidad que poseía esta mujer que "ni siquiera era joven", oración remarcada artificiosamente por el punto que la precede.

Alonso, por su parte, traduce así:

> TRAD. PALOMA ALONSO (PA): Era alta y delgada, pero tenía los senos firmes y vigorosos de la mujer morena y eso que ya no era joven.

Sustituye la coma por la conjunción copulativa ("era alta y delgada"), lo cual acaba con el ritmo de la frase original, utiliza un "pero" para marcar la oposición entre la delgadez y el hecho de tener los pechos "vigorosos" y, al igual que Abad, añade el sustantivo "mujer", precedido además por el artículo. La última frase es, a mi entender, la más atinada, pues con el "y eso que ya no era joven" la traductora reproduce tanto el sentido como el registro coloquial del TO.

Los traductores al catalán dicen:

> TRAD. ROSA M. PÉREZ FUSTER & XAVIER LLOVERAS (RPF & XL): Era alta, prima; només tenia uns pits durs i forts de morena i a més ja no era jove.

Resuelven mejor que los anteriores la cuestión del registro y el ritmo y aciertan al escribir solo "morena"; sin embargo, eliminan el valor adversativo del *e pure* original al traducirlo por "i a més" ('y además').

Por nuestra parte, al traducir el *incipit* hemos intentado reproducir hasta donde nos ha sido posible la cadencia y el registro del TO.

> TRAD. HELENA AGUILÀ RUZOLA & GIORGIA MARANGON (HAR & GM): Era alta, delgada, sólo que tenía un pecho firme y vigoroso de morena sin ser ya joven.

Avancemos ahora hasta la palabra *così* (*era pallida come se avesse sempre addosso la malaria, e su quel pallore due occhi grandi così*). Abad Baena traduce:

> TRAD. JAB: Era pálida como si sufriera permanentemente de malaria y, sobre esa palidez, tendía dos ojos así de grandes.

El primer problema lo plantea el "era", ya que, si concebimos la palidez como un estado, en español debería expresarse mediante el verbo 'estar', aunque aquí se hable de una condición permanente, como tiene a bien remarcar el traductor con ese adverbio que rompe la armonía de la frase, por su longitud y por la aliteración de nasal que produce junto a "malaria". Todo ello precedido del "sufriera", elección que eleva el registro y lo aleja sin remedio del empleado en el TO. Por último, también resulta llamativa la preposición "sobre", algo forzada en español y que parece un intento de traducción literal del *su* italiano.

Veamos el TM de Paloma Alonso:

> TRAD. PA: Era pálida, como si llevara siempre la malaria encima, y en aquella palidez dos ojos enormes.

Al igual que Abad Baena, opta por el uso discutible del verbo 'ser' en vez de 'estar', pero, a diferencia de aquel, intenta mantenerse en un registro cercano al del TO en la frase sobre la malaria, tan próximo que recurre casi a la literalidad y escribe una frase que resulta ajena al español o, cuando menos, muy poco natural. Llevar encima la malaria no funciona, es un intento fallido de traducir el *addosso*. Alonso acierta, en cambio, en la preposición, "en aquella palidez", pero vuelve a distanciarse del registro verguiano al trasladar el giro coloquial *grandi così* por "enormes".

Los traductores al catalán optan por esta solución:

TRAD. RPF & XL: Estava pàl·lida com si sempre tingués la malària, i sobre aquella pal·lidesa dos ulls aixi de grossos.

Son los únicos que utilizan el verbo "estar", aunque quizá no acabe de cuadrar por el hecho de mantener el adverbio "siempre" en la misma posición que en el TO, alejado del verbo 'ser' y referido a la malaria, colocación que en el texto italiano carga las tintas sobre lo enfermizo de dicha palidez y que no crea problemas con el verbo por no existir en dicha lengua nada semejante a nuestra diferenciación entre 'ser' y 'estar'.[2] Por otra parte, Pérez y Lloveras, al igual que Abad Baena, se exceden con la preposición al traducirla como "sobre".

En nuestro caso,

TRAD. HAR & GM: Siempre estaba pálida, como si tuviera la malaria, y en aquella palidez dos ojos así de grandes,

hemos apostado por la naturalidad en español, por crear unas frases que suenen tan espontáneas y populares como las que escribió Verga, de modo que hemos preferido usar el verbo 'estar' y trasladar el adverbio a la posición más habitual en nuestra reescritura, una colocación menos sorprendente que la del TO, aunque, en el fondo, ese "siempre" impregna también el inciso acerca de la malaria.

Analicemos ahora la última frase del *incipit* del relato (*e delle labbra fresche e rosse che vi mangiavano*). Observemos conjuntamente la traducción de Abad Baena y la versión en catalán:

TRAD. JAB: y labios frescos y rojos, que te comían
TRAD. RPF & XL: i uns llavis frescos i vermells, que se't menjaven

Curiosa y desafortunada la decisión de Abad Baena de prescindir de un determinante para labios, pero centrémonos en la última frase, ese *vi mangiavano* a medio camino entre lo que vendría a ser una forma impersonal, cuando menos en el plano semántico, y un apóstrofe al lector, en el que se usa la forma de cortesía *voi*, que podría ser tanto singular como plural. La solución no es fácil: vemos aquí que Abad y los traductores catalanes optan por una segunda persona del singular, un 'tú' que ciertamente es de uso habitual en español y en catalán en sentido impersonal, pero que se distancia de la forma de cortesía italiana y que desentona en el texto, máxime cuando en ambas traducciones el *voi* se traduce correctamente por las respectivas formas de cortesía en otros pasajes del relato.

---

2. Las analogías y diferencias entre el uso de los verbos 'ser' y 'estar' en italiano, español y catalán son una cuestión compleja que no puede tratarse aquí; baste señalar que, pese a las divergencias existentes entre su empleo en las dos LM, en el caso que nos ocupa lo correcto en ambas sería utilizar 'estar'.

Veamos ahora la opción de Alonso y la nuestra:

TRAD. PA: y unos labios frescos y rojos que se lo comían a uno vivo
TRAD. HAR & GM: y unos labios frescos y rojos que se lo comían a uno

Le dimos muchas vueltas a la frase hasta dar con el uso de la forma impersonal "a uno", que resuelve la cuestión: es natural en español y evitamos el problema del tratamiento, pues, si por un lado, como hemos visto, la traducción "que te comían" resulta errónea, debo admitir que, por otro, habría resultado muy forzado traducir, por ejemplo "que se lo comían a usted". Además, en el "se lo comían a uno" no se pierde esa especie de apóstrofe al lector al que me refería, pues la expresión no deja de involucrar al público en la descripción de los ojos de la protagonista y sus efectos. En cuanto a la frase de Alonso, descubrí que también había optado por traducir "a uno" cuando empecé a preparar el presente trabajo (pues mi colega y yo nos habíamos impuesto no consultar las traducciones anteriores mientras trabajábamos en nuestro texto para no dejarnos influenciar por ellas), y en ese instante sentí una afinidad con nuestra predecesora que acto seguido se vio empañada por el adjetivo "vivo" que ella añadió y que, si bien corresponde a una expresión común en español, en mi opinión causa un efecto casi hilarante que arruina el dramatismo pasional del TO.

3. En el nombre de la Loba

Drama y pasión, sí. La Loba, descrita y señalada por todos como un ser excesivo, sensual y pecaminoso, debe tal apodo a su insaciabilidad. De hecho, el término *lupa* "rimanda direttamente al modo di dire siciliano *aviri la lupa* che significa 'divorare', 'avere gran fame'" (Marangon 2019: 227), referencia perteneciente al acervo popular sículo que convive inevitablemente con el eco de otra *lupa*, esta vez de carácter literario y panitaliano: la del Infierno dantesco, símbolo de la concupiscencia. La mayoría de lectores de los TM no poseen estos referentes culturales; pese a ello, el nombre de la Loba o de la Lloba también los remitirá a imágenes de voracidad, fiereza y oscuridad que casan a la perfección con el retrato de la protagonista, cuyo nombre real es Pina. En la segunda secuencia del relato, así se dirige a ella por primera vez Nanni, el joven del que se ha enamorado: "O che avete, gnà Pina?" (Verga 1996: 198).

La palabra *gnà* significa 'señora' y procede del español "doña", pero es un tratamiento que se utilizaba en Sicilia para las mujeres de las clases populares (cf. Treccani). Veamos cómo queda reproducido en las distintas traducciones.

TRAD. JAB: ¿Qué le pasa, Doña Pina?
TRAD. PA: "¡Eh! ¿Qué le pasa, señá Pina?".
TRAD. RPF & XL: —Però què us passa, Pina?
TRAD. HAR & GM: —¿Qué le pasa, señá Pina?

Pese al origen del término, y habida cuenta del uso que se le daba en Sicilia, resulta del todo inadecuada la traducción de Abad Baena, puesto que "doña" en español está reservado para personas de alto rango. Enseguida se nos ocurrió la traducción "señá", forma sincopada de 'señora' con cierta tradición en la novela realista española más o menos contemporánea de Verga y empleada igualmente para reproducir el habla popular; más tarde, al preparar estas páginas, descubrí que Alonso había elegido la misma palabra. En cuanto a Pérez y Lloveras, optan aquí por eliminar el tratamiento, una estrategia de lo más pobre que contrasta con otras soluciones mucho más inspiradas que estos traductores ofrecen en no pocas ocasiones.

Lo que le pasa a la señá Pina, alias la Loba, es que suspira por Nanni. En un principio, este la rechaza, pues prefiere casarse con su hija Maricchia por motivos económicos y de estatus, deseo al que la madre accederá para poder tenerlo cerca. Así es como se fragua el triángulo incestuoso, pues el joven, una vez casado, acabará cayendo en la tentación en la tercera secuencia de la historia. A la postre, los hechos desembocarán en el desenlace trágico al que asistimos en la escena final, cuando atisbamos en toda su intensidad la negrura que impregna desde el principio la narración y nos quedamos sobrecogidos ante la elipsis en que se nos da a entender que el yerno acabará con la vida de su suegra y amante mientras esta, lejos de esforzarse por evitar el fatal desenlace, va resuelta a su encuentro, consciente, como el joven y como el lector, de que sólo la muerte puede poner punto final a tan desenfrenada pasión.

4. Arde la Loba

Volvamos sobre nuestros pasos en el relato hasta detenernos en otro pasaje, el último que examinaré, en el que se presenta un aspecto que define a nuestra protagonista. Así, para ilustrar la imagen de la Loba como mujer transgresora e independiente, que actúa y trabaja igual que un hombre y que, según el parecer tradicional, está fuera de casa cuando no debería, la voz coral de los vecinos bajo la que se camufla el narrador entona un refrán, un recurso muy propio de la narrativa verguiana, en la cual los proverbios "sintesi di una tradizione di vita familiare incontrastabile di sofferenza e di sconfitta, di espiazione per chi rompe i limiti della propria condizione, proverbi che nella loro assolutezza sono leggi cristallizzate e accoratamente accolte" (Piromalli: cap. 18)

Pues bien, el dicho en cuestión es el siguiente:

> In quell'ora fra vespero e nona, in cui non ne va in volta femmina buona, la gnà Pina era la sola anima viva che si vedesse errare per la campagna.
>
> (Verga 1996: 199)

Poco después, Nanni, al ver llegar a la Loba por enésima vez a la era con la intención de mantener relaciones con él, recita atormentado una *variatio* del proverbio:

> "No! non ne va in volta femmina buona tra vespero e nona", singhiozzava Nanni.
>
> (Verga 1996: 199)

La mujer anda con desasosiego por los campos que se describen poco más adelante en la narración, un paisaje árido, duro e inclemente que nadie más se atreve a pisar en las horas de calor intenso. Pina es un personaje errático en sentido físico, en calidad de caminante desesperada, pero también en sentido figurado, por su obsesión, por su locura de amor y deseo, por su talante osado. El uso del proverbio por parte del coro y por parte de Nanni ofrece una imagen muy potente del contraste radical entre lo que se espera de una mujer de la aldea y el temperamento de la protagonista, entre la inactividad de los aldeanos, que se refugian de las altas temperaturas, y la hiperactividad de la Loba, que arde de deseo como arden la tierra y las piedras cuando el sol está en lo más alto. Veamos primero la traducción catalana del refrán y su variación.

> TRAD. RPF & XL: En aquella hora entre vespres i nona, en què no volta cap dona bona, la Pina era l'única ànima viva que es veia errar pels camps
> —No! no volta cap dona bona a l'hora entre vespres i nona! — gemegava en Nanni

Los traductores consiguen recrear la rima, pero abusan de la repetición de fonemas y casi acaba pareciendo un trabalenguas: "nona, en què volta cap dona bona". Fijémonos ahora en el TM de Abad Baena.

> TRAD. JAB: A esa hora entre véspero y novena, cuando no sale de paseo ninguna mujer buena, Doña Pina era la única alma vagando por los campos
> —¡No! jamás sale de casa ninguna mujer buena, entre el véspero y la novena — sollozaba Nanni

El traductor complica innecesariamente la cuestión de las horas: como es sabido, según la división del tiempo diario empleada desde el Medievo en los países cristianos, cada hora o período del día estaba vinculado a un oficio religioso y recibía un nombre procedente del antiguo cómputo romano. En el proverbio aparecen dos horas: *vespero*, tras la puesta de sol, sobre las seis de la tarde, y *nona*, hacia las tres de la tarde.[3] Los respectivos nombres de dichas horas en español son habitualmente 'víspera' y 'nona', y resulta inverosímil que en un registro coloquial alguien diga "véspero" y "novena", por muy útil que resulte esta última palabra para rimar con "buena". Por otra parte, tenemos ese "no sale de paseo" que es más bien una salida de tono, porque el caminar de la Loba, lejos de ser un tranquilo paseo lúdico, constituye la manifestación, el signo del anhelo voraz de la mujer, un aullido silente que le quema la garganta como la tierra le abrasa los pies. Además, el suyo no es un errar sin rumbo, sino con un objetivo muy preciso: Nanni.

Examinemos ahora la versión de Alonso:

> TRAD. PA: En las horas que van de la víspera a la nona, en las que no hay buena mujer dando vueltas por ahí,* la señá Pina era la única alma que se veía vagabundear por el campo
> —¡No! ¡No hay mujer buena que salga a dar vueltas entre la víspera y la nona! — sollozaba Nanni

Aquí no hay nada parecido a la rima, y la traducción del proverbio es un desatino no solo por ello, sino por el "dando vueltas", una tentativa fallida de trasladar *non ne va in volta*, y por el "en las horas que van de", aclaración innecesaria y cacofónica. A continuación, el *errare* del TO se convierte en "vagabundear", otra elección desafortunada, pues las connotaciones de este verbo distan mucho del errar urgente y con meta de la Loba. Por último, cuando Nanni recita el dicho modificándolo, Alonso transforma el "dando vueltas" en "que salga a dar vueltas", lo cual empeora si cabe el efecto anterior. Tal vez la traductora justifique la falta de rima y de ritmo y el escaso rigor en la traducción por el hecho de haber incluido la siguiente nota explicativa a pie de página:

> *Viejo proverbio siciliano que se refiere a las primeras horas de la tarde en las que el sol cae a plomo y nadie se atreve a salir a la calle, que se consideran bajo el hechizo de los espíritus malignos.

La nota resulta confusa en la forma, a causa de una redacción torpe, y en el contenido, pues Alonso parece haber olvidado que, según el dicho popular incluido en el relato, son las mujeres buenas quienes no salen a la calle a esas horas y no ese "nadie" con el que engloba a ambos sexos y con el cual desvirtúa el sentido del TO, pues elimina la estigmatización de la mujer, y sólo de la mujer, que no

---

3. En puridad, el proverbio no debería aludir a la hora nona, sino a la sexta (de donde procede la palabra "siesta"), que corresponde a las doce del mediodía, pues es entre ese momento y la hora nona (15:00) cuando el calor aprieta y la gente suele descansar en el campo. Quizá Verga prefirió *tra vespero e nona* en vez de *tra sesta e nona* porque se trataba de una imprecisión introducida por la costumbre popular, algo habitual en muchos proverbios, o quizá simplemente le gustara más la sonoridad que aportaba *vespero*.

cumple el precepto, es decir, de la Loba. Por otra parte, mucho podría hablarse sobre la conveniencia de incluir o no aquí una nota, una decisión que depende de varios factores, entre los que sobresale el tipo de traducción y edición que uno se proponga ofrecer, o que a uno le hayan encargado; en cualquier caso, anotar el texto no exime al traductor de intentar dar con una traducción atinada y, por supuesto, la nota en cuestión debe proporcionar una información pertinente y acorde a cuanto se dice en el TO.

Por último, esta es nuestra traducción del pasaje:

> TRAD. HAR & GM: Entre vísperas y nona, hora en que una buena mujer por ahí no se deja ver, la señá Pina era la única alma que erraba por los llanos
> —¡No! Una buena mujer entre vísperas y nona por ahí no se deja ver — sollozaba Nanni

Hemos traducido las horas según la nomenclatura habitual en español y hemos desplazado la rima con respecto al TO, una licencia habitual en estos casos. Tras crear muchas versiones del refrán traducido, hemos optado por esta, en la que introducimos el verbo "ver", razón por la cual hemos eliminado dicho verbo en la frase que sigue al proverbio, que es donde aparecía en el original, "la gnà Pina era la sola anima viva che si vedesse errare per la campagna" y que en nuestra traducción queda así: "la señá Pina era la única alma que erraba por los llanos".

5. Las traductoras entran, no irrumpen (a modo de conclusión)

Traducir "La Lupa", o cualquier otro relato u obra verguiana, no es labor fácil. El propio Giovanni Verga era plenamente consciente de los retos que su escritura planteaba a la hora de ser traducida, tal como puso de manifiesto en la correspondencia que mantuvo con el escritor suizo Édouard Rod, su primer traductor al francés. Así, en una carta fechada en Milán el 4 de diciembre de 1881, Verga hace una serie de observaciones a Rod refiriéndose a la traducción de su novela *I Malavoglia*, en la que el suizo estaba trabajando, e incluso se ofrece a aclararle cualquier punto que no le resulte comprensible:

> Son certo che dalle sue mani escirà un lavoro perfetto per quanto le consente la diversità dell'indole delle due lingue, e la difficoltà enorme che Ella dovrà incontrare a rendere in francese uno stile che ho cercato di ridurre non solo personalmente ma possibilmente immedesimato all'argomento che si svolge in ambiente e fra personaggi assai diversi dal comune. Onde agevolare il suo compito io mi metto a sua disposizione per aiutarla in quelle parti della traduzione dove il carattere e l'indole dello stile siciliano sarebbero, non solo per lei straniero, ma anche per un italiano, di difficoltà insormontabile. [...] La prego soltanto di lasciare il

testo nella sua integrità. I tagli che ella vorrebbe fare non solo fanno sanguinare il mio cuore d'autore, ma parmi che nuocerebbero assai al libro. Sento che non ho scritto nei *Malavoglia* né un rigo, né una parola di superfluo, e faccio appello a tutta la sua buona volontà per accettarlo tale e quale è(Verga 1954: 38-39).

El párrafo está lleno de consideraciones muy dignas de ser tenidas en cuenta hoy en día al afrontar la traslación de obras de nuestro autor al español, el catalán u otras lenguas, al igual que el francés, afines a la italiana. Volviendo a la traducción de "La Lupa", cabe señalar que, si bien la presencia del *stile siciliano* es menor en este relato que en *I Malavoglia*, hay cuestiones semánticas y culturales, como hemos visto en los ejemplos examinados, que sólo pueden resolverse tras haber investigado y reconocido su origen isleño, de modo que resulta muy pertinente el comentario del autor acerca de los ambientes y personajes fuera de lo común que ha creado. En la parte final del fragmento, Verga insiste en la necesidad de que la traducción sea íntegra, sin cortes del TO, una advertencia que, en la actualidad, afortunadamente, resulta ociosa, puesto que el concepto de traducción contemporáneo no incluye semejantes licencias. Muy útil resulta, en cambio, la última aseveración, en la que Verga hace hincapié en la importancia que tienen cada línea y cada palabra de su novela y en que ninguna de ellas es prescindible, afirmación perfectamente aplicable a la narración que nos ocupa. Y es que "La Loba", en su *brevitas*, es un relato de una intensidad arrolladora, basado en un uso preciso y evocador del léxico y en la aplicación de las citadas técnicas veristas. Todo está medido: cada pausa, cada frase, cada gesto, cada imagen, cada elipsis contribuye a otorgar esa aura realista y trágica que tan bien representa la dinámica de un microcosmos y las reacciones de sus personajes, un mundo y unos protagonistas que son el producto de los usos, de las costumbres y problemáticas de su entorno, pero que, o quizá precisamente por ello, a la vez se erigen en representantes de conflictos y pasiones universales. Como traductoras, tenemos el deber de comprometernos a hacer todo lo posible por recrear ese equilibrio en el que una sola pieza fuera de lugar puede dar al traste con la armonía del conjunto.

Funding

Esta publicación es parte del Proyecto de I+D+i "Nuevo Catálogo histórico y crítico de traducciones españolas de obras italianas literarias y no literarias (1300-1939)" (referencia PID2020-118134GB-I00), financiado por MCIN/AEI/10.13039/501100011033.

Bibliografía

Base de datos de libros editados en España. ⟨https://www.culturaydeporte.gob.es/cultura/libro/bases-de-datos-del-isbn/base-de-datos-de-libros.html⟩

Bottari, Rosaria. 2020. "La lingua di Verga: Tra codice comunicativo e modello letterario". En *Italiano y español: Estudios de traducción, lingüística contrastiva y didáctica*, ed. Alicia M. López Márquez, y Fernando Molina Molina, 113–124. Berna, etc.: Peter Lang.

Guglielminetti, Marziano. 2007. *Struttura e sintassi del romanzo italiano del primo Novecento*. Vercelli: Mercurio.

La Magna, Franco. 2010. *Lo schermo trema. Letteratura siciliana e cinema*. Reggio Calabria: Città del Sole.

Marangon, Giorgia. 2019. "Una *Lupa* tra lupe. Riflessioni filologiche e traduttive nella combinazione linguistica italiano-spagnolo-francese." *Cuadernos de Filología Italiana*, 26: 221–232.

Piromalli, Antonio. *Storia della letteratura italiana*, cap. 18. ⟨http://www.storiadellaletteratura.it⟩

Proyecto Boscán. *Catálogo de las traducciones españolas de obras italianas (hasta 1939)*. ⟨http://www.ub.edu/boscan⟩

Verga, Giovanni. 1954. *Lettere al suo traduttore*, ed. Fredi Chiappelli. Florencia: Le Monnier.

Verga, Giovanni. 1990. *Vida dels camps (selecció)*, trad. Rosa M. Pérez Fuster & Xavier Lloveras. Barcelona: Diari de Barcelona.

Verga, Giovanni. 1991. *La Lupa: novella, dramma, tragedia lirica*, ed. Sarah Zappulla Muscarà. Palermo: Novecento.

Verga, Giovanni. 1996. *Tutte le novelle* [1979], introd., texto y notas de Carla Riccardi. Milán: Mondadori.

Verga, Giovanni. 2011. *Cavalleria rusticana y otros cuentos sicilianos*, trad. José Abad Baena. Barcelona: Traspiés.

Verga, Giovanni. 2017. *Historias sicilianas*, trad. Paloma Alonso. Madrid: La línea del horizonte.

Vocabolario della lingua italiana Treccani. ⟨https://www.treccani.it/vocabolario⟩

Reigen y la traducción de los referentes culturales en teatro

Elena Serrano Bertos
Departamento de Traducción e Interpretación, Universidad de Alicante

This paper addresses the translation of cultural references in dramatic literature from a double perspective: editorial translation and stage translation. In the reading and performance of a theatre play, both the channel (book/stage) and the space-time (that of each act of reading/performance) are factors that differ between both. The purpose of our paper is to analyze to what extent these factors (determined by the translation purpose, that is the editorial publication or the performance of the play) interfere in the treatment of cultural references for stage translation and editorial translation. For this aim, we will take as a model the theatre play *Reigen*, by the Austrian Arthur Schnitzler. We offer a brief theoretical framework on translation of cultural elements in theatrical texts and the characteristics of the theatrical text. The following is a comparison of the original play in German with the corresponding stage and editorial translations. This comparison allows us to observe, on the one hand, that the editorial translator employs an exoticising strategy for the translation of cultural elements. In the stage translation, on the other hand, the character of the original (Austrian) culture is maintained, but elements of the receiving culture are introduced to facilitate the understanding of the text. This apparent lack of coherence is due to the immediacy of the theatrical performance, in which the channel and space-time differ from the edited text, what determines the different translation techniques used.

Keywords: editorial translation, stage translation, cultural references, theater, Schnitzler

1. Introducción

Sabemos que la cantidad de literatura científica acerca de la traducción de referentes culturales es ingente. La celebración de seminarios y congresos, así como la publicación de las correspondientes actas, de artículos científicos y de monografías en torno a esta cuestión se remontan a comienzos de los años cincuenta y se han abordado desde diferentes ámbitos y perspectivas a lo largo de las décadas; trabajos como los de Mayoral y Muñoz (1997), Cartagena (1998), Katan (1999), Mayoral (2000) o Molina (2006) dan fe de su trascendencia.[1] Ya en el año 2000, Mayoral (2000: 67) apuntaba a las notables diferencias existentes en el plano conceptual y denominativo entre lo que cada autor o escuela sostiene que debe ser estudiado en este contexto, por lo que ya entonces, según el autor, resultaba difícil hacer nuevas aportaciones.

No obstante, el tratamiento de los culturemas en el marco de los estudios de traducción teatral merece mención aparte, también frente al campo de la traducción audiovisual, ámbito al que se ha dedicado mayor atención y con el que el teatro comparte algunas características.[2] Sin embargo, sabemos que el teatro es un género multisemiótico e híbrido, a caballo entre lo literario y lo audiovisual, y, por tanto, requiere, por sus características específicas, un tratamiento distinto también por lo que se refiere a la traducción de las distintas cuestiones culturales implicadas en el mismo. Esta necesidad de distinción es aún más notoria si sacamos a colación una de sus principales características, a saber, la dualidad del texto dramático, concebido para ser leído y para ser representado (Merino 1994). Si bien el fin último de todo texto teatral es su representación, el encargo de traducción frente a dicho tipo textual puede tener fines editoriales o bien escénicos. Uno u otro escenario podría condicionar la traducción de ciertos elementos en tanto que algunos de los factores imbricados son distintos en ambos, lo que redunda en una mayor complejidad de estudio de los procesos de manipulación textual. Entre estos elementos de análisis implicados en el estudio de una obra (no necesariamente teatral) y su correspondiente trasvase lingüístico (y que no siempre consideraron los estudios de traducción), señalaba Bassnett (1998a: 123–140) el modo en que se selecciona un texto para su traducción, el papel que desempeña el editor, los criterios que determinan las estrategias de traducción o el modo en que se recibe el texto en la cultura meta.

---

[1]. Una búsqueda en BITRA por palabra clave *cultura* arroja actualmente 2395 resultados (fecha de consulta: 11.1.2023) correspondientes a ese mismo número de artículos, capítulos, libros, revistas, etc. dedicados a cuestiones culturales en el ámbito de la traducción.

[2]. Así, pues, una nueva búsqueda en BITRA por palabras clave *cultura* y *teatro* ofrece 47 resultados, frente a los 233 que arroja la búsqueda por *cultura* y *audiovisual* (fecha de consulta: 11.1.2023). De hecho, una búsqueda en Google por las palabras clave *traducción de referentes culturales en teatro*, ofrece una mayoría de registros referidos al doblaje de series televisivas o películas como *Friends, This is us…* y pocos específicos de teatro. Esta falta de atención al teatro frente al género audiovisual podría quizás explicarse por la gran cantidad de productos audiovisuales que se importan, por ejemplo, a España frente al número de obras teatrales que, en la práctica, son traducidas.

En este contexto, nuestro trabajo tiene por objetivo analizar y cotejar el tratamiento de los culturemas en las traducciones editorial y escénica de la obra *Reigen (La Ronda)*, del austriaco Arthur Schnitzler, con el fin de arrojar luz sobre esta cuestión. Partimos de la premisa de que, más allá de los factores arriba mencionados, el canal, el espacio y el tiempo (distintos para la traducción escénica y la traducción editorial) determinarán el modo de traducción de estos elementos marcados culturalmente. En concreto buscamos analizar hasta qué punto estos tres componentes (canal, espacio y tiempo) condicionan su traducción escénica y editorial y, consiguientemente, si las estrategias y correspondientes técnicas traductológicas varían en función de uno u otro tipo de traducción. Discurriremos asimismo sobre cómo contribuyen las diferentes técnicas a la inteligibilidad del texto (o a la falta de esta) y las posibles diferencias en la creación de imágenes de la cultura origen a la cultura meta (en nuestro caso, las culturas austriaca y española, respectivamente).

Para ello, partiendo de una metodología descriptivo-comparativa, esbozaremos un breve marco teórico sobre el tratamiento que esta cuestión ha recibido en los estudios de traducción y expondremos asimismo las características del texto teatral, tomando el modelo de López Lapeña (2014), así como las diferencias existentes entre la traducción editorial y la escénica desde un punto de vista funcionalista (Serrano 2020). A continuación, procederemos al análisis de las traducciones editorial y escénica de *Reigen (La Ronda)*, por tratarse esta de una obra que está altamente marcada desde el punto de vista cultural. Para ello, extraeremos y clasificaremos los principales referentes culturales presentes en la obra y cotejaremos las estrategias y correspondientes técnicas de traducción empleadas.

2. Marco teórico

2.1 La traducción de la cultura: Traducción editorial y traducción escénica

En todo trasvase cultural, entre el universo de conocimiento del lector a quien fue dirigido el texto y el del destinatario que lo recibe en la cultura meta se produce una serie de asimetrías sistemáticas básicas en los planos lingüístico, cultural y textual, que se corresponden con los llamados anisomorfismos lingüísticos, interpretativos, pragmáticos y culturales, siendo estos últimos los referidos a los elementos culturales específicos en el discurso. Dichos elementos, independientemente de que se mantengan o no en el texto meta, nunca son iguales en traducción, lo que supone el principio fundamental por el cual se explica que un texto traducido nunca podrá ser igual que el original (Franco 2022). Sabemos que la traducción es, de hecho, considerada por autores como Reiss y Vermeer (1984) u

Oskaar (1988) como fenómenos de comunicación intercultural. En este sentido, Susan Bassnett y André Lefevere (1990) fueron pioneros en sugerir que los estudios de traducción adoptaran el *cultural turn* y se orientaran hacia el trabajo de los estudios culturales.

Existen distintas definiciones y clasificaciones de los elementos culturales (Nida 1945/1975; Vlakhov y Florin 1970; Bödeker y Freese 1987; Newmark 1988/1992; Katan 1999. En Petrescu 2011). En nuestro trabajo, partimos de la definición de Vermeer (1983: 8. En Petrescu 2011: 148), que los considera como: "un fenómeno social de una cultura A, que es considerado relevante por los miembros de esta cultura, y que, cuando se compara con un fenómeno social correspondiente en la cultura B, se encuentra que es específico de la Cultura A". De esta manera, podríamos afirmar que los referentes culturales, entre otros elementos, funcionarían como factor de encriptación del mensaje:

> No solamente las formas lingüísticas, bien deturpadas o bien estilizadas, son motivo de desautomatización (activa y pasiva, es decir, de emisión o de recepción) del lenguaje. También los contenidos y los referentes son causa de extrañamiento comunicativo. Los referentes no comunes, sino específicos de la realidad representada literariamente (en el sentido del término alemán *Darstellung*), son factores de encriptación y desautomatización que portan una carga de literariedad, sobre todo en los textos de carácter mimético, propios del historicismo, el realismo, el naturalismo o el neobjetivismo, aunque no solo.
>
> (Vega Cernuda y Serrano Bertos 2013: 1477)

Consiguientemente, el traductor actuaría como agente de *desautomatización* (en el sentido shklovskiano[3] del término). Por lo que respecta a la estrategia de descodificación de estos elementos propios de un determinado sistema cultural, de acuerdo con Espasa Borrás (2013: 326), tanto el proceso de traducción como el producto están condicionados por la función que deben cumplir el texto y la correspondiente puesta en escena en la cultura meta. En cuanto a este método, adoptamos en nuestro trabajo la distinción que propone Venuti (2008) entre domesticación y extranjerización.

De otro lado, por lo que se refiere al mencionado carácter dicotómico del texto dramático, los estudios de traducción distinguieron hace décadas entre dos estrategias de traducción dramática: estrategia de lectura (*reader oriented*) o estrategia de escenario (*performance oriented*), que, en la práctica, ha generado subtipos diversos (Lafarga 1989: 97), y que *grosso modo* recoge el binomio traducción editorial — traducción escénica. El punto de partida del traductor a la hora de abordar su labor será conocer cuál de las dos vías recorrerá el texto teatral, la edi-

---

3. Véase Shklovski 1980.

torial o la escénica, es decir, cuál es el propósito de la traducción: traducir un texto para ser leído (traducción editorial) o bien elaborar una traducción con el fin de que pueda ser representada (traducción escénica).

Si bien todo texto teatral es en esencia un texto para ser puesto en escena y, por consiguiente, la representación es su propósito o fin último, el marco comunicativo donde tiene lugar la traducción puede ser distinto y condicionar el tratamiento de algunos elementos. Como subrayábamos en la introducción de nuestro trabajo, conocer el contexto de la traducción resulta fundamental en este sentido en tanto que resulta un condicionante del proceso de traducción y del resultado final:

> Translation never takes place in a vacuum; it always happens in a continuum, and the context in which the translation takes place necessarily affects how the translation is made. Just as the norms and constraints of the source culture play their part in the creation of the source text, so the norms and conventions of the target culture play their inevitable role in the creation of the translation.
>
> (Bassnett 1998b: 93)

En la siguiente tabla analizamos las características contextuales de una y otra atendiendo al encargo o propósito de traducción. Dentro de la traducción escénica, establecemos una distinción entre la primera versión que elabora el traductor y la versión definitiva, ya adaptada por parte de los correspondientes miembros de la compañía. A la primera la hemos llamado *traducción preescénica*, y a la segunda, *traducción postescénica* (véase Serrano 2020:307).

Resultará, creemos, interesante observar en qué medida las diferencias entre dichos factores podrían determinar la traducción de los referentes culturales en los distintos tipos de traducción, en especial el canal, el espacio y el tiempo.

2.2 Características del texto dramático

Entre los géneros literarios, el teatro presenta quizás más peculiaridades propias, entre las que lo lingüístico es tan solo un elemento más. Existe en teatro una dimensión extratextual que incluye tanto componentes culturales y semióticos, como convenciones dramáticas y aspectos de la actuación y de la escenificación (Guirao 1999: 37) que el traductor teatral, consiguientemente, debe tener en consideración a la hora de desarrollar su actividad versora.

Lapeña distingue seis características referidas al texto dramático: la oralidad, la inmediatez, la multidimensionalidad, la publicidad, la teatralidad y la representabilidad (López Lapeña 2014: 153–157).

La *oralidad* se refiere a la oralidad fingida que crea el dramaturgo para dar credibilidad a los personajes o a los hechos, y se elabora a través de elementos como la fluidez, los encadenamientos, las cacofonías y eufonías, la puntuación y

Tabla 1. Diferencias entre la traducción editorial y escénica (Serrano 2020:307)

Encargo	Trad. editorial	Traducción escénica	
		Preescénica	Postescénica
Iniciador	**traductor** editor	**traductor** director empresario teatral	
Intervinientes	**traductor** editor corrector	**traductor** (con o sin pautas del director y/o empresario teatrales)	dramaturgista director ayudante de dirección asesor lingüístico **traductor** actores escenógrafo iluminación vestuario música producción espectador crítico teatral
Destinatarios	lector	director/empresario / adaptador	compañía teatral / espectador
Canal	libro	archivo (inédito)	escenario
Propósito	1º publicación (lectura) 2º posible representación	1º representación 2º posible publicación (lectura)	
Espacio-tiempo	Particular en función de cada uno de los elementos anteriores.		

los conectores o las onomatopeyas. Por su parte, la *inmediatez* viene dada por el hecho de que la representación escénica se da en un espacio-tiempo único e irrepetible. Por motivos evidentes, los espectadores no pueden intervenir en el ritmo, ni rebobinar para volver a ver una escena. Esta característica no se da, sin embargo, en la traducción editorial, en la que el lector puede releer cualquier fragmento del texto y para la que el traductor de teatro puede, además, usar la nota del traductor para aclarar algún juego de palabras o elemento cultural desconocido en la cultura de destino. Por este motivo, en la traducción escénica en ocasiones es necesario que se reemplacen unas frases por otras en aras de una mejor comprensión por parte del espectador, siempre que eso suponga una mejora para evitar "hiatos mentales" (Cantero y Braga 2011: 166). La *multidimensionalidad* tiene que ver con las tres estructuras de signos: verbal (los diálogos y los monólogos), no verbal (decoración, vestuario, maquillaje, atrezo, etc.) y cultural. Se trata de todos aquellos elementos de texto que aluden de forma más o menos directa a la cultura del autor y del TO, tales como las formas de tratamiento, el argot, los nombres propios y las referencias culturales. La *publicidad* también se refiere a la representación teatral en tanto que el teatro es un arte que requiere la copresencia del público y de los actores durante el acto de representación. Por último, la *teatralidad* es el "potencial teatral de los textos [...] la capacidad que tiene un texto dramático de generar diferentes signos teatrales" (Carvalho 2012:269. En López Lapeña 2014) y la *representabilidad*, todos aquellos elementos que permiten que un determinado texto teatral pueda ser puesto en escena.

Entre los elementos que abarca la multidimensionalidad se encuentran, pues, las referencias culturales, cuyo tratamiento en traducción teatral es objeto de nuestro trabajo, y que tienen a su vez un gran impacto en la inmediatez y la representabilidad del texto dramático, por lo que dicho tratamiento podría condicionar la recepción de la obra y del autor.

3. Análisis de traducción de los referentes culturales en *Reigen*

3.1 Metodología

La metodología empleada en nuestro trabajo es descriptivo-comparativa. Siguiendo a Toury (1980/1995), ponemos énfasis en la cultura receptora a través de un análisis empírico-descriptivo a partir del cual podamos extraer conclusiones de tipo teórico. Para llevar a cabo nuestro análisis, hemos cotejado dos traducciones de la obra *La Ronda*, una escénica y otra editorial, del austriaco Arthur Schnitzler (1862–1931), con su original *(Reigen)*.

Estamos de acuerdo con Bolaños (2016:12) cuando sostiene que, si bien no se trata de algo exclusivo del texto teatral, los referentes culturales en el teatro difieren de los de otros tipos textuales por la envergadura que tiene en este el componente no verbal: "La *mise en scène* de una obra de teatro revela que la información cultural que se transmite con información extralingüística (gestos, miradas, tono, ritmo, etc.) es incluso mayor que la que se transmite en el diálogo". No obstante, atenderemos únicamente a los aspectos lingüístico-culturales imbricados en el texto original y en las distintas prácticas de transferencia cultural.

Una vez extraídos, se expondrán según una clasificación propia atendiendo a la naturaleza de los mismos y se identificarán, siguiendo la clasificación de Venuti (2008), los métodos empleados para un tipo y otro de traducción con el objetivo de establecer el comportamiento traductor frente a estos elementos, analizar su impacto sobre la inmediatez y la representabilidad del texto y debatir sobre su funcionalidad. En último término, atenderemos a las eventuales pérdidas culturales producidas en cada traducción y a las diferentes imágenes creadas.

A continuación, indicamos los datos de las fuentes empleadas:

Traducción escénica:	Schnitzler, Arthur. (1987) *La ronda*. Barcelona: Institut del Teatre. Traducción de Carme Serrallonga y adaptación de Feliu Formosa. Todo apunta a que se trata de la traducción adaptada de que se sirvió Mario Gas para subir *La Ronda* a las tablas del Teatre Romea con la Companyia del Centre Dramàtic en 1986.[4] Por tanto, la traducción fue elaborada para la *mise en scène* de Gas y publicada con posterioridad a esta.
Traducción editorial:	Schnitzler, Arthur. (2004) *La ronda. Anatol. Ensayos y aforismos*. Madrid: Cátedra. 2ª ed. Traducción de Miguel Ángel Vega y Karl Rudolf.[5]
Texto original:	Schnitzler, Arthur. (2004) *Reigen. Liebelei*. Fráncfort del Meno: Fischer Verlag. 37ª ed. Se trata, pues, de dos traducciones procedentes de un mismo texto; la primera, con fines escénicos, se publica ya adaptada para la escena, y la segunda, para la editorial. Cabe decir en este contexto que, si bien la adaptación del texto la hace una segunda persona (en este caso, Feliu Formosa), supone también una práctica habitual encargar al traductor que él realice la adaptación de estos referentes o bien resuelva posibles juegos de palabras (entrevista realizada a Ronald Brouwer[6] 3.12.2020).

3.2 *Las referencias culturales en* Reigen (La Ronda), *de Arthur Schnitzler*

En términos generales, en toda manifestación artística y cultural, incluida la literatura, se plasman "modelos de realidad" que son genuinos de una civilización y sociedad determinadas (Petrescu 2011: 142). En este contexto, y atendiendo ahora

---

4. Datos extraídos del archivo digital histórico de los espectáculos del Teatro Romea.
5. A pesar de que las lenguas meta son distintas, el catalán y el español pertenecen a la misma familia lingüística y conviven en los teatros de aquellas comunidades autónomas españolas en las que constituyen la lengua oficial. Por este motivo ambas traducciones han sido tomadas como cala para extraer unas conclusiones aplicables a las correspondientes lenguas y culturas. Existe una grabación de *La Ronda* en español en el Centro de Documentación de las Artes Escénicas y de la Música, pero no está digitalizada, lo que no permite su reproducción (en sala ni mediante préstamo) y, consiguientemente, tampoco nos ha hecho posible el acceso a la traducción escénica. Se trata de un montaje dirigido por Javier Hernández Simón, estrenado el 10 de julio de 2009 en la sala Réplica de Madrid.
6. Ronald Brouwer es coordinador artístico del célebre teatro madrileño La Abadía.

a nuestro objeto de análisis, *Reigen,* la obra de Arthur Schnitzler más representada en España, está culturalmente muy arraigada a la época en la que se gestó, a saber, la Viena de entre siglos. Es por ello que contiene numerosos referentes culturales que, como en tantos otros casos, podrían dificultar la comprensión al espectador e interferir en la recepción:

> El valor referencial, documental y testimonial de la obra schnitzleriana inscribe al autor en la serie de autores que el crítico austriaco Egon Friedell calificó de poetas de la época, a saber, esos poetas que, frente a los 'genios milenarios', los que llenan un milenio (Dante, Cervantes, Goethe), transmiten a la posteridad, con toda la viveza de la representación literaria, el cuadro de la sociedad de la época en la que viven. [...] Sus obras son un cúmulo de datos sociológicos y de psicología humana de igual o mayor valor epistemológico que los aportados por la historia para el conocimiento de los entresijos de la época. (Vega 2004:10)

Los referentes culturales de *La Ronda* se han clasificado atendiendo a su naturaleza en antropónimos, personalidades, obras culturales y otros.[7]

3.3 Análisis de la traducción

3.3.1 *Antropónimos: Localidades, restaurantes, parques, puentes y calles*

(1) Primer ejemplo

Texto original:
DAS SÜSSE MÄDEL. Wir sind gefahren.
DER DICHTER. Ja, nach Haus — aber *in Weidling* am Bach sind wir doch drei volle Stunden herumgelaufen.

Traducción editorial:
LA MUCHACHITA INGENUA.— Sí, en coche.
EL POETA.— Para volver a casa, pero junto al arroyo, *en Weidling**, nos hemos dado un paseo de tres horas.
[*NdT: Localidad en el Wienerwald.]

Traducción escénica:
NOIETA: Hem viatjat.
ESCRIPTOR: Sí, per tornar a casa..., però *a Weidling*, ens hem passat tres hores caminant pel Prat, vora el riu.

---

7. En el presente trabajo no se han tenido en consideración las marcas dialectales y su correspondiente reproducción en español como elemento (cultural) de análisis. Consideramos que merecen atención aparte y, de hecho, existen numerosos estudios en torno a esta cuestión referidos precisamente a la traducción al español del teatro vienés (véanse al respecto los trabajos de Albaladejo 2005, 2008, 2011, 2012b y 2012b).

En el primer ejemplo, *Weidling*, localidad situada en el Wienerwald austriaco, el nombre propio se ha mantenido por no existir una traducción lingüística de este. En la traducción editorial, se añade una glosa extratextual que permite situar al lector geográficamente; en la traducción escénica, dicha información no se ofrece al espectador. Sin embargo, no es, creemos, un dato relevante que pueda afectar a la comprensión del texto (se sobreentiende que se trata de una localidad) ni el seguimiento de la obra por parte del espectador. En ambas traducciones se adopta una estrategia exotizante por la que se mantiene el escenario del original.

(2) Segundo ejemplo

Texto original:
STUBENMÄDCHEN. Es ist gar nicht so weit — *in der Porzellangasse*.

Traducción editorial:
LA CRIADA.— No está mu' lejos. *En la Porzellangasse**.
[*NdT: Calle del barrio del Augarten, en la margen izquierda del canal del Danubio]

Traducción escénica:
CAMBRERA: No gaire lluny... *Al passatge de la Porcellana*.

En el segundo ejemplo, el referente cultural es una calle vienesa. En la traducción editorial se ha traducido por repetición y, en nota a pie de página, se ofrece información sobre esta. Sin embargo, en la traducción escénica, el nombre de la calle se traduce por *passatge de la Porcellana*. Nos parece acertada esta domesticación del texto en tanto que permite al espectador conocer la naturaleza del antropónimo (si se trata de una calle, un restaurante o una localidad) y evitar al espectador un efecto de extrañamiento y pérdida de significado.

(3) Tercer ejemplo

Texto original:
DER GATTE. Jetzt sag einmal... Du hast mich schon früher bemerkt gehabt, was?
DAS SÜSSE MÄDEL. Natürlich. Schon *in der Singerstraße*.

Traducción editorial:
EL MARIDO.— Bueno, dime... ¿me habías echado el ojo antes?
LA MUCHACHITA INGENUA.— Por supuesto. Ya *en la Singerstrasse**...
[*NdT: Calle vienesa del distrito I, en la ciudad vieja, muy próxima a la catedral.]

Traducción escénica:
MARIT: Ara digues... Ja t'havies fixat en mi abans, eh?
NOIETA: És clar. *Al carrer Singer*.

El tercer ejemplo se corresponde de nuevo con el nombre de una calle y nos permite valorar la coherencia que presentan ambas traducciones. La traducción editorial ha mantenido de nuevo el nombre original y, en glosa extratextual, el traductor ofrece al lector más información sobre el referente. En la traducción escénica, sin embargo, se ha hecho una traducción lingüística por la que se informa al espectador de que se trata de una calle. Obsérvese que, en el ejemplo anterior, el traductor había hecho una traducción interlingüística del nombre de la calle.

(4) Cuarto ejemplo

Texto original:
DAS SÜSSE MÄDEL. Ja! Mit einem Buben von der Schul' vis-à-vis ist sie abends um halber acht *in der Strozzigasse* spazierengegangen. So ein Fratz!

Traducción editorial:
LA MUCHACHITA INGENUA.— ¡Fíjate! Con un chaval de la clase que vive enfrente, a las siete y media; estaban paseando *en la Strozzigasse**. ¡Qué pispajo! [*NdT: Calle de la Josefstadt, en el distrito VIII.]

Traducción escénica:
NOIETA: Sí! Amb un marrec de l'escola del davant. Es passejaven tots dos *pel carrer Strozzi* a dos quarts de vuit del vespre. Aquesta mocosa!

Lo mismo sucede en este cuarto ejemplo, referido a la *Strozzigasse* de Viena. Se realiza una traducción por repetición con glosa extratextual en la traducción editorial y una traducción lingüística en la traducción escénica. En ambas traducciones se sobreentiende que se trata de un antropónimo; la glosa extratextual permite al lector conocer la naturaleza del antropónimo, mientras que la traducción lingüística de la traducción escénica permite su comprensión al espectador. Ambas permiten tanto al lector como al espectador el seguimiento sin interferencias de la obra.

(5) Quinto ejemplo

Texto original:
SOLDAT. Also der Teufel soll mich holen, wenn eine heut *beim Swoboda* mollerter gewesen ist als Sie, Fräul'n Marie.

Traducción editorial:
EL SOLDADO.— ¡Que me zurzan si *en el Swoboda** había hoy una más blandita que usté, Fräulein Marie! [*NdT: Establecimiento de diversión y restauración en el Prater.]

Traducción escénica:
SOLDAT: Que em penguin si avui, *al ball*, n'hi havia alguna de més dolça que vostè.

En el quinto ejemplo aparece el *Swoboda*, local de diversión y restauración del célebre Prater vienés. La estrategia de la traducción editorial es la misma que en los casos anteriores: se traduce por repetición dado que no existe una traducción lingüística del nombre propio en España. Sin embargo, en lugar de emplear una glosa intratextual explicando la naturaleza del local, en la traducción escénica se ha optado por neutralizar el culturema al traducir por *al ball* ('en el baile'). En este caso podríamos hablar de una pérdida cultural debido a la neutralización del referente, a favor de una mayor naturalidad y mejor comprensión del texto.

(6) Sexto ejemplo

Texto original:
DER DICHTER. Gehst du denn nie ins Theater?
DAS SÜSSE MÄDEL. O ja — ich war erst neulich mit einem — weißt, mit dem Onkel von meiner Freundin und meiner Freundin sind wir in der Oper gewesen *bei der ›Cavalleria‹*.
DER DICHTER. Hm, also *ins Burgtheater* gehst du nie.
DAS SÜSSE MÄDEL. Da krieg' ich nie Karten geschenkt.

Traducción editorial:
EL POETA.— ¿No vas nunca al teatro?
LA MUCHACHITA INGENUA.— Sí, hace poco estuve con un… ¿sabes?, con el tío de mi amiga y mi amiga hemos ido a la ópera a ver la *Cavalleria*.
EL POETA.— Hum, entonces ¿no vas *al Burgtheater*?*.
[*NdT: El antiguo Teatro de la Corte fue el escenario más afamado del espacio cultural alemán.]
LA MUCHACHITA INGENUA.— Para ahí no me dan las entradas gratis.

Traducción escénica:
ESCRIPTOR: No vas mai al teatre?
NOIETA: Oh, sí… Hi vaig anar no fa gaire amb un… Saps? Amb l'oncle d'una amiga meva i amb la meva amiga va manar a l'òpera, a veure *la "Cavalleria rusticana".*
ESCRIPTOR: I *al Burgtheater*, no hi vas mai?
NOIETA: No em regalen entrades, d'aquest teatre.

En este sexto ejemplo, el referente cultural es el antropónimo *Burgtheater*, el celebérrimo teatro de la capital austriaca. En la traducción editorial se ha traducido por repetición y se ha añadido glosa extratextual en la que se explica acerca de este antiguo Teatro de la Corte. Esta información no aparece en la traducción escénica, en la que se mantiene el referente en el idioma original, pues no existe una traducción en catalán para el término. En este caso, se usa la glosa intratextual para aclarar al espectador que se trata de un teatro. No obstante, la palabra *Theater* no dista fonéticamente de su equivalente catalán ('teatre'), por lo que consideramos que no hay ningún problema de comprensión y refuerza el ambiente austriaco.

3.3.2 Obras artísticas y personalidades

(1) Primer ejemplo

Texto original:
DER JUNGE HERR. Kennst du *Stendhal*?
DIE JUNGE FRAU. Stendhal?
DER JUNGE HERR. Die ›*Psychologie de l'amour*‹.
DIE JUNGE FRAU. Nein, warum fragst du mich?

Traducción editorial:
EL SEÑORITO.— ¿Conoces a *Stendhal*?
LA JOVEN ESPOSA.— ¿Stendhal? No me suena.
EL SEÑORITO.— La *Psychologie de l'amour*.*
[*NdT: Se trata de la obra de Stendhal *De l'amour*, escrita en 1822.]

Traducción escénica:
SENYORET: Coneixes *Stendhal*?
JOVE CASADA: Stendhal?
SENYORET: La *"Psicologia de l'amor"*.

Por lo que a las personalidades se refiere, aparece el nombre de Stendhal, y también su obra *Psychologie de l'amour*. En la traducción editorial se mantiene el título en francés y en nota extratextual se indica la fecha de publicación. Esta información no aparece en la traducción escénica, en la que únicamente se mantiene el título, traducido al catalán. Por el contexto se sabe que la obra es de Stendhal, por lo que resultaría redundante añadir cualquier tipo de glosa (intrao extratextual). Respecto de la traducción al catalán, probablemente la comprensión del título no sería posible si se hubiese mantenido en el idioma original, por lo que la solución propuesta por la traductora y/o el adaptador resulta funcional.

(2) Segundo ejemplo

Texto original:
DIE JUNGE FRAU. Ich trag' nie ein Mieder. *Die Odilon* trägt auch keines. Aber die Schuh' kannst du mir aufknöpfeln.

Traducción editorial:
LA JOVEN ESPOSA.— Nunca lo llevo. *La Odilon** tampoco lo lleva. Pero me podías desabrochar los zapatos.
[*NdT: Actriz popular de la época.]

Traducción escénica:
JOVE CASADA: No em porto mai, de cotilla. *La Bella Otero* tampoco no en porta. Però pots descordar-me les botines.

El segundo personaje conocido que aparece en la obra es *la Odilon*, una actriz por entonces muy afamada. La estrategia que se emplea aquí es opuesta para la traducción editorial y la escénica. En la primera se traduce por repetición, manteniendo el nombre de la artista, desconocido para el lector español. No obstante, la glosa extratextual o nota del traductor permite la extranjerización sin que haya pérdida del matiz cultural ni del significado. Probablemente, debido a la inmediatez del espectáculo teatral a la que hemos aludido al comienzo de nuestro trabajo, en la traducción escénica se optó por la domesticación del referente, de modo que se tradujo por *la bella Otero,* conocida (en principio) por el espectador español de la época. Carolina Otero o La Bella Otero fue una bailarina, cantante, actriz y cortesana española muy destacada en los circuitos artísticos de la *Belle Époque*, afincada en Francia. Cabe señalar que la traducción escénica data de 1987, por lo que la puesta en escena del texto en la actualidad podría requerir una actualización del referente, desconocido para parte del público español actual.

(3) Tercer ejemplo

Texto original:
DER DICHTER. Gehst du denn nie ins Theater?
DAS SÜSSE MÄDEL. O ja — ich war erst neulich mit einem — weißt, mit dem Onkel von meiner Freundin und meiner Freundin sind wir in der Oper gewesen *bei der ›Cavalleria‹.*
DER DICHTER. Hm, also *ins Burgtheater* gehst du nie.
DAS SÜSSE MÄDEL. Da krieg' ich nie Karten geschenkt.

Traducción editorial:
EL POETA.— ¿No vas nunca al teatro?
LA MUCHACHITA INGENUA.— Sí, hace poco estuve con un… ¿sabes?, con el tío de mi amiga y mi amiga hemos ido a la ópera a ver la *Cavalleria.*

Traducción escénica:
ESCRIPTOR: No vas mai al teatre?
NOIETA: Oh, sí… Hi vaig anar no fa gaire amb un… Saps? Amb l'oncle d'una amiga meva i amb la meva amiga vam anar a l'òpera, a veure *la "Cavalleria rusticana".*

En este caso, el referente es la ópera de Mascagni *Cavalleria Rusticana*. No presenta ningún problema de comprensión pues en el texto queda explicado que se trata de una ópera.

3.3.3 Otros

(1) Primer ejemplo

Texto original:
SOLDAT zieht *an seiner Virginierzigarre.*

Traducción editorial:
EL SOLDADO.— (Da una calada [...] *a su virginia.**)
[*NdT: Habano barato].

Traducción escénica:
SOLDAT: (Xucla *el seu cigar*).

En este caso, el *Virginierzigarre* se traduce lingüísticamente con glosa extratextual en la traducción editorial y se neutraliza en la escénica. Se da una pérdida del matiz cultural (sin trascendencia aparente) en aras de una naturalidad y comprensión mayores.

(2) Segundo ejemplo

Texto original:
Prater. Sonntagabend. Ein Weg, der vom Wurstelprater aus in die dunkeln Alleen führt. Hier hört man noch die wirre Musik aus dem Wurstelprater; auch die Klänge vom Fünfkreuzertanz, eine ordinäre Polka, von Bläsern gespielt.

Traducción editorial:
(El Prater, tarde de domingo. Un camino que lleva del Wurstelprater hacia las oscuras alamedas del parque. Desde aquí se escucha todavía la algarabía musical del Wurstelprater. También *los sones de una polca barata, el baile de los cinco cruceros**.)
[*NdT: Una polca que llevaba tal denominación por el dinero que se pedía para los músicos. El crucero era una fracción de la corona.]

Traducción escénica:
El Prater, un diumenge al vespre. Un camí que des del Wurstelprater condueix a unes avingudes fosques. Se sent la música confusa que ve del Wurstelprater i *els sons d'un ball de patacada, una polca vulgar*, tocada amb instruments de vent.

En último lugar, el *Fünfkreuzertanz* se traduce interlingüísticamente en la traducción editorial y se añade una glosa extratextual en la que se informa al lector sobre esta polca. Para la traducción escénica se ha encontrado una equivalencia que permite la domesticación, el *ball de patacada,* baile que se celebra en locales de baja categoría y que parece tener su origen en los bailes que se celebraban los días de fiesta en el almacén de Antoni Nadal i Derrer, en la calle de Sant Pau de Barcelona, por la costumbre de los bailarines de saludarse con golpes en la espalda (enciclopedia.cat).

Podría resultar incoherente emplear aquí la estrategia domesticadora, cuando para la traducción escénica del resto de referentes se ha procurado mantener el ambiente del original, si bien en algunos otros casos se ha recurrido a la neutralización ("Virginierzigarre"-"cigar", "en el Swoboda"-"al ball") e incluso a la domesticación ("Porzellangasse"-"passatge de la porcellana", "die Odilon"-"la bella Otero"). Probablemente, esta aparente falta de cohesión en la estrategia de la traducción escécina se deba al hecho de que el canal, el tiempo y el espacio requieran la simplificación de algunos pasajes para facilitar la comprensión del espectador, que, al contrario del lector, no dispone de un soporte papel para releer algún pasaje más dificultoso (por una sintaxis más compleja, por la presencia de un elemento cultural desconocido o cualquier otro factor de encriptación del mensaje).

4. Conclusiones

El cotejo de la obra original *Reigen* con sus traducciones editorial y escénica nos permite realizar algunas observaciones acerca del tratamiento de los referentes culturales en el ámbito de la traducción teatral, que pasamos a exponer a continuación.

Tras analizar las técnicas empleadas para la traducción editorial y escénica, podemos afirmar que existen diferencias en el tratamiento de los culturemas para un tipo y otro de traducción. Así, pues, por lo que se refiere a la taxonomía de las técnicas traslatorias empleadas, que van desde una mayor conservación del universo cultural del TO hasta su sustitución por el universo cultural del TM o su omisión, las técnicas de traducción más empleadas han sido las siguientes: repetición, traducción lingüística, glosa extratextual, neutralización y omisión (Moya 2000: 173–182; Franco Aixelá 2000: 84–94). En la traducción editorial se ha adoptado una clara estrategia extranjerizante y se han aplicado las correspondientes técnicas. Las aclaraciones recogidas en la glosa extratextual han permitido conservar el aura connotativa de los referentes del original sin que se produzcan pérdidas de sentido ni efectos de extrañamiento que pudieran entorpecer la lectura. En este sentido, podríamos afirmar que dichas glosas extratextuales (también lo serían las intratextuales) o notas a pie de página formarían parte de la *literariedad (literaturnost)* del texto (el conjunto de los rasgos distintivos del objeto literario) y permiten una mayor conservación de la cultura origen (Vega y Serrano 2013:1475–1490) sin que la comprensión del mensaje se vea alterada.

Por lo que a la traducción escénica respecta, se ha adoptado mayormente una estrategia exotizante mediante el empleo de recursos como la glosa intratextual. No obstante, también se han hecho algunas adaptaciones ("die Odilon"-"la bella Otero") y neutralizaciones ("Virginierzigarre"-"cigar", "en el Swoboda"-"al ball") del texto cuando dichos referentes eran ajenos a la cultura receptora y podían provocar un efecto de extrañamiento y, consiguientemente, comprometer la comprensión del texto. De esta manera, si bien en líneas generales la voluntad del traductor es la de mantener la atmósfera de la cultura de origen, se producen en ciertas ocasiones pérdidas culturales en aras de una mayor comprensión de la trama. En este sentido, no parece que la naturaleza del referente cultural sea determinante por lo que a la técnica de traducción se refiere.

Si bien los comportamientos traductores analizados pueden ser sintomáticos de una práctica generalizada y funcional (y, de hecho, lo son en el caso de la traducción editorial), resulta evidente que dependerá de la voluntad del director de escena o del productor que un texto traducido conserve la cultura de origen o bien se adapte al contexto cultural de destino. No obstante, en caso de obras muy arraigadas a la cultura de origen, en las que la aplicación de las técnicas de adaptación podría acabar con el sentido de la obra original, no siempre será posible la domesticación del texto.

En cualquier caso, sí ha quedado demostrado que la inmediatez propia del canal y del espacio-tiempo de la representación obligan, en ciertos casos, a facilitar la comprensión del texto al espectador, que no dispone de la obra en papel para releer pasajes más complejos o que contengan referentes desconocidos. El tratamiento de los referentes culturales por parte del traductor teatral dependerá de los siguientes factores:

1. del propósito de traducción (editorial o escénica), que condicionará a su vez
2. el canal y el espacio-tiempo;
3. del encargo de traducción que reciba (mayor o menor libertad al traductor teatral).

Si bien para la traducción escénica son el adaptador o el director los principales responsables de realizar dichos cambios sobre la traducción que entrega el traductor, y no el propio traductor, también es posible que se pida al traductor que realice propuestas para estos y otros casos que muestren cierta complejidad, como sucede con la traducción de los juegos de palabras.

Por último, cabe subrayar que el proceso de *trasposición* o puesta en escena de un texto es muy complejo, en tanto que en él participan un sinfín de factores (desde criterios estéticos hasta cuestiones referidas a la pronunciación de los actores) y elementos dramatúrgicos que podrían justificar algunas aparentes incoherencias en el tratamiento de los referentes culturales y o de otros elementos en la traducción escénica.

Bibliografía

Albaladejo, Juan A. 2005. "Los clásicos marginados: Johann Nestroy o la traducción de lo imposible". En *La y traducción de los clásicos: problemas y perspectivas*, ed. por Miguel Á. Vega, 297–304. Madrid: Instituto Interuniversitario de Lenguas Modernas y Traductores.

Albaladejo, Juan A. 2008. "La traducción de los textos marcados del alemán al español". En *Reescrituras de lo global: traducción e interculturalidad*, ed. por Virgilio Tortosa, 301–334. Madrid: Biblioteca Nueva.

Albaladejo, Juan A. 2011. "La marca cultural como problema de traducción: interculturalidad diatópica y diacrónica". En *Traductions: langues et cultures*, ed. por Pedro Mogorrón, 71–84. Synergies Tunisie 3.

Albaladejo, Juan A. 2012a. *La literatura marcada: Problema de traducción y recepción ejemplificados a través del teatro popular vienés*. Soria: Diputación Provincial de Soria.

Albaladejo, Juan A. 2012b. "Problemas relacionados con la traducción de textos de teatro: marcación intralingüística, (in)equivalencia genérica y escenografía del Wiene Volkstheater". En *La traducción en las artes escénicas*, ed. por Pilar Martino, 167–178. Madrid: Dykinson.

Archivo digital histórico de los espectáculos del teatro Romea. *La Ronda*. https://www.teatreromeapropietat.cat/es/archivo-digital/espectaculos?view=espectaculo&id=3399

Bassnett, Susan. 1998a. "The Translation Turn in Cultural Studies". En *Constructing Cultures. Essays on Literary Translation*, ed. por Susan Bassnett, and André Lefevere, 90–180. Clevedon: Multilingual Matters.

Bassnett, Susan. 1998b. "Still Trapped in the Labyrinth: Further Reflections on Translation and Theatre". En *Constructing Cultures. Essays on Literary Translation*, ed. por Susan Bassnett, and André Lefevere, 123–140. Clevedon: Multilingual Matters.

Bassnett, Susan, & André Lefevere. 1990. *Translation, History and Culture*. London: Printer Publishers.

Bolaños, Alejandro. 2016. "La cultura en la traducción teatral: el caso de la versión de *Les Fourberies de Scapin* (1671) por Julio Gómez de la Serna". *Estudios de Traducción* 6: 9–23.

Brouwer, Ronald. 2020. Entrevista realizada (3 de diciembre).

Cantero, Susana, and Jorge Braga. 2011. "Del libro a las tablas: traducir para la escena". En *Últimas tendencias en traducción e interpretación*, ed. por Daniel Sáez, 157–177. Madrid: Iberoamericana Editorial Vervuert.

Cartagena, Nelson. 1998. "Teoría y práctica de la traducción de nombres de referentes culturales específicos". En *Por los caminos del lenguaje*, ed. por Mario Bernales and Constantino Contreras, 7–22. Temuco (Chile): Sociedad Chilena de Lingüística, Departamento de Lenguas, Literatura y Comunicación.

Enciclopedia.cat, "ball de patacada", https://www.enciclopedia.cat/gran-enciclopedia-catalana/ball-de-patacada-0

Espasa Borrás, Eva. 2013. "Stage translation". En *The Rout-ledge Handbook of Translation Studies*, ed. por C. Millán, and F. Bartrina, 317–331. Milton Park, Abingdon: Routledge.

Franco Aixelà, Javier. 2000. *La traducción condicionada de los nombres propios*. Salamanca: Almar.

Franco Aixelà, Javier. 2022. "Anisomorfismos" @ *ENTI (Enciclopedia de traducción e interpretación)*. AIETI.

Guirao, Marta. 1999. "Los problemas en la traducción de teatro: Ejemplos de tres traducciones al inglés de *Bodas de sangre*". *TRANS (Revista de Traductología)* 3: 37–51.

Katan, D. 1999. *Translating Cultures. An Introduction for Translators, Interpreters and Mediators*. Manchester: St. Jerome.

Lafarga Maduell, Francisco. 1989. "Traducciones y adaptaciones teatrales: ensayo de tipología". *Cuadernos de teatro clásico* 4: 95–112.

López Lapeña, Alejandro. 2014. "Recalificar el páramo. Bases para un nuevo modelo traductológico de análisis del texto teatral". *Sendebar* 25: 149–172.

Mayoral, Roberto. 2000. "La traducción de las referencias culturales". *Sendebar* 10-11: 67–68.

Mayoral, Roberto & Ricardo Muñoz. 1997. "Estrategias comunicativas en la traducción intercultural". En *Aproximaciones a los estudios de traducción*, ed. por Purificación Fernández and José Mª. Bravo, 143–192. Valladolid: Servicio de Apoyo a la Enseñanza, Universidad de Valladolid.

Merino, Raquel. 1994. *Traducción, tradición y manipulación: teatro inglés en España 1950-1990*. León: Servicio de Publicaciones de la Universidad de León y la Universidad del País Vasco.

Molina Martínez, L. 2006. *El otoño del pingüino. Análisis descriptivo de la traducción de los culturemas*. Castellón de la Plana: Universidad Jaime I, Castellón.

Moya, Virgilio. 2000. *La traducción de los nombres propios*. Madrid: Cátedra.

Oskaar, E. 1988. *Kulturemtheorie. Ein Beitrag zur Sprachverwendungsforschung*. Göttingen: Vandenhoeck & Ruprecht.

Petrescu, Olivia N. 2011. "La traducción de los culturemas (Discusión al margen de la traducción de una novela de Guillergo Arriaga". *Revista Valenciana, estudios de filosofía y letras* 8: 139–172.

Reiss, Katharina & Hans Vermeer. 1984. *Grundlegung einer allgemeinen Translationstheorie*. Tubinga: Niemeyer.

Schnitzler, Arthur. 1987. *La Ronda*. Barcelona: Institut del Teatre de la Diputació de Barcelona. [Traducción de Carme Serrallonga y adaptación de Feliu Formosa.]

Schnitzler, Arthur. 2004. *La ronda. Anatol. Ensayos y aforismos*. Madrid: Cátedra. [Traducción y edición de Miguel Ángel Vega Cernuda.]

Schnitzler, Arthur. 2004. *Reigen. Liebelei*. Fráncfort del Meno: Fischer Verlag. 37th ed.

Serrano Bertos, Elena. 2020. "La traducción teatral y la configuración de imágenes". En *Hispanística y traductología: dos pasiones*, ed. by Cuenca, Miguel José; Pilar Martino et al., 303–315. Madrid: OMMPRESS.

Shklovski, V. 1980. "El arte como artificio". En *Teoría de la literatura de los formalistas rusos*, ed. por Tz. Todorov. Madrid: Siglo XXI.

Vega Cernuda, Miguel Á. 2004. "Introducción". En *La Ronda. Anatol. Ensayos y aforismos*, ed. por Miguel Á. Vega, 9–98. Madrid: Cátedra.

Vega Cernuda, Miguel Á. & Elena Serrano Bertos. 2013. "La nota del traductor, ¿forma parte de la literariedad del texto terminal?". En *Translating culture*, coord. por Emilio Ortega Arjonilla, vol. 9, 1475–1490. Granada: Comares.

Venuti, L. 2008. *The Translator's Invisibility. A History of Translation*. Londres: Routledge.

Vermeer, H. J. 1983. "Translation theory and linguistics". En *Näkökhtia käänämisen tutkimuksesta*, ed. por P. Roinila, R. Orfanos, and S. Tirkkonen Condit, 1–10. Joensuu, University. of Joensuu.

El trasvase de los referentes culturales y la fraseología en las versiones españolas de I Viceré

Maria Carreras i Goicoechea
Dipartimento di Scienze Umanistiche, Università degli Studi di Catania

A study of some of the cultural references (CRs) in *I Viceré* (Federico De Roberto, 1894, 1920) and their translation into Spanish (*Virreyes* 1994a, *Virreyes* 1994b and *Virreyes* 2008) is presented. After a brief contextualisation of the author and his work and a quick review of translation theory with regard to CRs, all the examples have been compiled and classified and the translation techniques adopted by Monreal and Navarro Salazar have been compared in order to observe how the cultural transfer has been dealt with depending on the date of translation and/or the translator.

Keywords: *I Viceré* (1894, 1920), Federico De Roberto, Spanish translations (1994, 2008), cultural references, understanding and reception

> Non è dubbio, dunque, che *I Viceré* sia [...] dopo *I Promessi sposi*, il più grande romanzo che conti la letteratura italiana. Ma chi se ne è accorto, a suo tempo? Chi se ne accorge, oggi?
> (Leonardo Sciascia 1977)

1. Federico de Roberto: un estilo propio

Para afrontar el estudio de la traducción de la obra derobertiana al español, hay que tener en cuenta que la obra tomada en consideración aquí se redacta a finales del siglo XIX (*I Viceré* 1894) mientras que las versiones traducidas al castellano ven la luz entre finales del siglo XX y principios del XXI, es decir a partir de cien años más tarde. Otro elemento importante es que su autor, Federico De Roberto, publicó una segunda edición de la novela al cabo de unos pocos años (1920) la cual contiene una serie de correcciones realizadas por él mismo.[1] Como señala Hurtado Albir (2001: 597):

> Todo texto es fruto de su época. Los movimientos estéticos en boga, el estado de la lengua, las ideologías imperantes, etc., condicionan su forma y contenido. Toda traducción, immersa como está en un contexto sociocultural, no puede ser ajena a la época en que se efectúa y participa de esos condicionamientos históricos. La distancia temporal entre la época de aparición del texto original y el momento de la traducción es una de las variables que más complica el proceso traductor.

Efectivamente no se puede perder de vista que cuando De Roberto escribió *I Viceré* estaba buscando su propio registro literario para poder dirigirse al público de aquel joven Reino de Italia (17 de marzo de 1861) aún disgregado lingüísticamente. De hecho Spinazzola (1961: 158) sostenía que De Roberto lo había conseguido pues había construido la prosa de su novela haciendo que:

> [...] si scontrassero, pagina per pagina, l'italiano aulico e *i modi di dire vernacoli*, la moderna tecnica oratoria dei comizi elettorali e il linguaggio della narrativa patetica tardo romantica: un coraggioso esperimento di oggettivismo linguistico [...] Ma nello stesso tempo in cui moltiplicava i suoi moduli linguistici adattandoli alla varia individualità dei personaggi, egli li riconduceva tutti ad una fondamentale unità, ad *un tono medio che è quello dato dal parlar comune*.

Por otro lado, el mismo De Roberto — con *I Viceré* todavía por publicar[2] — aclaraba en una entrevista la causa de su pesimismo respecto a la literatura italiana del momento, insistiendo en la necesidad de encontrar un modelo lingüístico literario:

> Come ti dicevo, la seconda ragione del mio pessimismo, è la mancanza di una lingua agile e sicura. Tra la lingua nobile e aulica che Gabriele D'Annunzio predica e a volte usa, e *la lingua comune parlata viva e vivace*, che c'è? O meglio abbiamo una lingua che le comprende tutt'e due? Perché quella prima sarà adatta a formulare precisamente un'analisi psicologica o a descrivere uno stato d'animo o un paesaggio fine e poetico; *questa* seconda (e il Manzoni l'ha adoperata) *è più borghese, serve a nominare gli oggetti e gli uomini tra cui viviamo ogni giorno, serve a parlare e a intenderci nella vita comune*. (Ojietti 1894: 85)

---

1. Sobre dichas correcciones, Madrignani aclara que "Quando nel 1919 De Roberto stava curando il testo per la seconda edizione, i suoi interessi si erano da tempo allontanati dal primitivo orientamento naturalistico [...] *I Viceré* testimoniava un gusto e una teoria letteraria superate e forse rinnegate, anche se non pubblicamente." (1984: 1772-1773).
2. "Quindi io credo che non vi sia salvezza che nel romanzo di costume e il romanzo che sto per pubblicare è un romanzo di costume: *I Viceré*." (Para esta citación se ha consultado una edición de 1899:84).

Para intentar encontrar esta lengua, una 'lingua media borghese' como la llama Grana (1982: 537) que le ayude a lograr su objetivo, como recuerda Sardo, el autor catanés "non smise mai di condurre analisi sistematiche non solo su tutti i repertori lessicografici e fraseologici disponibili, ma anche sulla testualità narrativa coeva." (2010: 341). Asimismo, si quiere que la lengua de sus personajes sea comprensible para un público de cualquier zona de Italia y que a la vez no resulte ridícula, De Roberto tiene que encontrar su *iusta media via*:

> I popolani di Sicilia parlano un loro particolare dialetto; quando io li rappresento ho due partiti dinanzi a me: il primo, che è l'estremo della verità, consiste nel riprodurre tal e quale il dialetto — come hanno tentato per le loro regioni il D'Annunzio, lo Scarfoglio, il Lemonnier ed altri, — il secondo, che è l'estremo della convenzione, consiste nel farli parlare in lingua, con accento toscano e sapore classico. Ora, se nel primo caso io rischio soltanto di non farmi comprendere dai lettori che ignorano il dialetto, nel secondo rischio addirittura di farli ridere tutti. Fra i due estremi io tento, con l'esempio del Verga, una conciliazione: *sul canovaccio della lingua conduco il ricamo dialettale*, arrischio qua e là un solecismo, capovolgo certi periodi, traduco qualche volta alla lettera, *piglio di peso alcuni modi di dire, e riferisco molti proverbii*, pur di conseguire questo benedetto colore locale non solo nel dialogo, ma nella descrizione e nella narrazione ancora.
> (De Roberto, *Documenti umani*, 1888: XIV)

Dadas la importancia de nombrar los "objetos de cada día", como los llama De Roberto en la entrevista de Ojietti, y la relevancia que asumen los *modi di dire* a los que recurre el autor para conseguir 'ese bendito color local', se presenta una primera observación de su traducción al español para comprender si las distintas versiones publicadas resultan suficientemente eficaces.

2. Las diferencias de índole cultural y su traducción

Los objetos de cada día de los que habla De Roberto pertenecen a un polisistema, el de la Sicilia de finales del siglo XIX, lejano del público que accede a la obra por primera vez en español. Como recuerda Hurtado Albir (2001: 523), el primero en ocuparse del estudio de los problemas de traducción relacionados con "las diferencias de índole cultural" fue Nida (1945), autor que clasificó bajo cinco ámbitos las diferencias culturales que a su vez podrían causar dificultades de traducción: (a) la ecología; (b) la cultura material; (c) la cultura social; (d) la cultura religiosa y (e) la cultura lingüística. Sucesivamente Vlakhov y Florin (1970), dieron el nombre de *realia* a los elementos que confieren color local e histórico al texto y clasificaron los ámbitos culturales de modo un poco más extenso: (a) los elementos geográficos y etnográficos; (b) los folclóricos y mitológicos; (c) los objetos cotidianos y (d) los elementos sociohistóricos. Sin que cambie el concepto de fondo, Newmark (1988) prefiere la denominación de *palabras culturales extranjeras* y amplía los dos últimos puntos: (1) organizaciones, costumbres, actividades, procedimientos y conceptos; (2) hábitos y gestos, introduciendo por primera vez entre los elementos culturales el lenguaje no verbal. A finales de siglo, Agar (1992) introduce el concepto más complejo de *rich point* o *puntos ricos* procedentes de la antropología cultural, es decir aquellos puntos de fricción que pueden llegar a producir una *barrera cultural*; concepto que Nord (1994) relaciona con las funciones del lenguaje (Jakobson 1960) aclarando que, si estas últimas son universales, "su manifestación textual depende, además del material lingüístico, de las convenciones y normas de cada cultura." (Hurtado Albir 2001: 609). Aunque hay numerosos trabajos con nuevas propuestas, para el presente estudio es importante señalar especialmente aquellos que observan los textos de ficción, como la misma Nord o Mayoral Asensio (1999-2000), que afronta 'cosas de cada día' como las medidas, las monedas, los nombres propios, los tipos de comidas y de bebidas, etc. particularmente presentes en la novela *I Viceré*.

Algunos de estos autores sugieren distintos procedimientos para traducir los *realia*,[3] como la transcripción, el calco, la formación de una palabra nueva, la asimilación cultural, la traducción aproximada y la traducción descriptiva. Respecto a los elementos que se deben deben recoger bajo la etiqueta de la 'cultura lingüística' en la clasificación de Nida, y que esta primera novela de la saga de los Uzeda ofrece en gran cantidad, tanto las expresiones idiomáticas de vario tipo como los proverbios se denominarán aquí, para simplificar, unidades fraseológicas (UFs). A propósito de estas, la fraseología solamente se introduce como disciplina en España a principios de los años ochenta (Carneado y Tristá 1983)[4] y no se dispone de una primera clasificación global de las UFs hasta la publicación de la introducción a la fraseología de Casares (1993). De hecho, solo en 1996 Corpas Pastor marca el auténtico punto de partida de los estudios de esta disciplina en el país. Las teorías traductológicas relacionadas con la fraseología se remontan a la misma época y destaca por su aceptación el enfoque de la misma Corpas Pastor, que consi-

---

3. Se ha escogido este término del latín, 'las cosas reales', por resultar el más cercano a las necesidades expresivas señaladas por De Roberto. Christianne Nord prefiere hablar de 'referentes culturales' porque los *realia*, afirma, no se encuentran en el texto. Por su cuenta Jean René Ladmiral ha propuesto recientemente el término *tradctème* directamente relacionado con el *culturema*.

4. Téngase en cuenta que en los años sesenta Vinogradoy recogía la herencia de Charles Bally (el introductor del término 'fraseología' en 1909) contribuyendo de forma importante al desarrollo de la disciplina científica en Rusia. Desde allí su difusión a los países de la Europa oriental, luego a los de Europa occidental y finalmente a Estados Unidos donde a partir de los años noventa se reconoce la fraseología como componente fundamental de la gramática de una lengua.

dera cuatro posibilidades de traducción: equivalencia total o plena,[5] parcial,[6] aparente[7] y nula.[8] Según Vinay y Darbelnet (1958), las técnicas de traducción más usadas para las UFs son el préstamo, el calco, la traducción literal, la transposición, la modulación, la equivalencia (la más usada para la traducción de proverbios) y la adaptación. Nótese portanto que, respecto a cuando se tradujo por primera vez *I Viceré* al español, en 1994, la traductología española no había ahondado aún en la traducción de las UFs; en cuanto al concepto de *equivalencia*, fundamental en la traducción contemporánea, todavía no se había publicado el estudio de Reiss y Vermeer sobre la teoría del *skopos* (1991), estudio que conllevó una serie de rupturas importantes: "Se rompe, por un lado, con el concepto que hasta ahora se tenía de traducción, ya que las teorías anteriores propugnavan que la función del TO se mantuviera invariable en el TT o que el original no cambiara de función al traducirlo; se rompe también con el valor atribuido al TO; y, luego, con el papel asignado tradicionalmente al lector/traductor, que a partir de ahora se verá en cierto sentido revalorizado" (Moya, 2004: 90).

3. Los Virreyes

Actualmente existen tres traducciones de *I Viceré* al español, todas ellas con el título *Los Virreyes*; dos de ellas son del mismo traductor, Juan Ramón Monreal (*Virreyes* 1994a y *Virreyes* 2008) y la restante de María Teresa Navarro Salazar (*Virreyes* 1994b).

Virreyes (1994a) se presenta con una *Nota del traductor* (7-8) y la traducción del ensayo de Leonardo Sciascia *Perché Croce non aveva ragione*[9] (9-11), ensayo

---

5. La equivalencia total o plena debe contener el mismo significado connotativo y denotativo, pertenecer a los mismos niveles diafásicos, diastráticos y diatópicos, contener la misma base metafórica y la misma carga pragmática. Puede ocurrir raramente, solo con locuciones con significados literales.

6. La equivalencia parcial se presenta cuando entre la locución del TO y la del TT hay alguna discrepancia como por ejemplo un significado connotativo y denotativo diferentes, distintos contenidos semánticos o distinta base figurativa. La mayor parte de las UFS pertenecen a este segundo grupo.

7. La equivalencia aparente se verifica cuando dos locuciones presentan similitudes formales con respecto a sus componentes, pero manifiestan divergencias en los significados.

8. Se verifica cuando la locución de la lengua de origen no encuentra ninguna expresión adecuada en la lengua meta por razones culturales, históricas y lingüísticas.

9. Se trata del ensayo *Perché Croce aveva torto*, publicado en "La Repubblica" el 14-15 de agosto de 1977 y vuelto a editar en el mismo periódico el 10 de noviembre de 2007. De hecho fue el propio Sciascia quien sugirió a Monreal la traducción de la novela al español.

que pretendía devolver la obra al lugar que merecía tras los años de olvido provocados por la crítica de Benedetto Croce, quien sostenía que esta novela, a pesar de demostrar una importante laboriosidad cultural, e incluso habilidad en la escritura, resultaba pesada. Sigue un árbol genealógico de la familia Uzeda y cierra el texto un aparato crítico de 166 notas (643-652).

Comparada con la primera traducción, *Virreyes* (2008) resulta prácticamente 'amputada' de todo su paratexto mientras que las notas, once menos, cuya numeración se retoma ahora en cada página, se encuentran al pie. Sin adentrarnos en todos los cambios aportados en esta que se presenta como una segunda traducción, se observa sobre todo una actualización del texto que se acerca al público receptor con una propuesta más divulgativa y a la vez moderna que la anterior.

Por su cuenta, la traducción de Navarro Salazar, publicada en la prestigiosa colección *Letras Universales* de Cátedra, se presenta en la portada como 'edición' y en el frontispicio se aclara que se trata de una edición y una traducción de la misma autora. El volumen consta de dos partes, la primera, *Introducción*, contiene dos fotos del autor y otras tres de lugares emblemáticos (el *Liotru*, una fachada del convento de los Benedictinos y la puerta Uzeda); siguen nueve apartados –*La investigación y el arte* (9-19); *La travesía del método* (19-34), *Vida y obra de Federico De Roberto* (25-34), *La trilogía de los Uzeda* (34-50), *La forma lingüística* (50-52), *Los Virreyes y la crítica* (52-58), *De Roberto en España: un autor que nadie ha visto* (59-62), *Pertinencia de una traducción de "Los Virreyes"* (63-66) y *Bibliografía* (67-69)–. La segunda parte contiene la traducción de la obra –*Los Virreyes*– (75-805). Cierra el volumen el índice. La introducción presenta 97 notas a pie de página; la traducción 256.

Un último elemento a señalar es la presencia de los nombres de Navarro Salazar y Monreal en las portadas de *Virreyes* 1994b i 2008, mientras que en *Virreyes* 1994a el nombre de Monreal aparece solo en el frontispicio.

Tanto Monreal como Navarro Salazar hacen referencia explícita al centenario de la publicación de la obra, ya que ambas traducciones se habían preparado precisamente en ocasión del mismo.[10] El primero lamenta que todavía no exista una edición crítica en Italia que corrija las erratas y cambios queridos por el autor que siguen inéditos. Navarro Salazar explica que, a falta de una edición crítica definitiva que se estaba preparando,[11] ha seguido para su versión la edición de Madrignani de 1984, que se basa en la primera edición de la novela (1894). Ambos

---

10. A propóstito de esta coincidencia y de la reacción excesivamente crítica por parte de Navarro Salazar hacia la traducción de Monreal, puede verse Carreras i Goicoechea (2020).
11. Se refería a una edición de Gianvito Resta que al final quedó incompleta.

traductores declaran el propio objetivo; el intento traductivo de Monreal es respetar el estilo del autor que:

> Con ambición totalizadora [...] recrea mediante un plurilingüismo, de gran ductilidad y riqueza, los giros y expresiones del habla de las clases noble y popular, la terminología de las diversas actividades y disciplinas, buscando conciliar la lengua de sabor clásico con la regional. (Monreal 1994: 7–8)

Por lo que se refiere a Navarro Salazar, "La intención al emprender esa versión de *Los Virreyes* no es otra que la de dar a conocer una obra rica y compleja en sus planteamientos, plenamente actual." (1994b: 64). La traductora sostiene que se trata de una obra moderna "a pesar de la lejanía en el tiempo real en el que se desarrolla" pues refleja varios problemas plenamente actuales en el siglo XX como "la ambición por el poder, el camaleonismo político" etc. (ivi:63).

Obviamente, los dos traductores son conscientes de la riqueza y complejidad lingüística de la obra:

> Estilísticamente estamos ante una continua e inagotable caja de sorpresas.
> (Monreal 1994:7–8)

> Se ha hablado del "babelismo lingüístico" de *Los Virreyes*, babelismo que se manifiesta no sólo en la selección de formas lingüísticas determinadas que sirvan para dar el color local ansiado, imprescindible para crear la amalgama deseada de forma y contenido, sino también en los diferentes registros lingüísticos asignados a los personajes, en tanto que manifestación expresiva de los contrastes de pareceres y voluntades. [...] traduciendo al pie de la letra o adaptando modismos dialectales; y el color local lo consigue también a través de la introducción de términos dialectales, que denotan realidades específicamente regionales, o dando a ciertas formas italianas una regionalización fonológica.
> (Navarro Salazar 1997: 631)

Por ello recogen el fragmento del prólogo de *Documenti umani* citado más arriba donde De Roberto expone su técnica de bordado, Monreal en su Nota del traductor (8):

> Sobre el cañamazo de la lengua llevo a cabo el bordado dialectal, arriesgo aquí y allá un solecismo, invierto algunos períodos, traduzco en ocasiones al pie d ela letra, tomo directamente algunos modismos y hasta numerosos proverbios, con tal de conseguir ese tan deseadocolor local no sólo en el diálogo, sino también en la descripción e incluso en la narración.

y Navarro Salazar en el apartado *La forma lingüística* (51):

> [...] sobre el bastidor de la lengua, entretejo el bordado dialectal, aventuro aquí y allá un solecismo, desordeno algunos periodos, a veces traduzco al pie de la letra, me sirvo de ciertos modismos y de muchos refranes, con tal de conseguir el bendito color local, no sólo en el diálogo, sino también en la descripción y en la narración.

4. Estudio

Este estudio de la traducción de los referentes culturales presentes en *I Viceré* se ha circunscrito a la Parte I de la novela (1–368), que presenta centenares de ejemplos pertenecientes a los cuatro ámbitos culturales de Nida (1945): valgan como ejemplos "la lava secolare del Mongibello" (144) (medio natural), "fa la vita del Robinson Crusoè" (29) o "come un eroe del Tasso o dell'Ariosto" (116) (patrimonio cultural), "l'istituzione del maiorasco" (148) (cultura social) y "passa Savoia, passa Savoia" (189) (cultura lingüística); forman parte de esta última categoría los refranes, locuciones, colocaciones, frases hechas, etc. que, respecto a los 'objetos de cada día', son más del doble. En las tres versiones españolas muchos de los elementos procedentes de los *realia* aparecen acompañados de una Nota de traducción (166 notas de *Virreyes* 1994a vs. 256 notas de *Virreyes* 1994b); en las UFs en cambio las NdT se encuentran en contadas ocasiones, y son precisamente estas expresiones las que han ofrecido mayor interés desde la perpectiva traductológica.

4.1 Las notas de traducción

Como se ha adelantado, ambos traductores hacen uso de numerosas NdT para aclarar informaciones relacionadas con hechos y personajes históricos, medidas y monedas, topónimos y antropónimos y elementos culturales específicos del lugar y/o de la época en que se desarrolla la acción. La mayoría de las notas de Monreal y de Navarro Salazar son de tipo enciclopédico[12] con algunas ampliaciones quizás

---

12. Cfr. "¹⁶ Carlos V (1500–58) heredó el reino de Sicilia en 1516, cuando se convirtió en rey de Castilla y Aragón con el nombre de Carlos I." (*Virreyes* 1994a).

excesivas en la segunda traductora[13] que también redacta notas intertextuales[14] y algunas otras eruditas.[15]

Muchos topónimos sicilianos reciben una nota solamente en Navarro Salazar; notas que suelen resultar superfluas, tanto para la comprensión de los hechos narrados como de cara a la contextualización; de hecho quizás hubiera sido más práctico presentar un mapa con los lugares de la isla que aparecen en la novela para comprender los desplazamientos:

(1) [12] Messina: capital de la provincia del mismo nombre en el noroeste de la Isla.

(2) [5] Caltanissetta: capital de la provincia del mismo nombre situada en el centro de la isla.

(3) [Milazzo][22] Ciudad de la provincia de Messina.

(4) [63] Taormina: localidad situada al sur de la provincia de Messina.

Pocas y más oportunas son las notas relacionadas con algunos lugares emblemáticos de la ciudad:

---

13. Como esta: "[59] La anexión al estado italiano trajo consigo numerosos problemas para la isla, en primer lugar la imposición de un sistema tributario y fiscal que estaba previsto para un tipo de economía muy diferente de la siciliana. Además se estableció el servicio militar obligatorio, cuando los sicilianos habían gozado del privilegio secular de nos ser reclutados y con anterioridad a Garibaldi únicamente Fernando I, al instituirse el Reino de las Dos Sicilias, lo había hecho. Cfr. S. Correnti, *Storia di Sicilia come storia del popolo siciliano*, Milán, Longanesi, 1972, 192 y 242." (*Virreyes* 1994b).

14. Por ejemplo: "[1] De Roberto recoge (parte I, cap. II) la creencia popular de que los muertos se aparecen en sueños para dictar los números ganadores de la loto: "mientras la princesa de Roccasciano le contaba a la baronesa Cúrcuma un sueño: su madre se le había aparecido con tres números en la mano: 6, 39 y 70 "sobre los cuales había apostado doce marines a escondidas de su marido" (80)"; "[3] De Roberto define (parte I, cap. III) la antigua institución de los pelotilleros o familiares: "... esos noblecillos muertos de hambre que vivían haciendo casi las veces de criados de los grandes señores". Posteriormente da de ellos esta valoración: "...una vez cumplida la misión se la consideró como una boca inútil, inferior incluso a los pelotilleros; ya que, por lo menos, los pelotilleros adulaban a la familia y en caso de necesidad echaban una mano al mayordomo"".

15. Por ejemplo "[Antro infernal][7] En el original *bolgia*, 'lugar desagradable y muy ruidoso', término con el que Dante designa a cada una de las fosas circulares y concéntricas del octavo círculo del infierno"; "[peste][21] Ya en el *Decamerón* la epidemia de peste sirve de marco al desarrollo de las narraciones y otros precedentes histórico-literarios son *Los Novios* y también *Los Malavoglia*." o "[56] Según el *Diccionario heráldico y nobiliario de los reinos de España* de F. González Doria, Madrid, editorial Bitácora, 1987, p.769, el apellido Uceda es de origen castellano y procede de las montañas de Burgos." (*Virreyes* 1994b).

(5) [al Borgo][8] Barrio periférico situado fuera del recinto amurallado de la ciudad al norte de la *Via Etnea*, arteria principal de Catania.

(6) [al Crociferi][52] Calle del centro de Catania, en la zona barroca, y monumental, reconstruída en el siglo XVIII por el duque de Camastra.

Algunos fragmentos del TO en latín se dejan sin traducir, otros llevan una traducción en nota:

(7) [*Sic transit gloria mundi!*][9] ¡ Así se desvanecen las glorias mundanas!
(Virreyes 1994b)

(8) [*Brevi manu*][41] Por la vía rápida   (*Virreyes* 1994b)

(9) [*India moesta sedet...*][17] Afligidas están las Indias tras la muerte de Carlos V.
(Virreyes 1994a)

(10) [*India moesta sedet...*][24] La India permanece triste después de los funerales de Carlos V.   (*Virreyes* 1994b)

Navarro Salazar también redacta algunas notas lingüísticas probablemente para que su público pueda reconocer, a pesar de la traducción, el estilo del original; esto se observa tanto en algunas palabras de origen francés como *sansculotte* y *monsù* como en algunas expresiones dialectales italianizadas por De Roberto:

(11) [descamisados][15] En el original *sanscoulotte*.

(12) [monsù][67] Deformación popular del francés *Monsieur*.

(13) [el que presta sin prenda, pierde dinero, amigo y hacienda][50] Italianización del proverbio catanés: *Cui fa credenza senza averi pigna, perdi la roba, l'amicu e lu gnugnu* en Pitrè, *Biblioteca delle tradizioni popolari siciliane. Proverbi siciliani*, vol. II, 45.

(14) [había nivelado las finanzas[71] de nuestra casa?] En el original *mettere in piano*, traducción italiana del modismo siciliano; *mettiri nchianu*, 'nivelar'.

En realidad en (13) el TO reza "Chi presta senza pegno perde i denari, l'amico e l'ingegno" y la traducción de Navarro Salazar consigue mantener el estilo proverbial a pesar de ser literal. Sin embargo, hubiera resultado más eficaz decir "Traduzco así la italianización del proverbio catanés ...".

En muchas ocasiones los dos traductores coinciden en la elección del referente cultural que requiere una aclaración en nota, por ejemplo en las unidades de medida. Frente a referentes culturales internacionales, las mismas suelen tratar la información de modo semejante, como en el caso del personaje literario Anquises:

(15) ⁹ Padre de Eneas, quien, al huir del incendio de Troya hacia Italia, a donde los dioses lo habían destinado, se lo llevó consigo. Murió en Sicilia.
(*Virreyes* 1994a)

(16) ¹¹ Antiguo héroe troyano padre de Eneas que, según la tradición, murió en Sicilia, en la ciudad de Trapani. (*Virreyes* 1994b)

En cambio, frente a referentes culturales locales las notas suelen ser distintas, como en el caso de *i lavapiatti*:

(17) (…) guardate i *lavapiatti* che arrivano prima di tutti! (TO)

(18) ¡Vaya por Dios! ¡Mirad por dónde, los fregaplatos³ son los primeros en llegar!

(19) ³Lavapiatti en el original. Denominación despectiva para designar a los nobiluchos o gentes de más modesta condición que eran recibidos como amigos de la casa de los Virreyes. (*Virreyes* 1994a)

(20) ¡Vaya! ¡Mirad los pelotilleros³, son los primeros en llegar!

(21) ³De Roberto define (parte I, cap. III) la antigua institución de los pelotilleros o familiares (…). Posteriormente da de ellos esta valoración (…) (*Virreyes* 1994b)

Si es cierto que las notas de traducción deberían ser la última solución para una traducción fluida, en la versión de Navarro Salazar, que se presenta como una edición crítica, estas tienen una clara justificación en el proyecto editorial de Cátedra, incluso a pesar de que algunas sean superfluas. Por otro lado, las notas de Monreal, coherentemente con el proyecto editorial de Anaya, son más bien sencillas, sin pretensiones de exhaustividad ni de erudición. Los cambios entre las notas de *Virreyes* 1994a y 2008 son mínimos: se completa siempre la fecha respecto a la forma abreviada de la primera traducción ("⁴ Fernando II de Borbón (1810-59)." vs. "⁴ Fernando II de Borbón (1810-1959).") y alguna que otra vez el texto se reformula con un registro más sencillo corroborando la simplificación y actualización general que se señalaba respecto a esta tercera traducción:[16]

(22) ³ *Lavapiatti* en el original. *Denominación* despectiva para designar a los nobiluchos o *gentes* de más modesta condición que eran recibidos como *amigos* de la casa de los Virreyes. (*Virreyes* 1994a)

(23) ¹ *Lavapiatti* en el original. *Se trata de una palabra* despectiva *usada* para designar a los nobiluchos o *personas* de más modesta condición que eran recibidos como *clientes* de la casa de los Virreyes. (*Virreyes* 2008)

---

16. Cursiva mía.

El ejemplo de *lavapiatti*, que aparece 27 veces en la novela, es especialmente interesante porque De Roberto se divierte con un juego de palabras que contiene este término:

> A voi che importa?
> – A me ? Un fico secco ! Io non faccio il lavapiatti a nessuno !
> – I lavapiatti – rispose don Lorenzo – dovete sapere che io li ho tenuti sempre in cucina...
> – Silenzio! Siamo in chiesa... (*I Viceré*:32)

Monreal, que traduce *lavapiatti* de manera literal con *fregaplatos*, logra mantener la comicidad del TO con su propuesta en sendas versiones:

> – ¿Y a usted qué demonios le importa?
> – ¿A mí? ¡Una higa! ¡Yo no hago de fregaplatos a nadie!
> – Debéis saber – repuso don Lorenzo – que yo a los fregaplatos los he tenido siempre en la cocina...
> – ¡Silencio!... Estamos en la iglesia (*Virreyes* 1994a:46)

> – ¿Y a usted qué demonios le importa?
> – ¿A mí? ¡Un rábano! ¡Yo no hago de fregaplatos a nadie!
> – Ha de saber usted – repuso don Lorenzo – que yo a los fregaplatos los he tenido siempre en la cocina...
> – ¡Silencio!... Estamos en la iglesia (*Virreyes* 2008:39)

En cambio la réplica de don Lorenzo ha sido omitida en la versión de Navarro Salazar que había traducido *lavapiatti* con *pelotilleros*, pues esta elección no le ha permitido mantener el juego de palabras:

> – ¿Y a usted qué demonios le importa?
> – ¿A mí? ¡Un higo seco! Yo no soy pelotillero de nadie.
> – ¡Silencio! Estamos en la iglesia. (*Virreyes* 1994b:108)

Este ejemplo confirma cuán complicado es obtener un trasvase cultural completo en una obra de este tipo, que requiere aclaraciones tanto a causa de su historicidad como de la lengua con la que se construyen el registro de los personajes, de la narración y de la descripción.

4.2 Fraseología

Como ya se ha anticipado, *I Viceré* presenta numerosos ejemplos de UFs relacionadas con la cultura rural ("Un fulmine a ciel sereno!"), la cultura religiosa ("Predicava ai turchi"), las partes del cuerpo ("era una cosa, in verità, che andava con i suoi piedi", "non sarebbe partito così a rotta di collo"), la cultura gastronómica ("Aveva fatto la frittata"), hechos históricos ("Lo mandò a carte quarantotto"), etc.[17] La mayoría de estas expresiones son un auténtico desafío para su traducción. Véase, a modo de ejemplo, la densidad fraseológica del siguiente fragmento, que aparece en una de las primeras páginas de la I parte:

> Le donne pensavano alla signorina Lucrezia, alla principessa nuora: sapevano nulla, o avevano loro nascosto la notizia?... E Baldassarre, Baldassarre dove diamine aveva il capo, se non ordinava di chiudere ogni cosa?... Don Gaspare, il cocchiere maggiore, *verde in viso come un aglio*[(1)], *si stringeva nelle spalle*[(2)]:
> – Tutto *a rovescio*[(3)], qui dentro.
> Ma Pasqualino Riso, il secondo cocchiere, gli spiattellò *chiaro e tondo*[(4)]:
> – Non avrete il disturbo di restarci un pezzo!
> E l'altro, di rimando:
> – Tu no, che *hai fatto il ruffiano*[(5)] al tuo padrone!
> E Pasqualino, *botta e risposta*[(6)]:
> – E voi che lo faceste al contino!...
> Tanto che Salemi, il quale risaliva all'amministrazione, ammonì:
> – Che è questa vergogna?
> Ma don Gaspare, a cui la certezza di perdere il posto *toglieva il lume degli occhi*[(7)], continuava:
> – Quale vergogna?... Quella d'una casa dove madre e figli si soffrivano *come il fumo negli occhi*[(8)]?...
> Molte voci finalmente ingiunsero:
> – Silenzio, adesso! (1894:7-8; 1920:3-4)[18]

En este fragmento aparecen ocho locuciones fraseológicas:[19] cinco en boca de la voz narrante y tres pronunciadas por uno de los personajes que intervienen en el breve diálogo entre don Gaspare y Pasqualino Riso, el primer y el segundo cocheros de la casa. Su presencia fuera de la parte dialogada tiene especial importancia pues contribuye a dar credibilidad al registro del intercambio de insultos entre los dos siervos, obviamente coloquial. Por ello en la versión traducida es esencial mantener tanto la densidad fraseológica como su presencia en la narración sin dar más importancia al diálogo. Para obtener un resultado eficaz, no hay que olvidar el momento histórico en el que se redactaba la novela, así como la pluralidad de destinatarios: el público general contemporáneo que comparte o no la cultura

---

17. También hay muchos proverbios el estudio de cuya traducción se deja necesariamente para otra ocasión.
18. Cursiva mía.
19. Lo índices en el fragmento son míos y sirven para poder comparar el TO con las traducciones.

de la época, los lectores actuales que solo conocen el canon de forma parcial y el público moderno del texto traducido. Habrá que cuestionarse también qué querían decir estas UFs en aquel entonces pues, con el paso del tiempo, puede haber habido algún que otro desplazamiento semántico o incluso alguna de estas expresiones puede haber dejado de usarse.

A continuación, se recogen las tres traducciones al español de este fragmento y un breve comentario de las traducciones de cada UF teniendo en cuenta que en *Virreyes* 1994a y 2008 solo se han conservado cinco UFs, y en *Virreyes* 1994b cuatro.

Las mujeres pensaban en la señorita Lucrezia, en la princesa nuera: ¿sabían ellas algo, o les habían ocultado la noticia?... Y Baldassarre, ¿dónde diantres tenía *puesta* la cabeza Baldassarre, que no mandaba cerrar**lo** todo? Don Gaspare, el cochero mayor, *pálido el rostro* de *la ira*[1], *se encogía de hombros*[2]:

–Aquí *anda todo manga por hombro*[3].

Pero Pasqualino Riso, el segundo cochero, le espetó **en** la cara *sin pelos en la lengua*[4]:

–¡No, no *os molestéis* en quedar**os** un rato más!

Y el otro, devolviéndosela:

–¡Tú sí que no, *alcahuete* de tu amo[5]!

Y Pasqualino, *toma y daca*[6]:

¡**Vos** del condesito!...

La cosa se había encrespado de tal modo que Salemi, que subía de nuevo a la administración, les increpó:

–¿Qué es esta vergüenza?

Pero don Gaspare, a quien la certeza de perder su puesto *lo ponía fuera de sí*[7], replicó:

–¿Vergüenza de qué?... ¿De una casa donde madre e hijo *se llevan como perro y gato*[8]?...

Finalmente se sumaron muchas voces:

–¡Ahora, silencio! (*Virreyes* 1994a:19-20)[20]

***

Las mujeres pensaban en la señorita Lucrezia, en la princesa nuera: ¿sabían ellas algo, o les habían ocultado la noticia?... Y Baldassarre, ¿dónde diantres tenía la cabeza Baldassarre, que no mandaba cerrar todo?... Don Gaspare, el cochero mayor, *pálido el rostro* por *la ira*[1], *se encogía de hombros*[2]:

–Aquí *anda todo manga por hombro*[3].

Pero Pasqualino Riso, el segundo cochero, le espetó *a* la cara *sin pelos en la lengua*[4]:

–¡No, no *se moleste* en quedar*se* un rato más!

---

20. Cursiva y negrita mías.

Y el otro, devolviéndosela:
–¡Tú sí que no, *rufián* de tu amo[5]!
Y Pasqualino, *toma y daca*[6]:
¡Usted del condesito!...
La cosa se había encrespado de tal modo que Salemi, que subía de nuevo a la administración, les increpó:
–¿Qué es esta vergüenza?
Pero don Gaspare, a quien la certeza de perder su puesto *lo ponía fuera de sí*[7], continuaba:
–¿Vergüenza de qué?... ¿De una casa donde madre e hijo *se llevan como perro y gato*[8]?...
Finalmente se sumaron muchas voces:
–¡Ahora, Silencio!   (*Virreyes* 2008:7–8)[21]

Entre *Virreyes* 1994a y 2008, saltan a la vista los pocos cambios: el paso del tratamiento de cortesía *Vos* al mucho más actual *Usted* con todas las adaptaciones morfológicas que implica en el sistema verbal y la simplificación en el uso preposicional y del pronombre neutro *lo* en *cerrarlo todo* > *cerrar todo*, más cercano al registro coloquial del personaje que está hablando. El paso de *replicó* a *continuaba* proporciona un texto más fiel al original (*continuó*).

Las mujeres pensaban en la señorita Lucrezia, en la princesa nuera: ¿sabrían ya algo, o les habrían ocultado la noticia?... ¿Y Baldassarre? Baldassarre en qué demonios estaba pensando que no había dado la orden de cerrar todo?... Don Gaspare, el cochero mayor, con *la cara más verde que un ajo*[1], *se encogía de hombros*[2]:
– Aquí dentro *todo va manga por hombro*[3].
Pero Pasqualino Riso, el segundo cochero, le espetó *bien claro*[4]:
– ¡No tendréis que molestaros en seguir aquí ni por un momento!
Y el otro se la devolvió:
– ¡Tú no, que para eso has sido el *correveidile*[5] de tu amo.
Y Pasqualino, *devolviéndole el golpe*[6]:
– Igual que vos con el joven conde...
Hasta el punto que Salemi, que subía a la administración, les reprendió:
– ¿Nos os da vergüenza?
Pero don Gaspare, *ciego de ira*[7] porque estaba seguro de que iba a perder el empleo:
–¿Qué clase de vergüenza?... La de una casa en la que madre e hijos *se soportan igual que el humo en los ojos*[8]...
Por fin varias voces ordenaron:.
– ¡Silencio ahora mismo!   (*Virreyes* 1994b:77–78)[22]

---

21. Cursiva y negrita mías.
22. Cursiva mía.

4.2.1 (¹) *Essere verde in viso come un aglio*

Según el *Tommaseo/Bellini* (TB), diccionario que el mismo De Roberto podría haber consultado,[23] esta locución adjetiva puede hacer referencia a alguien que no tiene buen aspecto, como si estuviera enfermo:

> T. Prov. Tosc. 372. Verde come un aglio (di persona). / T. Prov. Tosc. 372. Verde come un aglio, come un ramarro. [G.M.] Minucc. Not. Malm. Dicendosi: Il tale è verde come un aglio,... alle volte s'intende uno di mala sanità. (TB apud 'verde')

Como demuestra la *Crusca*,[24] esta expresión inicialmente tenía un sentido positivo pero ha sufrido un desplazamiento semántico importante al pasar a signifcar también lo contrario, como señala el TB ("alle volte"): "2. Locuz. — (aglio) Essere verde come un aglio: avere un aspetto sano, vigoroso. — Anche al contrario: avere un aspetto malsano.". El sentido antitético, 'de poca salud', podría corresponder al actualizado por De Roberto en la novela, pero aún no debería haber adquirido el sentido extendido a la rabia recogido años más tarde por el GDLI:

> 4. Per estens. Che ha un colorito livido, olivastro, che è di un pallore grigiastro, in partic. per una condizione patologica, per lo stato avanzato dell'età o anche per un moto di rabbia, per un'emozione (anche con valore enfatico e iperb.).
>
> (GDLI, apud *aglio*)

En el contexto donde aparece esta expresión, dada la situación de caos que se ha venido a crear con la noticia de la muerte de la princesa, y el trajín entre cocheros para cambiar el caballo y permitir que el príncipe se fuera lo antes posible, lo más sensato parece que el cochero mayor tenga mala cara. Sin embargo, la interpretación de Monreal en sus dos versiones ha ido más allá suponiendo que don Gaspare está muy enfadado mientras Navarro Salazar ha optado en este primer ejemplo fraseológico por una traducción literal cuyo sentido resulta completamente opaco. Ninguno de los dos traductores parece conocer el equivalente fraseológico recogido por *Ambruzzi* (1949): "Essere verde come un — 'tener cara de viernes'" (apud *aglio*), es decir la expresión coloquial "cara macilenta y triste" (DLE, apud *cara*).

Si bien la elección de Monreal es el resultado de una interpretación personal del texto, es coherente con la penúltima locución del fragmento (cfr. *Infra* 4.2.7).

---

23. Esta obra no estaba en su biblioteca personal (cfr. Inserra 2017), que en cambio contenía otras obras de Tommaseo como el *Dizionario d'estetica* (1860), tres ediciones distintas del *Dizionario dei sinonimi della lingua italiana* (1838, 1867 y 19–), pero no hay que olvidar que De Roberto fue bibliotecario de la *Biblioteca civica* de Catania.

24. "Definiz: §. I. Esser verde com'un aglio; vale Esser di sanità perfetta". (Apud *aglio*).

I Viceré (1894, 1920)	*Virreyes* 1994a	*Virreyes* 2008	*Virreyes* 1994b
verde in viso come un aglio [1]	pálido el rostro de la ira	pálido el rostro por la ira	con la cara más verde que un ajo

4.2.2 [2] *Stringersi nelle spalle*

Stringersi nelle spalle, o Stringere le spalle. Scusarsi tacitamente per più non potere; e talora Cedere alla fortuna con pazienza. Franc. Sacch. Nov. 36. (M.) Strinsono le spalle, e ringraziaronlo, ed andossi con Dio. Nov. ant. 102. 21. Si diè ad intendere d'avere errato, e strettosi nelle spalle disse: per certo io sono stasera fuor di me.
(TB)

62. Assumere una posizione più raccolta; farsi piccolo per la paura o per la vergogna. — Stringersi nelle spalle, raccogliersi nelle spalle alzandole, per manifestare indifferenza, disinteresse, perplessità, indecisione, rassegnazione, per negare il proprio sostegno, facendo intendere di non volersi preoccupare di qualcosa o di non potere rimediare a una situazione ad altri molesta o sfavorevole.
(GDLI, apud *stringere*)

b. Con uso rifl., stringersi nelle spalle, alzarle contraendole, come espressione di dubbio, indecisione o disinteresse.
(Trecanni apud *spalla*)

I Viceré (1894, 1920)	*Virreyes* 1994a	*Virreyes* 2008	*Virreyes* 1994b
si stringeva nelle spalle[2]	se encogía de hombros	se encogía de hombros	se encogía de hombros

En el gesto de levantar los hombros hay que leer una disculpa tácita o una renuncia por parte del cochero Gaspare, a colaborar. En español existe una locución verbal equivalente, *encongerse alguien de hombros*, que tiene tres acepciones: "1. Hacer el movimiento natural que causa el miedo. 2. No saber, o no querer, responder a lo que se le pregunta. 3. Mostrarse o permanecer indiferente ante lo que oye o ve", todas ellas recogidas por *Academia* desde 1780. Esta pluralidad de significados permite traducir al español con una equivalencia total delegando la interpretación exacta al público al igual que ocurre en el TO.

4.2.3 [3] *A rovescio*

Esta locución, que no aparece aún en TB, se usa especialmente en expresiones figuradas y suele acompañar el verbo *andare*, aquí elidido. Ambos traductores recurren a la locución verbal coloquial *andar algo manga por hombro*; Navarro Salazar ha reemplazado el verbo *andar* con *ir* con una leve pérdida desde el punto de vista diastrático.

I Viceré (1894, 1920)	*Virreyes* 1994a	*Virreyes* 2008	*Virreyes* 1994b
Tutto a rovescio[3]	anda todo manga por hombro	anda todo manga por hombro	todo va manga por hombro

4.2.4 ([4]) Chiaro e tondo

> 16. Parlar chiaro e tondo; Dirle chiare e tonde (le cose). T. Senz'ambagi; Dirle anche troppo chiare a chi non vorrebbe ascoltarle, presa l'immagine dalla forma delle lettere, così più leggibili.
> (TB apud *tondo*)

Esta locución enfática o de refuerzo se usa con los verbos *parlare* y *dire* con función adverbial:

> In funzione avv., parlare, dire chiaro e tondo, con franchezza e apertamente, senza preamboli o reticenze, soprattutto quando si debbano dire cose spiacevoli: e io in vece vi dico chiaro e tondo che il cuore in pace non lo metterò mai (Manzoni).
> (Treccani apud *tondo*)

I Viceré (1894, 1920)	*Virreyes* 1994a	*Virreyes* 2008	*Virreyes* 1994b
gli spiattellò chiaro e tondo[4]	le espetó en la cara sin pelos en la lengua	le espetó a la cara sin pelos en la lengua	le espetó bien claro

En las tres traducciones se ha recurrido oportunamente al verbo 'espetar' para traducir el italiano *spiattellare*; sin embargo Monreal opta por traducir la locución del TO con la locución verbal coloquial *no tener alguien pelos en la lengua* en su forma sintética *sin pelos en la lengua* —con dos preposiciones distintas según la versión, ambas correctas— mientras que Navarro Salazar ha resuelto la traducción con una paráfrasis menos eficaz desde el punto de vista del registro.

4.2.5 ([5]) Fare il ruffiano

Respecto a esta expresión, es un interesante ejemplo de gramaticalización de *realia* cuyo resultado ha sido una UF:

> *Ruffiano*: "S. m. Mezzano prezzolato nelle cose veneree. Titolo disonesto." (TB)

> *Fare il ruffiano*: "2. fig. Chi cerca di acquistarsi il favore altrui con l'adulazione o con atteggiamento di ostentata sottomissione: *fa il r. con i superiori*."
> (Treccani *ad vocem*)

En español no existe una UF equivalente, de hecho en este caso se pueden ver tres propuestas distintas:

I Viceré (1894, 1920)	*Virreyes* 1994a	*Virreyes* 2008	*Virreyes* 1994b
hai fatto il ruffiano[5] al tuo padrone!	alcahuete de tu amo	rufián de tu amo	has sido el correveidile de tu amo

Monreal traduce primero con *alcahuete*[25] —que podía asociarse engañosamente a acepción que hace referencia a la profesión de la Celestina— y luego con *rufián*,[26] término que puede parecer más fiel al TO aunque en realidad no corresponde semánticamente al sentido de la locución italiana. En cambio la traductora de *Virreyes* 1994b ha sabido interpretar correctamente el sentido y ha recorrido a una transposición con el sustantivo coloquial *correveidile*, contracción de la frase *corre, ve y dile* en función atributiva, ya cristalizado en la época de ambientación de la novela (Salvá 1846).[27] Se trata de una voz documentada en la literatura española almenos desde 1765[28] y muy usada por Galdós, así pues un buen equivalente tanto desde el punto de vista semántico como respecto a los ejes diacrónico y diastrático.

4.2.6 ([6]) *Botta e risposta*

De esta expresión nominal TB da una definición muy clara: "Botta e risposta. Dicesi per lo più di colpi e repliche l'uno dopo l'altro, fatti prontamente", que es exactamente lo que ocurre en este breve diálogo entre los dos cocheros.

I Viceré (1894, 1920)	*Virreyes* 1994a	*Virreyes* 2008	*Virreyes* 1994b
botta e risposta[6]	toma y daca	toma y daca	devolviéndole el golpe

---

25. "*Alcahuete*: m. y f. Persona que solicita ó sonsaca á una mujer para usos lascivos con un hombre, ó encubre, concierta ó permite en su casa esta ilícita comunicación. fig. y fam. Persona ó cosa que sirve para encubrir lo que se quiere ocultar." Cfr. *Academia* desde 1884. "2. Persona o cosa que encubre u oculta algo: *fueron las cortinas alcahuetas de sus intrigas.*" (DLE, apud *alcahuete*).

26. "*Rufián*: m. El que hace el infame tráfico de mujeres públicas. Fig. Hombre sin honor, perverso, despreciable." Cfr. *Academia* desde 1884.

27. "*Correvedile* (y correveidile): El que lleva y trae cuentos y chismes de una parte á otra. Dícese también por el que es alcahuete."

28. "Esteban ¿Es usted correveidile?" Ramón de la Cruz, *El Prado por la noche*.

La locución sustantiva escogida por Monreal pertenece al registro coloquial que desaparece en la reformulación de Navarro Salazar, donde también se pierde el ritmo del TO.

4.2.7 (⁷) *Togliere il lume degli occhi*

El *lume degli occhi* corresponde a la facultad misma de ver las cosas, de modo que "i modi *Rendere, Riavere il lume degli occhi. Perderlo,* nel tr., intorbarsi la mente e l'animo." (TB apud *lume*). Monreal traduce de modo equivalente con la locución verbal *estar alguien fuera de sí* (DLE: "estar alterado por la furia", apud *fuera*), en este caso a través del verbo transitivo 'poner'. Navarro Salazar también obtiene un equivalente semántico con la colocación *ciego de ira* y se mantiene en el mismo ámbito de la visión, sin embargo no preserva la densidad fraseológica del texto.

I Viceré (1894, 1920)	*Virreyes* 1994a	*Virreyes* 2008	*Virreyes* 1994b
A cui... toglieva il lume degli occhi⁽⁷⁾	lo ponía fuera de sí	lo ponía fuera de sí	ciego de ira

4.2.8 (⁸) *Come il fumo negli occhi*

Esta última expresión, que en el texto refuerza el sentido negativo de *soffrirsi*, ya se encuentra en TB: "Avere uno a noja come il fumo agli occhi."

I Viceré (1894, 1920)	*Virreyes* 1994a	*Virreyes* 2008	*Virreyes* 1994b
si soffrivano come il fumo negli occhi⁽⁸⁾	se llevan como perro y gato	se llevan como perro y gato	se soportan igual que el humo en los ojos

Monreal traduce con un equivalente fraseológico, la locución adverbial coloquial sintética *como (el) perro y (el) gato* que no solo corresponde perfectamente al sentido del TO, sino que es una expresión sinonímica también usada por el mismo De Roberto en otras ocasiones ("come cane e gatto" 155). Navarro Salazar ha optado también esta vez por una traducción literal, ahora transparente, que se mantiene en el campo semántico de la vista pero se aleja de la densidad fraseológica.

El fragmento comentado no es más que un breve ejemplo para mostrar el grado de dificultad con el que tuvieron que enfrentarse ambos traductores, los cuales no siempre han logrado mantener el registro coloquial de don Gaspare. Navarro Salazar ha perdido también el de la voz narrante y no parece que haya conseguido preservar la densidad fraseológica para la que tanto se había documentado y esforzado De Roberto; respecto al ritmo, otro elemento fundamental en este diálogo, parece que la tendencia a realizar una traducción filológica como la de Navarro Salazar, muy fiel en relación a los campos semánticos, le impide mantener la velocidad en los intercambios de réplicas. La técnica de la traducción literal, a la que ha recurrido en más de una ocasión, tampoco ha dado resultados suficientemente transparentes.

5. Conclusión

La preocupación de De Roberto por encontrar una lengua literaria que le permitiera describir tanto paisajes como estados de ánimo se puede constatar en los ejemplos procedentes de la voz narrante aquí analizados; del mismo modo, su interés por 'nombrar los objetos y las personas de cada día' salta a la vista gracias a los numerosos *realia* comentados; una lengua la de *I Viceré* a medio camino entre el registro áulico y el burgués, que no solo tiene que ser creíble —esta es la función de los innumerables proverbios y expresiones idiomáticas—, sino también comprensible para todo el público de esa Italia recién unificada —por ello las expresiones dialectales aparecen a menudo italianizadas—. Tanto Monreal como Navarro Salazar son plenamente conscientes de ello y hacen todo lo que está en sus manos por ofrecer un trasvase lo más completo posible; sin embargo, el paso del tiempo —los cien años que median entre la obra original y su traducción— no facilitan las cosas, especialmente a causa del importante cambio cultural advenido en la cultura europea. Si por un lado la presencia de notas de traducción recarga el texto traducido, sobre todo en la versión de Navarro Salazar, por el otro el estilo pierde en eficacia, a pesar de la innegable labor filológica especialmente llevada a cabo por esta traductora. La falta de reconocimiento a veces de algunas expresiones idiomáticas y las técnicas de traducción escogidas en búsqueda de una traducción equivalente en otras no han conseguido reproducir la expresividad del texto, sobre todo en la voz narrante. Respecto a las traducciones de Monreal, no se puede negar que la estrategia de una simplificación en la versión de 2008 logra su cometido. Si hoy día, pasado casi el primer cuarto de nuestro siglo, *Los Virreyes* puede aspirar a un público, la última traducción atraerá sin duda el mayor número de personas que quizás no podrán percibir de pleno aquella *lingua viva e vivace* tan auspiciada por Federico de Roberto pero se leerán la novela entera fascinados por su trama. Al fin y al cabo, ¿cuál es hoy el público italiano de semejantes obras?

Referencias bibliográficas

Obras estudiadas

(*I Viceré* 1894) = De Roberto, Federico. 1894. *I Viceré*. Milano: Galli.
De Roberto, Federico. 1920. *I Viceré, Nuova edizione Treves (in 2 volumi)*. Milano: Treves.
(*Virreyes* 1994a) = De Roberto, Federico. 1994. *Los Virreyes. Con un prefacio de Leonardo Sciascia*. Traducido del italiano por José Ramón Monreal. Madrid: Anaya & Mario Muchnik.
(*Virreyes* 1994b) = De Roberto, Federico. 1994. *Los Virreyes*. Edición de M.T. Navarro. Madrid: Cátedra.
(*Virreyes* 2008) = De Roberto, Federico. 2008. *Los Virreyes*. Traducción de J.R. Monreal. Barcelona: Acantilado.
(Madrignani 1984) = De Roberto, Federico. 1984. *Romanzi, Novelle e Saggi a cura di Carlo Madrignani*. Milano: Arnoldo Mondadori.

Diccionarios

Ambruzzi = Ambruzzi, Lucio. 1949 [1960]. *Nuovo dizionario spagnolo-italiano e italiano-spagnolo. Quinta edizione accresciuta e corretta*. Torino: Paravia.
Crusca = *Vocabolario degli accademici della Crusca*. Versión electrónica: ⟨https://accademiadellacrusca.it/it/sezioni/scaffale-digitale/25⟩.
DLE = *REAL ACADEMIA ESPAÑOLA: Diccionario de la lengua española*, 23.ª ed., [versión 23.6 en línea]: ⟨https://dle.rae.es⟩ [enero de 2023].
GDLI = Battaglia, Salvatore. *Grande dizionario della lingua italiana*. Torino: UTET. Versión electrónica: ⟨https://www.gdli.it/⟩.
Salvá = Salvá, Vicente. 1846. *Nuevo diccionario de la lengua castellana, que comprende la última edición íntegra, muy rectificada y mejorada del publicado por la Academia Española, y unas veinte y seis mil voces, acepciones, frases y locuciones, entre ellas muchas americanas [...]*. París: Vicente Salvá.
TB = Tommaseo, Nicolò. *Dizionario della lingua italiana, nuovamente compilato dai signori Nicolò Tommaseo e Cav. Professore Bernardo Bellini con oltre centomila giunte ai dizionari precedenti raccolte da Nicolò Tommaseo, Gius. Campi, Gius. Meini, Pietro Fanfani e da molti altri distinti filologi e scienziati*. Torino: UTET (1861). Versión electrónica: ⟨https://www.tommaseobellini.it/#/⟩.
Treccani = *Vocabolario on line Treccani* ⟨https://www.treccani.it/vocabolario/⟩.

Obras consultadas

Agar, Michael. 1992. "The intercultural frame." *International Journal of intercultural relations* 18 2: 221–237.
Casares, Julio. 1993. *Introducción a la lexicografía moderna*. Madrid: CSIC.

Carreras i Goicoechea, Maria. 2020. "Nota alla polemica sulle traduzioni spagnole de *I Viceré*: il caso di M.T. Navarro y J.R. Monreal." *Annali della Fondazione Verga* XII: 251–271.

Carneado, Zoila y Antonia María Tristá. 1983. *Estudios de fraseología*. La Habana: Instituto de Literatura y Lingüística de la Academia de Ciencias de Cuba.

Corpas Pastor, Gloria. 1996. *Manual de fraseología española*. Madrid: Gredos.

Grana, Gianni. 1982. *I Viceré e la patologia del reale*. Milano: Marzorati.

Hurtado Albir, Amparo. 2001. *Traducción y traductología*. Madrid: Cátedra.

Inserra, Simona. 2017. *La biblioteca di Federico De Roberto*. Roma: Associazione Italiana Biblioteche.

Jakobson, Roman. 1960. "Linguistics and Poetics: Closing Statement." In *Style in Language*, ed by Thomas Sebeok, 350–377, Cambridge (Massachussets): MIT Press. Por la traducción de Ana María Gutiérrez Cabello, *Estilo del lenguaje*, 123–173, Madrid: Cátedra, 1974.

Mayoral Asensio, Roberto. 1999–2000. "La traducción de referencias culturales." *Sendebar* 10–11: 67–88.

Moya, Virgilio. 2004. *La selva de la traducción*. Madrid: Cátedra.

Navarro Salazar, María Teresa. 1997. "Adecuación de registros y equivalencias culturales en la traducción literaria." In *VI Encuentros: La Palabra Vertida. Investigaciones en torno a la Traducción*, ed. by Miguel Ángel Vega y Rafael Martín-Gaitero, 629–640, Madrid: Complutense.

Newmark, Peter. 1988. *A testbook of Translation*. Londres: Prentice Hall. Por la traducción de Virgilio Moya. *Manual de traducción*. Madrid: Cátedra, 1992.

Nida, Eugene A. 1945. "Linguistics and Ethnology in Translation Problems." *Word* 2: 194–208.

Ojietti, Ugo. 1894 [1899]. *Alla scoperta dei letterati*. Milano: Fratelli Bocca editori.

Reiss, Katharina y Hans J. Vermeer. 1991 [1996]. *Grundlegung Einer allgemeine Translationstheorie*. Tubingen: Max Niemeyer. Por la traducción de Sandra García Reina y Celia Martín de León. *Fundamentos para una teoría funcional de la traducción*. Madrid: Ediciones Akal.

Sardo, Rosaria. 2010. *"Al tocco magico del tuo lapis verde…". De Roberto novelliere e l'officina verista*. Acireale: Bonanno editore.

Spinazzola, Vittorio. 1961. *F. De Roberto e il verismo*. Milano: Feltrinelli.

Vinay, Jean Paul y Jean Darbelnet. 1958. *Stylistique comparée du français et de l'anglais*. Paris: Didier.

La metamorfosis del «lirio» (y del «lilio»)
De flor a símbolo

Monica Savoca
Università degli Studi di Messina

The article is composed of 5 paragraphs plus an introduction. In the first 4, a history of the «lirio» in language and literature is presented, showing how this flower has become an aesthetic, cultural and identity symbol. The aim of this paper is to investigate the presence and evolution of the «lirio» / «lilio» throughout the history of Spanish language and literature and to demonstrate how this flower has become an aesthetic, cultural and identity symbol. The localisation of occurrences and their contextualisation has been possible thanks to manual counts and the use of various computer resources (database, tools for concordance and text analysis, etc.). In the 5 paragraph, some traductological questions will be raised through the analysis of the Italian versions of a sonnet by Lorca in which the «lirio» plays a fundamental role.

Keywords: flower metaphor, Góngora, Lope de Vega, Lorca, poetic translation

1. Introducción

El presente trabajo pretende investigar la presencia y la evolución del «lirio» / «lilio» a lo largo de la historia de la lengua y la literatura españolas y demostrar cómo esta flor se ha convertido en un símbolo estético, cultural e identitario. La localización de las ocurrencias y su contextualización ha sido posible gracias a recuentos manuales y al uso de diversos recursos informáticos (banco de datos, herramientas para las concordancias y el análisis del texto, etc.). Finalmente, se plantearán unas cuestiones traductologicas a través del análisis de las versiones italianas de un soneto de Lorca en el que el «lirio» desempeña un papel fundamental.

1.1 «Lilio» / «lirio»: Definición

«Lirio» es la forma con la que se identifica, conforme a la definición (cuestionable, como se detallará a continuación) de la más reciente actualización del diccionario de la RAE (DLE), la

> planta herbácea, vivaz, de la familia de las iridáceas, con hojas radicales, erguidas, ensiformes, duras, envainadoras y de 30 a 40 cm de largo, tallo central ramoso, de 50 a 60 cm de altura, flores terminales grandes, de seis pétalos azules o morados y a veces blancos, fruto capsular con muchas semillas, y rizoma rastrero y nudoso.
>
> (*DLE, ad vocem*)

Sin embargo, en la historia de la lengua y de la literatura españolas, antes de la dominación de la variante «lirio», hubo alternancia y convivencia de formas entre «lirio» y «lilio». Este último, de hecho, vivió una larga temporada de esplendor.

La primera muestra del lema «lilio» en los diccionarios data de 1611 y se encuentra en el *Tesoro de la lengua castellana o española* de Sebastián Covarrubias, que se considera el primer vocabulario monolingüe y donde la voz lilio es subalterna a lirio y no tiene significado propio. «LILIO, o LIRIO» remite a «Açuzena», con la siguiente, sugestiva definición:

> AÇUZENA: La blanca flor del lilio real. Lat. Lilium, es nombre Hebreo, sosana [...], se dixo sosena, y susena, cõ el articulo Arabigo a-susena, y açucena. [...] Llamase el lilio, o açucena cerca de los Poetas. [...] Es el açucena simbolo de la castidad por su blancura, y de la buena fama por su olor;.
>
> (*Tesoro de la lengua castellana o española, ad vocem*)

Esta voz aparecerá a lo largo de los siglos XVII y XVIII en diccionarios bilingües (latín, francés, italiano, árabe) y en 1787 en el diccionario enciclopédico de Terreros y Pando donde queda definido como «lo mismo que lirio, ó azucena» (*ad vocem*). En 1803 la cuarta edición del diccionario de la RAE mantiene la relación de sinonimia: «s. m. ant. Lo mismo que LIRIO» (*ad vocem*). Todos los diccionarios del siglo XIX y XX le atribuirán carácter de arcaísmo, hasta desaparecer en algunos diccionarios de uso (vid. CLAVE 1997). En las ediciones del DLE del siglo XXI se le atribuirá la marca de «m. p. us.» (masculino poco usado).

Mejor fortuna corrió el lema «lirio» desde su primera aparición en las dos ediciones del diccionario español-latino de Nebrija (1495 y 1516), y en obras posteriores como el diccionario *arávigo*-castellano de Fray Pedro de Alcalá (1505), el toscano-castellano de Cristóbal de las Casas (1570), el inglés-castellano de Richard Percival y de John Stevens (1591 y 1706), el francés-castellano de Juan Palet, de César Oudin, de Sobrino (1604, 1607, 1705), los trilingües francés-italiano-español de Girolamo Vittori (1609) e «Hispanicum Latinum et anglicum» de John Minsheu (1617), el español-italiano de Lorenzo Franciosini (1620), el español-alemán de Nicolás Mez de Braidenbach (1670), el español-latín de Baltasar Henríquez (1679) y el castellano-portugués de Raphael Bluteau (1721).

En cuanto a su aparición en los diccionarios monolingües, también en esta ocasión, el primero en recogerlo es el de Covarrubias (1611); el «LIRIO [...] es una flor a modo de açucena cardeno; por otro nombre dicho iris, por tener las colores del arco celeste. Ay muchas especies de lilios [...]».

Además, está presente en el *Diccionario de Autoridades* en 1734 con una definición aún más técnica:

> Planta, que se halla sylvestre y doméstica. Produce las hojas como la espadaña cortas y agudas. Sus flores nacen de diversas partes del tallo, matizadas de varios colores, aunque lo más ordinario es ser cárdenas. Tiene las raices nudosas y macízas, y es útil para muchas enfermedades. [...]
>
> (*Diccionario de Autoridades, ad vocem*)

La RAE mantendrá intacta esta definición en las ediciones de 1780, 1783, 1791. En la del 1803 se modificará en «planta de hojas puntiagudas, cuyas flores están matizadas de varios colores; pero por lo común, son moradas. *Lilium*» y a partir del DLE de 1817 será «Yerba medicinal [...]. El tallo es derecho, redondo, de cinco ó seis nudos, que cada uno brota una hoja más pequeña [con] flores de seis hojas muy grandes y hermosas, de color más o menos azulado [...]» con integraciones de dos especies (blanco y hediondo) en 1852 (igual en 1869), para modificarse otra vez en 1884 y 1899 cuya definición es la cristalizada hasta la fecha.

Los diccionarios no académicos del siglo XX calcarían la última definición de la RAE (vid. Pagés 1914, Alemany y Bolufer 1917 y Rodríguez Navas 1918) salvo Toro y Gómez 1901 que proporcionan una sucinta descripción: «Planta medicinal, de flores grandes y hermosas ‖*Lirio blanco*. AZUCENA. *Lirio de los valles*. MUGUETE».

2. Primeras atestaciones (siglos XII–XIV)

El primer testimonio de «lilio»[1] en literatura se encuentra en el *Poema de Santa Oria* de Gonzalo de Berceo (1198?-1264?), precisamente en el cuarteto 31 de la *Pri-*

---

1. En la controvertida *Razón de amor* (1205?–1265?) de autor Anónimo aparece «liryo», forma que después no se repitió a lo largo de la historia de la lengua y literatura en castellano: «[...] Y es la salvia, y sson [l]as rosas, / Y el lyro e las violas; [...]» (edición y transcripción de A. Morel-Fatio). Otra variante — «lyrio» — se hallará en el Cancionero de Juan Fernández de Íxar (Anónimo, entre 1424 y 1520); en los *Sermones de Epístolas y Evangelios por todo el año* de auto-

mera visión que inauguró por un lado la retórica de la competencia entre mujer y flores y por el otro la pareja lilio-rosa, que gozará de gran popularidad en la literatura posterior:

> Cecilia fue tercera una mártir preciosa,
> que de don Jesu Christo quiso seer esposa,
> non quiso otra suegra si non la Gloriosa,
> que fue mucho más bella que nin lilio nin rosa.

El mismo par — aunque con la variante «lirio», que corresponde a la primera muestra de su uso — se dio en el *Libro de Alexandre* (Anónimo, 1240–1250):

> Fue la noche venida mala e peligrosa,
> amaneçió mañana çiega e tenebrosa,
> vinié robar el mundo de la su flor preçiosa,
> que era más preçiada que nin lirio nin rosa.

Sin embargo, aún antes de su uso en la literatura, al lilio se le otorgaban cualidades de planta intocable y digna de protección jurídica. Según el *Fuero de Zorita de los Canes*, tratado legislativo de 1218–1250, quienes cogieran «rosas o lilio o binbres o cardos o cannauera» tendrían que pagar una multa de unos cuantos maravedíes. Lo mismo acaecerá en el *Fuero de Béjar* de 1293, en el *Fuero de Sepúlveda* de 1295 y en el *Fuero de Alcaraz* de 1296. En el *Fuero de Alarcón* y en el *Fuero de Teruel*, ambos de 1300, se retoman estas normas con la variante «lirio»: en general, varios pasajes de todos estos tratados parecen calcos del original de Zorita de los Canes.

Asimismo, se le utilizaba como remedio para el bienestar de los halcones, conforme al relato de Abraham de Toledo en *Moamín. Libros de los animales que cazan*, tratado de cetrería que Alfonso X hizo traducir del árabe en torno al 1250. Este texto servirá de modelo para los tratados posteriores durante los siglos XIV y XV, cuando el lilio mantendrá dichas propriedades benéficas para los rapaces.

Alfonso X citará una vez el «lirio» en la *Estoria de España* de 1270 y 4 veces el «lilio» (3 en los *Libros de Salomón* y 1 en la *Cuarta parte*) en el seno de su *General Estoria* de 1280.

En los *Libros de Salomón* el rey se sirve de la metáfora floral para enaltecer la belleza de mujer — «El tu ombligo vaso tornable (como fecho en torno), e que nunca mengua de beveres. El tu vientre como montón de trigo cercado de lilio» (ed. Sánchez-Prieto Borja, Horcajada Diezma 1994: 181) — y para resaltar la com-

---

ría y fecha de composición dudosas (a lo largo del siglo XVI); en compendios de boticarios y tratados médicos de los siglos XVI y XVII; en la lírica romanceril y los poemas épicos del siglo XVII y en un libro de viajes de Antonio de Ulloa de 1748 (*Viaje al reino del Perú*).

paración entre la delicadeza del lilio entre espinas y el alma en pena de la amada — «Yo flor del campo e lilio de los valles. / Assí como el lilio entre las espinas, assí la mi amiga entre las fijas» (en *Ivi*: 169) —; en la *Cuarta parte* se exhortan los fieles a cultivar el lilio como flor de devoción — «ffloresced flores como lilio. & dad olor & fogeced en gracia & alabad el cantigo» (en *Ivi*: fol. 272r) —.

También procedían de la corte alfonsina *Las Cantigas de Santa María*, donde en 1284 el «lilio» aparece en *hápax* y se presta a ser cantado en cualidad de elemento laudatorio hacia la virgen. Además, en esta obra se relata con la forma «lirio» un milagro muy sugerente, que inspirará a muchos autores.

De hecho, más adelante, en los 702 capítulos divididos en 14 libros de la *Grant Cronica de Espanya. Primera partida. Libros I XIV / conpilada de diversos libros e ystorias por don Johan Ferrandez de Eredia, por la gracia de Dios de la sancta casa del Espital de Sant Johan de Jerusalem, maestro humil e aguardador de los pobres de Cristo* (1388–1393?) de Juan Fernández de Heredia se puede observar 2 veces la flor («lilio»). Igual número de apariciones se da en el *Libro de los exemplos por A. B. C.* de Clemente Sánchez Vercial compuesto entre 1400 y 1421, en el que el «lilio […] muy fermoso e preçioso» adquiere poderes milagrosos: crece en la boca de un monje muerto y sus hojas llevan la incisión dorada "Ave María", con un eco en el *Sermón* de San Vicente Ferrer que relata el mismo milagro (1411–1412).

En la primera y más extensa traducción al castellano de las *Sagradas Escrituras*, la *Biblia Escorial* de 1300, figura dos veces la forma «lirio» (en general, por su simbología y significación, esta flor está muy presente en las versiones bíblicas; véase, por ejemplo, la *Biblia Romanceada* de 1400). En el mismo periodo hace su aparición en un fragmento que representa por primera vez en la península la leyenda de Tristán; se trata del manuscrito Vaticano 6428, editado fragmentariamente a principios del siglo XX.[2]

La primera muestra en verso de «lirio» se detecta en el *Cancionero de Baena*. La obra que pretendía recoger poemas de autores que actuaron durante los reinados de Enrique II (1369–1379), Juan I (1379–1390), Enrique III (1390–1406) y Juan II (1406–1454), cuyas páginas acogen 576 composiciones de 56 poetas. En ella se vuelve a proponer el par «lirio-rosa» — «Vuestra vista, deleitosa / más que lirio nin que rosa» — en la cantiga de Alfonso Álvarez *Señora, flor de azucena*. Presencias de «lirio» se encuentran también en el *Cancionero castellano de París*, 1430–1470 y en el *Cancionero de Salvá* de la misma época.

---

2. Véase el iluminante artículo de Luzdivina Cuesta Torre, *La transmisión textual de Don Tristán de Leonís*.

3. Hacia el esplendor del «lilio» / «lirio»: Renacimiento y Barroco

El paralelismo lilio-virginidad se verbaliza muy temprano con las palabras de un pontífice, Benedicto XIII, cuando en el *Libro de las Consolaciones de la vida humana* de 1417 escribe «ca el lilio entre las espinas alanza sus flores, al cual la virginidad es comparada» (ed. Castillo Vinaròs 1998: 91), instaurando una exitosa correspondencia literaria entre esta flor y la pureza mujeril no necesariamente relacionada con la Virgen.

Y mientras el antipapa construía una imagen que a lo largo de los siglos tendría muchos seguidores y despojaba al lilio de su connotación religiosa atribuyéndole matices carnales, en 1431, en Sevilla, un escritor anónimo incluía por primera vez la flor en un tratado de medicina titulado! *Tesoro de la medicina (Tesoro de los remedios)* en el que se alababan detalladamente sus virtudes terapéuticas. Más tarde, en el *Arte complida de cirugía* de 1450 la forma «lilio» convive con la de «lirio»: la flor valía hasta para curar las llagas, así como en los tratados médicos venideros de los siglos XV y XVI. En los compendios de boticarios se convertía en decocción y hasta se aconsejaba su uso en libros del arte de las comadres del XVI para calmar los dolores del parto.

En un momento de la historia, esta planta herbácea vivaz entra en la esfera de la moda, precisamente en el 1477 con *De vestir y de calzar* del fraile jerónimo Hernando de Talavera. En esta obra el lilio es modelo de belleza y elegancia; ni siquiera «Salomón en todo su triunfo y gloria alcanzó vestidura tan hermosa como la del lilio y de la rosa» (ed. Sánchez-Prieto Borja, Horcajada Diezma 1994: 51).

En 1490 Alfonso de Palencia recoge en el *Universal vocabulario en latín y en romance* la forma latina «Susanna» definiéndola «lilio o ensalçamiento de gloria» conforme a los orígenes hebreos del nombre. Un estimonio del uso intensivo en hebreo es la copiosa presencia del lilio en la *Biblia de Ferrara* (1553) traducción al español del *Tanaj* (los veinticuatro libros sagrados del judaísmo).

Jorge de Montemayor retoma el paralelismo lilio-pureza en el *Diálogo espiritual* (1543–1548), ajustándolo a la virgen y acrecentando la simbología relativa al candor y a la inocencia que la imagen del lilio conlleva:

> Esto mostró en la sobredicha autoridad el Espíritu Santo diziendo que la Virgen concebiría y pariría con estimable gozo, como lilio alabando a Dios, porque el lilio -que llamamos azuçena- no concibe por mistión ni simiente, sino por la calor y rayos de sol, y desta manera echa la hermosa flor de olor tan suave que comprende toda la casa adonde está. Y de la misma manera la Virgen concibió sin corrupción ni simiente, sino por solo el calor grande y la virtud del Espíritu Santo que descendió a ella y parió quedando virgen. (ed. Esteva de Llobet 1998:127)

Las evidencias científicas desmienten a Montemayor puesto que, técnicamente, el *lilium candidum* o lirio de la virgen (al que presuntamente él hace referencia) es la única variedad de estas flores que necesita sol y calor para crecer, sin embargo, la diferencia en su cultivo respecto a las demás especies reside tan solo en la profundidad de plantación (a ras de tierra en lugar de 15-20 cm de hondura); por el resto, los métodos de propagación no difieren entre flores (propagación por semilla, escamas de bulbo, bulbillos de las hojas).

Los sintagmas poéticos «blanco lirio» / «lirio blanco» se presentan por primera vez en unas líricas de Garcilaso de la Vega recogidas entre 1526 y 1536. Es entonces que la flor empieza a convertirse en un elemento retórico esencial, asumiendo el valor de enlace entre la naturaleza y el ser humano, adquiriendo matices a la vez terrenales e inmateriales. Así en la *Égloga I*:

> [...]
> Por ti el silencio de la selva umbrosa,
> por ti la esquividad y apartamiento
> del solitario monte m'agradaba;
> por ti la verde hierba, el fresco viento,
> el blanco lirio y colorada rosa
> y dulce primavera deseaba.
> ¡Ay, cuánto m'engañaba!
> ¡Ay, cuán diferente era
> y cuán d'otra manera
> lo que en tu falso pecho se escondía!
> Bien claro con su voz me lo decía
> la siniestra corneja, repitiendo
> la desventura mía.
> Salid sin duelo, lágrimas, corriendo.
> [...]

El «lilio blanco» se presenta por primera vez de la mano de Fray Luis de León en sus traducciones de Virgilio con fecha oscilante entre 1550 y 1580. En 1561 también profundiza la etimología hebrea de la palabra en su variante de «lirio» en la *Exposición del Cantar de los Cantares*, además de ofrecer dilucidaciones sobre más variedades botánicas:

> Azucena de los valles: que por estar en lugar más húmedo, está más fresca, y de mejor parecer. Esto dice la Esposa del Esposo, como si más claro dijese: Yo soy rosa del campo, y tú Esposo mío, lirio de los valles. En lo cual muestra cuán bien dice la hermosura del uno con la beldad del otro, y que como se dice de los desposados, son para en uno; como lo son la rosa y el lirio, que juntos crecen la gen-

tileza de entrambos, y agradan á la vista, y al olor, más que cada uno por sí. Lo que traducimos, azucena, ó lirio, en el hebreo es sosanah, que quiere decir, flor de seis hojas. Cuál sea, ó cómo se llame acá, no está muy averiguado, ni va mucho en ello, y por esto ya la llamarémos azucena, ya alhelí, ya violeta.

(ed. Sánchez-Prieto Borja, Horcajada Diezma 1994:31)

«Lirio» y «lilio» encuentran el gusto pastoril respectivamente en las poesías de Francisco de Figueroa entre 1550 y 1600 y en las de Fernando de Herrera del mismo periodo.

En 1585, entre las líneas retocadas de *La Galatea*, Miguel de Cervantes inaugura la florida estación en prosa castellana de las guirnaldas hechas con flores, entre las que destaca el «lirio»:

¡Ay!, cuántas veces, sólo por contentarme a mí mesma y por dar lugar al tiempo que se pasase, andaba de ribera en ribera, de valle en valle, cogiendo aquí la blanca azucena, allí el cárdeno lirio, acá la colorada rosa, acullá la olorosa clavellina, haciendo de todas suertes de odoríferas flores una tejida guirnalda, con que adornaba y recogía mis cabellos;. (ed. Sevilla Arroyo 2001:66)

Y mientras el «lilio» iba desapareciendo y antes de la la definitiva suplantación por parte del «lirio», Lope de Vega hacía gran acopio de esta forma en su producción en poesía y en prosa. Cobra importancia el uso que el autor hace del «lirio» tanto en los romances incluidos en su poema pastoril *La Arcadia* como en las octavas reales de la narración épica *La Dragontea*, ambas obras de 1598.

En la primera, el dramaturgo condensa todos los elementos bucólicos y arcádicos que veían en las flores las protagonistas de una naturaleza que era a la vez patrón y marco de comparación:

¿Qué azar a tu aliento manso,
qué lirio a tus limpias venas,
qué mosquetas a tus pechos,
donde la nieve se engendra?
Jazmines, rosas, claveles,
alhelíes, azucenas,
junquillos y mirasoles,
azar, lirios y mosquetas,
ninguna se compara, ninfa bella,
a tu hermosura y celestial belleza.

Sin descuidar los recursos metáforicos aún más típicos de la época utilizados por Lope, entre otras cosas, para complacer al público (en una práctica frecuente y aceptada) y con el objeto de sustentar y dignificar sus estrategias expresivas. Escribe:

> Amaneció en tu cara
> un sol que el mundo
> en vivo fuego ardía;
> corrió la edad avara,
> pasó ligero el día,
> y vino en su lugar la noche fría.
> Cerróse el lirio ufano
> con la tiniebla del escuro cielo,
> y el almendro temprano,
> marchito con el hielo,
> sembró de flores el desierto suelo.

En *La Dragontea* el Fénix se aleja de la moda del tiempo, dando muestra de sus dotes de poeta erudito. El «lirio» en esta circunstancia se acompaña de elementos de la naturaleza en el seno de una visión identitaria que, a imitación de la *Gerusalemme liberata* de Tasso, propone la imagen de Cristo muerto y, en diferentes fragmentos, todo lo relativo a las cruzadas y a la épica religiosa:

> Si un pino, si un laurel alma tenia,
> Y esto la antigüedad tuvo por cierto,
> Tened, árbol dichoso en este día,
> Un vivo eternamente, y en Cruz muerto.
> Y vos, divina y celestial María,
> Ciprés, fuente, laurel, plátano, huerto,
> Olíva, cedro, lirio, rosa, y palma,
> También en éste quedaréis por alma.[3]

O se enfrenta a «una lectura mítica del mundo, en una visión procedente de los poemas homéricos, introducida por la Eneida en el contexto de la retórica medie-

---

3. Juan de Jáuregui y luego José de Valdivieso calcarán el modelo lopesco; el primero en las *Rimas* de 1618: «Sois lirio asido a la pungente y dura / rama de espinas, y jamás violado; / rosa cuya beldad intacta y pura / no marchitó la noche y viento helado. / ¡Oh sin igual, purísima criatura!, / que, preservada del común pecado, / sois, en desprecio suyo, victoriosa / palma, oliva, ciprés, vid, lirio y rosa.», *A Nuestra Señora. Aplicando algunos atributos a la limpieza de su Concepción*; el segundo en la obra teatral *El nacimiento de la meior. Comedia divina (doce actos sacramentales y dos comedias divinas)*, 1622: «Mírala entre el açul lirio, / entre la rosa encarnada, / entre el plátano y ciprés, / cedro, nardo, oliua, palma.».

val y finalmente recuperado por el Renacimiento para la épica del Siglo de Oro.» (Colomino Ruiz 2012: 92):

> Y no menos a vos imagen santa
> de Atocha y de mi patria ofrecen cirios
> los que esa mano celestial levanta
> de tan profundas penas y martirios.
> Ya en fin en tierra ponen boca y planta,
> donde las algas les parecen lirios,
> unos en Cádiz, y otros en Lisboa,
> que los perdiera el viento a dar en proa.

Hasta convertirse de nuevo el «lirio» en marca de identidad de españoles ilustres, con la cabeza coronada de laurel, palma y lirio:

> Los moros africanos andaluces,
> las conquistas de reyes castellanos,
> las órdenes e insignias de las cruces
> al pecho trasladadas de las manos;
> y las estrellas fúlgidas y luces,
> que al cielo dieron Decios y Dacianos,
> de españoles ilustres por martirio,
> de laurel coronados, palma y lirio.

El uso de esta flor se intensificará en las comedias y en las *Rimas*. En definitiva, Lope se compromete a proteger la imagen del «lirio» como elemento de unidad de una España que «se había hecho más sólida que nunca, afirmada en una ortodoxia religiosa sin reservas y en el más exaltado orgullo nacional» (Lapesa 1981: 283). Sin embargo, el mismo poeta consigue demostrar que el lirio representa una porción de la civilización española que no necesariamente coincide con la vertiente religiosa.

Con Francisco de la Torre (1535?-1594?), poeta italianizante cuyas *Poesías* fueron editadas por Quevedo en 1631, continúa la práctica que comenzó Garcilaso del uso del «lirio blanco» / «blanco lirio» que en las *Églogas* van juntamente a la «purpúrea rosa». En la *VI* — «adonde muestra Flora / los blancos lirios y purpúreas rosas» — y en la *VIII* — «más blanca y colorada / que el blanco lirio y la purpúrea rosa» —. Sintagmas idénticos se encuentran en la producción poética de Vicente Espinel (1550–1624).

Luis Carrillo y Sotomayor asocia la pureza del «lirio» a la imagen del *hortus conclusus*, abriendo paso a la simbología del poema-jardín que tanta influencia tendrá en la historia de la literatura posterior. De este modo, en su *Fábula de Acis y Galatea* de 1611 preanuncia, además, estilemas y retórica gongorinas:

> Compite al blando viento su blandura
> — de cisne blanca pluma — y en dudosa
> suerte la iguala de la leche pura
> la nata dulce y presunción hermosa;
> en su beldad promete y su frescura
> del hermoso jardín el lirio y rosa.
> Y si mis quejas, ninfa hermosa, oyeras,
> leche, pluma, jardín, flores vencieras.

Luis de Góngora se decanta por la forma «lilio». A lo largo de su producción literaria esta flor se encuentra en su única obra teatral acabada, *Las firmezas de Isabela* (1610), otra vez en bipartición con la rosa: «Desdichada Violante, / a la flor de tu nombre parecida; / celosa como amante, / tan de azul, / tan de púrpura teñida, / que es amante y celosa, / un lilio breve, una pequeña rosa» (ed. Dolfi 1999:133); «purpúreas rosas» y «lilios cándidos» se acoplan nuevamente en la *Fábula de Polifemo y Galatea* (1612); en la letrilla *No solo el campo nevado* (1615), vuelve el «blanco lilio», aunque «non occorre ricordare che il *lilio* di Góngora è, come la più ispanica *azucena*, il fiore bianco per antonomasia» (Poggi 2009: 122); en la *Soledad primera* se enlaza para siempre a la mitología. En los romances gongorinos es «blanco», «celoso», está acompañado por las rosas, «amatunto» (voz desusada y posiblemente utilizada tan solo por Góngora para referirse a la diosa Venus); en los sonetos es elemento de comparación central: es «lilio bello» en *Mientras por competir con tu cabello*, «lilio siempre real» y «muerto lilio» en *Lilio siempre real, nací en Medina*, son «blancos lilios» en *Los blancos lilios que de ciento en ciento*, y — al igual que en Quevedo en *Abundoso y feliz Licas en su palacio, sólo él es despreciable* — es morada para el áspid (*Si Amor entre las pulmas de su nido*: «Entre las violetas fui herido / de el áspid que hoy entre los lilios mora»).

Góngora «aprovecha metáforas que el uso había convertido en lugares comunes, [...] capaces, a pesar de su desgaste, de constituir la base de un lenguaje poético que alejara las cosas de su vulgar realidad» (Lapesa 1981: 293); y la nobleza del «lilio» forma parte del deseo de dignificar el código.

De hecho con Góngora la conversión en símbolo de pureza, candor, belleza complementa la transformación del «lilio» en elemento (además de simbólico), retórico y semántico, que se convertiría en *topos* literario durante la época barroca.

La flor se halla en mucha poesía sensible a la influencia del cordobés: un epígono, Juan de Tassis y Peralta conde de Villamediana (1582–1622) alterna las dos formas, «lilio» y «lirio» y condensa en la unión lilio-nieve-mitología-primavera imágenes que conducen al gongorismo más limpio:

> Freqüenta las primaveras
> este dilicioso sitio
> con su divina consorte;
> que este mayo no ha venido
> por dar púrpura al clavel,
> por que nieve aprenda el lilio,
> por que rayos beva el sol,
> o cristal la vsurpe el río,
> sino por celebrar sólo,
> con aparatos festivos,
> el sienpre natal dichoso
> de su semidiós marido.

En cambio, Francisco de Quevedo prefiere la forma «lirio» asociada a tonos más despreocupados y, en definitiva, menos "platónicos" como en este fragmento de romance XCIII, *Describe el río Manzanares*:

> Arrebócese sus baños,
> y cálese un papahígo,
> y séquese, pues le falta
> la fuente del Paraíso.
> Yo considero estas cosas,
> cuando estoy, el susodicho,
> tres años ha, sobre doce,
> entre cadenas y grillos,
> aquí donde es año enero,
> con remudar apellidos,
> tan capona primavera,
> que no puede abrir un lirio.

Después de su auge en el barroco, el uso de la variante «lilio» va menguando en los siglos siguientes, hasta su desaparición en el XIX. (En el siglo XX recobrará vigor aisladamente en el auto de Miguel Hernández *Quién te ha visto y quién te ve y sombra de lo que eras*, 1934).

En 1652, Pedro Soto de Rojas aprovechará la imagen del «cándido lirio» como recurso expresivo en su *Paraíso cerrado para muchos, jardines abiertos para pocos* completando la ruta emprendida por Carrillo y Sotomayor.

Pedro Calderón de la Barca conserva la condensación floral tan típica de la época («Vuelve a ver de esa falda / el ameno país, / donde imágenes son, / brotando mil a mil, / el lirio, el alhelí, / la azucena, la rosa y el jazmín.», *El diablo mudo*, 1660) y retoma unos estilemas que pertenecieron a Lope («siendo de todo ese bosque / a la palma más excelsa, / más alto ciprés, más fértil / plátano, oliva más bella, / más enamorado lirio, / durable cedro y vid tierna, [...]», *A María el corazón*, 1664) y otros ya conocidos por el público de Cervantes y Góngora («[...] cubrid de flores el suelo; haced / guirnaldas para ceñir / sus sienes, tejiendo en ellas /lirio, azucena y jazmín.», *Andrómeda y Perseo*, 1680), haciendo de las imágenes asociadas al lirio algo circular en literatura y recurrente entre eruditos.

4. Siglos XVIII–XX

En el siglo didáctico por antonomasia, el XVIII, escasean ejemplos literarios de utilización de las flores, a favor de unos dictámenes normativos típicos de la época ilustrada; así el bibliotecario de corte, Gregorio Mayans y Siscar, en su *Orígenes de la lengua española* de 1737 aclara el camino (purista) a quienquiera dude en elecciones léxicas:

> Quando se duda si un vocablo se ha de atribuir a una lengua, o a otra, deve preferirse la lengua en la qual se expresse mejor la significación. Azucena llamamos al lirio blanco. En vascuence a-cucena quiere decir, esto es derecho; i como la azucena tiene la vara derecha, quiere Oihenart que sea esse el origen; pero si los penos, frigianos i persas llaman souson al lirio según Estéfano, i el etimologista anónimo (de donde le vino a Susa su nombre) por la abundacia de azucenas, i a Susana el suyo por su hermosura, como si digéramos azucena, o rosa ¿quién puede negar que es mucho más provable esta etimología? I más no siendo las azucenas de Vizcaya las mejores del mundo. (Mayans y Siscar 1737:382)

A caballo entre el gusto protorromántico y los vestigios barrocos se sitúa Juan Meléndez Valdés que en su producción poética a finales de 1700 acompaña el empleo reiterado de ninfas fugitivas y metáforas florales (protagonista el «lirio» y también «la rosa», «el jazmín», «la azucena», «la clavellina», «el tomillo», «la madreselva») con el primitivo manejo de «pálidas lunas» o «noches infelicísimas», junto a más desdichas.

Manuel María Arjona, en el mismo periodo y sin originalidad así trata «azucena», «rosa», «lirio», «nardo», «mirto» y «clavel» en *XIV*:

> La azucena y rosa,
> Mezcladas se ven

> Al lirio y al nardo,
> Al mirto y clavel.
> De tan dulce encanto
> Gocemos, mi bien;
> Gocemos, que el tiempo
> No vuelve después.

Al igual que Juan Ignacio González del Castillo en las *Poesías* de 1795:

> A vos, en fin, a vos los sentimientos
> que le inspiró el amor, y la ternura,
> reverente consagra. ¿A quién pudiera
> más dignamente dedicar sus votos
> un fino corazón? Vos, entre todas
> las bellezas que adornan este suelo,
> sobresalís, al modo que en el prado
> entre el cárdeno lirio y la violeta,
> la rosa matutina, que hace alarde
> de toda su fragancia, dilatando
> el purpúreo azafate de sus hojas.

El siglo XVIII se concluye con acaecimientos poco relevantes desde una perspectiva literaria y el XIX se abre con una fase poética de imitación, si se tiene en cuenta la producción de Gaspar María de Nava Álvarez, conde de Noroña, que así dibuja «llanura», «lirio», «bosque» y más fragmentos de la naturaleza en *Descripción de un valle*:

> Mira allí la llanura verdi-roja,
> Que hinche de gozo al corazon valiente,
> Llena de aguas, de bosques, de jardines,
> Morada de famosos héroes digna;
> Tierra cual seda, con almizcle el aura,
> Agua de rosa sus vergeles riega,
> Se dobla el lirio por su mismo peso,
> El bosque á rosa en derredor trasciende,
> El faisan se pompea entre las flores,
> Y en el ciprés el ruiseñor discanta.
> Nunca marchitos sus pensiles, siempre
> Serán del bosque del Eden imágen.
> En el prado y colinas, reclinadas
> Verás doncellas, cual las hadas lindas;

O incluso, sin pretensión de exhaustividad, la producción de Juan Nicasio Gallego que en su poemario *Obras poéticas* de 1801 da muestra de ser fino imitador:

>¡Ay! tan gentil belleza
>Goza, Corina, impenetrable al sello
>Del tiempo y la tristeza,
>Y en rosa y lirio bello
>Cien Mayos enguirnalden tu cabello.
>Yo triste á crudo invierno,
>Y á llorar en tu ausencia condenado,
>Ni oigo á Favonio tierno
>Suspirar por el prado,
>Ni el trino de las aves concertado.

En cambio, a Juan Arolas Bonet, más allá de sus dotes de emulador, va el mérito de haber adelantado unos aspectos de abertura al orientalismo que caracterizará mucha poesía posterior, reuniendo lo que se fue convirtiendo en tradición (todo lo referente a la semántica del «lirio») en un adelanto de progreso:

>Con un misterioso arcano
>La odalisca del harén
>Véngase de su tirano,
>Que pérfido, que inhumano,
>La maltrata con desdén;
>Y un lirio que ha deslizado
>A los pies de un icoglán
>Le revela que es amado
>De aquella que no ha inflamado
>La tibieza del sultán.
>Si da su contestación
>Con una rosa el doncel
>Revela que la razón
>Contradice la pasión
>De la favorita infiel;

Durante el Romanticismo el «lirio» recobra la autonomía difuminada después de la exitosa temporada barroca. Se vuelve a dignificar en los endecasílabos de la épica del Duque de Rivas en 1834 con *El moro expósito o Córdoba y Burgos en el siglo décimo* y en los octosílabos asonantados de los *Romances históricos* de 1841, compuestos para revalorizar la tradición del romance en lengua castellana, aunque muchos fueron los detractores de esta operación que al parecer fue vacua y falta de contenidos.

El «lirio» también encuentra su espacio en la prosa de Bécquer sin nuevas aportaciones en cuanto a imágenes y semántica. También en la de Espronceda, precisamente en su única novela histórica, *Sancho Saldaña o el castellano de Cuéllar*, de 1834; en esta obra se encuentran resonancias renacentistas y barrocas entremezcladas con ecos del romanticismo más escueto. Es en este encuentro que se realiza la incorporación del «lirio» como elemento de tradición y homenaje al glorioso pasado literario en lengua castellana:

> Estaba de perfil a la puerta que había abierto para respirar el aire de la tarde, y sentada junto a la reja, a la que se enlazaban algunas ramas de árboles, con el laúd se entretenía en vibrar dulces sonidos acordes con su melancolía. Puestos los ojos al cielo, y acaso alguna lágrima solitaria bañando lentamente el lirio de sus mejillas, parecía la imagen de la hermosa Druida llorando al son de su lira en su sagrado bosque su funesto amor por el prisionero que va a perecer en las llamas, víctima de la superstición. (Espronceda 1834:pár. 440)

Benito Pérez Galdós en su novela de 1878 *La familia de León Roch* sostiene la tesis adelantada por Lope de Vega en *La Dragontea*. Así es como el narrador divisa en el lirio imágenes religiosas diferentes de las relacionadas a la pureza de la virgen: «Era, sí, un delicado lirio — dijo León, pálido y con nervioso temblor en su lengua, en sus ojos, en sus facciones todas —, un lirio que convidaba con su pureza y su aroma al amor cristiano, a los honestos goces de la vida...» (Galdós 1878:81). Y unos años más tarde Emilia Pardo Bazán en *Los Pazos de Ulloa* (1886) empareja la desnudez de un recién nacido a la «cosa más pura y santa del mundo: un lirio una azucena de candor» (Pardo Bazán 1886:293–94).

A lo largo de 1900, la Generación del '27 reconstituye la imagen del «lirio». Aquí se detallarán unos pocos ejemplos dentro de la diversidad de sugestiones que enriquecieron el siglo XX.

Rosa Chacel, en su deseo de continuidad con la tradición, ajusta el surrealismo de algunas formas a los homenajes clasicistas: en su poesía el lirio mantiene la idea de blancura (*Mariposa nocturna*: «[...] y leves voces laten en gargantas / entre el cieno que nutre al lirio blanco / mirado por la noche intensamente. [...]») y a la vez se convierte — inédita y personalmente — en «negro» (*Una música oscura, temblorosa*: «Una música oscura, temblorosa, / cruzada de relámpagos y trinos, / de maléficos hálitos, divinos, / del negro lirio y de la ebúrnea rosa. [...]»)

La simbología de esta flor asume aún más vigor y se llena ulteriormente de matices en la obra de Federico García Lorca, que ajusta el valor alegórico del lirio a sus exigencias expresivas, además de disfrazarlo de una semántica que si por un lado se ha criado en la tradición, por el otro se manifiesta como estrictamente inherente a su retórica, dando luz así a otras opciones de lectura de la flor.

5. El «lirio» en un soneto de Lorca y sus traducciones al italiano

El soneto de Lorca cuyo *incipit* es «¡Ay voz secreta del amor oscuro!» forma parte de los *Sonetos del amor oscuro*, editados entre 1981 y 1983, aunque compuestos entre 1935 y 1936. En esta recopilación póstuma el «lirio» se encuentra en *hápax*, pese a ser una flor que aparece constantemente, compasando en toda la producción poética y en prosa del granadino.

> ¡Ay voz secreta del amor oscuro!
> ¡ay balido sin lanas! ¡ay herida!
> ¡ay aguja de hiel, camelia hundida!
> ¡ay corriente sin mar, ciudad sin muro!
> ¡Ay noche inmensa de perfil seguro,
> montaña celestial de angustia erguida!
> ¡ay perro en corazón, voz perseguida!
> ¡silencio sin confín, lirio maduro!
> Huye de mí, caliente voz de hielo,
> no me quieras perder en la maleza
> donde sin fruto gimen carne y cielo.
> Deja el duro marfil de mi cabeza,
> apiádate de mí, ¡rompe mi duelo!
> ¡que soy amor, que soy naturaleza!

En 1994 Lorenzo Blini traduce este soneto en una edición al cuidado de Norbert Von Prellwitz:

> Voce segreta dell'amore oscuro!
> Belato senza lana! Ahi, ferita!
> Ago di fiele, camelia appassita!
> Corrente asciutta, città senza muro!
> Notte immensa dal profilo sicuro,
> d'eretta angoscia celestiale monte!
> Voce braccata, cane dentro il cuore,
> infinito silenzio, iris maturo!
> Fuggi da me, rovente voce gelida,
> e non farmi smarrire nella macchia
> dove sterili carne e cielo gemono.
> Lascia l'avorio duro del mio capo,
> abbi pietà di me, spezza il dolore,
> perché sono natura, sono amore!

En 2006 Glauco Felici edita y traduce el volumen *Sonetti dell'amore oscuro*, presentando la traducción de «¡Ay voz secreta del amor oscuro!» que aquí se lee:

> Ahi voce segreta dell'amore oscuro!
> ahi belato senza lana! ahi ferita!
> ahi ago di fiele, camelia reclinata!
> ahi corrente senza mare, città senza mura!
> Ahi notte immensa dal profilo netto,
> montagna celestiale d'angoscia eretta!
> Ahi cane nel cuore, voce inseguita,
> silenzio sconfinato, iris matura!
> Fuggi da me, calda voce di gelo,
> non volermi perduto nella boscaglia
> dove senza frutto gemono carne e cielo.
> Lascia il duro avorio della mia testa,
> abbi pietà di me, spezza il mio dolore!,
> ch'io sono amore, ch'io sono natura!

En 2021 Rosario Trovato propone una selección de traducciones de Lorca bajo el título de *Le più belle poesie d'amore*, en edición bilingüe con la siguiente propuesta del mismo soneto:

> Voce segreta dell'amore oscuro!
> Ahi belato senza lana, ahi ferita,
> ahi camelia sfiorita, ago di fiele!
> Flusso senz'acqua, città senza mura!
> Ahi notte immensa di linea sicura,
> monte celeste di protesa angoscia!
> Ahi cane nel cuore, voce inseguita!
> Silenzio senza fine, iris maturo!
> Fuggi da me, voce ardente di gelo,
> non farmi perdere nella sterpaglia
> dove carne e cielo gemono sterili.
> Della mia testa lascia il duro avorio,
> abbi di me pietà, spezza il dolore,
> perché sono natura, sono amore!

Los tres traducen «lirio» con «iris»: para Felici es «matura», para Blini y Trovato es «maturo», a pesar del género que en italiano es incuestionablemente femenino. ¿Por qué traducir «lirio» con «iris» cuando en italiano «lirio» tiene su exacto homólogo en la palabra «giglio»? De hecho, no hay que subestimar las notables ventajas de la traducción de «lirio» con «giglio»: lo primero, la feliz coincidencia del número de sílabas con acentuación llana; lo segundo, la contingencia de la asonancia en *i / o*, ambas circunstancias que en la traducción poética suponen un considerable provecho desde una perspectiva rímico-rítmico-fonosimbólica; además, no hay que considerar la traducción "unívoca" de lirio-giglio como una falta de atención, investigación o estudio, ya que no es cierto que una traducción transparente corresponda a una traducción superficial.

Cuestiones técnicas a parte (el «iris» florece en marzo, el «lirio» en verano; el «iris» forma parte de la familia de las iridáceas, el «lirio» de las liliáceas) y con la convicción de que la palabra «giglio» aparece la más apropiada para traducir al «lirio», se pueden llevar a cabo una serie de hipótesis para explicar el porqué de la aparición de «iris» en las versiones italianas; ante todo, es posible que los traductores en cuestión hayan sido engañados por la acepción de «lirio» del DLE que a partir del 1899 transmite una definición inexacta, puesto que el «lirio», como se ha dicho ya, no forma parte de la familia de las iridáceas, sino de las liliáceas; luego, puede que los mismos hayan sufrido una fuerte sugestión a partir de la traducción que del mismo soneto hizo por primera vez al italiano Mario Socrate en 1985[4] que aquí se presenta:

> Ah, voce occulta dell'amore oscuro,
> belato senza lana, ah ferita,
> ago di fiele, camelia reclina,
> foce senz'acque, città senza mura!
> Ah, notte immensa di linea sicura,
> vetta celeste d'angoscia protesa!
> Ah, cane dentro al cuore, ah voce offesa,
> silenzio senza fine, iris matura!
> Fuggi da me, calda voce di gelo,
> non farmi smarrire nella foresta
> dove sterili carne e cielo gemono.
> Sgombrami il duro avorio della testa,
> abbi pietà di me, sciogli il mio lutto,
> ché sono amore io, e natura è questa!

Pues, la traducción de «iris matura» de Socrate ha condicionado a las generaciones posteriores de traductores, que han "confiado" en el magisterio del gran hispanista y seguido fielmente sus huellas; además, una gestión superficial de las

---

[4]. Felici conocía sin duda la traducción en cuestión, ya que en esa misma edición se encargó de la redacción de las notas bio-bibliográficas.

actualizaciones del DLE por parte de la RAE ha completado el cuadro y ha permitido la transmisión de una ligereza por parte de experimentados traductores.

Sin embargo, en 2013 el joven estudioso Valerio Nardoni había propuesto una traducción «lungamente meditata» del soneto (Nardoni 2013:20), restituyendo el trasvase «lirio»-«giglio»:

> Ahi voce occulta dell'amore oscuro!
> belato senza lana, ahi ferita!
> ago di fiele, ahi camelia appassita!
> flusso senz'acqua, ahi città senza muro!
> Ahi notte immensa dal volto sicuro,
> celeste monte d'angoscia acuita!
> cane nel cuore, ahi voce inseguita!
> vasto silenzio, ahi giglio maturo!
> Fuggi da me, calda voce di gelo,
> io non mi perda nell'aspra radura
> del pianto sterile di carne e cielo.
> Lascia l'eburnea mia testa dura,
> abbi pietà, e rompi il mio sfacelo!
> che io sono amore, io sono natura!

Tomando como hilo conductor la evolución interna de la palabra y la historia de su uso, es posible afirmar que el «lirio» ha ido incorporando, conforme a su desarrollo a lo largo de los siglos, componentes reales y metafóricas que han contribuido a su completa formación como elemento identitario de la lengua, la literatura y la cultura españolas. El hecho de ser y haber sido palabra compartida y reconocible por una comunidad, el hecho de remitir a significaciones metafóricas (pureza, virginidad, belleza, en unos casos ortodoxia religiosa) además de denotativas, el hecho de que en unos casos literatos y literatas eligieran utilizar en su obra esta flor en forma intertextual con el deseo de que perdurara y sobreviviera al desgaste del tiempo, definen fuertemente al lirio y lo dotan de autonomía conceptual.

Siguiendo a Koller (1979) y a Bödeker y Freese (1987), se ha de tratar al «lirio» como un *realia*, por ser un elemento real y peculiar de una cultura en concreto, con todo lo que esto puede conllevar a la hora del trasvase de una lengua a otra. La operación nunca meramente lingüística de la traducción asume aún más connotaciones frente a la complejidad de la semántica de ciertos elementos.

La carga semántica de la flor se ha ido engrandeciendo a lo largo de su historia y — en línea intertextual y diacrónica — el «lirio» ha sido sometido, gracias a su uso, a constante renovación de significado. Estas circunstancias han facilitado su paso a palabra fuertemente connotada que en su contexto cultural, literario, lingüístico se yergue a elemento identitario. Al no traducir «lirio» con «giglio» se verifica una pérdida comunicativa que asume valor de *diminutio* de elementos de una cultura concreta. Esto no encuentra compensación alguna, ni en el renombre del traductor, ni en el deseo de obediencia de los discípulos al maestro.

Bibliografía

Benedicto XIII. 1998. *Libro de las consolaciones de la vida humana*, edición preparada y estudio preliminar por Juan B. Simó Castillo Vinaròs. Ayuntamiento de Peñíscola.

Bödeker, Birgit, and Katrin Freese. 1987. "Die Übersetzung von Realienbezeichnungen bei literarischen Texten: Eine Prototypologie." *TextContext* 2 (2): 137–165.

Castro, Teresa de. 2018. *El tratado sobre el vestir, calzar y comer del arzobispo Hernando de Talavera*. Alicante: Biblioteca Virtual Miguel de Cervantes. Versión electrónica: ⟨https://www.cervantesvirtual.com/nd/ark:/59851/bmc0924853⟩.

Cervantes, Miguel de. 2001. *La Galatea*, edición de Florencio Sevilla Arroyo. Alicante: Biblioteca Virtual Miguel de Cervantes. Versión electrónica: ⟨https://www.cervantesvirtual.com/nd/ark:/59851/bmcj9638⟩.

Colomino Ruiz, Sergio. 2012. *"La Dragontea" de Lope de Vega: una aproximación literaria e histórica*. Barcelona: Universitat Pompeu Fabra. Tesis doctoral inédita.

Cuesta Torre, Luzdivina. 1993. "La transmisión textual de Don Tristán de Leonís". *Revista de Literatura Medieval*, 5: 63-93.

Fantechi, Giancarlo. 2014. "La Bibbia Escoriale I.I.6, specchio di un'epoca: lingua e religione nella costruzione della identità castigliana nel XIII secolo." *Rivista Di Cultura Classica e Medioevale*, 56 (2): 435-74. Versión electrónica: ⟨http://www.jstor.org/stable/43923833⟩.

García Lorca, Federico. 1985. *Sonetti dell'amore oscuro. Suites*, introduzione di Carlo Bo, notizie biografiche e guida bibliografica di Glauco Felici, prefazione, traduzione e note di Mario Socrate. Milano: Garzanti.

García Lorca, Federico. 2013. *Sonetti dell'amore oscuro, a cura di Valerio Nardoni*. Firenze: Passigli.

Góngora y Argote, Luis de. 1999. *Las firmezas de Isabela*, edición de Laura Dolfi. Alicante: Biblioteca Virtual Miguel de Cervantes. Edición digital a partir del Manuscrito Chacón, *Obras*, vol. III, Biblioteca Nacional (España), Res. 46: 1-120. Versión electrónica: ⟨https://www.cervantesvirtual.com/nd/ark:/59851/bmc4x552⟩.

Koller, Werner. 1979. *Einführung in die Übersetzungswissenschaft*. Heidelberg-Wiesbaden: Quelle & Meyer.

Lapesa, Rafael. 1981. *Historia de la lengua española*, prólogo de Ramón Menéndez Pidal. Madrid: Editorial Gredos.

Los diccionarios consultados se encuentran en línea en ⟨https://www.rae.es/obras-academicas/diccionarios/nuevo-tesoro-lexicografico-0⟩

Mayans y Siscar, Gregorio. 1873. *Orígenes de la lengua española, compuestos por varios autores, recogidos por D. Gregorio Mayans y Siscar, bibliotecario del Rey, publicados por primera vez en 1737, y reimpresos ahora por la sociedad "La amistad librera", con un prólogo de D. Juan Eugenio Hartzenbusch, y notas al diálogo de las lenguas y a los orígenes de la lengua, de Mayans, por D. Eduardo de Mier*. Madrid: Librería de Victoriano Suárez.

Montemayor, Jorge de. 1998. *Diálogo espiritual*, edición de María Dolores Esteva de Llobet. Kassel: Reichenberger.

Morel-Fatio, Alfred. 1887. "Textes castillans inédits du XIIIe siècle". *Romania*, 62–64: 364–382.

Morreale, Margherita. 1962. "Alcuni aspetti filologici della storia delle volgarizzazioni castigliane medievali della Bibbia". En *Saggi e ricerche in memoria di Ettore Li Gotti*, Centro di studi filologici e linguistici Siciliani, Palermo: s. n.: 319–337.

Pardo Bazán, Emilia. 1886. *Los pazos de Ulloa*. Barcelona: Daniel Cortezo y C.a Editores.

Pérez Galdós, Benito. 1878. *La familia de León Roch*. Madrid: La Guirnalda.

Poggi, Giulia. 2009. *Gli occhi del pavone: quindici studi su Góngora*. Firenze: Alinea Editrice.

Orellana Calderón, Raúl. 2017. "La tradición bíblica en la cuarta parte de la *General estoria*. Fuentes y traducción". *Atalaya*, 17, sin páginas. Versión electrónica: ⟨http://journals.openedition.org/atalaya/2682⟩.

Sánchez-Prieto Borja, Pedro, and Bautista Horcajada Diezma. 1994. *General Estoria. Tercera Parte. Libros de Salomón: Cantar de los cantares, Proverbios, Sabiduría y Eclesiastés*. Edición de textos alfonsíes en REAL ACADEMIA ESPAÑOLA: Banco de datos (CORDE) [en línea]. Corpus diacrónico del español. Versión electrónica: ⟨http://www.rae.es⟩.

Sánchez-Prieto Borja, Pedro and Rocío Díaz Moreno, and Elena Trujillo Belso. 2002. *General Estoria. Cuarta parte*. Edición de textos alfonsíes en REAL ACADEMIA ESPAÑOLA: Banco de datos (CORDE) [en línea]. Corpus diacrónico del español. Versión electrónica: ⟨http://www.rae.es⟩.

L'intercompréhension en contexte universitaire
Traduction du *Petit Chaperon Rouge* de Charles Perrault dans différentes langues romanes

Alexandra Marti
Universidad de Alicante

The aim of this chapter is to show the two contradictory trends in the European plurilingual area: one that advocates European plurilingualism in the school environment and, at the same time, one that maintains a watertight education system in which the ideology of a single language prevails, thus excluding the diversity of languages. Can intercomprehension methodology be integrated into language teaching in the long term? This is what we propose to analyze in this chapter, first presenting intercomprehension as a means of achieving plurilingualism, then sharing a pedagogical experience via Charles Perrault's *Little Red Riding Hood*, translated into different Romance languages, with positive results. Finally, we will draw on the recommendations of advocates of intercomprehension in teacher training to enhance the plurality and understanding of languages in a university context.

Keywords: intercomprehension, plurilingualism, *Little Red Riding Hood*, translation, Romance languages

1. Introduction

Nombreux sont les chercheurs qui dénoncent le décalage évident entre les instances officielles prônant la diversité linguistique dans leurs textes officiels, ne donnant aucune instruction précise pour atteindre le plurilinguisme tant convoité, et la réalité des faits dans les classes, où règne un monolinguisme absolu. C'est le cas de la France, mais aussi de plusieurs pays européens, où l'école a hiérarchisé les langues en les rendant étanches. Les conséquences directes, qui en résultent, montrent l'inefficacité de l'enseignement des langues et le manque de légitimité accordé à l'intercompréhension, qui favorise justement, les interactions entre locuteurs de langues différentes (Modard 2010 ; Escudé et Janin 2010a). Chemin faisant, maints spécialistes considèrent que si l'intercompréhension prenait en compte cette réalité des systèmes éducatifs, alors elle pourrait les convaincre de ses atouts, et par là même, s'insérer à long terme dans l'enseignement en proposant de nouvelles méthodologies capables d'innover l'organisation scolaire via l'intégration du plurilinguisme. (Escudé et Janin 2010a).

Dans un premier temps, nous exposerons les avantages de l'intercompréhension en milieu éducatif, puissant instrument pédagogique, permettant de consolider la diversité linguistique. Par la suite, nous présenterons une expérience pédagogique d'intercompréhension moyennant un conte connu par tous, *Le Petit Chaperon Rouge*, de Charles Perrault, traduit en neuf langues romanes (occitan, catalan, valencien, castillan, portugais du Portugal, portugais du Brésil, galicien, italien et roumain). Finalement, nous prendrons appui sur les recommandations des défenseurs de l'intercompréhension dans la formation des enseignants.

2. L'intercompréhension comme moyen d'atteindre le plurilinguisme

Escudé et Janin (2010b) prônent l'intégration des langues afin de développer la compétence métalinguistique. Pour ces auteurs, l'intercompréhension permet d'établir des relations entre les langues grâce aux ponts, comparaisons, transferts et retours vers la langue maternelle, etc. Pour eux :

> Plus on travaillera sur des langues de même famille, plus il y aura de passerelles de langue à langue : la frontalité qui fait par exemple de l'espagnol et du français des langues *étrangères* s'affaisse. Les *frontières* entre langues ne sont plus jamais définitives et se déplacent : parfois le français sera proche d'un groupe portugais, castillan, catalan, occitan et parfois éloigné, plus proche d'un groupe italien-roumain. Ces traits communs sur une ligne de continuum élastique permettent l'assimilabilité des langues voisines. (Escudé & Janin, 2010b : 54)

L'apprentissage traditionnel va dans un seul sens, en juxtaposition et opposition, alors que l'apprentissage en intercompréhension prend en compte les langues et les intègre. Comme l'expliquent Escudé et Janin (2010b : 56) :

> (…) croiser les langues, les comparer, travailler en aller-retour entre la langue source et les langues cibles est le fondement de l'intercompréhension, ce qui construit de fait la compétence métalangagière (…). L'intercompréhension, tout en ne travaillant que sur une base plus restreinte de compétences, apporte d'autres bénéfices : aire de compréhension plus développée ; construction de compétences métalangagières ; désinhibition et efficacité d'apprentissage.

Croiser les deux apprentissages serait favorable au plurilinguisme et permettrait d'améliorer l'apprentissage des langues en qualité et en quantité. Comme l'indiquent Escudé et Janin (2010b : 56) :

> Si les autorités éducatives ouvraient l'apprentissage des langues à l'intercompréhension, cela permettrait de faire évoluer les curricula, les méthodes et les manuels et d'obtenir des résultats beaucoup plus efficaces, non seulement pour chaque apprenant, mais plus généralement par rapport à l'investissement collectif consenti dans ce domaine.

Comme l'explique Castagne (2011), le programme InterCompréhension Européenne (ICE) a montré que les règles linguistiques sont pas importantes en soi mais ce qui le sont ce sont les relations et les interactions existantes entre elles. Autrement dit, la rencontre entre différentes règles est à l'origine d'une nouvelle systémique donnant lieu à d'autres règles accessibles à leur tour par le biais d'inférences.

Partageant la remarque de Castagne (2011 : 84), « les langues ont toujours été en contact avec d'autres langues et partagent ainsi des convergences qui facilitent le phénomène général de leur (inter)compréhension par les textes ».

Voici la typologie des langues que dresse Castagne (2011 : 86) à partir des résultats obtenus par les membres du programme ICE :

- langues voisines et parentes du français : espagnol, italien, portugais ;
- langues voisines et non parentes du français : anglais, allemand, néerlandais ;
- langues non voisines et parentes du français : roumain ;
- langues non voisines et non parentes du français : suédois, russe, turc...

Les années 90 voient la notion de plurilinguisme se construire tout comme celle d'intercompréhension visant de nouvelles orientations pour l'enseignement des langues. L'acceptation totale de l'intercompréhension comme un complément à l'apprentissage des langues doit passer nécessairement par l'identification immédiate de ses perspectives par rapport à celles déjà existantes (Caddéo et Jamet 2013 : 25-27). Dès les années 90, les premiers outils d'intercompréhension ont vu le jour dans différents pays européens :

Dans les années 2000, de nombreux travaux sont publiés sur l'intercompréhension. Chemin faisant, l'approche d'intercompréhension devient à la mode, enseignée dans maintes institutions universitaires, expérimenter dans le milieu professionnel et dans les écoles par le biais de projets. De nombreuses formations existent pour les enseignants (programmes Euro-forma et Formica). Au-delà de l'Europe, l'Amérique Latine et les États-Unis l'adoptent. Le but est d'intégrer l'intercompréhension dans les programmes scolaires de chaque pays (Caddéo et Jamet 2013).

Tableau 1.

Pays	France	France	Allemagne	Danemark
Chercheur	Claire Blanche-Benveniste	Louise Dabène et Christian Degache	Franz-Joseph Meissner / Horst G et al.	Jorgen Schmitt Jensen
Université	Université de Provence	Université de Grenoble 3	Universität Giesse / Goethe Universität	Univerité d'Aarhus
Projet	Méthode EuRom4	Méthodes Galatea et Galanet	Méthode EuroComRom	Publication d'ouvrages de grammaire comparée

Source: Caddéo et Jamet (2013 : 28)

De surcroît, comme l'indique Escudé (2020), il existe des ressources scolaires qui favorisent le plurilinguisme. Le manuel *Euromania* en est un formidable exemple didactique, offrant aux apprenants des contenus disciplinaires par le biais de « l'intercompréhension intégrée » et permettant :

> De ne pas mettre en concurrence sur le marché scolaire les langues romanes entre elles : souvent, français, espagnol, italien, sont au choix pour la seconde langue apprise. L'intercompréhension permet d'entrer dans le système commun de ces langues et de développer des compétences fortes et abouties en compréhension écrite, puis par des enseignements complémentaires et choisis, l'apprenant pourra développer grâce au système scolaire ou par son propre trajet biographique, sa compétence plus globale en telle ou telle langue (Escudé 2020 : 79).

Selon Tyvaert (2008), l'intercompréhension révèle la richesse de la variation linguistique indépendamment que l'espace soit ample ou restreint. Il suggère la désensibilisation aux langues étrangères (LE), autrement, l'allergie aux LE doit laisser place à la découverte des langues. C'est là que l'intercompréhension acquiert toute son importance pouvant être la clé de voûte de « tous les espaces de rencontre en Europe, entre individus et collectivités de toutes tailles, entre personnes et cultures de tous les niveaux de socialisation » (Tyvaert 2008 : 275).

Andrade et Aráujo e Sá (2008), quant à elles, argumentent que l'intercompréhension est au cœur de la didactique des langues et des politiques linguistiques européennes prônant la diversité des langues et des cultures. C'est ainsi que leur projet européen ILTE (*Intercomprehension in Language Teacher Education*) a vu le jour dont l'objectif principal était l'intégration de l'intercompréhension dans la formation didactique des enseignants. Les modules proposés prétendaient sensibiliser à :

- la diversité linguistique
- la communication interculturelle
- la réflexion métalinguistique
- la mise en place de stratégies de compréhension et de lecture

3. Expérience pédagogique d'intercompréhension via le conte du *Petit Chaperon Rouge* de Charles Perrault

La perspective « applicative » via l'intercompréhension donne donc un souffle de renouveau aux études en philologie, ayant connu un déclin considérable en Europe et notamment en France. Les similitudes entre les langues redeviennent un thème de recherche dont le noyau dur est de didactiser la façon dont les apprenants pourront en bénéficier (Caddéo et Jamet 2013).

Le conte, genre narratif canonique, qui provient d'une tradition orale véhiculant des valeurs ou des stéréotypes universels, se présente opportunément, comme un support didactique de qualité, en matière d'échange interculturel, dans le contexte d'une exploitation en classe. Comme il fonctionne souvent sur des invariants linguistiques récurrents (titres, formules magiques, vœux, malédictions, tics de langage ou sentences préférées d'un protagoniste, etc.), il est très intéressant d'établir des passerelles d'une langue à l'autre, voire de comparer les liens linguistiques que le français entretient avec les langues romanes.

Cette expérience pédagogique d'intercompréhension par le biais du conte *Le Petit Chaperon Rouge*, de Charles Perrault, s'inscrit dans la matière « Langue CIV : français » auprès d'étudiants de deuxième année de LEA (Langues Étrangères Appliquées) à l'Université d'Alicante. Nous tenons d'ailleurs à remercier Carmen González Aranda, Iris Cots Penalva et David Castillo Navarro pour leur participation dans ce projet d'innovation ainsi que notre collègue, Andréa Marques de Almeida Bouix, pour sa collaboration.

Les objectifs principaux étaient les suivants :

- Promouvoir une éducation plurilingue à partir du conte *Le Petit Chaperon Rouge*
- Développer des capacités d'intercompréhension chez les étudiants
- Favoriser le respect des apprenants envers d'autres langues et cultures voisines
- Comparer les langues romanes : alphabets, sons, orthographe, syntaxe
- Développer l'autonomie des étudiants

Nous pouvons observer, dans le tableau ci-dessous, les différences et les ressemblances entre les titres du *Petit Chaperon Rouge* traduits dans différentes langues romanes. C'est ainsi que nous remarquons la présence de diminutifs divers dans chacune des langues (-et, -eta, -ita, -inho, -iña, -etto), les marques du masculin et féminin varient dans les dix langues. Notons également qu'il n'y a pas d'articles en valencien, castillan, portugais, galicien, italien et roumain. En revanche, il y a un article en français, en occitan et en catalan. Remarquons aussi qu'en français, en occitan, en portugais le titre est au masculin. Enfin, une autre similarité, il y a une majuscule dans les différentes langues romanes.

Tableau 2.

Français	Le petit Chaperon Rouge
Occitan	Lo Capaironet Roge
Catalan	La Caputxeta Vermella
Valencien	Caputxeta Roja
Castillan	Caperucita Roja
Portugais (Brésil)	Chapeuzinho Vermelho
Portugais (Portugal)	Capuchinho Vermelho
Galicien	Carapuchiña Vermella
Italien	Cappuccetto Rosso
Roumain	Scufita Rosie

Passons maintenant au début du conte du *Petit Chaperon Rouge* où les personnages nous sont présentés :

Tableau 3.

Français	Il était une fois une petite fille de village, la plus jolie qu'on eût su voir ; sa mère en était folle, et sa mère-grand plus folle encore. Cette bonne femme lui fit faire un petit chaperon rouge, qui lui seyait si bien, que partout on l'appelait le Petit Chaperon rouge.
Occitan	I aviá un còp una drolleta de vilatge, la pus polida que s'agèsse vista; sa maire n'èra emmascada, e sa grand emmascada que mai. Aquel bona vièlha li faguèt far un capairon roge, que li estava tan plan, que li disián pertot lo Capaironet roge.
Castillan	Érase una vez en una aldea una niñita, la más bonita que jamás se hubiera visto; su madre estaba enloquecida con ella y su abuela mucho más todavía. Esta buena mujer le había mandado hacer una caperucita roja y le sentaba tan bien que todos la llamaban Caperucita Roja.
Catalan	Vet aquí que una vegada hi havia una nena petita que vivia en un poblet. Era la nena més bonica que us pugueu imaginar; la seva mare n'estava encantada, i la seva àvia encara més. Aquesta bona dona li va fer una petita caputxa de color vermell. I li esqueia tan bé que tothom l'anomenava la Caputxeta Vermella.
Valencien	Hi havia una vegada en un poble una xiqueta molt xicoteta, la més bonica que mai s'haguera vist; la seua mare estava boja amb ella i la seua àvia molt més encara. Aquesta bona dona li havia manat fer una caputxeta roja i li asseia tan bé que tots la cridaven Caputxeta Roja.
Italien	C'era una volta in un villaggio una bambina, la più carina che si potesse mai vedere. La sua mamma la adorava, e sua nonna ancor di più. La mamma le aveva fatto cucire un cappuccetto rosso, che le stava molto bene, tanto che la chiamavano tutti Cappuccetto Rosso.

Tableau 3. *(continuación)*

Portugais (Portugal)	Era uma vez uma jovem aldeã, a mais bonita que fosse dado ver; a sua mãe era louca por ela e a avó mais ainda. Esta boa mulher mandou fazer-lhe um capucho vermelho, que lhe ficava tão bem que em todo o lado lhe chamavam Capuchinho Vermelho
Portugais (Brésil)	Era uma vez uma menina que vivia numa aldeia e ela era a coisa mais linda que se podia imaginar! Sua mãe era louca por ela e, a avó, mais ainda. A boa velhinha mandou fazer para ela um chapeuzinho vermelho. Esse chapéu assentou-lhe tão bem que a menina passou a ser chamada por todos de Chapeuzinho Vermelho
Galicien	Había unha vez nun pobo unha meniña, a máis fermosa que nunca se vira; a súa nai estaba tola por ela e a súa avoa aínda máis. Esta boa muller fixéralle unha carapuchiña vermella e lle quedaba tan ben que todo o mundo lle chamaba Carapuchiña.
Roumain	A fost odată o fetiță care locuia într-un sat, cea mai frumoasă dintre câte se puteau vedea. Mama sa o iubea nespus, iar bunica ei încă și mai mult. Această femeie de treabă îi făcuse fetei o scufiță roșie, care îi stătea așa de bine, încât toți oamenii o numeau Scufița Roșie.

Partageant l'opinion d'Escudé (2014), l'intégration des langues entre elles permet aux apprenants de découvrir qu'elles ont des familles, qu'elles appartiennent à un système cohérent et ouvert. L'intercompréhension est au cœur même de ce continuum qui prend en considération les apports linguistiques des langues souvent marginalisées de la sphère d'enseignement, comme par exemple, les Langues Vivantes Régionales.

L'observation et la comparaison des formes lexicales, morphologiques, l'ordre syntaxique et le nombre de mots de plusieurs langues de même famille via le dialogue du Petit Chaperon Rouge a permis aux étudiants d'avoir une autre approche des langues.

Tableau 4.

Français	Un jour, sa mère, ayant cuit et fait des galettes, lui dit: – Va voir comme se porte ta mère-grand, car on m'a dit qu'elle était malade. Porte-lui une galette et ce petit pot de beurre. Le Petit Chaperon rouge partit aussitôt pour aller chez sa mère-grand, qui demeurait dans un autre Village. En passant dans un bois elle rencontra compère le Loup, qui eut bien envie de la manger ; mais il n'osa, à cause de quelques Bûcherons qui étaient dans la Forêt. Il lui demanda où elle allait ; la pauvre enfant, qui ne savait pas qu'il est dangereux de s'arrêter à écouter un Loup, lui dit : – Je vais voir ma Mère-grand, et lui porter une galette, avec un petit pot de beurre, que ma Mère lui envoie.

Tableau 4. *(continuación)*

Castillan	Un día su madre, habiendo cocinado unas tortas, le dijo: – Ve a ver cómo está tu abuela, pues me dicen que ha estado enferma; llévale una torta y este tarrito de mantequilla. Caperucita Roja partió enseguida a ver a su abuela, que vivía en otra aldea. Al pasar por un bosque, se encontró al taimado lobo, que tenía muchas ganas de comérsela, pero no se atrevió porque unos leñadores andaban por allí cerca. Le preguntó adónde iba. La pobre niña, que no sabía que era peligroso detenerse a hablar con un lobo, le dijo: – Voy a ver a mi abuela, y le llevo una torta y un tarrito de mantequilla que le envía mi madre.
Catalan	Un bon dia, la seva mare va amassar i va fer una coca, i li va dir: – Vés a veure què fa la teva àvia, que m'han dit que no es troba gaire bé. I li portes aquesta coca i aquest pot de mantega. La caputxeta Vermella va agafar tot seguit el camí per anar a veure a la seva àvia, que vivia en un altre poble. Tot passant pel bosc, la Caputxeta Vermella va trobar el temut llop, el qual se l'hauria menjada amb molt de gust; però no ho va gosar fer, perquè molt a prop d'allà hi havia una colla de llenyataires. Li va preguntar on anava; i la pobra filleta, que no sabia que és molt perillós aturar-se a escoltar un llop, li va dir: – Me'n vaig a veureu a la meva àvia, a dur-li una coca i un pot de mantega que li ha fet la meva mare.
Valencien	Un dia la seua mare, havent cuinat unes coques, li va dir: – Camina a veure com està la teua àvia, perquè em diuen que ha estat malalta; porta-li una coca i aquest potet de mantega. Caputxeta Roja va partir de seguida a veure a la seua àvia, que vivia en un altre poble. En passar per un bosc, es va trobar a l'enfadat llop, que va tindre moltes ganes de menjar-se-la, però no es va atrevir perquè uns llenyataires caminaven per ací a prop. Li va preguntar a on anava. La pobra xiqueta, que no sabia que era perillós detindre's a parlar amb un llop, li va explicar: – Veuré a la meua àvia, i li porte una coca i un potet de mantega que la meua mare li envia.
Italien	Un giorno sua madre, avendo preparato alcune focacce, le disse: "Va' a visitare la nonna, perché mi hanno detto che è indisposta: e portale questa focaccia e questo vasetto di burro". Cappuccetto Rosso, senza farselo dire due volte, partì per andare dalla nonna, la quale stava in un altro villaggio. E passando per un bosco s'imbatté in quel brutto ceffo del Lupo, al quale venne una gran voglia di mangiarla; ma poi non ebbe il coraggio di farlo, a motivo di certi taglialegna che erano nei paraggi. Egli le domandò dove andava. La povera bambina, che non sapeva quanto fosse pericoloso fermarsi a dar retta al Lupo, gli disse: "Vado a trovare mia nonna e a portarle una focaccia, con questo vasetto di burro, che le manda mia madre".

Tableau 4. *(continuación)*

Portugais (Portugal)	Um dia a mãe, tendo cozido pão e feito bôlas, disse-lhe: «Vai ver como está a tua avó, porque me disseram que está doente; leva-lhe uma bôla e este potinho de manteiga». Capuchinho Vermelho partiu imediatamente para a casa da avó, que morava numa outra aldeia. Ao passar num bosque encontrou o compadre Lobo, que tinha muita vontade de comê-la, mas não se atrevia a tal por causa de alguns lenhadores que estavam na floresta. Perguntou-lhe aonde ela ia; a pobre criança, que não sabia que é perigoso deter-se para escutar um Lobo, disse-lhe:«Vou ver a minha avó e levar-lhe uma bôla com um potinho de manteiga que a minha mãe lhe manda».
Portugais (Brésil)	Um dia, tendo feito alguns bolos, sua mãe disse-lhe: – Vá ver como está passando a sua avó, pois fiquei sabendo que ela está um pouco adoentada. Leve-lhe um bolo e este potinho de manteiga. Chapeuzinho Vermelho partiu logo para a casa da avó, que morava numa aldeia vizinha. Ao atravessar a floresta, ela encontrou o senhor Lobo, que ficou louco de vontade de comê-la. Mas não ousou fazer isso, só por causa da presença de alguns lenhadores na floresta. Perguntou a ela aonde ia, e a pobre menina, que ignorava ser perigoso parar para conversar com um lobo, respondeu: — Vou à casa da minha avó, para levar-lhe um bolo e um potinho de manteiga que mamãe mandou.
Galicien	Un día, súa nai, despois de cociñar uns bolos, díxolle: – Vai ver como está a túa avoa, porque me din que estivo enferma; lévalle unha torta e este tarro de manteiga. Carapuchiña Vermella marchou inmediatamente para visitar á súa avoa, que vivía noutro pobo. Ao pasar por un bosque, atopou ao lobo astuto, que a quería comer, pero non se atreveu porque había uns leñadores preto. Preguntou onde ía. A pobre rapaza, que non sabía que era perigoso parar a falar cun lobo, explicoulle: – Vou ver á miña avoa, e voulle levar unha torta e unha cazola de manteiga que lle manda miña nai.
Roumain	Într-o zi, mama, care făcuse niște plăcinte, îi zise: – Du-te până la bunica să vezi ce mai face, căci mi-a spus că e bolnavă, și du-i și niște plăcinte și ulcica aceasta cu unt! Mica Scufiță Roșie porni îndată spre bunica ei, care locuia în alt sat. Trecând printr-o pădure, ea îl întâlni pe cumătrul lup, care avea mare poftă să o mănânce, dar nu îndrăznea, din cauza unor tăietori de lemne ce se aflau prin preajmă. El o întrebă unde merge, iar biata copilă, care nu știa cât de primejdios e să te oprești să asculți un lup, îi zise: – Merg să o văd pe bunica, să-i duc niște plăcinte și o ulcică de unt, pe care mama i le trimite.

Le travail de repérage a permis de systématiser les éléments communs à toutes les langues (au système) et les spécificités propres à chaque langue. Les étudiants ont manipulé les langues tout en redécouvrirant leur langue maternelle. La fin du *Petit Chaperon Rouge* a aussi permis de comparer les formes lexicales, morphologiques, l'ordre syntaxique et le nombre de mots de plusieurs langues de même famille.

Tableau 5.

Français	– Ma mère-grand, que vous avez de grands bras ?
	– C'est pour mieux t'embrasser, ma fille.
	– Ma mère-grand, que vous avez de grandes jambes ?
	– C'est pour mieux courir, mon enfant.
	– Ma mère-grand, que vous avez de grandes oreilles ?
	– C'est pour mieux écouter, mon enfant.
	– Ma mère-grand, que vous avez de grands yeux ?
	– C'est pour mieux voir, mon enfant.
	– Ma mère-grand, que vous avez de grandes dents.
	– C'est pour te manger.
	Et en disant ces mots, ce méchant Loup se jeta sur le Petit Chaperon rouge, et la mangea.
Castillan	– Abuelita, ¡qué brazos tan largos tienes!
	– Son para abrazarte mejor, hija mía.
	– Abuelita, ¡qué piernas tan largas tienes!
	– Son para correr mejor, hija mía.
	– Abuelita, ¡qué orejas tan grandes tienes!
	– Son para oírte mejor, hija mía.
	– Abuelita, ¡qué ojos tan grandes tienes!
	– Son para verte mejor, hija mía.
	– Abuelita, ¡qué dientes tan grandes tienes!
	– ¡Son para comerte mejor!
	Y al decir estas palabras, este malvado lobo se abalanzó sobre Caperucita Roja y se la comió.
Catalan	– Àvia, quins braços més llargs que tens!
	– És per abraçar-te millor, filla meva!
	– Àvia, quines cames més llargues que tens!
	– És per corre més, filla meva!
	– Àvia, quines orelles més llargues que tens!
	– És per sentir-te millor, filla meva!
	– Àvia, quins ulls més grossos que tens!
	– És per veure't millor, filla meva!
	– Àvia, quines dents més llargues que tens!
	– És per menjar-te!
	I havent dit aquestes paraules el malvat llop es va llançar sobre la Caputxeta i se la va menjar.
Valencien	– Àvia, i quins braços més llargs que tens !
	– És per abraçar-te millor, filla meua !
	– Àvia, quines cames més llargues que tens !
	– És per córrer més, filla meua !
	– Àvia, quines orelles més llargues que tens !

Tableau 5. *(continuación)*

	– És per sentir-te millor, filla meua ! – Àvia, quins ulls més grossos que tens ! – És per veure't millor, filla meua ! – Àvia, quines dents més llargues que tens ! – És per menjar-te ! I havent dit aquestes paraules el malvat llop és va llançar sobre la Caputxeta i se lañ va menjar."
Italien	– Nonna, che braccia grandi che hai!. – È per abbracciarti meglio, bambina mia. – Nonna, che gambe grandi che hai! – È per correr meglio, bambina mia. – Nonna, che orecchie grandi che hai! – È per sentirti meglio, bambina mia. – Nonna, che occhioni grandi che hai! – È per vederti meglio, bambina mia. – Nonna, che bocca grande che hai! – È per mangiarti meglio! E nel dir così, quell'avido Lupo si gettò sulla povera Cappuccetto Rosso, e ne fece un sol boccone.
Portugais (Portugal)	– Avó, que braços tão grandes! – É para abraçar-te melhor, filha minha. – E, avó, que pernas tão grandes! – É para correr melhor, filha minha. – E, avó, que orelhas tão grandes! – É para ouvir-te melhor, filha minha. – Avó, que olhos tão grandes! – É para ver-te melhor, filha minha. – Avó, que dentes tão grandes! – Para comer-te melhor!
Portugais (Brésil)	– Vovó, como são grandes os seus braços. – É para melhor te abraçar, minha filha. – Vovó, como são grandes as suas pernas. – É para poder correr melhor, minha netinha. – Vovó, como são grandes as suas orelhas. – É para ouvir melhor, netinha. – Vovó, como são grandes os seus dentes. – É para te comer! E assim dizendo, o malvado lobo se atirou sobre Chapeuzinho Vermelho e a devorou.

Tableau 5. *(continuación)*

Galicien	– Avoa, que brazos tan grandes!
	– Son para abrazarte mellor, miña filla.
	– E, avoa, que grandes pernas!
	– Son para correr mellor, miña filla.
	– E, avoa, que grandes orellas!
	– Son para escoitarte mellor, miña filla.
	– Avoa, que ollos grandes!
	– Son para verte mellor, miña filla.
	– Avoa, que dentes tan grandes!
	– Para comerte mellor!
	E dicindo estas palabras, este lobo malvado abalanzouse sobre Carapuchiña Vermella e comeuna.
Roumain	– Bunica, de ce ai brațele așa de lungi?
	– Ca să te pot îmbrățișa mai bine, fetița mea!
	– Bunica, de ce ai picioarele așa de lungi?
	– Ca să port alerga mai bine, copila mea!
	– Bunica, de ce ai urechile atât de mari?
	– Ca să te pot auzi mai bine, copila mea!
	– Bunica, de ce ai ochii așa de mari?
	– Ca să te pot vedea mai bine, copila mea!
	– Bunica, dar de ce ai dinții atât de mari?
	– Ca să te pot mânca pe tine!
	Și zicând aceste cuvinte, lupul cel rău se năpusti asupra Scufiței Roșii și o înghiți.

4. Recommandations des défenseurs de l'intercompréhension

Pour Bertucci (2010) la mise en place d'une didactique du plurilinguisme dans les institutions scolaires françaises implique une réorganisation de l'enseignement des langues notamment la relation entre le français et les autres langues. De surcroît, cette approche s'interroge aussi sur les compétences plurilingues des apprenants. Selon l'auteure, réfléchir à une didactique du plurilinguisme est nécessaire et les approches de l'éveil aux langues à l'école primaire s'avèrent bénéfiques pour les apprenants qui ne se familiarisent pas seulement avec les langues enseignées à l'école mais aussi avec les langues étrangères, les langues régionales ou minorisées, les parlers bilingues et les variétés d'une même langue. Les résultats montrent que les élèves sont sensibles à la diversité culturelle et linguistique et motivés pour apprendre d'autres langues.

Escudé et Janin (2010b: 110) recommandent trois niveaux d'implication à l'intercompréhension : **(1)** La sensibilisation, **(2)** L'initiation, **(3)** L'apprentissage.

Partageant le constat des deux auteurs, il est vrai que la méthodologie de l'éveil aux langues a permis de familiariser les apprenants à la diversité des langues, et de s'en servir dans des tâches menant à une conscience et une pratique métalangagières.

Escudé et Janin (2010b : 111) énumèrent des propositions de réorganisation : **(1)** Dès 3 ans : enseigner une heure par semaine les langues romanes à partir de la littérature de jeunesse (contes, albums, BD, etc.). **(2)** Dès 3 ans : enseigner une heure par jour une langue romane dans les disciplines comme le sport, les sciences, la géographie. Tout cela contribue au développement des compétences en compréhension et en production. Les résultats qui en découleraient seraient très bénéfiques : **(1)** Renforcement de la LM, **(2)** Maîtrise des codes, **(3)** Fluidité des langues, **(4)** Conscience d'un citoyen européen, **(5)** Transfert vers d'autres langues.

Comme indiquent Escudé et Janin (2010b), l'objectif est de changer la perspective sur les langues en les appréhendant d'un point de vue comparatif et simultané. Les pratiques intégratrices (EMILE, intercompréhension de langues apparentées) souvent mises à l'écart par les instances éducatives et, par conséquent, par les maisons d'édition, ont un avenir prometteur. De plus, sachant que la majorité des méthodes d'intercompréhension vise un public adulte et prépare à la mobilité européenne et internationale, à la maîtrise de plusieurs langues, au transfert de compétences, etc., de nouvelles méthodes devraient voir le jour et s'ajouter à celles qui existent déjà. Les auteurs recommandent aussi de diversifier les enseignements universitaires en intégrant l'intercompréhension dans les licences et les masters, ce qui doterait les cursus universitaires d'un nouvel apprentissage.

Les recommandations d'Escudé et Janin (2010a : 122) sont donc très pertinentes : **(1)** Intégrer en Europe la langue d'enseignement avec les langues apparentées. **(2)** Prendre appui sur les langues connues des apprenants pour aller vers d'autres langues. **(3)** Aider les apprenants à s'ouvrir à la diversité des langues.

Castagne (2016 : 136-137) énumère trois choix fondateurs ayant comme noyau dur la langue et la culture romanes : **(1)** Utiliser la compréhension réciproque romane en préservant sa LM en suivant une formation à l'intercompréhension et en promouvant le plurilinguisme roman à court, moyen et long terme. L'objectif ultime serait de créer des synergies entre toutes les formes d'intercommunication romanes et d'éduquer les locuteurs romanophones à s'y habituer sans ayant systématiquement recours à l'anglais. **(2)** Utiliser la compréhension réciproque romane pour faciliter les échanges, les mobilités, etc. **(3)** Utiliser la compréhension réciproque romane pour générer de la croissance économique.

Pour Rho Mas (2016), il s'avère nécessaire de poursuivre les recherches et d'analyser l'impact de la biographie langagière des apprenants dans le processus d'intercompréhension auprès de publics variés. D'où l'importance de s'intéresser au bagage linguistique et culturel de tous les apprenants car bien souvent celui-ci est marginalisé au détriment de la langue française.

Or, l'histoire de la France est jalonnée de rencontres et de métissages ayant profondément enrichi la langue française tant au niveau culturel que linguistique. L'espace francophone est le témoin direct de toutes ces différentes communautés qui le constituent. Il représente une aubaine pour le rayonnement du français et pour mieux cerner la diversité culturelle et linguistique. Certaines « passerelles culturelles », déjà existantes, méritent d'être scrutées car l'extension du français à des pays si divers est une source d'enrichissement pour tout un chacun. (Modard, 2010).

En partant du principe que la variation constitue le noyau dur de toute langue, il est impossible de ne pas la prendre en considération. Pour familiariser les jeunes apprenants à la variation linguistique d'une langue, certains matériels s'avèrent très bénéfiques comme celui des *Lettres de francophonie*. Ce matériel offre, via des supports vidéo, de multiples situations authentiques illustrant la diversité culturelle et linguistique de l'espace francophone. (Modard, 2010).

5. Conclusion

Le décalage entre les instances officielles prônant la diversité linguistique et la réalité des classes, où règne un monolinguisme omnipotent, est incontestable. La France est un bon exemple de cela, tout comme de nombreux pays européens, qui n'ont de cesse de valoriser le plurilinguisme dans leurs textes officiels mais qui, sur le terrain, hiérarchisent les langues en les rendant étanches. Chemin faisant, l'enseignement des langues étrangères s'avère inefficace et cantonné à la langue anglaise.

Nonobstant, partant du constat que le plurilinguisme est le principal objectif pédagogique de l'Europe, l'intercompréhension se présente comme l'un des moyens pour l'atteindre, ce qui vaincrait le monolinguisme absolu au sein de la majorité des systèmes éducatifs européens. L'expérience pédagogique de l'intercompréhension par le biais du *Petit Chaperon Rouge*, dans différentes langues romanes, se révèle être une innovation dans l'enseignement/apprentissage des langues, favorisant ainsi l'éducation plurilingue. Pour ce faire, l'intercompréhension doit convaincre tout un chacun des avantages de son approche, afin de s'insérer durablement dans l'enseignement et de l'innover via l'intégration du plurilinguisme.

Le chemin est encore long, certes, mais l'intercompréhension augure de belles perspectives d'avenir dans l'enseignement/apprentissage des langues. D'où l'importance de prendre en considération les recommandations de ses défenseurs et de proposer de nouvelles méthodes ayant pour ADN l'intercompréhension.

Références bibliographiques

Andrade, A. I. & Aráujo e Sá, M-H. 2008. Intercompréhension et formation des enseignants : parcours et possibilités de développement. *S'entendre entre langues voisines : vers l'intercompréhension*, Conti, Virginie et Grin, François, p.277-298. Genève: Georg.

Bertucci, M-M. 2010. Politiques linguistiques-éducatives : propositions pour une didactique du plurilinguisme. Dans *L'enseignement des langues vivantes étrangères à l'école. Impacts sur le développement de la langue maternelle*, Corblin, C.; Sauvage, J., p.145-156. Paris: L'Harmattan.

Caddéo, S. & Jamet, M-C. 2013. *L'intercompréhension : une autre approche pour l'enseignement des langues*. Paris: Hachette

Castagne, É. 2016. L'intercompréhension des langues romanes comme vecteur de développement géopolitique. *Hermès, La Revue*, n°75, 131-138.

Castagne, É. 2011. Intercompréhension et dynamique des inférences : des langues voisines aux langues non voisine. *Redinter-Intercompreensão, 3, Attraverso le lingue. L'Intercomprensione in ricordo di Claire Blanche-Benveniste*. Chamusca, Edições Cosmos / REDINTER, 81-94.

Escudé, P. 2020. Apprendre des langues et des disciplines scolaires ensemble: la fonction centrale des « langues médianes ». L'exemple du manuel *euromania*. Dans Schädlich, B. (eds) *Regards croisés sur le plurilinguisme et l'apprentissage des langues*. Berlin: Heidelberg.

Escudé, P. 2014. De l'intercompréhension comme moteur d'activités en classe. *Tréma* 42: 46-53.

Escudé, P. & Janin, P. 2010a. L'école, la langue unique et l'intercompréhension : obstacles et enjeux de l'intégration. *Synergie Europe* 5: 115-125.

Escudé, P. & Janin, P. 2010b. *L'Intercompréhension, clé du plurilinguisme*. Didactique des langues étrangères. Paris: CLEInternational.

Modard, D. 2010. Familiariser des jeunes apprenants avec la diversité linguistique et culturelle d'une langue : le français d'ici et d'ailleurs. *L'enseignement des langues vivantes étrangères à l'école. Impacts sur le développement de la langue maternelle*, Corblin, C.; Sauvage, J., p.55-77. Paris: L'Harmattan.

Rho Mas, P. 2016. Intercompréhension entre langues romanes : séquence informatisée pour CM2. *Adjectif.net* [En ligne] http://www.adjectif.net/spip/spip.php?article376

Tyvaert, J-E. 2008. Pour une refondation de la didactique des langues sur la base de l'intercompréhension. *S'entendre entre langues voisines : vers l'intercompréhension*, Conti, Virginie et Grin, François, p.251-276. Genève: Georg.

La traducción al castellano de los culturemas de *Le pays des autres*

María del Mar Jiménez-Cervantes Arnao
Universidad Nacional de Educación a Distancia (UNED)

Le pays des autres is the first novel of a trilogy published in 2020 in which the author, Leïla Slimani, narrates the arrival and adaptation of Mathide, a young Alsatian, to Meknes before the independence of Morocco. The novel, written in French, presents many cultural references through the use of loanwords and code-switching, which imbues the work with a linguistic and cultural heterogeneity as well as a sense of veracity and exotism. This study aims to identify these novel culturems, classify loanwords and moments of code-switching and carry out an analysis of the translation into Spanish, carried out by Malika Embarek López, in order to verify whether the linguistic and cultural richness of the original work has been retained.

Keywords: literature translation, Moroccan culturems, loanwords, code-switching, French, Spanish

1. Introducción

La guerre, la guerre, la guerre, (Slimani 2021) es la primera parte de una trilogía titulada *Le pays des autres* inspirada en la historia familiar de la autora. A pesar de tener título propio, esta primera novela es conocida por el nombre de la trilogía en lugar de por el suyo, por lo que en este trabajo nos vamos a referir de esta manera a ella.

El texto original, escrito en francés, muestra una hibridez lingüística y cultural al presentar numerosas referencias culturales mediante préstamos y la transcripción de expresiones en árabe. Encontramos la mayor parte de estas referencias culturales en préstamos relativos a la indumentaria típica marroquí, referencias a partes de la ciudad, paisajes, etc. Además, Slimani utiliza la alternancia de código al incluir expresiones en árabe que normalmente traduce en notas al pie. En nuestra opinión, ambos recursos, los préstamos y la alternancia de código, tienen un claro propósito comunicativo y estilístico: ayudar al lector a contextualizar la narración y darle veracidad, por un lado, al tiempo que le confiere un carácter exótico por otro lado (Ali 2020).

Al realizar la lectura de la novela nos planteamos de qué forma habrían sido traducidos esos términos culturales marroquíes en la traducción al castellano, teniendo en cuenta la relación dispar que el árabe ha tenido con la lengua francesa y la castellana. Con este objetivo, realizamos una clasificación de los culturemas con la taxonomía de Molina Martínez (2006) y analizamos de qué forma han sido trasladados en la traducción realizada por Malika Embarek López, publicada en 2021 por la editorial Cabaret Voltaire, siguiendo la clasificación las técnicas de traducción de Molina y Hurtado (2002).

2. Le pays des autres y su traducción

Como hemos avanzado, *La guerre, la guerre, la guerre* es la primera parte una trilogía escrita por Leïla Slimani y publicada en 2020 por Éditions Gallimard. La segunda parte, que ha visto la luz en esta misma editorial en 2022, se titula *Regardez-nous danser*. Slimani, nacida en 1981 en Rabat, estudió en París en el Institut d'Études Politiques y en la École Supérieure de Commerce. Antes de dedicarse por completo a la literatura, trabajó como periodista para *L'Express* y *Jeune Afrique*. Además, en el año 2017 fue designada por el presidente Macron para ser la representante francesa en el Conseil de la Francophonie.

Escritora de novelas como *Dans le jardin de l'ogre* (Slimani 2014) o *Chanson douce* (Slimani 2016), con el que ganó el Premio Goncourt, Leïla Slimani presenta en sus obras, ya sea en su producción de ficción como en ensayos (*Sexe et mensonges: la vie sexuelle au Maroc* 2017) o álbum ilustrado (*À mains nues* I 2020, *À mains nues II* 2021) un interés por mostrar la imagen de la mujer y el papel que desempeña en la sociedad (Fernández Erquizia 2019). En *Le pays des autres,* Slimani presenta una saga familiar inspirada en su propia familia. Escrita en francés y situada en Meknes, Marruecos, la primera parte de esta trilogía se desarrolla tras la Segunda Guerra Mundial y durante el inicio del movimiento de independencia, que llegó en 1956. Mathilde, una joven recién casada, llega a Marruecos para encontrarse con Amine, su esposo, y establecerse en la casa heredada de su padre en el campo. Desde los primeros días en el país africano, Mathilde ve cómo el Amine que conoció en Francia se muestra diferente y su vida poco se parece a la que había soñado. El lector de la novela acompaña a la protagonista en su primer contacto y progresiva inmersión en la cultura marroquí mediante para la que Slimani recurre al uso de términos específicos, buena parte de ellos ya pertenecientes a la lengua francesa actual, en el caso de los préstamos adaptados.

La artífice de la versión en castellano, Malika Embarek López, es hispanista de formación y se dedica profesionalmente a la traducción literaria. Está especializada en literatura magrebí escrita en lengua francesa, desde 1989 ha publicado más de cincuenta obras de autores como Tajar Ben Jelloun, Edmond El Maleh o Fatima Daas, entre otros. En 2017 recibió el Premio Nacional a la Obra de un Traductor concedido por el Ministerio de Educación, Cultura y Deporte por "su plena dedicación a la labor de traducción y por constituir un ejemplo único de mestizaje, de relación fructífera entre el norte y el sur, de diálogo de culturas y de difusión de la mejor literatura magrebí y francesa" (AECID 2017).

3. Marco teórico

A lo largo de la Historia de la Traducción se han propuesto diferentes denominaciones y clasificaciones para lo que hoy conocemos como culturemas. Soto-Almela (2013) los define como

> [...] términos de índole cultural, pertenecientes a ámbitos diferentes de una misma cultura, conocidos y compartidos por todos los miembros de una sociedad que, al ser transferidos a otra cultura, pueden dar lugar a problemas traductológicos, lo que supondrá una posible adaptación lingüística del término por medio de diversas técnicas de traducción para hacerlas comprensibles en la cultura receptora.   (Soto-Almela 2013: 18)

De acuerdo con esta definición, cuando el autor o el traductor literario se encuentran frente a un culturema, este normalmente presenta una dificultad, a no ser que el autor recurra a uno perteneciente a su cultura o a la del traductor. Sin embargo, cuando el autor incluye referencias culturales ajenas a la propia o a la de la futura cultura meta, estos términos plantean una dificultad, como señala Soto-Almela (2013). Según Martínez de Sousa (2003), este es el motivo por el que escritores y traductores son a menudo los responsables de la introducción de préstamos en sus respectivas lenguas de trabajo si no pueden trasladarlos o incorporarlos mediante otro recurso que no sea el préstamo, cuando el autor del texto original recurre a un culturema.

En cuanto a la manera de clasificar los culturemas, vamos a seguir la taxonomía realizada por Molina Martínez (2006), quien, tras analizar las clasificaciones anteriores realizadas por autores como Nida, Newmark o Nord, establece cuatro ámbitos culturales:

1. Medio natural: en este ámbito se encuentran elementos culturales como la flora, fauna, clima, paisajes o incluso topónimos.
2. Patrimonio cultural: aquí encontramos las "referencias físicas o ideológicas que comparte una cultura" (Molina Martínez 2006: 81) como personajes, hechos históricos, creencias populares, folklore, viviendas, utensilios, herramientas o instrumentos musicales entre otros.
3. Cultura social. Molina Martínez distingue aquí dos subapartados: Convenciones y hábitos sociales y Organización social. En el primero se incluyen formas de comer y vestir, costumbres, saludos, tratamientos y cortesía, gestos, etc. mientras que el segundo engloba sistemas políticos, legales o educativos, organizaciones, monedas, medidas, etc.
4. Cultura lingüística: en este ámbito se recogen transliteraciones, refranes, frases hechas, nombres propios con significado, interjecciones, insultos y blasfemias.

Como hemos avanzado, buena parte de los culturemas se presentan en francés mediante el uso del préstamo lingüístico. De acuerdo con el *Dictionaire de linguistique*:

> Il y a *emprunt* linguistique quand un parler A utilise et finit par intégrer une unité ou un trait linguistique qui existait précédemment dans un parler B (dit langue source) et que A ne possédait pas; l'unité ou le trait emprunté sont eux-mêmes qualifiés d'*emprunts*. (Dubois et al. 2001: 177)

Buena parte de los elementos culturales que aparecen en el texto original son considerados préstamos adaptados: están recogidos en diccionarios de lengua francesa y adaptados a la grafía y pronunciación de la lengua que los toma prestados, en este caso el francés. Por el contrario, aquellos préstamos que mantienen la forma de la lengua original y no han sido recogidos por el diccionario, son los llamados préstamos puros o crudos (Real Academia Española 2010). En cuanto a la clasificación y el tratamiento tipográfico de los préstamos, estos son análogos en las dos lenguas del estudio realizado. Los préstamos puros deben ir marcados tipográficamente con cursiva mientras que los adaptados no deben llevar ninguna marca, tanto en castellano (Martínez de Sousa 2012; RAE 2009, 2010, 2018) como en francés (Gravisse y Goosse 2008, Imprimerie Nationale 2014, Bureau de la traduction 2015, Ramat de la typographie 2017) puesto que son considerados como ya pertenecientes a la lengua receptora.

Por otro lado, la alternancia de código consiste en la introducción de términos o expresiones de una lengua en un texto escrito en otra lengua y es particularmente habitual encontrar este recurso en novelas en las que hay una situación de bilingüismo, donde se presenta un personaje en una cultura o lengua procedente de otra, como es el caso de la literatura chicana con el binomio inglés-castellano (Jiménez Carra 2004; Jiménez Carra 2011; Quintero Ocaña y Zaro Vera 2014, Womble 2017). Sin embargo, también hay estudios que analizan este recurso en la combinación francés-árabe en textos literarios (Ali 2020, Díaz Alarcón 2017, Miloudi 2022). En cualquier caso, la alternancia de código muestra la hibridez lingüística en la que el autor se expresa y decide trasladar a su texto, aportando veracidad a la narración y a los personajes. Además, Miloudi (2022) señala que aquellos relatos de carácter autobiográfico, como es el caso de *Le pays des autres*, son más propensos a utilizar la alternancia de código.

Este es un recurso estilístico ciertamente emparentado con el préstamo o extranjerismo, dado que supone utilizar términos o expresiones de una lengua en otra. Sin embargo, la alternancia de código no permite nombrar un concepto o realidad que no exista en otra lengua, como ocurre con el préstamo, sino que se utiliza para mostrar una hibridez lingüística propia de los contextos bilingües. Dicho de otra forma, se recurre al préstamo (puro) en primer lugar cuando hay un vacío léxico y no existe término equivalente en la lengua de llegada y con el uso y el tiempo, dicho préstamo puede incorporarse a la lengua mediante una adaptación de la misma. Sin embargo, la alternancia de código utiliza otra lengua para expresar realidades que normalmente tienen equivalencia en la primera; se trata de un recurso que aparece en contextos de bilingüismo, como ya hemos señalado arriba. Grosjean (1995: 263), por su parte, establece la diferencia entre ambos recursos de la siguiente manera: "Code-switching is shifting (switching) completely to the other language for a word, a phrase, a sentence, etc. 'Borrowing' is taking a word or short expression and (usually phonologically or morphologically) adapting it to the base-language".

Por su parte, Miloudi (2022: 5) indica que

> la fonction du code-switching littéraire est celle d'introduire un contraste qui fait ressortir un personnage, une réaction particulière, un certain cadre situationnel, susceptible de créer un ancrage référentiel authentique par rapport au texte global.

En el caso de la novela analizada, la alternancia recuerda al lector, al igual que lo hace el uso de los préstamos, dónde se desarrolla la acción y quiénes son los personajes, añadiendo un matiz de veracidad y de exotismo a la obra.

El cambio de código puede ser de dos tipos: intersentencial, cuando a una frase en una lengua le sigue otra en la otra lengua, o intrasentencial, cuando el cambio de lengua se produce dentro de una misma cláusula (Poplack 1980, Hamminck 2000, Miloudi 2022). En cuanto a la representación gráfica de la alternancia de códigos, los autores que recurren a ella no son partidarios de establecer diferencias entre las lenguas del texto, evitando así una posible jerarquización de las mismas y mostrando esta interlengua como algo natural (Womble 2017).

Ante la cuestión de si la alternancia de código literaria es auténtica o artificial, se ha acordado por buena parte de los investigadores que han de cumplirse dos requisitos para que sea auténtica. En primer lugar, los personajes deben pertenecer a una comunidad de hablantes en la que la alternancia de código sea la norma; y, en segundo lugar, el autor debe pertenecer a esa comunidad (Montes-Alcalá 2012). En el caso de *Le pays des autres*, nos encontramos con una distancia temporal entre la autora y el relato y desconocemos si en el Marruecos de mediados del siglo XX la alternancia de código era una estrategia usada por todos los hablantes o si se encontraba limitada a un sector determinado de la población del país. Pero, en cualquier caso, estaríamos ante una alternancia de código auténtica, ya que existe una situación de bilingüismo real, tanto para la autora de la novela como para la familia formada por un marroquí y una francesa.

Como ya hemos avanzado, en la obra analizada, tanto los préstamos como la alternancia de código están trasladando referencias culturales. Los préstamos son utilizados para los tres primeros ámbitos culturales establecidos por Molina Martínez (2006), Medio natural, Patrimonio cultural y Cultura social, mientras que la alternancia de código presenta refranes, interjecciones, blasfemias, etc. que no han sido traducidas al francés por Slimani. Estas expresiones están incluidas en el cuarto ámbito cultural de Molina Martínez (2006): Cultura lingüística.

Por otro lado, el lector monolingüe que se enfrenta a un texto literario híbrido con préstamos o alternancia de código que no han sido traducidos, debe hacer un esfuerzo mayor para comprender ese texto del que haría en la lectura de un texto escrito en una lengua conocida por él (Wecksteen 2009, Womble 2017). En este sentido, Womble (2017) considera lo siguiente:

> If (a) CS texts give readers access to moments of translation, and b) translation inherently involves conflict and an exchange of power, then c) readers encounter a confluence of these various elements. Ultimately, I argue d) CS texts create readers-as-translators, enacting unique hermeneutical, rhetorical, and narratological implications. (Womble 2017: 64)

Como veremos en el análisis, en esta novela se presenta la alternancia de código siempre acompañada de una nota al pie. Slimani recurre a la glosa extratextual para facilitar al lector la comprensión de su texto y ahorrarle ese nuevo rol que indica Womble (2017), aunque esto implique la interrupción del proceso lector.

Un aspecto determinante para nuestro trabajo es la diferente relación que el francés y el castellano han tenido con la lengua árabe. De acuerdo con el estudio realizado por Baiwir (2014), la inclusión de préstamos directos procedentes del árabe en el *Trésor de la langue française* comenzó en el siglo XII, alcanzando su punto más alto en el siglo XIX. La lengua francesa ha recibido y sigue recibiendo términos procedentes del árabe que hoy día forman parte de la interlengua que utilizan los jóvenes franceses en la actualidad, además de otros procedentes de otras lenguas (Lievois y Noureddine 2018). Aunque el castellano cuenta con un importante número de arabismos en su haber, estos son en su mayoría "procedentes del árabe andalusí que pasaron al romance, [...] legado de la presencia durante casi nueve siglos de los árabes en España" (Embarek 2016: 34). En consonancia con esto último, Lievois y Noureddine (2018) reflexionan en su estudio sobre la traducción al árabe, al neerlandés y al castellano de la traducción de *Kiffe kiffe demain* de qué manera la dispar relación que el francés y el castellano han tenido con la lengua árabe ha podido repercutir en la traducción de la obra de Faiza:

> Si l'espagnol n'a pas nécessairement été en contact avec l'arabe aux mêmes moments que ne l'a été le français, son vocabulaire de base a été fort influencé par l'arabe et ily a probablement plus facilement moyen de rendre compte du caractère hybride que vehiculent les emprunts dans la traduction espagnole.
> (Lievois y Noureddine 2018: 56)

En este sentido, como afirma El Hag Hassan El Dannanah (2021), es posible que el traductor recurra a arabismos con una intención estilística:

> [A] veces recurrir a arabismos trasciende el mero intento de colmar los vacíos culturales. Son palabras mayormente extrañas por sus referentes culturales que tienen poco que ver con la cultura española de hoy en día y que, por lo tanto, dejan un regusto exótico y un colorido local, semejante al producido por el uso del préstamo o la transliteración de las voces culturales
> (El Hag Hassan El Dannanah 2021: 225)

Dando un paso más allá de lo expuesto arriba, Malika Embarek (2016), traductora de *El país de los otros* (Slimani 2021b), se muestra a favor de la intervención en el texto traducido, dejando atrás la supuesta objetividad del traductor, debido tanto a sus circunstancias personales como al tipo de textos que ella traduce, la literatura magrebí escrita en francés. Para ello, utiliza los arabismos como estrategia para reproducir la mirada y la voz de esos autores que, aunque se sirvan de la lengua del antiguo colonizador, son diferentes a las de los autores europeos:

> [M]i modesta intención [...] es conseguir revitalizar aquellos términos que poco a poco han sido desclasados, condenados a la obsolescencia forzosa, tildados de arcaicos, de poco usados, arrumbados en diccionarios o enciclopedias del idioma. [...] La traducción literaria permite reactualizar esos arabismos, puesto que nos llegan de una cultura en la que *no* quedaron obsoletos.
> (Embarek 2016: 34)

La traductora comenta en este mismo texto el disgusto que le supuso ver que el corrector de la editorial que publicó su traducción de *Harruda*, de Ben Jelloun, introdujo sin contar con ella notas al pie para explicar los arabismos que ella había seleccionado para traducir "unos términos que el autor transcribía del árabe al francés" (Embarek 2016: 36) y que el lector podía haber consultado en el diccionario si no los entendía por el contexto. De esta forma, Embarek muestra su opinión sobre el uso de la glosa extratextual como herramienta para favorecer la comprensión del lector, estrategia a la que recurre en ocasiones Slimani en *Le pays des autres*.

4. Objetivos de estudio y metodología

Ya hemos avanzado que este estudio descriptivo surgió para responder a la pregunta que nos planteamos al realizar la lectura de *Le pays des autres*: conocer de qué forma se habían tratado los culturemas en la traducción al castellano y si se había reproducido la hibridez lingüística y cultural del original. Para alcanzar este objetivo se diseñó una metodología de trabajo que permitiese comparar ambos textos. En primer lugar, se identificaron los términos referentes a elementos culturales marroquíes presentes en el texto escrito por Slimani. Después, se procedió de manera análoga en la versión traducida por Malika Embarek, de forma que resultaron dos registros (uno para los préstamos y otro para las expresiones en lengua árabe) en el que se recopilaron los casos encontrados en francés y castellano.

Con el corpus de préstamos registrados, se realizó en primer lugar una clasificación de los mismos siguiendo la taxonomía establecida por Molina Martínez (2006) porque consideramos interesante averiguar a qué ámbito pertenecían. Después, se comprobó si estos culturemas eran préstamos puros o crudos o, si, por el contrario, se trataba de préstamos adaptados a la lengua francesa, y replicamos el análisis en la versión en castellano. Para ello, se revisó si estos términos estaban incluidos en diccionarios de referencia de ambas lenguas: el *Diccionario de la lengua española* (2020) de la Real Academia para el castellano y *Le Dico en ligne* (2021) de Éditions Le Robert y *Dictionnaire Larousse* (2020) para el francés. La distinción entre préstamos puros y adaptados en nuestro estudio obedece, por un lado, al interés por conocer y cuantificar el tipo de préstamos que se utilizan para presentar los culturemas en la novela, y, por otro, para comprobar si la diferente naturaleza de los préstamos conlleva elecciones de traducción diferentes, tal y como indican Lievois y Noureddine (2018) en su estudio. Por último, la traducción de estos términos al castellano ha sido analizada para ver cómo se ha resuelto la problemática de la traducción de los culturemas señalada por Soto-Almela (2013) en su definición de los mismos; para ello, se ha seguido la clasificación de las técnicas de traducción realizada por Molina y Hurtado (2002).

En cuanto a la alternancia de código, de menor incidencia que los préstamos, se analizó el tipo de alternancia se producía en el original para después ver cómo se trasladó al texto traducido.

5. Resultados del estudio

Como hemos avanzado, el corpus estudiado se repartió en dos tablas, una para los préstamos identificados y otra para la alternancia de código. Presentamos a continuación los resultados del estudio.

5.1 Préstamos

Esta tabla cuenta con 104 registros extraídos del texto original que pueden aparecer varias veces, ya que nos interesaba ver cómo habían sido trasladados al castellano en todas las ocasiones. Estos términos fueron clasificados en dos grupos: préstamos puros para aquellos que no están incorporados en los diccionarios de consulta de la lengua francesa y préstamos adaptados para los que sí lo están. Encontramos ochenta y cuatro préstamos adaptados, algunos ejemplos son: *bled*, *djellaba* o *djinn*. La presencia de préstamos puros es sustancialmente menor, ya que se reduce a veinte. Algunos préstamos puros son: *chouafa*, *nassarania* o *adoul*. El texto original no los presenta con marcas tipográficas, pero en ocasiones la autora recurre a una nota al pie de página para explicar su significado.

En el texto traducido, esos ochenta y cuatro términos clasificados como préstamos adaptados se reparten entre préstamos puros (20), préstamos adaptados (43), omisión (1) y otras soluciones traductológicas (20). Presentamos a continuación una tabla para ilustrar estos números.

Tabla 1. Presencia de préstamos adaptados en el TO y su traducción

TO	TM
84 préstamos adaptados	43 préstamos adaptados
	20 préstamos puros
	20 traducciones
	1 omisión

Los números de la tabla muestran que los ochenta y cuatro términos seleccionados son considerados préstamos adaptados en francés y en el texto meta se reducen a cuarenta y tres, algo más de la mitad. Los términos restantes son trasladados al castellano mediante préstamos puros, traducciones u omisiones. Algunos de estos préstamos puros en el texto traducido son los siguientes: *yinn*, *felah*, aduar y su forma en plural, aduares, *hamam* o Sidi.[1]

---

1. Reproducimos aquí la grafía que presentan estos términos en la versión en castellano, mostrando que el uso de la cursiva no sigue la norma establecida por la Real Academia de la Lengua (2009, 2010, 2018). Procedemos de igual forma en los ejemplos extraídos de forma literal de los

Las técnicas de traducción a las que ha recurrido Malika Embarek para trasladar veinte de esos ochenta y cuatro préstamos adaptados al castellano son las siguientes: descripción (5 casos), generalización (7), equivalente acuñado (7) y compresión lingüística (1).

En los casos en los que la traductora recurre a la descripción, no existe un préstamo adaptado al castellano y tampoco utiliza un préstamo puro como en otras ocasiones. En tres ocasiones traslada el término *riad* como *casa tradicional*; efectivamente, este término no está incluido en el *Diccionario de la lengua española*, pero pensamos que sí podría haberse mantenido el término ya que es relativamente conocido. Los otros dos casos en los que se recurre a una descripción son *bled* y su derivado *blédard*.

Bled es un término que se ha incorporado con uso habitual en la lengua francesa actual, pero no lo es en la lengua castellana. La traductora salva este problema de la siguiente manera:

(1) "Ses parents lui interdisent d'aller au bled" (259)
"Sus padres le tienen prohibido ir donde viven los campesinos de las cabilas" (278)

(2) "Le garçon n'était qu'un paysan, un pauvre blédard [...]" (374)
"Era un campesino, originario de alguna aldea perdida [...]" (399)

En el primer caso, vemos cómo además de la técnica de descripción, la traductora recurre a la compensación al introducir el término *cabila*. En el segundo, Slimani utiliza el despectivo *blédard* para especificar el término neutro *paysan*, y Embarek lo soluciona describiendo el origen recóndito del personaje.

El término *bled* aparece más adelante como complemento del nombre y la traductora recure a una técnica diferente, la compresión lingüística, que resulta también en la pérdida de un préstamo.

(3) "[...] et il fallut moins de trois semaines pour que les gens du bled le haïssent" (278)
"[...] en tres semanas Murad se había granjeado el odio de los obreros" (298)

A pesar de que este ejemplo puede ser considerado también una generalización, pensamos que encaja mejor como compresión.

Entre los siete casos de equivalente acuñado volvemos a encontrar *bled* en tres ocasiones, en dos de ellas se traduce como *campo* y en otra como *tierras*. Los cuatro casos restantes en los que se recurre a la técnica de equivalente acuñado son los siguientes:

---

dos textos (origen y meta), que se presentan a continuación numerados. En los casos restantes, hemos respetado la norma establecida.

(4) "[...] et ses ouvriers durent arracher le doum à la pioche [...]" (54)
 "[...] y sus obreros tuvieron que arrancar el palmito a golpes de pico [...]" (58)

(5) "Le douar était constitué de cinq masures misérables [...]" (110)
 "La aldea se componía de cinco casuchas miserables [...] (116)

(6) "[...] et Mourad insistait pour porter le barda d'Amine" (273)
 "[...] y Murad insistía en cargar el petate de Amín" (292)

(7) "Ce type, se plaignaient les fellahs, était pire qu'un étranger" (278)
 "Este tipo — se quejaban algunos jornaleros — era peor que un extranjero"
 (298)

En cuanto a la generalización, en dos ocasiones se traduce el viento *chergui* por *siroco*. Este mismo término se traslada en otra ocasión como "el viento del chergui", lo que supone el mantenimiento del préstamo, aunque en castellano es puro en lugar de adaptado, y una amplificación. Encontramos de nuevo el término *riad*, trasladado en esta ocasión como *casa*. Finalmente, los cuatro casos restantes de generalización pertenecen a la indumentaria típica y a agrupaciones. Presentamos uno de ellos a continuación porque pensamos que es significativo, dado que nos ofrece tres términos resueltos de diferente manera:

(8) "Mais il mourut en 1939, alors que son fils s'était engagé dans le regiment des spahis et portait fièrement le burnous et le sarouel" (16)
 "Pero murió en 1939, mientras su hijo de había alistado en el regimiento de los espahíes, vistiendo con orgullo su uniforme: la capa y los zaragüelles" (16)

El primer préstamo que aparece en la oración se traslada de la misma manera en castellano, dado que los dos son préstamos adaptados, recogidos por los diccionarios de ambas lenguas. Sin embargo, pensamos que *espahí* es un término no muy conocido por la población española, motivo por el cual un lector español podría considerar que se trata de un préstamo puro. En cualquier caso, el contexto permite deducir su significado. En cuanto a los términos que se utilizan para describir el uniforme de estos militares, en el primer caso se realiza una generalización al traducir *burnous*, que es "Grand manteau de laine sans manches, à capuchon, en usage chez les Arabes" (Larousse 2020) por *capa*, por lo que se pierde la especificidad del término original al utilizar el término más general. *Zaragüelles* es también un préstamo adaptado procedente de la lengua árabe, pero es posible que el lector no conozca tal procedencia y pueda pensar que se trata de un término castellano, como ocurre con *capa*, ya que se usa para designar los pantalones del traje típico de algunas regiones españolas (RAE 2020).

Presentamos a continuación los resultados de los préstamos puros.

Tabla 2. Presencia de préstamos puros en el TO y su traducción

TO	TM
20 préstamos puros	11 préstamos puros
	6 préstamos adaptados
	3 traducciones

Los veinte préstamos puros del texto original han sido trasladados al castellano como préstamos puros (11), préstamos adaptados (6) y traducciones (3). Algunos ejemplos de préstamos puros que se mantienen en castellano son: *chouafa*, que Embarek adapta a la grafía castellana como *chuafa*; *sebsi* o *nassarania*, que es de nuevo adaptada por la traductora a *nasranía*. Los préstamos puros pasan a ser préstamos adaptados en seis ocasiones únicamente, una para el término *moqaddem*, que en el *Diccionario de la lengua española* (RAE 2020) está recogido con la forma *almocadén*, y las cinco veces en las que aparece *adoul*, que no está incluido en los dos diccionarios de lengua francesa consultados, mientras que *adul* sí que lo está en el de la Real Academia.

Finalmente, en tres ocasiones la traductora recurre a equivalentes acuñados en castellano para trasladar sendos préstamos puros que aparecen solo en una ocasión en el texto origen.

(9) "Ils mâchouaillaient sans entrain les rares pousses de pissenlits, l'herbe jaunie, les bouquets de bakkoula" (100)
"Masticaban sin entusiasmo las escasas matas de diente de león, de una hierba amarillenta, de hojas de malva" (105)

(10) "Elle arriva sur la place El-Hedim et se gara en haut du derb" (120)
"Llegó a la plaza El-Hedim y aparcó en la parte alta de una callejuela" (126)

(11) "Allez, va-t'en, bouge-toi, on dirait un gros sac de smid !" (239)
"Venga, largo de aquí, muévete, pareces un saco de sémola" (254)

En nuestra opinión, estos tres ejemplos muestran cómo la elección de Slimani por los préstamos que no son necesarios, ya que podría haber utilizado términos en francés (*mauve, ruelle* o *semoule*), responde a un objetivo: dar a su texto una hibridez lingüística que lo defina y distinga de otros textos. Señalamos además que la autora introduce una nota al pie con el equivalente acuñado en francés de *smid*.

En cuanto al uso de las marcas tipográficas, los préstamos puros aparecen en el texto original sin ninguna marca y con letra redonda, por lo que en francés no se sigue lo establecido por la norma. Sin embargo, ocho de estos préstamos van acompañados de una nota al pie de página que ayudan al lector a comprenderlos.

Algunos de estos términos acompañados de glosa extratextual son formas de cortesía incluidos entre los culturemas del ámbito Cultura social, y dentro de este, en el apartado de Convenciones y hábitos sociales (*benti, ya Ba, ya moui, ya ouldi*); los otros casos con nota al pie explicativa son *smid, moqaddem, nassarania* y *le Bousbir*. Al recurrir a la nota al pie, Slimani muestra que es consciente de que estos términos pueden dificultar la comprensión del lector de la novela que no conozca estos culturemas marroquíes, pero eso no le impide utilizarlos.

En el texto en castellano encontramos en dieciséis ocasiones la letra cursiva, siempre para términos considerados préstamos puros, aunque en total suman treinta y uno, hay catorce que aparecen con letra redonda, por lo que no sabemos por qué algunos están marcados tipográficamente y otros no. Estas son las palabras que aparecen en cursiva: *chuafa, sebsi, yinn* (en cuatro ocasiones), *felah, zelliyes, nesranía* (dos veces), *benti, mellah, ia uldi, hamam, haram* y *chergui*. Por otro lado, las notas al pie de página desaparecen en castellano y en ocasiones la información que se incluía en las mismas se incorpora al texto, en consonancia con lo que había declarado Embarek (2016) con lo ocurrido en su traducción de Ben Jelloun. Presentamos a continuación un ejemplo en el que se dan ambos casos:

(12) "«Ne lui fais pas peur, ya Ba[1]! Ne t'inquiète pas, benti[2], chez vous à la ferme il n'y a pas de petites souris comme celle-là»". (112)
  1. Ô père.
  2. Ma fille.

"«¡No asustes a la niña, Ba!» «No te preocupes, *benti*, hija mía, en vuestra finca no hay ratoncitos como ese»". (119)

Como muestra el ejemplo 12, el texto en castellano no traslada de la misma forma dos casos similares: dos préstamos puros relativos al tratamiento de personas con nota al pie de página. En el primer caso, *ya Ba*, se reduce a *Ba*, se elimina la nota al pie, así como la información que aporta, y no está marcado tipográficamente, por lo que el lector puede pensar que se trata de un nombre propio al utilizar la mayúscula inicial. Sin embargo, *benti*, el segundo caso, incorpora la información de la nota al pie yuxtaponiéndola al término, que además es uno de los préstamos puros que han sido marcados con letra cursiva en la versión en castellano.

La presencia de préstamos es, como presuponíamos al inicio del estudio, diferente en ambas lenguas, lo que refleja la diferente relación que el francés y el castellano han tenido con el árabe. En la Tabla 3 se muestran los tipos y el número total de préstamos que aparecen en cada texto.

En esta tabla se han incluido las tres compensaciones que ha realizado Embarek al introducir tres términos: *cabila, adul* y *jaique*. Recordemos además que hay veintitrés préstamos traducidos y una omisión, lo que justifica la diferencia en la comparación de números en las dos versiones.

Tabla 3. Presencia y tipos de préstamos en el TO y el TM

	TO	TM
Préstamos adaptados	84	52
Préstamos puros	20	31
Total	104	83

En cuanto al uso de marcas tipográficas, en el texto en francés se recurre a la nota al pie para explicar o describir nueve préstamos, los ocho puros enumerados arriba y uno adaptado (*haram*), pero no se marcan nunca con cursiva. En la versión traducida se incluye la información para ayudar a la comprensión del lector en el propio texto y se marcan con cursiva catorce de los treinta y un préstamos puros.

5.2 Alternancia de código

La presencia de la alternancia de código en la primera parte de *Le pays des autres* es menor que la de los préstamos, ya que la encontramos en nueve ocasiones, pero contribuye posiblemente de forma más explícita a la hibridez lingüística de la novela y a proporcionarle exotismo. Este recurso se presenta de forma más homogénea que los préstamos en el texto original ya que los nueve casos son tratados de forma análoga: aparecen entre comillas y están marcados con letra cursiva y acompañados de una nota al pie de página con su traducción salvo en un caso. En cuanto al tipo de alternancia que se produce, encontramos cuatro alternancias intersentenciales frente a cinco intrasentenciales.

En el texto traducido, con también nueve ocurrencias de alternancia de código, se presenta igualmente un tratamiento más homogéneo, aunque diferente del texto en francés en cuanto a las notas al pie de página, que han sido eliminadas e incorporadas al texto en algunas ocasiones. Hay cinco casos de alternancia intersentencial y cuatro intrasentenciales y no se mantiene la cursiva ni las comillas en todos los casos. Encontramos dos casos en letra redonda frente a siete en cursiva y ocho con comillas y uno sin ellas, por lo que el lector no puede deducir el motivo del uso de estos recursos, como ya vimos que ocurrió con la marca en cursiva en los préstamos puros en el texto en castellano. En la siguiente tabla se muestran estos datos para ayudar a la comparación entre textos.

Gracias a la tabla podemos ver que la mayor diferencia entre las dos versiones radica en el uso de las notas al pie en el texto en francés y su eliminación en la versión en castellano. Como ya habíamos señalado en el estudio de los préstamos, Embarek incorpora al texto la información aportada en el pie de página.

Tabla 4. Alternancia de código en el TO y el TM

	TO	TM
Alternancia intersentencial	4	5
Alternancia intrasentencial	5	4
Comillas	9	8
Letra cursiva	8	7
Notas al pie	8	0

Presentamos a continuación algunos ejemplos representativos del tratamiento que se ha dado a la alternancia de código en francés y su traducción.

(13)   "Cachée par un petit muret, Mathilde répétait les quelques insultes qu'elle connaissait pour parfaire son accent et les passants levaient la tête et l'insultaient en retour. «*Lay atik typhus*[1]!»"   (35)
[1] "Que Dieu te donne le typhus!"
"Escondida tras el pretil, repetía algunos insultos en árabe que había aprendido, y la gente que pasaba por la calle alzaba la cabeza y la insultaba a su vez, deseando que Dios condenara al descarado con alguna enfermedad, como el tifus: «*Allah iatik tifus!*»"   (37)

En este ejemplo vemos cómo en el texto de Slimani se presenta la alternancia de código de forma intersentencial, con la llamada de la nota al pie de página y su traducción. La versión de Embarek mantiene la alternacia intersentencial, pero incorpora el significado del insulto al texto, evitando así recurrir a la nota al pie. Ambas versiones presentan la oración con letra cursiva y entre comillas, y la traducción adapta además la grafía de la expresión en árabe.

Presentamos a continuación dos alternancias de código similares que se han trasladado de forma diferente:

(14)   "«*Lalla Fatima*[1]», dit-il à l'écolière qui s'avançait vers lui, et Aïcha se demanda pourquoi cette enfant, qui couvrait ses leçons de salive à force de dormir sur ses cahiers, était traitée comme une dame"   (92)
[1] Titre respectueux pour désigner une femme.
"«Lala Fatima», dijo, dirigiéndose a la niña que avanzaba hacia él, y Aicha se preguntó por qué a esa cría, que manchaba sus libros de baba de tanto dormirse sobre ellos, la trataban como a una señora"   (98)

(15)   "Elles l'appelaient «*Bent Tajer*[1]» avec une déférence moqueuse et elles ajoutaient: «Tu n'est pas mieux que nous, si?»"   (114)
[1] "La fille du maître"
"La llamaban *Bent Tayer*, la hija del rico, con una deferencia burlona, y añadían: «¿A que tú no eres mejor que nosotras?»"   (121)

En los dos casos anteriores la alternancia en el texto en francés se realiza al introducir dos apelativos de forma intrasentencial, con el uso de la letra cursiva, las comillas y nota al pie de página. En el primer caso, la nota es explicativa mientras que en el segundo se utiliza para aportar la traducción al francés. En el texto en castellano vemos cómo la nota explicativa desaparece, probablemente debido a que la parte final de la oración cumple con esa misma función. En la oración original de Slimani también aparece, pero la autora decide incluir igualmente la nota al pie de página, quizás por mantener la hegemonía del tratamiento de las alternancias de código. En la traducción vemos de nuevo una adaptación a la grafía española: *Lalla* pasa a ser *Lala*, aunque *Fatima* no incorpora la tilde. Por otro lado, en la versión de Embarek se mantienen las comillas, pero desaparece la letra en cursiva.

En el Ejemplo (15) el texto meta sí incorpora la traducción de la alternancia en la oración, incluida como aposición, pero se eliminan las comillas y se mantiene el uso de la cursiva.

6. Conclusiones

A la vista de los resultados del análisis realizado podemos valorar cómo se ha trasladado la hibridez lingüística y cultural del texto en francés en la versión en castellano. En primer lugar, en el original se han presentado culturemas marroquíes pertenecientes a los cuatro ámbitos culturales establecidos por Molina Martínez (2006) principalmente gracias a préstamos adaptados, que, con ochenta y cuatro ocurrencias, superan ampliamente el número de préstamos puros. En cuanto a la presentación de los mismos, no se hace distinción tipográfica entre los puros y los adaptados, no siguiendo la norma establecida para la lengua francesa. El texto de Slimani presenta notas al pie de página en algunos de los préstamos puros para facilitar la comprensión del lector.

En el texto traducido encontramos una menor ocurrencia de préstamos, se reducen a ochenta y tres frente a los ciento cuatro del original. Además, estos se reparten de diferente forma: los adaptados se reducen a cincuenta y dos frente a los puros, que aumentan a treinta y uno. La primera diferencia numérica muestra la labor de la traductora, quien, como hemos visto en el apartado anterior, ha recurrido a la omisión en una ocasión, así como a compensaciones y traducciones. El aumento de los préstamos puros en la traducción muestra que la lengua castellana no ha adaptado tantos términos procedentes del árabe como lo ha hecho el francés. Tipográficamente sí encontramos dieciséis préstamos puros marcados con letra cursiva, pero hay quince más que no lo están, por lo que el recurso tipográfico no cumple su función del todo y puede incluso confundir al lector. Por último, las notas al pie de página que acompañaban a ciertos préstamos puros en el texto de Slimani desaparecen, aunque se incorporan en ocasiones al texto para salvar las dificultades de comprensión.

Como hemos visto, la problemática de los culturemas señalada por Soto-Almela (2013) en su definición, se ha resuelto de tres formas: mediante el uso de préstamos, una omisión y recurriendo a la traducción en veintitrés casos.

En cuanto a la alternancia de código, como hemos visto arriba, la diferencia más notable se encuentra de igual manera en la desaparición de las notas al pie de página que Slimani incluye en su texto para ayudar al lector. El texto en castellano evita la interrupción de la lectura con este recurso y presenta también un uso menos homogéneo de las comillas y la cursiva de lo que hace el original, como hemos visto en los ejemplos presentados.

El objetivo de este estudio era comprobar de qué forma se había trasladado al castellano la hibridez lingüística encontrada en el original mediante el uso de préstamos y de la alternancia de código para trasladar culturemas y de qué forma se presentaban en ambos textos estos recursos. Pensamos que el análisis nos permite concluir en primer lugar que en la traducción se ha perdido dicha hibridez debido a la reducción del uso de préstamos y, por ende, de la presencia de culturemas. Por otro lado, el texto francés es más homogéneo al eliminar las marcas tipográficas para los préstamos, aunque eso supone no seguir la norma, al mismo tiempo que iguala el tratamiento de la alternancia de código. El texto en castellano, sin embargo, sigue la norma establecida para los préstamos puros, pero solo en la mitad de los casos, lo que hace que se pierda en cierta manera el sentido del uso de la marca tipográfica y que pueda confundir al lector. Por último, pensamos que la supresión de las notas al pie en favor de la inclusión de su contenido en el propio texto favorece la lectura del mismo al permitir que esta se haga sin interrupciones de este tipo.

En nuestra opinión, un análisis de la recepción de ambos textos sería determinante, ya que es posible que buena parte de los préstamos adaptados en francés no sean percibidos como arabismos por los lectores franceses, reduciendo así el carácter exótico de la lengua utilizada e igualándose a la de la versión en castellano, que había reducido la presencia de préstamos adaptados y aumentado la de los puros. Esto mismo puede ocurrir al lector español, ya que es posible que desconozca la procedencia de términos como *zaragüelles* o *azulejos* y, por lo tanto, no sea consciente de la variedad lingüística del texto.

Por último, sería interesante ampliar este análisis a otras lenguas, para mostrar de qué manera se han solventado los problemas de traducción que han podido plantear los culturemas, así como para evidenciar si se ha mantenido la hibridez lingüística y cultural en el texto traducido. Sería particularmente interesante un estudio que presente cómo se han trasladado dichos elementos en la traducción al árabe y si se ha conseguido un texto heterogéneo o si, por el contrario, dicha hibridez se ha perdido.

Referencias

Ali, Mohammed Saad. 2020. "L'impact de l'arabe dans le roman francophone". *La linguistique*, LVI, pp. 159-178.

Baiwir, Esther. 2014. "Les arabismes dans le TLF: Tentative de classement historique". *Revue de Linguistique Romane* 78, pp. 367-402.

Bureau de la Traduction. 2015. *Le guide du rédacteur*. ⟨https://www.btb.termium-plus.gc.ca/tpv2guides/guides/redac/index-fra.html?lang=fra⟩

Díaz Alarcón, Soledad. 2018. "Análisis y traducción de los rasgos de oralidad de la novela *Béni ou le paradis* de Azouz Begag". *Thélème. Revista Complutense de Estudios Franceses* 33 (1), pp. 9-28.

Éditions Le Robert. 2021. *Le dico en ligne*. ⟨https://dictionnaire.lerobert.com⟩

El Hag Hassan El Dannanah, Noha. 2021. "El uso de arabismos en la traducción literaria del árabe al español: estudio de tres casos de narrativa contemporánea." *TRANS. Revista de Traductología* 25, pp. 223-243.

Embarek López, Malika. 2016. "Traducir entre las dos orillas del Mediterráneo". *Vasos comunicantes* 47, pp. 33-36.

Fernández Erquicia, Irati. 2019. "La présence de la femme dans l'oeuvre de Leïla Slimani." *Thélème. Revista Complutense de Estudios Franceses*, 34 (1), pp.173-189.

Grevisse, Maurice & André Goosse. 2008. *Le bon usage*. Bruselas: Éditions de Boeck.

Hammink, Julianne. 2000. *A Comparison of the Code-Switching behavior and knowledge of adults and children*. El Paso (Texas): University of Texas.

Imprimerie Nationale. 2014. *Lexique des règles typographiques en usage à l'Imprimerie Nationale*. París: Imprimerie Nationale.

Jiménez Carra, Nieves. 2004. "Estrategias de cambio de código y su traducción en la novela de Sandra Cisneros *Caramelo or Puro cuento*". *TRANS. Revista de Traductología* 8, pp. 37-59.

Jiménez Carra, Nieves. 2011. "La traducción del cambio de código inglés-español en la obra de *The brief wondrous life of Oscar Wao*, de Junot Díaz". *Sendebar* 22, pp. 159-180.

Larousse. 2020. *Dictionnaire de français*. ⟨https://www.larousse.fr/dictionnaires/francais-monolingue⟩

Lievois, Katrien y Nahed Nadia Noureddine. 2018. "La traduction des arabismes dans Kiffe kiffe demain de Faïza Guène". *Atelier de traduction* 29, pp. 51-69.

Martínez de Sousa, José. 2003. "La contravención de la norma en el lenguaje". ⟨http://martinezdesousa.net⟩

Martínez de Sousa, José. 2012. *Manual de estilo de la lengua española. MELE 4*. 4ª edición, revisada y ampliada. Gijón: Trea.

Miloudi, Imene. 2022. "Hétérolinguisme et pluristylisme dans *La robe blanche* de Barkahoun de Farida Saffidine". *Multilinguales* 17, pp. 1-11.

Molina Martínez, Lucía. 2006. *El otoño del pingüino. Análisis descriptivo de la traducción de los culturemas*. Castellón de la Plana: Universitat Jaume I.

Molina, Lucía & Amparo Hurtado Albir. 2002. "Translation Techniques Revisited: A Dynamic and Functionalist Approach". *Meta: journal des traducteurs / Meta: Translators' Journal* 47, pp. 498–512.

Montes-Alcala, Cecilia. 2012. "Code-Switching in US-Latino Novels." En: Sebb, Mark; Mahootian, Shahrzad y Carla Jonsson (eds.) 2012. *Language Mixing and Code-Switching in Writing: Approaches to Mixed-Language Written Discourse*. Nueva York: Routledge, pp. 68–88.

Poplack, Shana. 1980. "Sometimes I'll start a sentence in English y termino en español: Towards a typology or codeswitching". *Linguistic* 18, pp. 581–618.

Quintero Ocaña, Marinella & Juan Jesús Zaro Vera. 2014. "Problemas y estrategias de traducción del cambio de código en la literatura chicana al español. El caso de *From this Wicked Patch of Dust* de Sergio Troncoso". *Núcleo* 31, pp. 247–273.

Ramat, Aurel & Anne-Marie Benoît. 2017. *Le Ramat de la typographie*. 11e édition. Saint-Laurent: Diffusion.

Real Academia Española. 2009. *Nueva gramática de la lengua española. Morfología. Sintaxis. Fonética y fonología*. Madrid: Espasa.

Real Academia Española. 2010. *Ortografía de la lengua española*. Madrid: Espasa.

Real Academia Española. 2018. *Libro de estilo de la lengua española según la norma panhispánica*. Madrid: Espasa.

Real Academia Española. 2020. *Diccionario de la lengua española*. Edición en línea. (https://dle.rae.es)

Slimani, Leïla. 2014. *Dans le jardin de l'ogre*. París: Gallimard.

Slimani, Leïla. 2016. *Chanson douce*. París: Gallimard.

Slimani, Leïla. 2017. *Sexe et mensonges. La vie sexuelle au Maroc*. París: Les Arènes.

Slimani, Leïla. 2020. *À mains nues I*. París: Les Arènes.

Slimani, Leïla. 2021a. *Le pays des autres*. París: Folio.

Slimani, Leïla. 2021b. *El país de los otros*. Cabaret Voltaire. Traducción de Malika Embarek López.

Slimani, Leïla. 2022. *À mains nues II*. París: Les Arènes.

Soto-Almela, Jorge. 2013. "La traducción de culturemas en el ámbito del patrimonio cultural: análisis de folletos turísticos de la Región de Murcia". *Tonos Digital: Revista de Estudios Filológicos* 24, pp. 1–26.

Varios autores (AECID). 2017. "Página de inicio" (https://www.aecid.es/ES)

Wecksteen, Corinne. 2009. "La traduction de l'emprunt: *coup de théâtre ou coup de grâce?*". *Lexis* 3, 137–156.

Womble, Todd. 2017. "Non-Translation, Code-Swiching, and the Reader-as-Translator". *CLINA* 3-1, pp. 57–76.

Index

A
Adaptación   155, 164, 172, 178, 179, 227, 234
Adaptaciones morfológicas   244

C
Código   293, 294, 295, 303, 304
Comprensión lectora   143, 152
Comunicación intercultural   214
Conocimientos extralingüísticos   143
Conocimientos lingüísticos   143
Contexto cultural   227
Contexto lingüístico   53
Contexto sociocultural   231
Cultura gastronómica   242
Cultura general   156
Cultura lingüística   232, 293
Cultura receptora   217
Cultura religiosa   241
Cultura rural   241
Cultura social   293
Culturemas   212, 226, 291, 292, 297, 302, 306

D
Doblaje   44

E
Equivalente domesticante   51
Equivalente fraseológico   249
Equivalente semántico   249
Estrategia domesticante   47, 56, 57
Estrategia extranjerizante   58, 226
Estrategia exotizante   220, 226
Estrategias expresivas   261
Estrategias traslativas   155

F
Fraseología   233, 241

P
Préstamos puros   293, 297

R
Referencia cultural   51
Referencias culturales   42, 43, 45, 46, 48, 49, 58, 147, 217, 218, 290
Referencia geográfica   46, 48
Referencia monocultural   52
Referencia transcultural   53
Referente cultural   44, 227, 239
Referentes universales   158
Registro coloquial   202, 244

S
Subtitulación   43, 44, 45, 51, 54, 58, 60, 65
Subtitulación interlingüística   43

T
Técnicas domesticantes   56
Técnicas extranjerizantes   45, 56
Traducción audiovisual   43
Traducción editorial   213, 216, 220
Traducción literaria   179, 296
Traducción teatral   164